1634479

S0-BSF-874

DATE DUE

THE OLD TESTAMENT

ARTHUR J.
BELLINZONI

THE OLD
TESTAMENT

An Introduction to
Biblical Scholarship

Prometheus Books

59 John Glenn Drive
Amherst, New York 14228–2119

Published 2009 by Prometheus Books

Inquiries should be addressed to
Prometheus Books
59 John Glenn Drive
Amherst, New York 14228–2119
VOICE: 716–691–0133, ext. 210
FAX: 716–691–0137
WWW.PROMETHEUSBOOKS.COM

13 12 11 10 09   5 4 3 2 1

Library of Congress Cataloging-in-Publication Data

Bellinzoni, Arthur J.
     The Old Testament : an introduction to biblical scholarship / by Arthur J. Bellinzoni.
          p. cm.
     ISBN 978–1–59102–673–0 (hardcover)
     1. Bible. O.T.—Criticism and interpretation. 2. Jews—History—To 70 A.D.
3. Judaism—History—To 70 A.D. I. Title.
     BS1178.H4B43 2008
     221.072—dc22

                                                                                    2008030897

Printed in the United States of America on acid-free paper

CONTENTS

CHAPTER 5: MEDIATORS BETWEEN YAHWEH AND ISRAEL   151

CHAPTER 6: THE NORTHERN KINGDOM'S EPIC: THE ELOHIST   181

CHAPTER 7: MEDIATORS BETWEEN YAHWEH AND JUDAH   187

MAPS AND DIAGRAMS

PREFACE

There are a myriad of introductions to both the Hebrew Bible and the New Testament. Many of these introductions are committed to the historical method of investigation; many, unfortunately, are not. Yet, even those introductions that make use of the historical method rarely speak directly to the foundational principles of contemporary biblical scholarship.

Both as an undergraduate at Princeton and as a graduate student at Harvard, I was introduced to the historical study of the Bible without actually understanding the basis and the justification for such a scholarly approach. A friend called to my attention a few years ago the value of having an introductory textbook that addresses clearly and directly issues of methodology in order to enable students of the Bible to understand better the reasons for and the implications of the best results of biblical scholarship.

Accordingly, this volume has a twofold purpose: (1) to introduce readers to the origins of and the reasons for the basic methodology of biblical scholarship; and (2) to provide an overview of the origins and the evolution of Hebrew beginnings by employing those methods in an examination of the relevant primary sources, specifically the books of the Old Testament. In writing this book, I have been especially mindful of college undergraduates, seminary students, and even graduate students in the field of religion. I have also been mindful of laypersons who already have some knowledge of the Bible but who are unaware of the methodological basis of contemporary biblical scholarship and its results. It is essential that people at every level of understanding have an awareness of the kinds of conclusions that come with the rigorous application of the historical method of biblical interpretation.

On numerous occasions, former students returning to Wells College for reunion or some other reason thank me for what they learned years earlier in my classes. Most tell me that what they learned from me was *how* to read the Bible. They often comment that they do not remember the details of the courses they took with me but that they did learn and still remember how to think clearly, to reason wisely, and to read the Bible with a much clearer eye with regard to what the Bible is and what the Bible is not. Hence this book focuses primarily on the reasoning process.

This volume is not an introduction to the Bible, or even to the Old Testament. There are already many excellent introductions to the Bible as a whole, and separate introductions to the Old and the New Testaments. Typically such introductions afford basic information about all of the books of the Bible. I am, however, not aware of any introductory study that tries to accomplish what I am attempting with this volume.

In the introduction, I provide the reader with insight into the origins and the principles of modern biblical scholarship, including a discussion of the rules of evidence for the writing of history, whether biblical history or any other history. The rules and methods for the writing of history are always the same whatever the specific subject matter. Nonetheless, the systematic application of the historical method to the Bible has come only with a long and painful struggle that has spanned several centuries and that is still not deeply implanted in the minds of many millions of people.

The introduction to this volume is among the most important and most challenging chapters, although it is this material that is generally lacking in introductions to the Old and the New Testaments. An understanding of the origins, the ascendancy, and the ultimate preeminence of biblical scholarship as the single most important way of understanding and reconstructing Hebrew and Christian beginnings is, in my opinion, essential to an appreciation of what unfolds in the subsequent chapters of this volume.

To present the reader with a book that is both faithful to the rigors of biblical scholarship and, at the same time, readable and engaging, I have focused on two issues: first, I have developed detailed arguments in some portions of the book in order to allow the reader to understand more clearly how a historical reconstruction of the past is built upon an interpretation of the relevant data. The work of biblical scholars is generally based on the study of original texts that ideally requires knowledge of ancient languages, minimally Hebrew and Greek, of which few laypersons have any knowledge. In the course of this volume, I will introduce some issues involving texts in their original languages in order to expose the reader to an understanding of the ways in which biblical scholars build detailed cases.

Second, I have in other instances avoided detailed arguments and discussion and have provided the reader instead with what are scholarly conclusions based on a careful reading and interpretation of the evidence, at least as I understand the evidence and the consensus of sound scholarship. Without taking such shortcuts, it would be impossible to cover in detail two thousand years of history in a modest volume of the sort that I propose to offer here.

My intention is to provide the reader with meaningful insight into both the methods of biblical scholarship and the results of the application of these methods to the ancient texts. Such an effort is designed to afford the reader a reasoned reconstruction of what likely happened in the ancient past, which is after all our ultimate goal. Although not everyone will agree with all of my conclusions, hopefully everyone will agree with the value and the rigor of the method used to reach these conclusions. It is my hope that this blend of a rigorous application of the historical method and introductory overviews of the history of ancient Israelite religion will stimulate the reader who wants more information about the subject to pursue elsewhere individual issues in greater detail.

Writing an introduction means making compromises regarding what to include and what not to include, and I have indeed made such compromises. I do not cover every book of the Old Testament, as most introductions attempt to do. I am more interested in addressing certain issues more deeply than in providing a summary of every book of the Hebrew Bible. In making the decisions I have made, I hope to remain faithful to the text, to scholars who have written before me, and I hope to be as faithful as possible to the history that unfolded in the distant past. It is essential in this regard to remind the reader that biblical scholarship is not an exact science in the way in which physics and astronomy are more-or-less exact sciences with strong foundations in mathematics.

The study of the origins of Judaism and Christianity is especially problematic because the earliest period of both religions is far removed not only from us, but even more important it is far removed even from our earliest written sources. This is especially the case with the earliest stages in the emergence of Hebrew religion.

Consequently, in the course of what follows in this volume, we shall have ample opportunity to understand the limitations of reconstructing the past.

The writing of history uses what we call the historical method, or the scientific method, and aims at objectivity to the extent that objectivity is possible in trying to reconstruct events that occurred thousands of years ago. Equally competent scholars often draw very different conclusions from the same evidence. The important word here is *evidence*. Ideally, scholars look at the same evidence, all of the available data, and at what other scholars have had to say in the past about that data. Then, and only then, can historians try to connect all of the dots in a way that is faithful both to the data and to the methodology of historical investigation. Scholars can do no more than draw conclusions within the limits of historical reason; they can never be certain that their conclusions conform to what actually happened in the distant past. Scholars build models of the past or renovate models built by their learned predecessors. The historical method is nothing more and nothing less. Accordingly, it is essential to understand at the outset the limits of the method, the limits of the discipline, and the uncertain nature of many of our conclusions.

The doing of history is at all times a secular exercise. The Bible presents a special challenge because it represents Israel's history as a history of the acts of Israel's God Yahweh. Accordingly, a historical study of the Bible poses serious concerns and sometimes grave personal challenges for many readers, because it is exactly that impartial, detached, neutral, unbiased, dispassionate, and objective perspective that not only troubles some students but that lies necessarily at the heart of all rigorous and serious biblical scholarship.

Although I am ultimately responsible for everything that I have gathered into this book, the final version is better because of the generous suggestions and criticisms of two good friends and professional colleagues: Marvin A. Breslow, professor of history emeritus at the University of Maryland and my roommate for four years at the Harvard University Graduate School of Arts and Sciences; and David M. Reis, formerly visiting assistant professor of religion at Wells College and currently assistant professor of religion at Bridgewater College. Both of these men labored tirelessly and unselfishly over every word of every chapter of this manuscript and made invaluable contributions to this volume. I want also to acknowledge the generous technical assistance I received from Dimitrios Dimopoulos, as I could not have prepared this manuscript without him.

This book is dedicated to the memory of those professors at Princeton University who first introduced me to the academic study of religion, especially George Thomas, Malcolm Diamond, R. B. Y. Scott, and W. D. Davies, who have influenced my life in more ways than they could have ever imagined.

Arthur J. Bellinzoni
Wells College
Aurora, New York
November 29, 2008

INTRODUCTION

The term generally used for biblical scholarship in professional circles is "biblical criticism." The English word "criticism"—which has its roots in the Greek verb *krinein*, meaning "to separate," "to think," "to discern," "to decide," "to distinguish," "to judge"—unfortunately conjures up the English word "criticize" with its connotations of attacking, subverting, or undermining. The intention of biblical scholarship is, however, not to criticize, to attack, to subvert, or to undermine the Bible. Rather, biblical scholarship endeavors to better understand the Bible, using the same methodology that historians use when they investigate documents from ancient Greece, medieval Europe, or modern America. In other words, the goal of the historian is always the same: to analyze available evidence in order to make informed and discriminating judgments about the past.

THE ORIGINS OF MODERN BIBLICAL SCHOLARSHIP

Already in antiquity, Jews and Christians applied critical methods to establish the canons of the Hebrew Bible (what Christians call the Old Testament) and of the New Testament. Ancient Jewish scribes were not only copyists, jurists, and lawyers; they were also teachers and scholars who established rules for copying biblical manuscripts in a conscious effort to standardize the biblical texts. Nevertheless, different versions of the books of the Hebrew Bible continued to exist as late as 70 CE[1] in manuscripts known as the Dead Sea Scrolls, and also in the so-called Septuagint, a translation into Greek of ancient Hebrew manuscripts undertaken in Alexandria, Egypt, circa 250–150 BCE. It was likely sometime around 500 CE that the text of the Hebrew Bible was standardized by the scholars known as Masoretes, whose responsibility it was to maintain the tradition and rules that governed the production of all copies of the Hebrew Bible (the so-called Masoretic text, which is the basis of all modern Hebrew Bibles, or Old Testaments).

In the second and third centuries CE, early Fathers of the Christian Church exercised judgments when deciding which Christian writings to include in the New Testament and whether or not to defend the authority of the Jewish Bible and to include it in the Christian canon of sacred scripture. Accordingly, critical study of the Bible, in one form or another, reaches back about two thousand years. Nonetheless, although Jewish scribes and early Christian Fathers were encouraged by intellectual curiosity, they were clearly motivated more by doctrinal presuppositions than by what we would consider today to be impartial inquiry and objective research.

Ancient Jewish rabbis and early Christian Fathers basically assumed that individual books of the Old and New Testaments ultimately had God as their author, although they acknowledged several stages in the development of these books. First, there was the divine utterance itself, the words that God actually spoke in the past; second, there was the hearing of that divine utterance by an inspired prophet or mediator chosen or otherwise designated by God to deliver his divine utterance to the people; and third, there was the faithful transcription of the prophet's or the mediator's words into writing by a faithful scribe, presumably under the inspiration of the Spirit of God or the Holy Spirit, whose role it was to guarantee the authenticity and the accuracy of the written word and its faithfulness to the divine utterance. This process, it was believed, guaranteed the authenticity, the accuracy, and the authority of these writings as "holy books," set apart by God himself as the record of his message for the Jews, and later for Christians, and ultimately for the whole of humankind.

It is not sufficient to rely on the fanciful conjectures of ancient authors or even on long-standing traditions regarding such serious matters as the authorship and date of composition of ancient books. The criterion for such determination needs rather to be a critical examination of internal evidence furnished by the individual books themselves and any relevant and available external evidence that can assist in the process of making an informed judgment.

Many early Fathers of the Church were aware, at least in nascent form, of problems that have become focuses of modern biblical scholarship. These men were, however, generally concerned with the content and the authority of the church's sacred scripture and, for the most part, simply accepted the traditions of Judaism and of the early Christian church regarding matters of authorship, date, and place of composition of the books of the Bible.

In his monumental *Introduction to the Old Testament*, Robert Pfeiffer maintained that

> the crude beginnings of a critical and historical investigation of the Old Testament reach back at least to the second century of our era, when **Celsus** maintained that the Pentateuch could not have been written by a single author, and **Ptolemy** (a disciple of the Gnostic teacher Valentinus), in his epistle to Flora, distinguished in the Pentateuchal law parts inspired by God, parts written by Moses, and parts written by the elders.[2]

Pfeiffer notes that several ancient writers, some of them early Christian Fathers, made significant contributions to historical criticism of the Bible, but he confers especially strong praise on **Porphyry**:

> Porphyry, a Syrian Neoplatonist philosopher who lived in Alexandria (ca. 233–304), attacked the historicity of the Book of Daniel, proving conclusively that it was written in the Maccabean period, and that chapter 11 was not a prophecy, but a veiled history of Syria from Alexander to Antiochus Epiphanes.[3]

Likewise,

> **Jerome** (d. 420) refused to commit himself to the view either that Moses wrote the Pentateuch or that Ezra published it, but by identifying Deuteronomy as the lawbook discovered in the Temple during the reign of Josiah (*Commentary on Ezekiel, ad* 1:1) he unwittingly found the key to Pentateuchal criticism.[4]

So too,

> **Theodore of Mopsuestia**, a theologian belonging to the school of Antioch (d. ca. 428), not only perceived that the titles and superscriptions of the Psalms were added to the original compositions, but also that a number of psalms (seventeen, in his opinion) were Maccabean in date.[5]

In addition to these examples cited by Pfeiffer, **Origen** (185–254 CE), one of the greatest of all Christian theologians, concluded on the basis of internal evidence, specifically stylistic criteria, that Paul was likely not the author of Hebrews (cf. Eusebius, *Hist. Eccl.* VI.25.11ff.), and Origen's disciple **Dionysius of Alexandria** (ca. 190–265 CE) found linguistic and stylistic reasons to dismiss the traditional view that the apostle John was the author of the book of Revelation (Jerome, *De Viris Illustribus* 1).

These learned and critical Fathers of the Church were the exception in their times, and there is no uninterrupted line of succession to connect them and their findings to modern biblical scholarship. Their observations had to be rediscovered many centuries later.

Modern biblical scholarship has its earliest foundations in the sixteenth century. The invention of printing about 1440, the advent of the Protestant Reformation in 1517, and the revival of scholarship during the Renaissance in the fourteenth, fifteenth, and sixteenth centuries all contributed to the rediscovery of a method that had long since been set aside, perhaps even forgotten. Print disseminated texts as never before, accelerating the spread of information.

The humanistic revival of critical scholarship meant that Europeans rediscovered and relearned biblical Hebrew, classical and biblical Greek, and other languages of the ancient Near East. The convergence of these movements resulted in the emergence and spread of modern biblical scholarship, although the road to the future proved to be extremely treacherous because the church would surrender authority in critical areas only after a series of fierce fights.

With a new focus on impartial inquiry, scholars for the first time asked with authority whether the beliefs and the practices of the medieval Roman Catholic Church reflected faithfully the beliefs and the practices of their ancient forebears. With that question very much in his mind, **Martin Luther** and other Protestant reformers maintained that there should be a return to the authority of the scriptures and an abandonment of the authority heretofore vested in the church, and most especially in the bishop of Rome, the pope. The renewal of interest in the Old and New Testaments in their original Hebrew and Greek was, accordingly, imperative.

The German Protestant reformer **Andreas Rudolph Bodenstein** (1477–1541), known also as Andreas Carlstadt, or simply as Karlstadt after the city of his birth, presented theses denying free will as early as 1516. He asserted the doctrine of salvation by grace alone and was, by 1518, an ardent supporter of Martin Luther. Karlstadt was apparently the first person since Celsus and Jerome, more than a thousand years earlier, to break with the ancient tradition that Moses was the author of the Pentateuch, because, he argued, the account of Moses' death in Deuteronomy 34 is in the same style as the rest of the Pentateuch and could not have been written by Moses.

Louis Cappel (1585–1658), a French Protestant theologian and Hebrew scholar, was the first trained specialist who had the requisite skills and the courage to carry out, with meticulousness, insight, and reason, a systematic and linguistic investigation of the text of the Hebrew Bible. In his *Arcanum Punctationis Revelatum* (*The Secret of the Pointing Revealed*; 1624), Cappel proved that vowels had been added to the text of the Hebrew Bible during the Christian period and that until that time the text of the Hebrew Bible consisted only of consonants. In his *Critica Sacra* (*Sacred Literary Criticism*; 1650), Cappel proved that even the earlier consonantal text without vowel pointings had not been transmitted without errors and required correction with help from ancient translations as well as some element of speculation on the part of biblical scholars.[6]

Jean Morin (1591–1659), a French Roman Catholic priest, has been called the most learned Roman Catholic author of the seventeenth century. Born a Calvinist, Morin converted to Roman Catholicism and in 1618 joined the Oratory at Paris. Several of Morin's writings address questions of the text of the Old Testament: *Exercitationes ecclesiastiae in utrumque Samaritorium Pentateuchum* (*Ecclesiastic Exercises in the Samaritan Pentateuch*; 1631), in which he argued that the Samaritan text and the Greek Septuagint are often superior to the extant Hebrew text of the Old Testament, a position he later took up once again in his *Exercitationes biblicae de Hebraei Graecique textus sinceritate* (*Exercises regarding the Reliability of the Text of the Hebrew and Greek Bibles*; 1663, 1669, 1686). Morin also published the text of the Greek Septuagint in *Biblia graecae sive Vetus testamentum secundum Septuaginta* (*The Greek Bible of the Old Testament according to the Septuagint*; 1628) and the text of the Hebrew-Samaritan Pentateuch in *Pentateuchus hebraeo-samaritanus* (*The Hebrew-Samaritan Pentateuch*) and *Pentateuchus samaritanus* (*The Samaritan Pentateuch*; 1645).

In 1637, French philosopher **René Descartes** (1596–1650) published *Discours de la Méthode* (*Discourse concerning Method*), in which he elevated the principle of doubt to a valid historical, philosophical, and scientific principle. Descartes' approach involved three principles:

(1) Man, as a thinking being, stands at the center of all investigation. Descartes' famous phrase *cogito, ergo sum* (I think, therefore I am) summarizes that standpoint.

(2) Tradition alone is not a legitimate or convincing reason for acknowledging something as true. It is necessary to question everything except what is so patently obvious that there can be no reasonable basis for doubt.

(3) Human reason is the one and only criterion of all truth.

A consequence of Descartes' philosophy was that human reason became a legitimate principle, indeed *the* legitimate principle, for examining religion and the Bible.

Frenchman **Isaac La Peyrère** (1596–1676) published in Amsterdam in 1655 *Prae-Adamitae* (*Humans before Adam*), in which he concluded that the biblical time span of six thousand years since creation was insufficient to derive Turkish, Chinese, Arabic, and the European languages from a single original language. La Peyrère also argued that Adam was not the first man but merely the earliest ancestor of the Israelites. He also attacked, although only in passing, the Mosaic authorship of the Pentateuch.

La Peyrère's work was considered heretical by the French clergy, by the faculty at the Sorbonne, and by the violent crowd that burned his book and that tried also to burn him—presumably just treatment for the first scientist to extend the age of the earth beyond the restrictive mathematics of the Bible. Religious orthodoxy responded predictably and dogmatically by requiring a *sacrificium intellectus*, a submission of the intellect or of reason to the authority of the Bible and the church. The argument was made that fallen reason could serve as no guide to knowledge, and certainly not as a guide to sacred scripture.

In chapter 33 of *The Leviathan* (1660), English philosopher of natural law **Thomas Hobbes** (1588–1679) summarized the purposes and the methods of the critical study of the Bible by asking such questions as: Who were the actual authors and what were the dates of composition of the several books of the Bible? How did the books of the New Testament gain authority as scripture, if not through the decisions of bishops assembled in 354 CE at the Council of Laodicea? How can we judge the source of the authority by which we interpret scripture? Hobbes concluded that Moses wrote only a few chapters of the book of Deuteronomy and that most of the books of the Old Testament were written following the Babylonian exile in the late sixth century BCE.

One of the most influential figures in the development of historical criticism of the Bible was the Jewish philosopher **Baruch Spinoza** (1632–1677), whose invaluable contribution to the subject appears in chapters 7–10 of his *Tractatus theologico-politicus* (*Theological-Political Treatise*). By the time of the publication of this work in 1670, there was nothing particularly new about the claim that Moses was not the author of the whole of the Pentateuch. What was new, however, was Spinoza's claim that the issue of authorship has major importance with regard to determining how scripture is to be understood and interpreted. Specifically, Spinoza was troubled by the fact that the scripture itself had become an object of veneration and that more attention was sometimes paid to the words on the printed page than to the message conveyed by those words.

Spinoza maintained that if the Bible is a historical (i.e., natural) document, then it should be examined like any other phenomenon. The study of the Bible should, therefore, be conducted as one would conduct the study of any other object in nature: by collecting and evaluating empirical data within the book itself and by then setting that data within the context of its time and place of composition.

Spinoza states his position clearly in chapter 7 of the *Tractatus*:

I hold that the method of interpreting Scripture is no different from the method of interpreting Nature, and is in fact in complete accord with it. For the method of interpreting Nature consists essentially in composing a detailed study of Nature from which, as being the source of our assured data, we can deduce the definitions of the things of Nature. Now in exactly the same way the task of Scriptural interpretation requires us to make a straightforward study of Scripture, and from this, as the source of our fixed data and principles, to deduce by logical inference the meaning of the authors of Scripture. In this way—that is, by allowing no other principles or data for the interpretation of Scripture and study of its contents except those that can be gathered only from Scripture itself and from a historical study of Scripture—steady progress can be made without any danger of error, and one can deal with matters that surpass our understanding with no less confidence than those matters that are known to us by the natural light of reason.[7]

In precisely the same way in which knowledge about nature is derived from nature alone, so too knowledge about scripture, for Spinoza, must be derived from scripture alone, and in both instances that is accomplished only through the clear and untheological exercise of rational inquiry. Spinoza maintained that the universal message conveyed in the scripture was a simple moral message, namely, "to know and love God, and to love one's neighbor as oneself." This and this alone is the *true* word of God, and it lies unadulterated in a defective, flawed, distorted, and corrupted text (the Bible), articulated imperfectly and imprecisely in the words of men (the authors of the various books of the Bible). This simple message preserved within the Bible requires no philosophical or metaphysical speculation about the universe or about God; it requires no formal training in philosophy or history. "Scriptural doctrine," Spinzoa maintained, "contains not abstruse speculation or philosophic reasoning, but very simple matters able to be understood by the most sluggish mind."[8]

Another major figure in the emergence of biblical scholarship is **Richard Simon** (1638–1712), a French Roman Catholic priest and biblical scholar. Simon studied theology at Paris, where he developed an interest in Hebrew and other ancient Near Eastern languages. Simon's *Histoire critique du Vieux Testament* (*Critical History of the Old Testament*; 1678, 1685) raised once again the question of whether Moses could have written material in the books traditionally attributed to him. Simon's views raised strong opposition within France leading to the issuance of a council of state that ordered the seizure and destruction of the total impression of thirteen hundred copies of Simon's book, and Simon himself was expelled by his colleagues from his religious order. The book was republished in the Netherlands in 1685. In his study, Simon called attention to the fact that there is sometimes more than one version of the same story and that these doublets show variations in their literary styles. Consequently, apart from the legal portions of the Pentateuch, which Simon attributed to Moses, the remainder of the Pentateuch was the work of several different authors.

Simon's study was in three volumes. The first dealt with issues of biblical scholarship, such as the transmission of the text of the Hebrew Bible from ancient until modern times and the question of the authorship of the Pentateuch and of other books of the Hebrew Bible. Volume 2 provided an account of the principal translations of the Old Testament, both ancient and modern. Volume 3 consisted of an examination of the Old Testament's principal commentators.

Although many critical positions had been advanced earlier by scholars such as Cappel and Morin, the special value of Simon's work was that it brought together in one place the established results of Old Testament scholarship up to his time. Simon's work provoked a great deal of hostility not only from the Roman Catholic Church but also from Protestants, who saw in Simon's work a frontal attack on their single most important stronghold, an infallible Bible. Simon responded to attacks leveled against his work in his *Réponse aux Sentiments de quelques théologiens de Hollande* (*Response to the Opinions of Some Theologians from Holland*). Simon's later work consisted of his *Histoire critique du texte du Nouveau Testament* (*Critical History of the Text of the New Testament*; 1689), in which he discussed the origin and character of the various books of the New Testament, and by his *Histoire critique des versions du Nouveau Testament* (*Critical History of the Versions of the New Testament*; 1690), in which he provided an account of the various translations of the New Testament, both ancient and modern.

In 1693, Simon published what was perhaps his single most valuable contribution to biblical scholarship, *Histoire critique des principaux commentateurs du Nouveau Testament depuis le commencement du Christianisme jusques à notre temps* (*Critical History of the Principal Commentators of the New Testament from the Beginning of Christianity until the Present Time*), and in 1695 he published *Nouvelles Observations sur le texte et les versions du Nouveau Testament* (*New Observations on the Text and the Versions of the New Testament*). Simon's contribution to the emerging discipline of biblical scholarship cannot be overestimated. Simon's use of internal evidence has led to his being considered as the father of modern biblical criticism.

In addition to challenges from philosophy and from the emerging field of biblical scholarship, science began to deal a series of blows to the inerrancy of scripture. Although it was not intentional, a major assault on the Bible came in the sixteenth and seventeenth centuries from the field of astronomy. Polish astronomer **Nicolaus Copernicus** (1473–1543) began his work on *De revolutionibus orbium coelestium* (*On the Revolutions of the Heavenly Spheres*) in 1515, but it was not until 1543, the year of his death, that he finally published his findings and in a crushing blow displaced the earth, and therefore humankind, from the center of the universe, and even from the center of our own solar system, and advanced the model of a heliocentric universe.

Italian philosopher, poet, and Roman Catholic priest **Giordano (Filippo) Bruno** (1548–1600) spread Copernicus's system as well as his own view that there were infinite worlds in the physical universe and that the stars are other suns. Bruno was rewarded for his work by being burned at the stake for heresy.

Galileo Galilei (1564–1642) was an Italian mathematician, astronomer, and physicist who published in 1632 *Dialogo sopra i due massimi sistemi del mondo* (*Dialogue concerning the Two Chief Systems of the World* [Ptolemaic and Copernican]). For his support of Copernicus's theory, Galileo was tortured at Rome both physically and mentally and remained under house arrest for the remainder of his life, ironically to be absolved by the Roman Catholic Church more than three hundred fifty years later in 1989.

Copernicus's model of the universe was substantially strengthened by German mathematician **Johannes Kepler** (1571–1630), who was the first to recognize that the planets go around the sun in elliptical rather than in circular orbits. Kepler formulated the laws of planetary motion that describe mathematically the elliptical orbits of all celestial objects. By working independently of the Bible and the church, Copernicus, Bruno, Galileo, and Kepler diminished significantly the influence of the Bible as a source for scientific knowledge.

As a result of the growing influence of reason during the seventeenth century, science, philosophy, and history began to emerge as separate and distinct branches of learning, increasingly independent of biblical and ecclesiastical authority. These new approaches to knowledge were certain to spill over increasingly into the field of biblical studies. Although the Bible was acknowledged as the final word in virtually all fields of knowledge at the beginning of the seventeenth century, by the end of that century the Bible's universal authority was being eroded, and it was being treated increasingly like any other historical document.

The eighteenth century brought additional support for the progressive views of these earlier scholars. In 1753, prominent French Roman Catholic physician **Jean Astruc** (1684–1766) published *Conjectures sur les mémoires originaux dont il paraît que Moïse s'est servi pour composer le livre de Genèse* (*Conjectures on the Original Memoirs that Moses Appears to Have Used in Composing the Book of Genesis*), in which he postulated the existence of two distinct sources in the book of Genesis, based on the alternating use of two names for God, one of which sources used Elohim, and the other Yahweh or Jehovah.

This thesis of two sources in the book of Genesis received little attention until **Johann Gottfried Eichhorn** (1752–1827) published the first great modern introduction to the Old Testament, his *Einleitung in das Alte Testament* (*Introduction to the Old Testament*, 3 volumes; 1780–83). Eichhorn built on Astruc's hypothesis of two documents in Genesis and expanded the theory by noting that the separate documents have other characteristics, both literary and substantive, and applied his analysis of the sources to the whole of the Pentateuch (Genesis, Exodus, Leviticus, Numbers, and Deuteronomy). Eichhorn's analysis was more radical than Astruc's because Eichhorn was also writing under the influence of eighteenth century German rationalism, English deism, and skepticism, and he was, therefore, asking questions and raising doubts much more penetrating than the relatively innocuous issue of the multiple sources of the book of Genesis.

In doing so, Eichhorn may have been aware of the writings of Englishman **Charles Blount** (1654–93), most especially his short pamphlet on the nature of miracles, *Miracles, No Violation of the Laws of Nature* (1683), the publication of which attracted a great deal of hostile criticism; and of **Anthony Collins** (1676–1729), an English theologian who defined the position of the English deists and defended the cause of rational theology in his *A Discourse concerning Free-Thinking* (1713). In their writings, Blount and Collins dismissed out of hand specifically both miracles and predictive prophecy and, in addition, the authority of the Old Testament. The writings of Blount and Collins likely afforded Eichhorn the philosophical underpinning for his more radical positions on these issues.

It was, however, **Hermann Samuel Reimarus** (1694–1768), German philosopher, man of letters, and professor of Oriental languages, who first expressed an unequivocal and uncompromising opposition to the supernatural in the Bible. Reimarus studied theology, ancient languages, and philosophy and in 1720–21 visited Holland and England, where he likely encountered the English deist movement. Reimarus is best known for his *Apologie oder Schutzschrift für die vernünftigen Verehrer Gottes* (*Apology or Defense for the Rational Worshippers of God*), carefully withheld from publication during his lifetime, but from which, following his death, his friend **Gotthold Ephraim Lessing** published several chapters under the title of *Fragmente eines Ungennannten* (*Anonymous Fragments*), generally referred to as the *Wolfenbüttel Fragments* (1778). The position of the *Apologie* is pure naturalistic deism, allowing for no miracles and no intrusion of the supernatural into the natural order. Natural religion advances everything that is the opposite of revealed religion and uses doubt with its rationalist presuppositions as the basic principle of all historical investigation. The basic truths of this natural religion are the existence of a good and wise Creator and the immortality of the human soul, truths that are discoverable only on the basis of human reason and that can and should constitute the foundation of universal religion.

Reimarus's work is the starting point of **Albert Schweitzer's** masterpiece *The Quest of the Historical Jesus* (*Von Reimarus zu Wrede*, 1906 [*From Reimarus to Wrede* is the title in the original German]). Schweitzer opens his chapter on

Reimarus with these words: "Before Reimarus, no one had attempted to form a historical conception of the life of Jesus."[9] Reimarus's bold work was the first effort to apply systematically and consistently the tools of historical criticism to the life of Jesus, and its results were devastating to Christian orthodoxy of the time. According to Schweitzer, Reimarus stated, "we are justified in drawing an absolute distinction between the teaching of the Apostles in their writings and what Jesus Himself in His own lifetime proclaimed and taught."[10] Schweitzer goes on to state: "What belongs to the teaching of Jesus is clearly to be recognized. It is contained in two phrases of identical meaning, 'Repent, and believe in the Gospel,' or, as it is put elsewhere, 'Repent, for the Kingdom of Heaven is at hand.'"[11] According to Reimarus, Jesus took his personal stand within first-century Judaism and accepted its Messianic expectations without modifying or correcting them in any way. What is new in Jesus' teaching is the timetable, namely, that the arrival of the Kingdom (or Rule) of God was imminent.

According to Reimarus, Jesus had no intention of setting aside Judaism and putting a new religion, Christianity, in its place. Drawing a clue from the difficulty that the Easter event was first proclaimed at Pentecost, fifty days after Jesus' death, Reimarus came to the conclusion that following Jesus' unexpected and inexplicable death, his disciples stole his body, hid it, and proclaimed a spiritual resurrection as well as Jesus' second coming in glory in the very near future. It is no wonder that Reimarus chose not to publish his work during his lifetime; his conclusions struck at the very heart of Christianity.

In spite of Reimarus's sometimes far-fetched conclusions, his work is extraordinarily significant because of his remarkable eye for detail and his systematic application of the principle of historical reason to the texts of the canonical gospels. Many of Reimarus's insights still remain at the center of biblical scholarship two hundred fifty years after his death: the understanding of Jesus as an eschatological prophet; the problem of the Messianic Secret; the difficulties associated with Jesus' prediction of his own passion, death, and resurrection, the *miracles stories* of the gospels as opposed to the *miracles* of Jesus, the striking difference between the Jesus of the gospel of John and the Jesus of the synoptic gospels (Matthew, Mark, and Luke), and much more.

Reimarus's work was followed by a series of rationalist lives of Jesus to which Schweitzer devotes several chapters in his *Quest*. It was, however, **David Friedrich Strauss** (1808–74) who provided for New Testament scholars a critical key that is essentially still a working principle of contemporary biblical scholarship. "Religion," Strauss maintained, "is not concerned with supra-mundane beings and a divinely glorious future, but with present spiritual realities which appear as 'moments' in the eternal being and becoming of Absolute Spirit."[12] Strauss maintained "immortality is not something which stretches out into the future, but simply and solely the present quality of the spirit, its inner universality, its power of rising above everything finite to the Idea."[13]

Strauss's masterpiece, *Das Leben-Jesu* (*The Life of Jesus*), published in two volumes of 1,480 pages in 1835 and 1836, when Strauss was still in his twenties, is one of the most brilliant works in the entire corpus of biblical scholarship. Although the concept of myth had frequently been applied by scholars to the literature of the Old Testament, prior to the work of David Friedrich Strauss it had never been fully appreciated or consistently applied to the life of Jesus. The word myth was, and to many Christians still is, an offense to religious belief. However, as used by Strauss, religious myth is "nothing else than the clothing in historic form of religious ideas, shaped by the unconscious power of legend, and embodied in a historic personality."[14]

For Strauss, Christianity introduced into history the idea of God-manhood as that idea was realized and expressed in the historical personality of Jesus of Nazareth. For early Christians, it was frankly impossible to advance a purely historical representation of Jesus, because the early church was confident that Jesus was the incarnation of God-manhood, an ideal that, they believed, is now open to everyone and that remains the ultimate goal of all humanity. As a thoroughgoing Hegelian, Strauss sought, through his mythological interpretation of the New Testament, to bring together and synthesize the *thesis*, as represented by the supernaturalistic explanation of the Bible, with its opposite or *antithesis*, as represented by the rationalistic interpretation of the Bible, both of which were in Strauss's opinion unacceptable ways of reading and understanding the text.

For Strauss, all of the stories relating to Jesus before his baptism are myths, woven on Old Testament prototypes. As for the accounts of the baptism of Jesus in the four gospels, the historical residue of these stories is only that Jesus was, in fact, baptized by John the Baptist and was, for a period of time, probably a disciple of John. In their present forms, however, the stories of Jesus' baptism serve to state that either for Jesus or more likely for the early church, the baptism was the moment in Jesus' life in which his Messiahship either dawned on him, or served, more probably, as the moment from which Jesus' Messiahship was traced by his followers. So too the story of the temptation of Jesus is primitive Christian legend, woven out of stories from the Old Testament, designed to show Jesus' inner struggle concerning his own self-identity.

As for the healing miracles, some of them may have their roots in actual exorcisms that Jesus performed, but in their present form, in which evil spirits or demons recognize Jesus as Messiah, these stories reflect nothing more than the church's effort to show that the supernatural powers of evil recognized and submitted themselves to Jesus' supernatural power during his lifetime. Reports of healings of the blind, of the deaf, of paralytics, of the dumb, and raisings of the dead all belong to the expectations of contemporary Judaism regarding what will transpire in the Messianic age and have their roots not in history, but in passages in the Old Testament (e.g., Isaiah 35:5–6a, "Then the eyes of the blind shall be opened, and the ears of the deaf unstopped; then shall the lame man leap like a deer, and the tongue of the speechless sing for joy").

Strauss maintained, moreover, that the stories of the resurrection appearances of Jesus to his disciples and to others are all mythical. Matthew knew of such appearances only in Galilee, Luke of appearances only in Jerusalem, and Mark of no appearances at all. For Strauss, if there were appearances of the risen Lord, then he had, indeed, not died; and if Jesus had actually died, then there were, pure and simple, no such appearances. The mythical character of the ascension into heaven is, for Strauss, self-evident.

What Strauss did, story by story, gospel by gospel, was to demonstrate down to the most minute detail that what we have in the gospels of the New Testament are not reliably historical accounts of virgin births, theophanies at baptisms, healings of the sick, and raisings of the dead, culminating in Jesus' own resurrection from the dead and ascension into heaven. Rather what we have are "stories" that *clothe in historical form* the church's claim or idea that Jesus was a divinely ordained messenger of God. The *stories about Jesus* in the gospels are the "historicizing" of that Idea.

Going a step farther, Strauss was the first to take the position that the Gospel of John has little historical value. The Jesus of the Gospel of John is totally dominated by the theological conviction of the early church. Unlike the gospels of Matthew, Mark, and Luke, in which history is carefully interwoven with myth, in John there is little more than dogma pretending to be history:

> John represents a more advanced stage in the mythopoeic process, inasmuch as he
> has substituted for the Jewish Messianic conception, the Greek metaphysical con-

ception of the Divine Sonship, and, on the basis of his acquaintance with the Alexandrian Logos doctrine, even makes Jesus apply to Himself the Greek speculative conception of pre-existence.[15]

It has not been my purpose in this section to trace the long and detailed history of the emergence of modern biblical scholarship.[16] I have, however, tried to point to some of the major players who made particularly significant contributions to the emergence of the modern method of biblical scholarship with its deference to rationalism as the primary criterion of historical reason.

THE HISTORICAL METHOD

As we have seen above, the historical method (or what I prefer to call the tools of biblical scholarship) emerged and evolved over a period of several centuries and in the larger context of learning nourished by the Renaissance, the Reformation, and the Age of Reason.[17] However, the basic tenets of that method, the canons of biblical scholarship, have been firmly in place for more than a century, although some scholars and many Christians refuse to acknowledge that fact. Although the war is over, the battle against biblical scholarship rages on in some quarters because of the perceived threat of biblical scholarship to Christian orthodoxy.

Before the rules of biblical scholarship were entirely clear, a number of smaller streams had to flow into a single great river. The first and the simplest of these small streams was an examination of internal evidence within the books of the Bible themselves. That methodology was already evident almost two thousand years ago in the early work of Celsus, Ptolemy, Porphyry, Jerome, Theodore of Mopsuestia, Origen, and Dionysius of Alexandria. The findings of these men had to be rediscovered, relearned, and further developed in the last few centuries. That work began with Karlstadt in Germany in the early sixteenth century, and continued with Cappel, Morin, and La Peyrère in France in the seventeenth century. Even Hobbes writing in England in the seventeenth century built his arguments essentially on an examination of evidence internal to the Bible.

It was likely Spinoza, a Portuguese Jew, born and raised in Amsterdam, who first understood the importance of examining the Bible as one would study any other object in nature. Spinoza appealed to much more than the issue of internal evidence.

He claimed that the Bible was a collection of books written by men and that it was, therefore, subject to the same vicissitudes as any other human endeavor. The Bible is simply one more object within the natural order.

In the late eighteenth century in his introduction to the Old Testament, Eichhorn embraced for the first time the systematic philosophical perspective of German rationalism and English deism. At about the same time, Lessing published Reimarus's application of an unequivocal opposition to supernaturalism to the books of the New Testament and, more specifically, to the life of Jesus. The final nails were being hammered into the coffin of the old order of biblical interpretation. The rules of biblical scholarship were changing dramatically; they now had an uncompromising philosophical foundation: rationalism.

To understand the significance of this final blow to the old order, it is important to look briefly at the foundational contribution of movements variously called German rationalism, the German Enlightenment, English deism, and skepticism to see how they collectively provided the philosophical underpinning for modern biblical scholarship. German scholarship began to question and eventually to reject the divine authority of the traditional canon of the Bible and, more specifically, the inspiration and presumed correctness of the texts of the Old and New Testaments. It questioned whether it was appropriate to equate scripture with revelation.

The term "rationalism" was used to designate the view that human reason, or human understanding, is the sole source, the final test, and the competent judge of all truth. As these insights invaded the study of the Bible, this seemly destructive criticism was leveled especially against the miracles recorded in the Bible and against the inerrancy and authenticity of the scriptures. Most specifically, David Hume (1711–76) directed his celebrated critique of miracles against the justification of religion by any means other than the rational. Hume weighed the possibility of error on the part of the observer of miracles or the historian against the possibility of miraculous occurrences themselves.[18] Human experience, affected by ignorance, fancy, and the imaginings of fear and hope, explains sufficiently the growth of religion and the presence of the element of the miraculous and the supernatural in virtually all religious traditions.

Once the special authority of the Bible had been questioned and its place in the natural order firmly established, it was essential to understand more clearly the original meanings of the ancient texts in their ancient contexts. Scholars understood that a detached and objective reading of the Bible, free from dogmatic preconceptions and with special attention to the ancient languages and the original historical circumstances, would alone produce a more informed and less biased reconstruction and appreciation of the origins of ancient Judaism and early Christianity. Once scholars had established the principle that ancient documents should be examined in their own historical contexts, in a spirit of impartial inquiry and total freedom without predisposition or prejudice, it was only a matter of time until the methodology and tools of modern biblical scholarship emerged.

By the nineteenth century, archeological discoveries in Palestine, Egypt, and Mesopotamia and the decipherment of Egyptian hieroglyphs and ancient cuneiform[19] scripts aroused even greater interest in setting the Bible and biblical religion within the historical, social, and religious contexts of the ancient Near East. Scholars soon understood that ancient Israelite religion could and should be understood within the larger context of ancient Semitic religions and that early Christianity could and should be understood within the historical, social, and religious contexts of the Greco-Roman Hellenistic world. The issue of *contextuality* was paramount to the new method. It was evident that it was essential to look at the Bible itself and the historical figures in the biblical narratives within the historical, social, and religious contexts of the world in which these individuals lived and out of which these written documents arose.

It was suddenly obvious that each of the sixty-six books of the Christian Bible (thirty-nine from the Old Testament and twenty-seven from the New Testament) had its own unique history. Each of the sixty-six books was written in a particular time, in a particular place, by a particular author, and for a particular purpose, and it fell to historians to develop the particular tools and skills needed to discover the origin and history of each book.

Ulrich Wilckens has provided an excellent formal definition of the historical method of biblical scholarship:

> The only scientifically responsible interpretation of the Bible is that investigation of the biblical texts that, with a methodologically consistent use of historical understanding in the present state of its art, seeks via reconstruction to recognize and describe the meaning these texts have had in the context of the tradition history of early [Judaism and] Christianity.[20]

In other words, biblical scholarship is committed to providing a systematic statement of what probably happened in the past after assessing carefully and objectively the authenticity, the reliability, and the veridicality of the ancient sources, free from centuries of interpretative theological overlay. The biblical scholar must be a person of integrity with a passionate and unqualified commitment to the truth, wherever that may lead.

Before proceeding to discuss the rules of evidence for what I consider sound biblical scholarship, it might be helpful to clarify what does and what does not constitute the purview of biblical scholarship by focusing on just two examples: one from the Old Testament and one from the New Testament.

However much evidence conservative Jewish or Christian scholars may muster to argue that God led the people of Israel out of Egypt in the Exodus, the exercise is doomed to failure. No body of evidence can possibly authenticate an act of God, or even the purported "events" described in the book of Exodus. Historians can establish the likelihood that there was an escape from Egypt by a relatively small band of Hebrew slaves, but the magnitude of the event as described in the book of Exodus falls beyond the purview of the historian, who cannot deal with miraculous crossings of seas or with voices from burning bushes, as if they were actual events subject to verification or falsification. They are the language of ancient myth. At best historians can discuss the ways in which a simple event might have been interpreted by Moses and others as an act of Israel's God Yahweh and how such a simple event was exaggerated in the oral retelling and subsequently by authors in their writings. Scholars can discuss the biblical accounts of the exodus, but they can never know from those accounts that they reflect a reliable retelling of what actually happened.

Likewise no body of evidence can ever establish the historicity of Jesus' birth from a virgin. Science dictates that all children are born of a mother and a father, and there is a great deal of evidence in the New Testament that suggests, in fact, that Mary and Joseph were Jesus' biological parents. Historians can also speculate about how and why the early church initially created oral traditions and then somewhat later written accounts in two different gospels, Matthew and Luke (which, by the way, disagree in significant details as to what is purported to have "happened"). What we have in the early chapters of the gospels of Matthew and Luke are *birth narratives* that demand our attention, but we obviously do not have *reliable accounts* of Jesus' birth. There is a fundamental difference between *miracle stories* and *miracles*. The latter falls totally outside the purview of the historian, who would properly characterize such *stories* as legends that served a particular purpose for early Christian communities.

THE RULES OF EVIDENCE

It should be eminently clear that biblical scholars make no assumptions about the Bible except that they are committed to studying its books in the same manner in which they would study any literature from antiquity, or from any other period. Indeed, because the Bible focuses on *history* and purports to tell the *story* of God's active involvement in *history*, then *history* must be a primary concern, a sine qua non, for anyone who wants to understand the Bible in as full and objective a way as is humanly possible.

Biblical scholars apply to the books of the Bible the same critical tools that they would apply to any writing that is a human production. In doing so, scholars apply greater value to evidence found within the books themselves than they do to external traditions *about* the Bible, which are generally considerably later than the writing of the books themselves and which often reflect the biases of subsequent generations.

Scholars assume that the books of the Bible were composed by men in specific historical environments of both time and place and that those documents will, therefore, almost always betray some evidence about the time and place of their composition. It is essential to acknowledge that these ancient documents will reflect methods of composition and worldviews contemporary with the world in which they arose and that those methods of composition and those worldviews will be substantially alien to our own. This simple fact means that the reader will have to try to place himself or herself into the time and place in which these books were written in order to be able to understand them properly.

Biblical scholars have determined that there are vast differences in the historical value of the books of the Old and New Testaments, and even differences within specific books insofar as history is the paramount concern. Having said that, it is important to lay out the rules and criteria whereby we can reasonably determine what likely did and did not happen in the ancient past. That is, however, not an easy task, and equally competent unbiased scholars will often examine the same evidence and come to very different conclusions. The problem sometimes lies in the inadequacy or the insufficiency of the evidence, when drawing conclusions leaves a great deal of room for reasonable doubt. We shall, therefore, often speak about what is probable and even possible *within the limits of historical reason*.

Whatever else there may be in the sixty-six books that Christians call their canon of sacred scripture, there is a human component, and that human component suffers from the same limitations, deficiencies, shortcomings, errors, and biases that we find in any body of literature from which we attempt to reconstruct what likely happened at some time in the past, in our case at various times in the very distant past. That endeavor poses enormous but not insurmountable challenges. It is, however, essential to approach our task with a measure of humility, because there is so much that we do not know and will probably never know with any degree of certainty.

Biblical scholars with a strong personal religious predisposition sometimes fall into the trap of exercising the principles of biblical criticism until they reach the point where the application of rationalist principles appears to conflict with what they consider revealed truth. For the historian as historian, nothing, not even so-called revealed truth, can stand in the way of the consistent application of the canons of historical reason. There are no exceptions, no exemptions, no bending of the rules, and no retreating from the consistent application of the principles of historical reason.

At this juncture, it is important to state clearly and unequivocally that history and theology are by no means the same. The historian attempts to reconstruct the past; the theologian tries to identify and unfold the meaning and relevance of the texts. Although the two are closely interrelated, they are distinct. Our purpose in this volume will be to focus exclusively on the question of history, what we can and cannot know, and with what measure of certainty.

Whatever the historian's particular subject matter, history is much more than a simple retelling of what is written in the sources. History is a narrative account of the past, based on the sources, but only after their reliability, their competence, their authenticity, their truthfulness, and their clarity have been carefully examined and critically questioned. Biblical scholars must hone their analytical acumen in examining and evaluating the relevant biblical and nonbiblical texts in order to provide the best possible explanation of what happened in the past.

In order to appreciate better the methodology used by biblical scholars, let me by analogy consider the example of the courtroom, because historical sources are like witnesses in a courtroom and must be questioned and have their testimony evaluated. John Smith is on trial for murdering Mary Jones, and you, the reader, are a member of the jury. It is, on the one hand, the burden of the state, through the office of the district attorney, to set forth persuasively the evidence needed to convince you and the other jurors that John is guilty. It is, on the other hand, the responsibility of John's defense attorney to cast doubt in the minds of the jurors that John is, in fact, guilty. Typically, witnesses are introduced, examined, and cross-examined to build the case and to influence the jury. Wherever appropriate, physical evidence is admitted for consideration. In the end, the jurors retreat to the privacy of a room, where they are expected to discuss and evaluate the evidence and ultimately to pass judgment on John's guilt, which the state must establish in their minds *beyond reasonable doubt.*

The standard by which the historian makes judgments is understandably somewhat less than the courtroom threshold of *beyond reasonable doubt.* Nevertheless, the principle for making judgments is basically the same: to collect and evaluate the evidence (the witnesses) impartially and without bias in order to make an informed and reasoned decision or determination about what actually happened at some time in the past.

Just as there are basic rules of evidence in the courtroom, so too there are basic rules of evidence for the historian as well. Typically, historians, in dealing with a primary source, ask of that source the *who*, the *where*, the *when*, and the *why* questions. To use the book of Genesis as an example, is there either internal or external evidence that enables the historian to determine *where*, *when*, *why*, and *by whom* Genesis was written?

The **time and place** criterion generally affirms that the closer in time and place a source or the author of a source is to an event, the more reliable that source is likely to be. Conversely, the farther in time and place a source or the author of a source is from an event, the less reliable that source is likely to be. The historian looks for direct testimony of an event. Most reliable are accounts from multiple independent eyewitnesses. Next in reliability would be accounts of an event, created after the event itself, by multiple individuals who themselves had direct access to independent eyewitnesses to the actual event. Obviously, the farther removed a source is from the purported event, the less reliable the testimony is likely to be.

A second criterion to which historians generally appeal is **the bias rule.** Every source is biased in some way. Documents invariably tell us what the author of the document thought happened, or perhaps in all too many instances what the author of the document wanted his audience to believe happened. Accordingly, every source and every piece of evidence must be examined critically and skeptically. No evidence and no testimony can be taken entirely at its face value, especially evidence or testimony whose primary purpose is to advance the agenda of the witness (or the author) or the agenda of the in-group to which the source is addressed. The Bible is especially problematic in this regard because it is a collection of in-group writings for in-group readers and does not purport to be objective.

Wherever possible, evidence from **external written sources** and **circumstantial evidence**, such as linguistic studies and archaeological data, can and should be called upon to confirm or to question what we find in our biblical sources. Fortunately, we have many written sources from ancient Mesopotamia, ancient Egypt, ancient Canaan, and the Greco-Roman world that enable us to read the Old and New Testaments against the background and within the context of ancient Near Eastern history, religion, and culture. In addition, we now know much more about the languages of the ancient world and we have substantial raw data from archaeological excavations that we can use as objective, perhaps even scientific and unbiased, evidence in reconstructing the past.

We are in a better position today than we have ever been before to understand the Bible. It would appear, therefore, that we have an obligation to use all of the available methodologies and tools to the fullest extent possible in order to place our feet firmly on as solid a foundation of history as is humanly reasonable. What distinguishes the Bible from most other great religious literature is that throughout the sixty-six books, from Genesis to Revelation, the Bible claims that God has revealed himself in *history*. History is, therefore, paramount for both Jews and Christians, and a clear understanding of the ancient history can and will only enrich our understanding of the origins of both Judaism and Christianity. Faith is, of course, very different from history and science. Nevertheless, history can and should afford an important corrective to unexamined and uncritical religious faith.

Throughout this volume, I will be applying the basic principles of the historical method of biblical scholarship and the rules of evidence as outlined above. I hope to show how these principles work by applying them to particular stories and traditions. At times, I will also introduce or allude to additional principles or criteria that have guided biblical scholars in their efforts to reconstruct the past. At every step, our single-minded objective must always be a quest for the truth—an honest reconstruction of the past within the limits of historical reason. That quest will sometimes lead us to likely conclusions, sometimes to possible conclusions, and sometimes to no conclusion at all. We must be prepared to know when there is not sufficient evidence to know what happened in the past, just as there is in the courtroom sometimes insufficient evidence to convict a suspect. My goal in this volume is to lead the reader, wherever possible, through the method of biblical scholarship to what I consider the best conclusions based on a rigorous application of that method.

NOTES

1. In using the designations BCE (Before the Common Era) and CE (of the Common Era), I am using terminology that is more current and more inclusive than the designations BC (Before Christ) and AD (*Anno Domini*, in the year of the Lord), which are specifically Christian. There is, otherwise, no difference between BCE and BC, or between CE and AD.

2. Robert H. Pfeiffer, *Introduction to the Old Testament* (New York: Harper & Brothers, 1948), p. 43.

3. Ibid.

4. Ibid.

5. Ibid.

6. The Hebrew language is written from right to left and was originally written only with consonants. Vowel sounds between the consonants were understood but not written. Only later, when Hebrew was no longer a spoken language, and when Jews spoke Aramaic, or Greek, or Latin, or some other vernacular language, did rabbinic scholars add the requisite vowel signs to the Hebrew text as dots and dashes above and below the consonants. These vowel pointings were standardized about 500 CE.

Imagine the confusion in trying to understand a text without vowels. For example, try to pronounce the English word NTRL. That could, of course, be NeuTRaL, or NaTuRaL, or even NoT ReaL, words with very different meanings, yet all written with the same consonants. The opportunity for confusion in reading a text without vowels is enormous. The adding of vowel pointings to the Hebrew Bible much later than when the books were originally written means that those later rabbinical scholars added the vowels that suited their understanding of the texts. There is, of course, no guarantee that their vowels reflected the intentions of the original authors.

7. Baruch Spinoza, *Tractatus Theologico-Politicus* (*Theological-Political Treatise*), trans. Samuel Shirley (Leiden: Brill Academic Publishers, 1997), p. 177.

8. Ibid.

9. Albert Schweitzer, *The Quest of the Historical Jesus*, trans. W. Montgomery, with a new introduction by James M. Robinson (New York: Macmillan Company, 1968), p. 13.

10. Ibid., p. 16.

11. Ibid.

12. Ibid., p. 73.

13. Ibid.

14. Ibid.

15. Ibid., p. 86.

16. A good summary of that history can be found in succinct form in Edgar Krentz, *The Historical-Critical Method* (Philadelphia: Fortress Press, 1975).

17. The reader can find a brilliant and comprehensive treatment of the history of Western thought in Richard Tarnas's *The Passion of the Western Mind: Understanding the Ideas That Have Shaped Our World View* (New York: Ballantine Books, 1991). Of special interest for our purposes here is chapter 5: "The Modern World View," in which Tarnas discusses the Renaissance, the Reformation, the Scientific Revolution, the Philosophical Revolution, Foundations of the Modern World View, and the Triumph of Secularism. What Tarnas accomplishes in five hundred pages is monumental and far more than I can hope to communicate in a short chapter.

18. Trying to find historical evidence to support the miracles of the Bible is like trying to find evidence to refute Darwin. The methodology of much evangelical Christian biblical scholarship is the historical equivalent of intelligent design in the realm of natural science. There is no distinction between bad biblical scholarship and bad science, because the presuppositions of biblical historians and of all historians and of all scientists are and must remain essentially the same. All employ a "scientific" (i.e., a secular, naturalist, nonsupernatural) methodology in their work.

19. Cuneiform refers to the wedge-shaped characters in the inscriptions of ancient Akkadians, Assyrians, Babylonians, and Persians. It is the method of writing, not a particular language, just as many people in the world use the convention of the Roman alphabet to write their own individual languages.

20. Ulrich Wilckens, "Über die Bedeutung historischer Kritik in der modernen Bibelexegese," in *Was heisst Auslegung der Heiligen Schrift?* (Regensburg: Friedrich Pustet, 1966), p. 133; English translation by Edgar Krentz, *The Historical Method* (Philadelphia: Fortress Press, 1975), p. 33.

CHAPTER 1

THE AUTHORSHIP
OF THE PENTATEUCH

Inasmuch as the Mosaic authorship of the Pentateuch[1] (the books of Genesis, Exodus, Leviticus, Numbers, and Deuteronomy) was one of the earliest areas of investigation, both in ancient times and at the beginning of the period of modern biblical scholarship, it is fitting to begin our study with an examination of this subject. The question of the authorship of the Pentateuch raises important issues about the reliability and the credibility of these five books as sources for a historical reconstruction of Israel's earliest history. Hence, a review of the evidence is central to evaluating the dependability of this material as a historical source.

Although tradition holds that Moses wrote these five books, upon rigorous examination of the evidence, that tradition proves to be unreliable. It is, therefore, essential before embarking on a study of Israel's early history to consider the question of the authorship of the Pentateuch, for it matters considerably when, where, why, and by whom these five books were written.[2]

THE CASE FOR MOSAIC AUTHORSHIP
OF THE PENTATEUCH

Even if it could be established that Moses was the author of the Pentateuch, and, in particular, of the book of Genesis, it is crucial to acknowledge that Moses would not have been a particularly credible witness to the events from the time of Adam and Eve to the period of the Hebrew patriarchs, Abraham, Isaac, and Jacob. Moses lived in the latter part of the fourteenth and early part of the thirteenth century BCE. The "events" of the primordial history "occurred" millennia earlier, and the period of the patriarchs should probably be dated a half millennium before the time of Moses. Even more problematic: from whence should we suppose Moses learned about the activities concerning Creation as described in the opening chapters of Genesis?

Conservative Christians, often with a clear bias, tend to claim that there is strong evidence that Moses wrote the books of Genesis, Exodus, Leviticus, Numbers, and Deuteronomy.[3] In support of their position, they point, for example, to the following passages:

(1) Exodus 17:14

"Then the LORD (= Yah or Yahweh) said to Moses, '*Write* this as a reminder *in a book* and recite it in the hearing of Joshua'" (italics mine).[4]

This verse is the Bible's earliest reference to writing and an indication of the first words that Moses was ordered to write. The text implies a directive to Moses to record something in writing, but not necessarily in a book, as the Hebrew word used here can refer to any document. In any event, it is evident that this verse is not a reference to the Pentateuch or to any portion of the Pentateuch.

(2) Exodus 24:4a

"And Moses *wrote down* all the words of the LORD (Yahweh)" (italics mine).

At this point in the story, Moses presumably wrote the Ten Commandments on parchment to deposit in the ark of the covenant. The stone tablets of the Ten Commandments are referred to only later in Exodus 24:12 and 31:18. In any event, this is clearly not a reference to the Pentateuch.

(3) Exodus 34:27

"The LORD (Yahweh) said to Moses: '*Write* these words; in accordance with these words I have made a covenant with you and with Israel'" (italics mine).

The reference here is presumably to Exodus 34:11–26, the substance of which is the new tablets of the Ten Commandments (see Exodus 34:28b), written to replace the tablets that Moses had previously broken (Exodus 32:19). Once again, this is clearly not a reference to the Pentateuch.

(4) Numbers 33:1–2a

"These are the stages by which the Israelites went out of the land of Egypt in military formation under the leadership of Moses and Aaron. Moses *wrote down* their starting points, stage by stage, by command of the LORD (Yahweh)" (italics mine).

This verse implies that Moses wrote down an itinerary for the Israelites to follow for the course of their exodus from Egypt.

(5) Deuteronomy 31:9

"Then Moses *wrote down* this law, and gave it to the priests, the sons of Levi, who carried the ark of the covenant of the LORD (Yahweh), and to all the elders of Israel" (italics mine).

The reference is presumably to the Deuteronomistic Law referred to in Deuteronomy 4:14 and discovered in 621 BCE by Hilkiah the priest during a major repair and renovation of the Jerusalem temple (see 2 Kings 22). That body of law, generally referred to by scholars as D, now likely found in Deuteronomy 12–26, was probably written somewhat earlier in the seventh century BCE and was likely based on older oral and written legal tradition. Apparently sometime in the sixth century BCE, this D material (basically but not exclusively Deuteronomy 12–26) was set within the framework of Moses' valedictory address to Israel on the plains of Moab shortly before his death and the Israelites' entry into the promised land in order to assure the Mosaic legacy of Israel's covenantal law—namely, the claim that *all* covenantal law came directly from Moses.

(6) Joshua 1:7–8a

"Only be strong and very courageous, being careful to act in accordance with all the law that my servant Moses commanded you; do not turn from it to the right hand or to the left, so that you may be successful wherever you go. *This book of the law* shall not depart out of your mouth; you shall meditate on it day and night, so that you may be careful to act in accordance with all *that is written in it*" (italics mine).

This reference to the *book of the law* refers once again to D, the earlier edition of Deuteronomy, basically but not exclusively chapters 12–26, mentioned above.

(7) Joshua 8:30–31a

"Then Joshua built on Mount Ebal an altar to the LORD (Yahweh), the God of Israel, just as Moses the servant of the LORD (Yahweh) had commanded the

Israelites, *as it is written in the book of the law* of Moses, 'an altar of unhewn stones, on which no iron tool has been used'" (italics mine).

Once again, a probable reference to D, rediscovered in 621 BCE during the reign of King Josiah (see Deuteronomy 27:5–6 for the specific reference to building an altar of unhewn stones on which no iron tool has been used).

(8) Joshua 23:6

"Therefore be very steadfast to observe and do all that is written in *the book of the law of Moses*, turning aside from it neither to the right nor to the left" (italics mine).

This *book of the law* refers once again to the earlier edition of Deuteronomy, containing legal lore such as is contained basically but not exclusively in Deuteronomy 12–26.

(9) 1 Kings 2:3

"Keep the charge of the LORD (Yahweh) your God, walking in his ways and keeping his statutes, his commandments, his ordinances, and his testimonies, *as it is written in the law of Moses*, so that you may prosper in all that you do and wherever you turn" (italics mine).

Once again a reference to D, especially reminiscent of the theme expressed in Deuteronomy 4:40; 6:5; 8:6; 10:12–13; and 11:1, 22.

(10) 2 Kings 14:6

"But he did not put to death the children of the murderers, according to *what is written in the book of the law of Moses*, where the LORD (Yahweh) commanded, 'The parents shall not be put to death for the children, or the children be put to death for the parents; but all shall be put to death for their own sins'" (italics mine).

This citation of the *law of Moses* is from Deuteronomy 24:16, and therefore another reference to D.

(11) Ezra 6:18

"Then they set the priests in their divisions and the Levites in their courses for the service of God at Jerusalem, *as it is written in the book of Moses*" (italics mine).

In the biblical tradition, it was David, not Moses, who arranged the divisions for the priests and the courses for the Levites (see 1 Chronicles 23–26). Moses simply established the two classes, the priests and the Levites (see Exodus 29; Leviticus 8; and Numbers 3, 4, and 8). The reference to "the book of Moses" in this verse is probably to a recension of the Pentateuch available to the author of the book of Ezra in about 400 BCE.

(12) Ezra 7:6

"This Ezra went up from Babylonia. He was a scribe skilled in *the law of Moses that the LORD (Yahweh) the God of Israel had given*; and the king granted him all that he asked, for the hand of the LORD (Yahweh) his God was upon him" (italics mine).

"The law of Moses" probably refers to a recension of the Pentateuch available to the author of the book of Ezra in about 400 BCE.

(13) Nehemiah 8:1

"All of the people gathered together into the square before the Water Gate. They told the scribe Ezra to bring *the book of the law of Moses*, which the LORD (Yahweh) had given to Israel" (italics mine).

"The book of the law of Moses" refers to a recension of the Pentateuch available in about 400 BCE.

We know from archaeological evidence that the art of writing was developed well before the time of the Exodus from Egypt and that both law codes and historical records existed in the ancient Near East long before the time of Moses. Nevertheless, there is little, in fact probably nothing, in the verses cited above to suggest that these passages refer to the completed Pentateuch. Even the reference in Nehemiah, which seems to be most detailed, may refer to only a portion of the Pentateuch, the so-called Deuteronomistic Law, or to the JED document,[5] the latest recension of the Pentateuch available toward the end of the fifth century, when Ezra and Nehemiah were presumably active in Jerusalem. It is possible that an early recension of the entire Pentateuch, referred to as "the book of the law of Moses," was available by about 400 BCE, but that is not certain.

Apart from the possible allusions to the Pentateuch in Ezra and Nehemiah, the earliest testimony that Moses was the author of the Pentateuch comes from Ecclesiasticus, or the Wisdom of Jesus Son of Sirach, written sometime shortly after 200 BCE: "All this is the book of the covenant of the Most High God, the law that Moses commanded us as an inheritance for the congregations of Jacob" (Sirach 24:23).[6] Yet, even in this verse, the meaning of the phrase "the book of the covenant of the Most High God" is not entirely clear.

Outside the biblical texts, the Jewish philosopher Philo of Alexandria, who was born circa 20 CE, likely believed the tradition of Mosaic authorship of the Pentateuch (*On Abraham* 1,[7] and possibly *The Contemplative Life* 28[8]). Flavius Josephus, a first-century CE Jewish historian, is more specific on the subject:

> I say that we do not possess myriads of inconsistent books, conflicting with each other (as the Greeks have). Our books, those which are justly accredited, are but two and twenty, and they contain the record of all time. Of these, five are the books of Moses, comprising the laws and the traditional history from the birth of man down to the death of the lawgiver. (*Against Apion* 1.39; Loeb Classical Library translation).[9]

Mosaic authorship of the Pentateuch is obviously a late Jewish tradition, originating in a period perhaps eight hundred to a thousand years after Moses' death. The modern historian would have to find convincing internal evidence to support this late tradition of Mosaic authorship, but no such evidence is forthcoming in the passages cited above.

The only certain conclusions that emerge from the evidence that has been assembled above in support of Mosaic authorship of the Pentateuch are that: (1) there is evidence in several passages in the Old Testament for an early seventh-century BCE legal code that was discovered during renovations of the Jerusalem temple in 621 BCE, more than six hundred years after Moses' death; (2) exiles who returned to Jerusalem in the late fifth century BCE, more than eight hundred years after Moses' death, brought with them a book, possibly comprised of the JEDP traditions, that was known as "the book of the law of Moses"; (3) sometime between the late fifth century BCE (ca. 400 BCE) and the beginning of the translation of the Old Testament into Greek in the mid-third century BCE (ca. 250 BCE) in Alexandria, the Pentateuch reached its final form; and (4) shortly thereafter Jews began to ascribe unequivocally the authorship of the Pentateuch to Moses.

It is clear from the New Testament that Jesus and the early Christian community believed that Moses was the author of the Pentateuch:

(1) Matthew 8:4

"Then Jesus said to him, 'See that you say nothing to anyone; but go, show yourself to the priest, and offer the gift that Moses commanded, as a testimony to them.'"

(Compare this with the intended reference in Leviticus 14:3b–4, 10–11: "If the disease is healed in the leprous person, the priest shall command that two living clean birds and cedarwood and crimson yarn and hyssop be brought for the one who is to be cleansed. . . . On the eighth day he shall take two male lambs without blemish, and one ewe lamb in its first year without blemish, and a grain offering of three-tenths of an ephah of choice flour mixed with oil, and one log of oil. The priest who cleanses shall set the person to be cleansed, along with these things, before the LORD [Yahweh], at the entrance of the tent of meeting.")

(2) Matthew 19:7–8

"They said to him, 'Why then did Moses command us to give a certificate of dismissal and to divorce her?' He said to them, 'It was because you were so hard-hearted that Moses allowed you to divorce your wives, but from the beginning it was not so.'"

(Compare this with the intended reference in Deuteronomy 24:1–2: "Suppose a man enters into marriage with a woman, but she does not please him because he finds something objectionable about her, and so he writes her a certificate of divorce, puts it in her hand, and sends her out of his house; she then leaves his house and goes off to become another man's wife.")

(3) Luke 24:27, 44

"Then beginning with Moses and all the prophets, he [Jesus] interpreted to them the things about himself in all the scriptures. . . . Then he said to them, 'These are my words that I spoke to you while I was still with you—that everything written about me in the law of Moses, the prophets, and the psalms must be fulfilled.'"

The citations from the Torah, the prophets, and the psalms to which the risen Christ (i.e., the church) refers in these verses are far too numerous to cite.

(4) John 5:46–47

"If you believed Moses, you would believe me, for he wrote about me. But if you do not believe what he wrote, how will you believe what I say?"

This is a typical Johannine testimony in which Jesus makes claims about his own divine sonship. Again, the references John alludes to in the Pentateuch are far too numerous to cite.

It is important to note in this regard that the passages cited above from the gospels are evidence from individuals who were not themselves eyewitnesses, or, more accurately, ear-witnesses to the reported events. Furthermore, the gospel writers regularly put words into Jesus' mouth.

That Jesus believed the tradition of Mosaic authorship of the Pentateuch is no surprise; presumably all Jews of his generation believed that Moses was the author of the Pentateuch. Conservative Christians often maintain that if Jesus believed in Mosaic authorship of the Pentateuch, then that must be true, inasmuch as he is the divine Son of God. Such an argument, however, carries no weight with the modern historian, as it is nothing more than a faith claim. It is not evidence as discussed in the section on "The Rules of Evidence" in the introduction. Stated succinctly, the case for Mosaic authorship of the Pentateuch is very weak, if not totally unconvincing.

THE CASE AGAINST MOSAIC AUTHORSHIP OF THE PENTATEUCH

In contrast to the above accumulated evidence, scholars have since ancient times advanced a number of arguments to demonstrate that Moses did not and could not have written the Pentateuch. Apart from the obvious, namely, that Moses is spoken of throughout the Pentateuch in the third person, never the first person; that there is no claim within the Pentateuch that it was written by Moses; and that the author of Deuteronomy 34:5–8 describes Moses' death and burial, there is even more convincing internal evidence against Mosaic authorship.

(1) There are obvious anachronisms in the text. Parts of the Pentateuch were obviously written much later than the time of Moses, even as late as the period of the monarchy.

- In Genesis 21:34;[10] 26:1;[11] and Exodus 13:17;[12] 15:14,[13] a Philistine presence in the land of Canaan is taken for granted as early as the period of the Hebrew patriarchs, even though the Philistines began to settle the coastal area of Canaan about a century after the time of the Exodus and many decades after Moses' death. Moses would not have known of the Philistines; neither could he have referred to "the land of the Philistines."

- Exodus 15:17, the Song of Moses, refers to Mount Zion ("you . . . planted them on the mountain of your own possession") and to the Jerusalem temple ("your abode, the sanctuary . . . that your hands have established"). These specific allusions to Jerusalem and its temple would have been impossible until at least three centuries after Moses' death.

- There are several passages that indicate their author wrote them a time long after Moses had died: "*At that time* the Canaanites were in the land" (Genesis 12:6b; italics mine); "*At that time* the Canaanites and the Perizzites lived in the land" (Genesis 13:7b; italics mine); "Abram passed through the land to the place of Shechem, to the oak or Moreh. *At the time* the Canaanites were in the land" (Genesis 12:6; italics mine). These and other passages indicate that the author was writing at a time when the Canaanites were no longer in the land, something that did not happen until many centuries after Moses' death.

- Deuteronomy 4:37b–38 shows that a considerable time had elapsed since Moses' death: "He brought you out of Egypt with his own presence, by his power, driving out before you nations greater and mightier than yourselves, to bring you in, giving you their land for your possession, *as it is still today*" (italics mine). "As it is still today" points to a time long after the events described, and the events described transpired long after Moses' death.

- Likewise Genesis 36:31: "These are the kings who reigned in the land of Edom, before any king reigned over the Israelites." This passage indicates it was written during the period of Israel's kings, at least three centuries after Moses' death.

(2) The Pentateuch is not a literary unity, a single story. There are, in fact, many instances of repetition and numerous inconsistencies.

- Compare
    (1) Exodus 3:1 ("Moses was keeping the flock of his father-in-law Jethro, the priest of Midian")[14]
    (2) Numbers 10:29 ("Moses said to Hobab son of Reuel the Midianite, Moses' father-in-law")[15]
    (3) Exodus 2:18 ("When they [Moses' brothers-in-law to be] returned to their father Reuel, he said . . .).
- Looking carefully at these passages: who exactly was Moses' father-in-law: (1) Jethro, (2) Hobab, or (3) Reuel? There are clearly conflicting traditions,

and Moses would surely have known the name of his own father-in-law if he were the author of these passages in the Pentateuch.

- There are significant disagreements between the two creation stories in Genesis 1:1–2:4a and Genesis 2:4b–25. Among the differences: in Genesis 1, humankind is God's (Elohim's) final act of creation (Genesis 1:26) on the sixth day, following the creation of the animals; in Genesis 2, the LORD (Yahweh) created man first (2:7), then the animals (2:19–20).
- There are in Genesis three versions of a story that I refer to as "the wife-sister-herem story" in which one of the patriarchs claims that his wife is actually his sister in order to avoid the wrath of the king. The characters differ, however, in the three versions of the story:

Patriarch	Wife	King	Verses in Genesis
Abram	Sarai	Pharaoh of Egypt	12:10–20
Abraham	Sarah	Abimelech of Gerar	20:1–18
Isaac	Rebekah	Abimelech of Gerar	26:6–11

These three passages are clearly the same story in different form. Abram and Abraham are variations of the same name, as are Sarai and Sarah. One would think that Abraham might have learned his lesson the first time in Egypt and would not have repeated his mistake once again in Gerar. Even more preposterous is the likelihood that Abraham and his son Isaac would have experienced exactly the same situation with the same King Abimelech of Gerar. Inasmuch as Isaac had not yet been born at the time of Abraham's folly, King Abimelech of Gerar must have had a very long reign to have encountered the same situation with the next generation of patriarchs in the person of Abraham's son Isaac. Rather, the three accounts are obviously three distinct versions of the same story.

(3) The author of the Pentateuch clearly lived west of the Jordan River, an area that Moses never reached.

- Deuteronomy 1:1 states: "These are the words that Moses spoke to all Israel *beyond the Jordan*—in the wilderness, on the plain opposite Suph, between Paran and Tophel, Laban, Hazeroth, and Di-zahab" (italics mine).

- Deuteronomy 1:5 states: *"Beyond the Jordan in the land of Moab,* Moses undertook to expound his law" (italics mine). Moses never entered the promised land; he never lived on the west side of the Jordan River. He died in Transjordan, so referring to the land of Moab as "beyond the Jordan" betrays that fact that the author of this passage lived west of the Jordan River and could not, therefore, have been Moses.

I could continue for pages with more examples, but the instances cited above are representative of the issues involved in claiming that Moses wrote the Pentateuch, or even a significant part of it. Perhaps none of these arguments alone would be convincing, but their cumulative weight eliminates entirely the possibility that Moses could have written the Pentateuch.

The issue of who actually did write the Pentateuch can be addressed only by an impartial examination of the evidence within the texts themselves, and that is what I have attempted to demonstrate in this chapter. It is absurd for anyone to continue to claim Mosaic authorship of the Pentateuch in light of such overwhelmingly irrefutable and indisputable evidence to the contrary.

If Moses did not write the Pentateuch, then who did? Modern scholarship identifies several layers of tradition in the Pentateuch and suggests multiple authors writing or editing existing oral and written tradition at different times and under different historical circumstances. Unfortunately, one of the first challenges we must address before examining the earliest traditions in Genesis is among the most complex: the documentary hypothesis of the authorship of the Pentateuch.[16]

As we noted in the introduction, French physician Jean Astruc made a significant observation in 1753 when he discovered that some narratives in Genesis, when referring to God, call him by his personal name, Yahweh, whereas other passages, often parallel accounts of the same story, call God by the generic word Elohim. Astruc concluded that Genesis was, therefore, composed of two originally independent sources. Although Astruc's initial observation was significant, beginning with Johann Gottfried Eichhorn, scholars have gone much further than Astruc by building on his initial observation and have concluded that there are probably four distinct sources or layers of tradition that comprise our current Pentateuch.

There were, it is thought, originally two accounts of the national history, the older version, identified as J (for its use of the divine name Yahweh),[17] probably composed in Judah, the southern capital of the United Kingdom of Israel, about 950

FIGURE 1. THE COMPOSITION OF THE PENTATEUCH

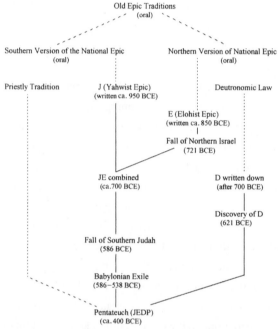

Broken lines signify oral tradition, solid lines signify written documents.

BCE during the reign of King Solomon.[18] A northern version of that same epic tradition appeared a century later in about 850 BCE in Ephraim, the northern kingdom of Israel, following the civil war of 922 BCE and the division of Israel into two nations, Ephraim (or Israel) in the north and Judah in the south. This northern version of the national epic used the generic word Elohim for God.[19] Following the fall of the northern kingdom of Israel to the Assyrians in 722–21 BCE, the northern version (E) and the southern version (J) of the national epic were fused together in the surviving southern kingdom of Judah in about 700 BCE into what scholars refer to as JE. About 400 BCE, priests in Jerusalem fused this JE tradition with the Deuteronomic Law,[20] the law code discovered in the Jerusalem temple in 621 BCE but composed a generation earlier, and provided their own framework (P)[21] for the final narrative, our Pentateuch (JEDP). This hypothesis is critical to an understanding of what follows and will be taken up again in more detail in subsequent chapters when the various components (J, E, D, and P) can be better understood in their proper historical contexts. Figure 1 serves the reader as a visual illustration of the complex process that likely reflects the composition of the Pentateuch.

CONCLUSIONS

My intention in this book is to afford the reader an insight into both the principles and the methods of biblical scholarship and the results of the application of these principles and methods to the biblical texts. The goal is ultimately to provide a reasoned reconstruction of what likely happened in the past.

With regard to the arguments in support of Mosaic authorship of the Pentateuch, I have shown that many of the passages cited as evidence of Mosaic authorship support, in fact, knowledge of the existence of an early version of Deuteronomy from the late seventh century BCE. I have also shown that the tradition of Mosaic authorship of the Pentateuch is a very late tradition, originating between eight hundred and a thousand years after Moses' death, sometime between circa 400 BCE (the date of the final conflation of earlier sources into a document very similar to our current text of the Pentateuch) and circa 200 BCE (the date of the reference in Ecclesiasticus to "the book of the covenant of the Most High God, the law that Moses commanded us"). The purpose of that late tradition is evident. As in the case of most pseudonymity, there is an obvious agenda involved: to afford greater credibility to a written work by assigning its authorship to an authoritative person from the past, in this instance by ascribing the authorship of the final text of the Pentateuch to none other than Moses, the likely father of the worship of Yahweh that subsequently evolved into Judaism.

On the other hand, the arguments against Mosaic authorship are multiple and compelling. The evidence against Mosaic authorship stands on its own merit, and there is certainly no theological bias involved in drawing this conclusion, as there often is in the case of the arguments in favor of Mosaic authorship. I can, in fact, think of no respected Old Testament scholar who advocates Mosaic authorship of the Pentateuch.

More substantive arguments in support of the various components of the four-document hypothesis (J, E, D, and P) will be introduced in subsequent chapters. Suffice it to say for now that the four-source hypothesis is the result of a scholarly historical analysis of the literary structure of the Pentateuch and is based on a detailed study of the text of the five books by many biblical scholars over a period of more than two and a half centuries.

NOTES

1. The word Pentateuch comes from the Greek *penta* = five, and *teuchos* = implement or book.

2. The following sections contain considerable detail, which the reader may follow closely or choose to skim. The arguments for and against Mosaic authorship of the Pentateuch are complicated and technical and require an examination of details in biblical texts. For those who wish to follow the fine points of this discussion, the evidence is here. For those who prefer to skim this section, the conclusions are set forth clearly at the end of this chapter.

3. Unless otherwise noted, scriptural quotations contained throughout this volume are from the *New Revised Standard Version Bible*, copyright 1989 by the Division of Christian Education of the National Council of Churches of Christ in the U.S.A. I have specifically used *The HarperCollins Study Bible*, New Revised Standard Version (HarperCollins, 1993) because of its extensive and helpful notes.

4. Throughout the Old Testament the divine name Yah or Yahweh is ordinarily translated into English as "the LORD," with all capital letters. In each instance where this occurs, I have taken the liberty of inserting the divine name Yahweh in parentheses, inasmuch as that was the actual name by which people called the god of Israel in the period before the Babylonian exile in the sixth century BCE. This particular verse is, by the way, the Bible's earliest reference to writing.

5. The significance of these earlier documents J, E, and D will become clearer later in this chapter and in subsequent chapters when we review the question of the sources of the Pentateuch.

6. See also Sirach, The Prologue: "Many great teachings have been given to us through the Law and the Prophets, and the others that followed them, and for these we should praise Israel for instruction and wisdom."

7. "The first of the five books in which the holy laws are written bears the name and inscription of Genesis or creation of the world, an account of which it contains at the beginning. . . . ; for in these men we have laws endowed with life and reason, and Moses extolled them for two reasons" (*Philo*, volume 6; Loeb Classical Library translation).

8. "They [an ascetic community of Jews known to Philo and settled near Alexandria] read the Holy Scriptures and seek wisdom from their ancestral philosophy by taking it as an allegory. . . ." (*Philo*, volume 9; Loeb Classical Library Translation).

9. Even ancient authors were troubled by the fact that in Deuteronomy 34:5 Moses was presumably writing about his own death.

10. "And Abraham resided as an alien many days *in the land of the Philistines*" (italics mine).

11. "Now there was a famine in the land, besides the former famine that had occurred in the days of Abraham. And Isaac went to Gerar, to *King Abimelech of the Philistines*" (italics mine).

12. "When the Pharaoh let the people go, God did not lead them by way of *the land of the Philistines*, although that was nearer; for God thought, 'If the people face war, they may change their minds and return to Egypt'" (italics mine).

13. "The peoples heard, they trembled; pangs seized *the inhabitants of Philistia*" (italics mine).

14. See also Exodus 4:18 ("Moses went back to his father-in-law Jethro and said to him. . . .); and 18:1, 12 ("Jethro, the priest of Midian, Moses' father-in-law . . .).

15. See also Judges 4:11 ("Now Heber the Kenite had separated from the other Kenites, that is, the descendants of Hobab the father-in-law of Moses . . .).

16. These five books were actually a single literary document in their final form. The division into five separate books had to do with the fact that a single parchment scroll could not contain the entire text. Biblical scrolls were typically no more than about twenty-four feet in length. The text of the Pentateuch had to be written on five separate scrolls, hence our current five books.

17. Yahweh is written as Jahweh with a J in German, the language of most of the original modern historical research on this subject.

18. As a mnemonic device, remember J for Yahweh (Jahweh) and J for Judah.

19. As a mnemonic device, remember E for Elohim (the generic Hebrew word for God) and E for Ephraim, the seat of the northern kingdom of Israel following the division of the United Kingdom into two nations, (northern) Israel and (southern) Judah.

20. Remember D for Deuteronomic Law.

21. Remember P for Priestly Code.

CHAPTER 2

ISRAEL'S PRIMORDIAL AND PATRIARCHAL HISTORY

ESTABLISHING A CHRONOLOGY

Fundamental to the writing of history is good chronology, the ability to agree on the raw facts and to date them in an unbiased manner, free of interpretation. Between 1650 and 1654, Archbishop James Ussher of Armagh, Ireland (1581–1656) published his *Chronology* or *Annales Veteris et Novi Testamenti* (*Annals of the Old and the New Testament*). In this two-volume work, Ussher calculated his long-accepted chronology by counting backward from certain known dates and by using the lengths of lives of people as provided in the Old Testament. His dates for events found their way into print by an unknown authority of the Authorized Version of the Bible (King James), which dated the creation of the world to October 22, 4004 BCE. This date was quickly accepted as authoritative in the English-speaking world and found its way into the margin of reference versions of the King James Bible, thereby affording legitimacy to this date for God's creation of the universe. Ussher was a well-educated scholar and used basically sound methods in developing his chronology. Although his dating of Creation has absolutely no historical value, Ussher's chronology is generally reliable, and modern scholarship has not deviated significantly from many of his dates.

There were, however, prior to Archbishop Ussher, much earlier efforts at writing chronologies of the world. As early as the early third century BCE, Demetrius of

Phaleron (ca. 350 BCE–ca. 280 BCE), writing in Alexandria, dated historical events with reference to Adam and the flood. However, the first serious steps to synchronize the dates of events in the Bible with existing secular calendars were undertaken by Christian writers, such as Julius Africanus (ca. 160–ca. 240) and Eusebius of Caesarea (ca. 260–before 341). Julius Africanus's five-volume *Chronicle* (Greek *Chronographiai*) covers the time from Creation, which he dates to 5499 BCE, to the third year of Eliogabalus (221 CE). This work is an attempt to reconcile events in the Bible with the Greek and Roman history known to Julius Africanus, who used as sources first the Bible, then Greek, Roman, and Jewish historians, especially Justus of Tiberias (last third of the first century CE), who had used Flavius Josephus (37 CE–ca. 100 CE). Julius was probably influenced also by the *Miscellanies* (Greek *Stromata*) of Clement of Alexandria (date of birth unknown–died ca. 215 CE). Julius Africanus's *Chronicle* was the first earnest attempt to write a comprehensive history of the world and influenced all subsequent Christian chronographies.

Eusebius of Caesarea made Julius's work the foundation of his *Chronicle*, a composition in two parts: the first called the *Chronography*, the second the *Canons* or the *Chronological Canons*. The *Chronography*, which contains quotations from several lost sources, was an attempt to write a comprehensive history of the world. It was in five parts: (1) the history of the Chaldeans and the Assyrians, followed by lists of Assyrian, Median, Lydian, and Persian kings; (2) Old Testament history; (3) Egyptian history; (4) Greek history; and (5) Roman history. Archbishop Ussher's work significantly advanced these earlier efforts by setting events of ancient history within the context of a more reliable modern calendar.

THE PRIMORDIAL HISTORY

Scholars generally agree that Israelite history and Israelite religion began with the Exodus, one of the watershed moments in Israel's history. The Exodus was the event whereby Moses led Hebrew slaves out of Egypt, delivered to them the Ten Commandments at Mount Sinai, and set them in the direction of the land of Canaan. Yet the earliest account of Israelite history, generally referred to as the Yahwist account (or J), has a considerable record in the book of Genesis of what is best called prehistory before the story of the Exodus. Priests in Jerusalem sometime before 400 BCE later incorporated the Yahwist account into the final redaction of the Pentateuch.

A Priestly or P version of that Primordial History serves as the framework for the text of Genesis 1–11 and is generally divided by scholars into two periods, the Antediluvian Period (the period before the great flood) and the Postdiluvian Period (the period following the great flood). The record of this Primordial History is contained in two parallel traditions, Genesis 4:17–26, the earlier J or Yahwist version, and Genesis 5:1–32, the later P or Priestly version.

Within that Primordial History, the Priestly tradition introduces chronological material within a genealogical table composed in a well-defined literary form:

> When a had lived x years, he became the father of b; a lived y years after the birth of b, and he had other sons and daughters; thus all the days of a were $x + y$.

The total number of years for the Antediluvian Period is 1,656 years, with most of the men living extraordinarily long lives (see the first table below). The second age, the Postdiluvian Period of the dispersion following the flood, is reported in Genesis 9:28–29; 11:10–26. Both are P or Priestly traditions. This period covers 290 years, with the life spans of those men gradually diminishing to life spans of relatively more normal lengths (see the second table below).

ANTEDILUVIAN ANCESTORS[1]

Ancestor	Age at Fathering	Years after Fathering	Age at Death	Reference in Genesis
Adam[2]	130	800	930	5:3–5
Seth[3]	105	807	912	5:6–8
Enosh[4]	90	815	905	5:9–11
Kenan[5]	70	840	910	5:12–14
Mahalalel[6]	65	830	895	5:15–17
Jared[7]	162	800	962	5:18–20
Enoch[8]	65	300	365	5:21–24
Methuselah[9]	187	782	969	5:25–27
Lamech[10]	182	595	777	5:28–31
Noah[11]	500	350	950	5:32 (and 9:28–29)

Total   1,656 years for the Antediluvian Period

POSTDILUVIAN ANCESTORS

Ancestor	Age at Fathering	Years after Fathering	Age at Death	Reference in Genesis
Shem[12]	100	500	600	11:10–11
Arpachshad[13]	35	403	438	11:12–13
Shelah[14]	30	403	433	11:14–15
Eber[15]	34	430	464	11:16–17
Peleg[16]	30	209	239	11:18–19
Reu[17]	32	207	239	11:20–21
Serug[18]	30	200	230	11:22–23
Nahor[19]	29	119	148	11:24–26
Terah[20]	70	138	208	11:26

Total   290 years for the Postdiluvian Period

What historical value can we assign to these primordial traditions? Probably little to none! The stories of the primordial ancestors fail both tests: the time and place rule and the bias rule. Clearly we are millennia removed from most of the "people" listed in these two genealogies, which may be little more than an effort to account for the long period of time between the first couple, Adam and Eve, and the beginning of the Patriarchal Period.

The division of time into antediluvian and postdiluvian ancestors replicates other ancient Near Eastern traditions with which our authors were likely familiar. More specifically, ancient Sumerian sources report that the world's first kings from the period before the flood lived for tens of thousands of years. Specifically eight (or possibly ten) Sumerian kings ruled for a total period of 241,000 years, the shortest reign being 18,600 years and the longest nearly 65,000 years.[21] In the period following the flood, Sumerian kings still lived long lives, but not nearly as long as the lives of the antediluvian rulers. Attempting to place the lives of the world's primordial ancestors into a time frame is senseless for two reasons: (1) the genealogical lists in Genesis cannot be synchronized with any extrabiblical chronologies, and (2) there is no reason to take seriously the names and certainly not the life spans of these probably fictitious "ancestors," who seem to mirror archetypes or to replicate place names in northwest Mesopotamia and northern Syria.

It seems appropriate in the context of our glance at the primordial history to focus on the best-known story from the primordial history, the story that divides that history into the antediluvian and postdiluvian periods, namely, the story of Noah and the flood. Although the story covers several chapters (Genesis 6:9–8:22), I will focus only on the account of the flood itself in Genesis 7 to illustrate, on the one hand, the issue of the J and P sources of the Pentateuch and also to show, on the other hand, how this story relates to other ancient Near Eastern stories.

In the account below, the earlier Yahwist or J tradition is printed in Arial Narrow letters and the later Priestly or P tradition in *italics*.

₁Then the LORD (Yahweh) said to Noah, "Go into the ark, you and your household, for I have seen that you alone are righteous before me in this generation. ₂Take with you seven pairs of all clean animals, the male and its mate; and a pair of the animals that are not clean, the male and its mate; ₃and seven pairs of the birds of the air also, male and female, to keep their kind alive on the face of all the earth. ₄For in seven days I will send rain on the earth for forty days and forty nights; and every living thing that I have made I will blot out from the face of the ground." ₅And Noah did all that the LORD (Yahweh) had commanded him.

₆Noah was six hundred years old when the flood of waters came on the earth. ₇And Noah with his sons and his wife and his sons' wives went into the ark to escape the waters of the flood. ₈Of clean animals, and of animals that are not clean, and of birds, and of everything that creeps on the ground, ₉*two and two*, male and female, went into the ark with Noah, as *God (Elohim)* had commanded Noah.

₁₀And after seven days the waters of the flood came on the earth.

₁₁*In the six hundredth year of Noah's life, in the second month, on the seventeenth day of the month, on that day all the fountains of the great deep burst forth, and the windows of the heavens were opened.* ₁₂The rain fell on the earth forty days and forty nights. ₁₃*On the very same day, Noah with his sons, Shem and Ham and Japheth, and Noah's wife and the three wives of his sons, entered the ark,* ₁₄*they and every wild animal of every kind, and all domestic animals of every kind, and every creeping thing that creeps on the earth, and every bird of every kind—every bird, every winged creature.* ₁₅*They went into the ark with Noah, two and two of all flesh in which there was the breath of life.* ₁₆*And those that entered, male and female of all flesh, went in as God (Elohim) had commanded him;* and the LORD (Yahweh) shut him in.

₁₇*The flood continued* forty days *on the earth;* and the waters increased, and bore up the ark, and it rose high above the earth. ₁₈*The waters swelled and increased greatly on the earth; and the ark floated on the face of the waters.* ₁₉*The waters swelled so mightily on the earth that all the high mountains under the whole heaven were cov-*

ered; 20*the waters swelled above the mountains, covering them fifteen cubits deep.* 21*And all flesh died that moved on the earth, birds, domestic animals, wild animals, all swarming creatures that swarm on the earth, and all human beings;* 22everything on dry land in whose nostrils was the breath of life died. 23He blotted out every living thing that was on the face of the ground, human beings and animals and creeping things and birds of the air; they were blotted out from the earth. Only Noah was left, and those that were with him in the ark. 24*And the waters swelled on the earth for one hundred fifty days.*

Taking an initial clue from Jean Astruc (see introduction), we notice that the divine name Yahweh is used in verses 1, 5, and 16b, and that the word Elohim is used in verses 9 and 16a. Unlike the Priestly and Yahwist versions of creation, which are coherent and distinct literary units (Genesis 1:1–2:4a = P; and Genesis 2:4b–24 = J), the J and P accounts of the flood have been intricately intertwined into a single fabric. Nevertheless—and this is a testimony to P's method of redaction—the separate components are still largely visible:

> J = verses 1–5, 7–10, (except for the words *two and two* and *God [Elohim]* in
>   verse 9, which probably reflect final editing by P),[22] 12, 16b, 17b, 22–23;
>   and
> P = verses 6, 11, 13–16a, 17a (except for the words *forty days*), 18–21, 24.

There are other differences between the Yahwist and the Priestly versions, not only in Genesis 7 but also in the surrounding material in chapters 6 and 8:

> In the Yahwist account seven pairs of clean and one pair of unclean animals
>   are taken aboard the ark (verses 2–3), whereas in the Priestly account
>   one pair of all animals is taken aboard (verses 14–15; see also Genesis
>   6:19–20).
> In the Yahwist account it rained for forty days and forty nights (verses 4,
>   12, and possibly 17), whereas in the Priestly account there is mention
>   of floodwaters that lasted for one hundred fifty days (verse 24).

There are other accounts of a flood elsewhere in ancient Near Eastern mythology, most notably in Sumerian and Babylonian versions, both of which are from Mesopotamia, where the Tigris-Euphrates Valley was frequently subject to severe flooding. By contrast, Canaan/Israel was not subject to such floods. The fact that the

Mesopotamian versions of the flood are much older than both the Yahwist and Priestly versions suggests that the biblical storytellers probably borrowed freely from popular traditions of the ancient Near Eastern world, although they clearly adapted and reworked those older stories to suit their own cultural and religious points of view.

Many of the Hebrew traditions concerning Creation (Genesis 1:1–2:4a), the Garden of Eden (Genesis 2:4b–3:24), the flood (Genesis 6:5–8:22), Nimrod (Genesis 10:8–12), and the Tower of Babel (Genesis 11:1–9), although clearly myths or legends, reflect remembrances of a time when Israel's ancestors lived in Mesopotamia. Most of these stories have parallels or roots in Mesopotamian cosmology, myths, and legends. Why did Mesopotamia, an area of the ancient Near East relatively far removed from Palestine, influence these Hebrew narratives, whereas the primordial history in the Bible shows little influence from the literature of Egypt and Canaan, areas that were much closer to Israel, both historically and geographically? The answer likely lies in the fact that essential ingredients of these stories were brought by Israel's forebears from the ancestral homeland in Haran in northwest Mesopotamia when they migrated into Canaan.

With regard to the Primordial History, biblical scholars have generally concluded that the ancient authors of Genesis wrote within the context of their own time and place and were influenced by living oral and written traditions from neighboring cultures. This is not surprising, since these authors otherwise had little "information" to fill the long time span between Creation and the beginnings of their Patriarchal History. What is clear is that the author(s) of the Primordial History in Genesis 1–11 were providing a universal context for the ancestral history of one particular people, the Hebrews, whose beginnings are reported in Genesis 12–50.

THE HEBREW PATRIARCHS

The Primordial History is followed in Genesis by the so-called Patriarchal History (Genesis 11:31–50:26). The problem of history is rather complicated with regard to the stories of the patriarchs and matriarchs, those men and women whom Israel considered its ancestors, indeed the founders of their history and of their religious tradition.

In the time of Abraham, assuming for a moment that there was such a person, world history centered in the region of the Fertile Crescent, an area of the Middle

East extending in a semicircle from Egypt through Palestine and Syria down the Tigris-Euphrates Valley to the Persian Gulf. The dates of these presumed ancestors cannot be easily synchronized with extrabiblical chronologies, but most scholars set them in the period 2000 to 1800 BCE, in part because the wanderings of the patriarchs may reflect the memory of Amorite migrations known, from ancient Mari documents[23] and from archaeological evidence, to have occurred at about that time. Some scholars place the patriarchs a bit later because of similarities between social customs reflected in the narrative in Genesis and those described in the Nuzi texts.[24]

The account of the movements of Abraham, Isaac, and Jacob into Canaan almost certainly preserves vestiges of historical memory about clan movements and social relationships that served as the background for the establishment of the Israelite Kingdom by Saul and David beginning about 1000 BCE, but the issue is exceedingly complex.

The story of the ancestors begins in Genesis 11:31[25] with the call of Abraham from Ur in the southernmost area of Mesopotamia, a city that at that time lay near the shore of the Persian Gulf. Abraham's father, Terah, moved the family from Ur to the city of Haran in northwestern Mesopotamia, six hundred miles away. From Haran, Abraham migrated south-southwest about four hundred fifty miles into Canaan, stopping first at Shechem (Genesis 12:6), an important city in central Canaan, and then heading south to Hebron, where he settled by the oaks of Moreh at Hebron (Genesis 13:18).[26] There the LORD (Yahweh) made a covenant with Abraham, promising him that he and his descendants would occupy the land from the river of Egypt to the river Euphrates (Genesis 15:18–21),[27] basically the boundaries of King David's empire in the early tenth century BCE, almost a millennium later than the presumed period of the patriarchs.

Because his wife, Sarah, was unable to bear him children, Abraham had a son, Ishmael, by Sarah's Egyptian slave-girl Hagar (Genesis 16). In an appearance at the oaks of Mamre several years after the birth of Ishmael, the LORD (Yahweh) promised Abraham a son by his wife, Sarah (Genesis 18). Sarah bore Abraham a son, Isaac (Genesis 21:1–7), and consequently Abraham banished the slave-girl Hagar and their son, Ishmael (Genesis 21:8–21), who later became the father of the Ishmaelites, the Arab nations, still one more etiological legend designed to connect in a single family tree all of the people in the area immediately surrounding what would later become the land of Israel (see the genealogical chart on p. 68).

Following Sarah's death, Abraham directed his servant to return to the ancestral

FIGURE 2. THE ANCIENT NEAR EAST BEFORE THE EXODUS

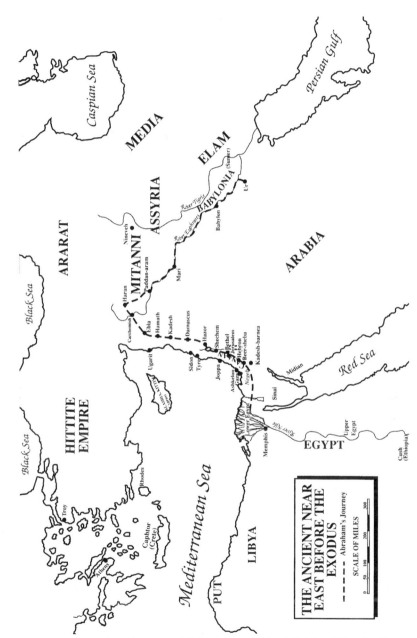

This map can be viewed at www.bible.ca; copyright, 1994 by Abingdon Press.
Used by permission.

FIGURE 3. GENEALOGICAL HISTORY OF THE PATRIARCHS

The patriarchal history in Genesis 12–50 can be understood more easily by referring to the following family tree:

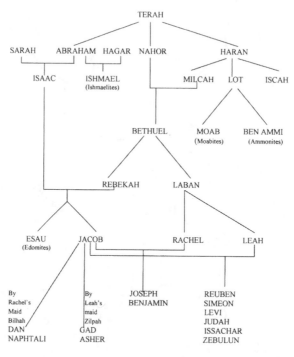

homeland of Haran to find a suitable wife for his son Isaac, lest he marry a Canaanite woman (Genesis 24). Isaac married Rebekah, his first cousin twice-removed, according to the tradition two generations younger than him (see the genealogical chart). Abraham died (Genesis 25:7–11), and shortly thereafter Isaac and Rebekah had twin sons (25:19–26), Jacob, who would become Israel, and Esau, who would be the father of the Edomites, still one more etiological legend linking Israel to her closest neighbors.

The patriarchal history in Genesis 12–50 can be understood more easily by referring to the family tree on page 68.

Although Jacob was the younger of the twins, it was he who, through a ruse (Genesis 25:29–34), inherited Yahweh's promise to Abraham that he would make of his descendants a great nation.

Jacob returned to the ancestral home and married two sisters, Leah and Rachel, his first cousins, the daughters of his uncle Laban (Genesis 29). Jacob's wife Leah then bore him four sons: Reuben, Simeon, Levi, and Judah (Genesis 29:31–35). Then Rachel's maid Bilhah bore Jacob two sons: Dan and Naphtali (Genesis 30:1–8). Then Leah's maid Zilpah bore him two sons: Gad and Asher (Genesis 30:9–13). Then Jacob's wife Leah bore him two more sons: Issachar and Zebulun, and a daughter, Dinah (Genesis 30:14–21). At long last, Jacob's favorite wife, Rachel, conceived and bore him two sons: Joseph (Genesis 30:22–24) and, as she died in childbirth, Jacob's youngest son, Benjamin (Genesis 35:16–21).

Genesis comes to a close with the Joseph cycle (Genesis 37–50). Following his dreams of greatness (Genesis 37:1–11), Joseph's brothers sold him to a caravan of Ishmaelites or Midianites (Genesis 37:12–36),[28] who took him to Egypt. There Joseph interpreted pharaoh's dreams (Genesis 41:1–36) and thereby rose to power in pharaoh's court (Genesis 41:37–57). Because of a famine in Canaan, Jacob sent ten of his sons, Joseph's brothers (but not Benjamin), to Egypt to buy grain (Genesis 42:1–25). Joseph recognized his brothers, gave them grain, detained his brother Simeon, and ordered the others to return to Canaan and come back to Egypt with their youngest brother, Benjamin (Genesis 42:26–38). The brothers returned to Canaan to their father, Jacob, and eventually returned to Egypt with Benjamin (43:1–34), at which time Joseph disclosed his identity to his brothers (Genesis 45:1–15). The brothers returned to Canaan to their father, Jacob (Genesis 45:21–28), who, when he learned that Joseph was alive, went with his sons to Egypt and settled in the land of Goshen in the Nile Delta in the north (Genesis 46:1–47:12). After Jacob's death in Egypt, his body was taken to Canaan to be buried with his grandparents Abraham and Sarah; his parents, Isaac and Rebekah; and his first wife, Leah (Genesis 49:29–50:14). The cycle ends with Joseph's death in Egypt (Genesis 50:22–26).

The story of the patriarchs is probably just that: a story—with little merit as history. The narrative is schematic, as the genealogical tree clearly discloses. In fact, it seems safe to say that biblical genealogies were obviously not intended to preserve historical information. They had a totally different purpose: they served economic, political, social, and religious functions. They told the people who they were in relationship to one another and to the people surrounding them. The patriarchal narrative reflects the enmity between the Israelites and the Ishmaelites, kinship with the Moabites and the Ammonites, and the complex relationship between the Rachel and the Leah tribes, which we will address in some detail in chapter 3.

In the account in Genesis, members of Abraham's immediate family populated the entire region surrounding what would, almost a millennium later, become the empire of kings David and Solomon of Israel. Most obvious in the scheme is the fact that Jacob, whose name was changed to Israel (Genesis 32:28), became the father of twelve sons, each of whom was, in turn, the father of one of the twelve tribes that would eventually become the nation of Israel. Most important, however, the story of the patriarchs served as a backdrop for the account of the Exodus from Egypt, where Israel's history really begins.

A final comment about the religion of the patriarchs is important at this point. Although the final editors of Genesis would have us believe that Israel's ancestors worshiped Yahweh,[29] the god of the Exodus, and that, indeed, this same Yahweh was also the god of creation (Genesis 2:4b–25), there is substantial evidence in the tradition to refute that view.

Polytheism was the normative practice in the ancient Near East, and gods and goddesses, accordingly, had personal names to distinguish them. Knowing the name of a god had significant importance, because it enabled an individual, through magic, divination, and incantations, to invoke the name of that god to acquire power. The religion of the patriarchs should be understood against this polytheistic background and was itself certainly polytheistic, or polydaemonistic.[30] There are in the Bible clues that support this observation.

Israel's understanding of Yahweh is best understood within the context of the divinities of the ancient Near Eastern world. It appears that the name of the patriarchal god was actually not Yahweh, but rather El Shaddai. Genesis 17:1 reports "When Abram was ninety-nine years old, the LORD (Yahweh) appeared to him, and said to him 'I am El Shaddai; walk before me and be blameless." Although generally rendered in English translations as "God Almighty,"[31] the word Shaddai has northern Mesopotamian roots, and El Shaddai likely came into Canaan as a family god, perhaps the personal god of the tribe or clan, with the migration into Canaan of the ancestors from the area of Haran. In support of that view, there is an interesting story about Jacob's wife Rachel, who appropriated her father Laban's images of the household gods without his knowledge (Genesis 31:19, 30–32, 34–35)[32] and carried them under her saddle. These figurines, presumably in human form and small enough to be hidden under the saddle of Rachel's camel, were probably used for talismanic or cultic purposes or for divination. Possession of these figurines sometimes signified legal title to an estate.

El Shaddai's function as a family god or clan deity may underlie the later covenantal relationship between Yahweh and Israel. In the patriarchal stories, the family god, the god of Abraham, the god of Isaac, and the god of Jacob, entered into a personal relationship, a covenant or contract that involved both demands and promises involving both parties. Inasmuch as the name Shaddai probably means "the Mountain One," El Shaddai was likely a deity from the mountainous regions of northwest Mesopotamia, the ancestral home. Other references to El Shaddai appear in Genesis 28:3; 35:11; 43:14; 48:3; and 49:25.

Elsewhere in Genesis there are references to:

- **El Elyon**

  El Elyon, meaning God Most High, was apparently worshiped in Jerusalem in pre-Davidic times as creator of the world and as the high god of that city's pantheon (Genesis 14:18–20, 22–23).[33]

- **El Olam**

  El Olam, meaning Everlasting God, was apparently worshiped in Beersheba (Genesis 21:33).[34]

- **El Roi**

  El Roi, meaning God of Seeing or God Who Sees, was apparently worshiped at Beerlahairoi (Genesis 16:13–14).[35]

- **El Berith** or **Baal Berith**

  El Berith or Baal Berith, meaning the God or the Lord of the Covenant, was worshiped at Shechem as the god of the covenant long before the arrival in Canaan of the Exodus tribes.[36]

Some additional interesting information about the religion of the patriarchs is relevant:

- Abraham (Abram) is often associated with *holy trees*
- The oak of Moreh[37] (meaning a place of instruction or divination)
    - a sacred tree near Shechem (Genesis 12:6–8)
    - a Canaanite sacred tree prior to Abraham's time (Deuteronomy 11:30; see also Elon-meonenim, the "Diviner's Oak," in Judges 9:37)
- The oaks of Mamre[38]
    - Abraham built an altar to Yahweh there (Genesis 13:18)
    - Yahweh appeared to Abraham there (Genesis 18:1)

- A tamarisk tree in Beersheba
  - ○ Abraham planted a tree in Beersheba and called on the name of the LORD (Yahweh), El Olam (Genesis 21:33)
  - ○ Abraham is associated principally with Mamre

- Isaac is often associated with *watering places*
  - ○ Isaac found Rebekah by a well (Genesis 24:10–49)
  - ○ Isaac dwelt near the well at Lahai-roi (Genesis 25:11)
  - ○ Isaac quarreled with others over wells (Genesis 26:17–22)
  - ○ Isaac built an altar at the well of Shibah (Genesis 26:23–33)
  - ○ Isaac's well is associated principally with Beersheba (the well at Sheba, or the well of the oath)

- Jacob is associated primarily with *stones*
  - ○ Jacob's famous dream occurred while he was sleeping with his head on a stone (Genesis 28:10–17)
  - ○ That stone was later set up as a pillar for a sanctuary at Bethel (Genesis 28:18–22)
  - ○ Jacob erected a pillar of stone at Bethel in the place where he had spoken with God (Genesis 35:9–15)
  - ○ Jacob is associated principally with Bethel

It is tempting to find in this data a recollection of an animistic or polydaemonistic period in the religion of the patriarchs, in which it was believed that natural phenomena and objects such as trees, watering places, and stones were alive and had indwelling spirits. There are without doubt elements of animism and polydaemonism in the patriarchal religion. Abraham's sacred trees at Moreh, Mamre, and Beersheba; Isaac's sacred watering places at Lahai-roi and Beersheba; and Jacob's sacred stone on which he had his famous dream and which he later set up as a sacred pillar at Bethel (the house of God) were, even in the accounts in Genesis, clearly places where the ancestors consulted oracles, spoke to the local god or spirit, and set up altars or small shrines.

Although the names of some of these Canaanite gods or spirits were later considered as titles, alternative names, or epithets for Yahweh, their survival in the text of Genesis (and elsewhere) serves as an indication of early developments in the course of Israel's religious history and as expressions of the way in which the old animism or polydaemonism survived, even though it has been overlaid with the later Yahwism. Our biblical texts attempt to subsume all of these gods and/or spirits under the name of Yahweh, the god of Moses, the god of the Exodus, who was evidently the god of a much later period.

The Patriarchal Tradition tells the story of Israel's ancestors, who lived centuries before the Exodus. It is important to observe, however, that the Patriarchal Traditions were written down only after a long period of oral transmission and that they were consciously shaped to promote subsequent faith in Yahweh, the god of the Exodus and the Sinai covenant, who, the written tradition would have us believe, was the same as the god of Israel's ancestors. The written tradition in Genesis intentionally pushed the relatively late, post-Exodus concept of Israel, the chosen people of Yahweh, back into the ancestral history. Accordingly, the story in Genesis unfolds with a theme of *the promise to the patriarchs* anticipating the subsequent *fulfillment of that promise* in the Exodus from Egypt, the ensuing covenant at Sinai, and the subsequent conquest and entrenchment of the land of Canaan.

Therefore, many scholars, including myself, are skeptical about the historical reliability of these patriarchal stories. Although there are obviously vestiges of ancient traditions and ancient memories in these stories, in their present form the report of these early events is more schematic and legendary than historical.

CONCLUSIONS

As with the question of the authorship of the Pentateuch, responsible biblical scholars are virtually unanimous in their conclusions regarding the Primordial History. The material in Genesis 1–11 has no merit whatsoever as history. There are no reliable witnesses for any of the "events" described in the early chapters of Genesis. The Creation, the Garden of Eden and the fall of man, the beginnings of civilization, Noah and the great flood, the multiplication of languages at the Tower of Babel, and so forth have no status whatsoever as history. They are myths and legends related to myths and legends from Mesopotamia, many of which are known to us from modern archaeological discoveries. Additionally, the names in the antediluvian and postdiluvian genealogies probably do not refer to actual historical persons. These genealogies are, at best, schematic efforts to provide what is essentially the world's prehistory before the call of father Abraham.

When viewed within the context of ancient Near Eastern history, these stories have been shown to parallel substantially some of the myths and legends in ancient Mesopotamian literature, where creation stories, flood stories, and ancestral genealogies abound. Genesis 1–11 affords a collection of myths and legends that reveals familiarity with these Mesopotamian antecedents.[39]

The Priestly antediluvian genealogy is certainly not a reliable genealogy of actual people from antiquity, and its merit is compromised further by the parallel J or Yahwist genealogy in Genesis 4:17–26, which duplicates some of the same names, but a different family line and in a different order: Adam, the father of Cain, the father of Enoch, the father of Irad, the father of Mehujael, the father of Methushael, the father of Lamech, the father of Jabal and Tubal-Cain; and, in addition, a second line from Adam: Adam, the father of Seth, the father of Enosh. There is no merit in trying to reconcile these genealogies because they will ultimately remain irreconcilable forever.

The postdiluvian Priestly genealogy is of no more historical merit than the antediluvian genealogy. The appearance of these names in ancient Mesopotamian sources proves very little—likely not much more than the fact that the ancient Israelite stories had their origin in northwest Mesopotamia and that some ancestral names (or place names) were remembered by those who migrated from this region into Canaan. It is essential to note that the appearance of some of the same names in extrabiblical sources does not establish the reliability of an entire tradition.

The matter of the Patriarchal History is far more complicated, and equally qualified scholars differ considerably in the way in which they read the evidence. The problem is that although there are data, the data are scanty and inconclusive, allowing equally competent, unbiased scholars to draw very different conclusions from the same evidence. Admittedly, I am more skeptical than many about the reliability of the patriarchal tradition, but that is because the evidence is often contradictory. Even father Abraham may be an archetypal creation of an ancient storyteller's imagination. The name itself comes down to us in two forms, which were apparently preserved in separate traditions: Abram, meaning "exalted father"; and Abraham, which was apparently understood to mean "father of a multitude."[40]

When there is conflicting evidence in the text, I am inclined to follow the principle that the more difficult reading, the more problematic evidence, is probably more reliable. This principle is called the criterion of dissimilarity or the criterion of embarrassment and is widely used by biblical scholars. As an example, there is a tendency throughout Genesis 12–50 to promote the view that Yahweh, first worshiped in the days of Adam's grandson Enosh (Genesis 4:26), was worshiped consistently as the god of Israel by the ancestors, Abraham, Isaac, Jacob, and his twelve sons. I have already identified evidence to the contrary, namely, that the ancestral god was probably El Shaddai and that some ancestors likely also worshiped other gods, such as El Elyon, El Olam, El Roi, and El Berith. Both of these positions cannot be true, and the criterion of embarrassment suggests that the more difficult reading is likely the more authentic.

It is, I contend, apparent that the evidence for polytheism and polydaemonism would not have found its way into the stories in Genesis if it did not reflect some modicum of ancient historical memory. It is, otherwise, impossible to explain with any measure of reason the origin of these unorthodox (indeed heretical) traditions. It is, on the other hand, quite easy to understand that once Yahweh worship was firmly implanted in Israel centuries later the belief that Israel's ancestors had always worshiped Yahweh was worked back into the earlier stories, both in their oral and subsequently in their written forms.

Fortunately, the final editors of the Pentateuch did not have consistency in mind when they brought together different sources, which were often not in agreement on matters of detail. The discrepancies, the differences, the inconsistencies, the doublets, and the problematic verses often afford scholars important evidence or clues for insights and glimpses into the ancient history. Regrettably, the evidence is insufficient to enable biblical scholars to draw their conclusions with the kind of certainty that they would like. Accordingly, it is important to learn to use words like "possibly," "probably," "likely," "unlikely," and so forth to qualify conclusions. There are even times when we should admit that in the face of inadequate evidence we simply do not know.

I will have more to say about the reconstruction of the patriarchal history and religion in the following chapter, especially in the sections on the conquest and entrenchment of Canaan and the establishment of the tribal confederacy. We will be able to draw fuller conclusions and justify our skepticism much more clearly once we have had an opportunity to review some of that subsequent history.

NOTES

1. Whereas the P or Priestly source in the following table lists the descendants of Adam through Seth, the Yahwist or J version of the genealogy in Genesis 4:17–26 lists as successive generations of the antediluvian ancestors Adam's descendants through Cain, the father of Enoch, the father of Irad, the father of Mehujael, the father of Methushael, the father of Lamech, the father of Jabal and Jubal (by his wife Adah), and the father of Tubal-Cain (by his wife Zillah). This J version of the genealogy also mentions that Adam later fathered Seth, who was the father of Enosh. The similarities and differences between the J and the P genealogies are striking, as both genealogies list Enoch and Lamech as descendants of Adam, but through different sons.

2. The Hebrew noun *'ādām* is used widely throughout the Old Testament to mean "human being" or "humankind." The word *'dm* means "human being" in two related languages, Ugaritic and Phoenician, suggesting that it is of northwest Semitic origin. It may be related to the Hebrew word *'dm*, meaning "red."

3. Seth was the third son of Adam and Eve and the ancestor of Noah. Seth, through Noah, was the ancestor of all of postdiluvian humankind.

4. Enosh means "man" in Hebrew. The name may possibly serve as a symbolic reference to the first man born from the new line of Seth, following Cain's murder of Abel. Enosh is possibly represented as a new beginning, a new Adam.

5. The name Kenan may be related to the name Cain. The first three consonants of both names are the same in Hebrew: *qyn*. Scholars have suggested that just as Cain was the son of Adam, meaning "humankind," so too Kenan was the son of Enosh, whose name also means "man" or "humankind."

6. The name Mahalalel is based on two Hebrew roots: *hll* meaning "to praise," and *'l* meaning "God." The initial *m* suggests a participial form of the verb, meaning "praising God."

7. The Hebrew name Jered (*yered*) or Jared (*yāred*) may be related to the Hebrew verb *yrd*, "to descend," but this verb does not appear in any other West Semitic names.

8. The name Enoch may derive from the West Semitic *ḥnk*, meaning "to initiate" or "to introduce." Some scholars have suggested that the name may mean "founder" because of Enoch's association with the first city in Genesis 4:17.

9. The name Methuselah contains two elements: *mutu*, the West Semitic word for "man" or "husband," and *šlḥ*, probably a divine name, possibly Selah or Shelah, who was a Canaanite god of the underworld river, in which case the name might mean "a follower or devotee of the god Selah." Methuselah has the distinction of being the Bible's oldest living person.

10. The root *lmk* does not exist in West Semitic languages; however, a few personal

names with the root *lmk* appear in the Mari tablets from the second millennium BCE. Lamech has the distinction of being the Bible's first polygamist (Genesis 4:19).

11. The name Noah (*nōaḥ*) is generally thought to be derived from the Hebrew verb *nwḥ*, meaning "to rest" or "to repose." Genesis 5:28–29 gives us a folk etymology "to bring us relief or comfort [from our work]."

12. Shem means "name" in Hebrew, and secondarily "renown." Shem, the oldest of Noah's sons, is represented as the father of all Semites, particularly the Hebrews and the Arabs.

13. Arpachshad, probably a non-Semitic name, may be Arrapachitis of the Greek geographer Ptolemy, or, more likely, the Assyrian city of Arrapkha, probably modern Kirkuk.

14. The name Shelah is related to the West Semitic root *šlḥ*, possibly a Canaanite god of the underworld river, and is found in combination in the name Methuselah.

15. The name Eber (*'ēber*) signifies "the other side" or "across," and has basically the same root as the word used for "Hebrews," possibly signifying those people who came "from the other side" of the river Euphrates (Joshua 24:2–3). The word generally has social rather than ethnic significance, not unlike our words "sojourner" and "foreigner."

16. The etymology of the name Peleg is disputed. The reference may be geographical, *phalga* in the Upper Euphrates, but this seems unlikely. The Hebrew word *plg* ordinarily means "to divide," hence the obscure verse in Genesis 10:25: "In his (Peleg's) day the earth was divided." The passage may be referring to the division of the peoples of the earth into nations, as described in Genesis 10.

17. The name Reu suggests the West Semitic word meaning "shepherd" or "friend," and is often compounded in Semitic names in many times and places (e.g., Moses' father-in-law Reuel, "a friend of God").

18. The root of the name Serug (*šrg*) appears in northwest Mesopotamian place names of the first millennium BCE. In fact, several names in this list of Abraham's ancestors suggest geographic locations in northern Syria, Abraham's ancestral homeland.

19. Nahor's name is likely related to Nahur, a city referred to in the Mari tablets in the second millennium BCE and located near Haran, Abraham's ancestral home.

20. As with other names in the genealogy of postdiluvian ancestors in Genesis 11, Terah may have been a place name in northwest Mesopotamia, although the etymology of this name is still debated.

21. Thorkild Jacobsen, *The Sumerian King List*, Assyriological Studies, vol. 11 (Chicago: University of Chicago Press, 1939), pp. 70ff.

22. Although the name "Elohim" appears in the traditional Hebrew (Masoretic) text of Genesis 7:9 instead of "Yahweh," which we would expect if this is originally J material, the name "Yahweh" does appear in the Samaritan Pentateuch, in the Syriac Peshitta, and in the Latin Vulgate versions of Genesis 7:9, possible evidence that "Yahweh" and not Elohim is

original to the text of this verse. Further justification for accepting the reading of the Samaritan Pentateuch in this instance will become even clearer in the final chapter of this volume.

23. Beginning in the 1930s and continuing into the period after World War II, archaeologists discovered a library of more than twenty thousand clay tablets at the site of the ancient kingdom of Mari in northwest Mesopotamia, near the border between Syria and Iraq. These cuneiform tablets provide information on virtually every aspect of everyday life in Mari, which controlled northern Mesopotamia before and, possibly, during the time of the Hebrew patriarchs. The tablets contain names that appear in early biblical traditions: e.g.,

> Peleg (Genesis 10:25; 11:16–19; 1 Chronicles 1:19, 25);
> Serug (Genesis 11:20–23; 1 Chronicles 1:26);
> Terah (Genesis 11:24–28, 31–32; Joshua 24:2; 1 Chronicles 1:26); and
> Nahor (Genesis 11:22–27, 29; 22:20, 23; 24:10, 15, 24, 47; 29:5; 31:53; 1 Chronicles 1:26).

They also mention Haran, the patriarchs' ancestral city in northwest Mesopotamia, from which Abraham migrated to Canaan. See the names of the postdiluvian ancestors in the chart on p. 62.

24. In 1919, archaeologists discovered at the Hurrian city of Nuzi on the Tigris River a library of about thirty-five hundred cuneiform tablets dating from 1500 to 1350 BCE. Among the more interesting discoveries in the tablets was information about some of the social, economic, and legal practices of the period as recorded in deeds, wills, adoptions, and marriage agreements—information that sheds light on many of the customs referred to in Genesis 12–50. Similarities between practices reported in the Nuzi tablets and the patriarchal narratives indicate that the two traditions shared a common background in the ancient Near East in the early to mid-second millennium BCE.

25. "Terah took his son Abram and his grandson Lot, son of Haran, and his daughter-in-law Sarai, his son Abram's wife, and they went out together from Ur of the Chaldeans to go into the land of Canaan; but when they came to Haran, they settled there."

26. Intervening passages in Genesis 12:10–13:17 describe Abraham and Sarah's sojourn in Egypt (12:10–20) and Abraham and his nephew Lot's decision to separate, with Abraham staying in Canaan and Lot settling in Transjordan (13:1–13). This latter story is clearly an etiological legend, an attempt to trace Israel's genealogical relationship with neighboring people: Lot's sons Moab and Ben Ammi are the fathers of the Moabites and the Ammonites, respectively (see the genealogical chart on p. 54).

27. There are other intervening stories, Lot's capture and rescue (14:1–16) and Abraham's blessing by Melchizedek, the king of Jerusalem (14:17–24). I intend in this summary to trace only the essential events in the patriarchal story, and will pass over these inter-

vening stories, which have merit in their own right but interrupt the basic narrative and would require extended detail that is unnecessary to our current discussion.

28. There are obviously two conflicting traditions that have been combined here: Ishmaelites in Genesis 37:25–27, 28b and Midianites in the version in Genesis 37:21–24, 28a.

29. See especially Genesis 4:26b, which claims that the worship of Yahweh goes back to the Antediluvian Period: "At that time [shortly after Cain killed Abel] people began to invoke the name of the LORD (Yahweh)."

30. *Webster's Deluxe Unabridged Dictionary* defines *polydaemonism* as "a form of religion in which a multitude of demons or spirits are thought to govern natural phenomena."

31. The rendering of El Shaddai as God Almighty has its roots in the third-century BCE Greek translation known as the Septuagint and in Jerome's Latin Vulgate and is probably nothing more than a free rendering of the Hebrew, whose meaning was by then obscure.

32. 19"Now Laban had gone to shear his sheep, and Rachel stole her father's household gods. . . . 30[Laban spoke to Jacob] 'Even though you had to go because you longed greatly for your father's house, why did you steal my gods?' 31Jacob answered Laban, 'Because I was afraid, for I thought that you would take your daughters from me by force. 32But anyone with whom you find your gods shall not live. In the presence of our kinfolk, point out what I have that is yours, and take it.' Now Jacob did not know that Rachel had stolen the gods. . . . 34Now Rachel had taken the household gods and put them in the camel's saddle, and sat on them. Laban felt all about in the tent, but did not find them. 35And she said to her father, 'Let not my lord be angry that I cannot rise before you, for the way of women is upon me.' So he searched, but did not find the household gods."

33. "And King Melchizedek of Salem (= Jerusalem) brought out bread and wine; he was the priest of El Elyon. He blessed him [Abraham] and said, 'Blessed be Abram by El Elyon, maker of heaven and earth; and blessed be El Elyon who has delivered your enemies into your hand.' . . . But Abraham said to the king of Sodom, 'I have sworn to the lord El Elyon, maker of heaven and earth, that I would not take a thread or a sandal-thong or anything that is yours, so that you may not say, "I made Abraham rich."'"

34. "Abraham planted a tamarisk tree in Beersheba, and called there on the name of the LORD (Yahweh), El Olam."

35. "So she named the LORD (Yahweh) who spoke to her, 'You are El Roi'; for she said, 'Have I really seen God and remained alive after seeing him?'"

36. El Berith or Baal Berith will be discussed in more detail in the next chapter in the context of Joshua's renewal ceremony at Shechem as reported in Joshua 24.

37. The word traditionally translated as "oak" was probably a terebinth or turpentine tree. The word Moreh means "teacher," suggesting that, following ancient Canaanite practice, a seer or priest sat under the sacred tree and delivered "oracles."

38. As in the case of Moreh, once again the terebinth or turpentine tree at Mamre.

39. James B. Pritchard, *Ancient Near Eastern Texts Relating to the Old Testament with Supplement* (Princeton, NJ: Princeton University Press, 1969) and Theodor H. Gaster, *The Oldest Stories in the World* (Boston: Beacon Press, 1959) provide English translations of relevant myths and legends with extensive notes indicating Mesopotamian and other ancient Near East parallels to relevant biblical passages.

40. Genesis 17:5 provides a creative etymological explanation for the presumed name change: "No longer shall your name be Abram [exalted father], but you shall be called Abraham [father of a multitude]; for I have made you the ancestor of a multitude of nations."

CHAPTER 3

FROM THE EXODUS TO THE CONQUEST AND ENTRENCHMENT OF CANAAN

THE DELIVERANCE FROM BONDAGE

The Exodus is the defining event in Israel's history. The patriarchal stories notwithstanding, Israel understood that its history originated in the marvelous deliverance from suffering and subjugation at the hands of the Egyptian pharaoh. Although it was Moses who apparently led the people out of Egypt, the narrative in Exodus tells the story of Yahweh's intervention in history to lead the people out of slavery, to establish a covenant with them in the Sinai wilderness, and ultimately to lead them to the promised land of Canaan where he would establish them as a nation.

Obviously, the historian cannot talk about "acts of God" in history, but the rigors of biblical scholarship have no difficulty in looking at the story from the perspective of historical objectivity. From the historian's perspective, the central figure in the story is, of course, Moses, and so we turn now to look at Moses.

Unfortunately, there is no mention of Moses or of the Exodus in any extant non-biblical records. Although some scholars have, therefore, questioned whether Moses was an actual person, Moses so towers over the event of the Exodus that there can be little question that he was a historical figure. Nonetheless, it is not easy to substantiate details either in Moses' life or in the events surrounding the Exodus.

The tradition in Exodus 2 that Moses was born and raised in Egypt is probably reliable, although there is obviously a great deal of legendary material surrounding the stories of his early years. The account of Moses floating on the Nile on a basket of bulrushes (Exodus 2:1–10) is reminiscent of a similar legend about the Mesopotamian king Sargon of Akkad from about 2300 BCE.[1] An inscription tells that after Sargon's mother bore him, she placed him in a basket of rushes that had been sealed with bitumen and cast the basket on the river. Akki, the drawer of water, lifted Sargon out of the river and raised him as his own son. From these humble origins, Sargon rose to become king of Agage (Akkad). The dependence of the story about Moses in the book of Exodus on the tradition about Sargon of Akkad is obvious.

Moses' name is a clear indication of his Egyptian roots. The biblical writer obviously did not know that Moses was an abbreviated Egyptian name; hence, Exodus tries to connect the name (Hebrew: *mōšeh*) with the Hebrew verb *māšâ* meaning "to draw out." It is incomprehensible that pharaoh's daughter could be expected to have given Moses a name related to this Hebrew verb after she *drew him out* of the water. The name is actually the Hebrew equivalent of the Egyptian word *msy*, which means "to give birth" and appears, usually in combination with the name of a god, in such Egyptian names as Tuth-mose (the god Thoth is born), Ra-meses (the god Ra is born), and Ptah-mose (the god Ptah is born). Pharaohs of the nineteenth dynasty were sometimes referred to simply as *Mose*, without the name of the god. It is beyond the realm of historical objectivity to know definitively whether Moses was originally Hebrew or Egyptian. If Moses was Hebrew, then it is improbable that he was raised as a prince in pharaoh's court. If he was Egyptian, we need to explain why he took an interest in liberating Hebrew slaves. Neither position is self-evident.

The events surrounding Moses' early life and the use of slave labor for large-scale building recall imperial projects in the Nile Delta during the reign of pharaoh Seti I. The story of Moses' murder of an Egyptian taskmaster for beating a Hebrew slave may be true and could explain Moses' flight from Egypt to "the land of Midian," apparently in the Sinai Peninsula, just east of Egypt. There Moses was welcomed by "the priest of Midian," a chieftain of the Kenite tribe of Midianites, who is variously called Jethro (Exodus 3:1; 4:18; 18:1–27); Hobab (Numbers 10:29; Judges 1:16; 4:11); and Reuel, meaning in Hebrew "a friend of El (god)" (Exodus 2:18). Moses eventually married Jethro's daughter, Zipporah.

What is most important about this tradition is that Moses' connection with the Kenites is probably authentic and that it was Moses' Kenite father-in-law Jethro, the priest of Yahweh at Sinai, who first introduced Moses to Yahweh, who was apparently a Kenite tribal god. It seems unlikely that prior to his Sinai experience Moses and the Hebrew slaves had ever heard of this god Yahweh. As we have seen, there are numerous clues in the text that point to this conclusion in spite of the fact that it contradicts what tradition would otherwise have us believe——namely, that Yahweh goes back as far as Abraham, and perhaps even to the period of the Primordial History, and even to creation. The criterion of dissimilarity or embarrassment is operative here——historical probability is greater if there is evidence that is dissimilar to the received tradition of later generations.

The account of Moses' encounter with Yahweh in the burning bush (Exodus 3) is a classic example of the call and commission of a prophet, evident in the calls and commissions of much later prophets such as Amos (Amos 7:14–15), Isaiah (Isaiah 6:1–13), and Jeremiah (Jeremiah 1:4–10). Moses is often considered the prototype of Hebrew prophets, but it may be more accurate to say that the account of Moses' call and commission assumed its written form in E, the ninth-century Elohist source, in light of stories of the calls and commissions of subsequent Hebrew prophets with which the Elohist was familiar. The historical Moses predates by several centuries the period of Israel's great prophets, but the accounts of Moses' call and commission were written after Hebrew prophecy had already begun to make its mark on Israelite religion. Hence the literary form of Moses' call and commission in E assumed the literary form of stories about the calls and commissions of later prophetic figures, similar to what we find subsequently in the calls of Amos (eighth century BCE), Isaiah of Jerusalem (eighth century BCE), and Jeremiah (seventh century BCE). Although these prophets all lived after the writing of the Elohist epic, there were earlier prophets about whom we know much less, but who, presumably, also experienced "calls"—among them Micaiah, Elijah, and Elisha, all from the ninth century BCE (see chapter 5).

A study of the phenomenon of prophetic types (*homines religiosi*) across time and cultures suggests that the qualities we find in these individuals are very similar, despite time and place. Such people are invariably convinced that they are under some sort of supernatural or superhuman constraint; they generally experience a feeling of personal worthlessness and absolute dependence on a higher power or being, and many experience an ecstatic or psychical state in which they receive divine revelations. They often become speakers who are compelled to announce to others what they have received in their divine revelations, and most can point to a single moment in which they received their special calls, from which they more often than not tend to shirk because of a feeling of utter worthlessness. To quote the words of Johannes Lindblom in addressing the phenomenon of prophecy:

> In the technical language of psychology, it might be described rather differently, thus: the characteristic of inspiration in a general sense is that certain ideas, images, emotions, impulses from the subconscious, subliminal, unconscious, co-conscious (whichever term may be used) arise in the mind so spontaneously and so independently of reflection and meditation, that the inspired person feels as though his ideas were coming not from himself, but from another realm, and are given him by a power other than himself.[2]

It appears that the phenomenon of prophecy is deeply rooted in the human psyche, although few experience it in the manner of a Moses, an Amos, or an Isaiah.

Whatever it was that Moses experienced on the mountain, the story is clear: Moses came away from his *vision* or *audition* convinced that Yahweh had called him to go back to Egypt to deliver the Hebrew slaves from Egypt and to bring them to the foot of the holy mountain where he had received his call and commission. The newness of Yahweh worship is reinforced in Moses' question (Exodus 3:13–15):

> If I come to the Israelites and say to them, "The God of your ancestors has sent me to you," and they ask me, "What is his name?" what shall I say to them? . . . God also said to Moses, "Thus you shall say to the Israelites, 'The LORD (Yahweh), the God of your ancestors, the God of Abraham, the God of Isaac, and the God of Jacob, has sent me to you.'"

The current form of this "conversation" makes little or no sense. Moses asks this god who he is and what his name is. The answer is eminently clear: Yahweh. But the narrative goes on to link what was certainly a new god Yahweh to the god of the patriarchal tradition, who was not Yahweh, except in the later revisions of the history. It was obviously important for Moses to know the name of this god. The story makes much more sense if Moses is simply asking this god who he is, so that he knows and will be able to communicate that information to the Hebrew slaves, who will want to know whose command they are following.

The divine name Yahweh is actually the third personal singular imperfect of the Hebrew verb *hwh* "to be" and may suggest that Yahweh "will be" with his people in the events that ensue.[3] Exodus 3:15 indicates quite clearly that a new god, not merely a new name for the patriarchal god, was being introduced at this time.

The important text in Exodus 6:2–3 simultaneously contrasts and connects patriarchal religion and Yahweh religion: "I am the LORD (Yahweh). I appeared to Abraham, Isaac, and Jacob as God Almighty (El Shaddai), but by my name 'The LORD (Yahweh)' I did not make myself known to them." This passage attempts, somewhat unsuccessfully, to link the religion of the ancestors (the god El Shaddai) with Israel's current religious focus (Yahweh, the god of the Exodus). Yahweh is the god who brought Israel out of Egypt. The patriarchal history is the prehistory of Israel; therefore, patriarchal religion must reflect the prehistory of Yahwism. In other words, when the ancestors left Mesopotamia, they brought with them their own religious beliefs and practices, including the worship of their familial clan god El Shaddai, who was likely of Amorite origin. In light of the Exodus and Sinai experience, the former Egyptian slaves began to worship Yahweh. Was this Yahweh a new god, or just a new name for the old god? I think the answer to the question is clear: Yahweh was a new god, who was later understood to be the same god as El Shaddai of the patriarchs. The criterion of dissimilarity or embarrassment is, once again, helpful in sorting out this particular dilemma.

In support of the view that Yahweh was, indeed, a new god, at least for the Hebrews, it is useful to note that there are no personal names containing the element Yah or Yahweh among the Hebrews in the period before the Exodus. Such names, however, became common in the period following the Exodus: Hoshea's name was changed by Moses to Joshua = Yah(weh) is salvation. Isaiah, Josiah, Jeremiah, Hezekiah, Nehemiah, Obadiah, Zephaniah, Zechariah, and so on are all Yah or Yahweh names in combination with different prefixes.

To summarize, Yahweh was likely originally the god of the Kenites, a clan of the Midianites. Moses was introduced to Yahweh by his father-in-law Jethro, the priest of Midian at Mount Sinai, apparently a Midianite holy site. Moses went back to Egypt and introduced the Hebrew slaves to this new god, whom they had heretofore not known or worshiped. Moses then urged the slaves to leave Egypt and to go with him to the holy mountain of this new god Yahweh, the presumed author of their deliverance. We are, at this point, advancing a hypothesis, one designed to address the evidence. We do not and cannot ever know definitively what happened. However, this is, in my opinion, a good theory, the one that speaks best to the evidence and addresses most satisfactorily the sometimes conflicting data. This interpretation also makes better sense of the later defection in the wilderness of many of the Israelites and of the account of the covenant ceremony at Shechem in Joshua 24, both of which will be addressed later in this chapter.

The focus of the story on Jethro, the Kenites, and Mount Sinai, which is well outside the territory of both the patriarchs and of the land of Canaan, points conclusively to the probability that Jethro, a priest of Yahweh at Mount Sinai, was the one who introduced Moses to this Yahweh, who presumably dwelt on this imposing mountain in the south-central Sinai wilderness. Despite the legendary accretion of miraculous powers to Moses, it appears that Moses returned quite simply to the Nile Delta to plot the liberation of the Hebrew slaves from Egyptian servitude. I have serious doubts about Moses' alleged interviews with the pharaoh,[4] presumably Rameses II, and even more doubts about what are certainly legendary accounts of the plagues. There can, however, be little doubt that under Moses' leadership a band of several hundred slaves left Egypt sometime around 1290 BCE, shortly after the beginning of the reign of Rameses II, presumably the king "who did not know Joseph" (Exodus 1:8).

Who were these slaves? Who took part in the Exodus? It is important to be mindful of three details. First, the text would have us believe that they were the descendants of the children of Jacob, who went down to Egypt centuries earlier. Second, the text at one point describes them as a "mixed crowd" or a "mixed multitude" (Exodus 12:37–38).[5] And third, they were Hebrews. We need to look more closely at this word, because it may not be an equivalent of Israelites. The term "Hebrews" is used most often in the Joseph cycle (Genesis 39:17; 40:15; 41:12), in the story of the Exodus (Exodus 1:16; 2:7; 3:18; 5:3; 7:16), and in the story of the wars between Israel and the Philistines (1 Samuel 4:6; 13:19; 14:11). In those passages, the word does not seem to express the same sense of national identity conveyed in the name "Israel," inasmuch as some individuals who were apparently not Israelites are described as Hebrews.

There are numerous references in documents of the second millennium BCE to people known as Habiru or 'Apiru. According to Mesopotamian and Egyptian texts (specifically the Amarna letters) the 'Apiru seem to have been rootless people, whom we might call "sojourners" or "foreigners," who settled in the midst of more established peoples, probably on empty land between larger cities or settlements. Certainly this meaning fits the patriarchs Abraham, Isaac, and Jacob. The term "Hebrew" was in the earliest texts apparently more inclusive than it is in the biblical books.

Exodus would have us believe that six hundred thousand men took part in the escape (see the text of Exodus 12:37–38 in footnote 5). With women and children, it is estimated that over two million people would have been involved.[6] Although Cecil B. DeMille and Charlton Heston would have us believe this excessive number, it is a later exaggeration, reflecting perhaps a census taken in the tenth century BCE during the reign of King David.[7] The text of Exodus, however, is probably correct in describing the escapees as a "mixed multitude" representing not only the "Israelites-to-be," but Habiru of other origins as well.[8] In fact, it is probably an anachronism to use the term "Israelites" at this period in the national history. The group of slaves was undoubtedly small, probably no more than two or three hundred people. The Sinai wilderness, an arid area with small oases, could not possibly have supported the millions the text of the book of Exodus reports.

The route of the Exodus is uncertain, but the people apparently left the area of Rameses (Goshen) in the Nile Delta under Moses' leadership and traveled eastward toward the area that currently borders on the Suez Canal, presumably en route to the sacred mountain where Moses had received his call and commission.[9] The fugitives soon arrived at the *yam sûp*, which means "the sea of reeds" or "papyrus lake," not the Red Sea, which was much farther to the south. The mistake in translation was first made by the Septuagint and has been passed on to our modern translations, courtesy of the Latin Vulgate. The term probably refers to a marshy lake, perhaps Lake Timsah, on the border between the Egyptian delta and the northern Sinai. There is no merit whatsoever to the claim that it was the Red Sea that the people crossed, or even the Gulf of Suez, an arm of the Red Sea, where reeds do not grow.

With the Egyptian army in pursuit behind them and the sea in front of them, the people were apparently prepared to return to slavery in Egypt (Exodus 14:11–12). Apparently, under Moses' direction, the people decided to cross the shallow marshy lake on foot, something that pharaoh's chariots were unable to maneuver. The details of the story are obviously shrouded by later accretions designed to heighten the account, but there is little question among biblical scholars that there was an escape across the water, perhaps facilitated by wind and tide. The details of the Exodus will be forever obscure, but that does not diminish the probability that, under Moses' leadership, the band of former slaves succeeded in escaping from Egypt into the wilderness of the northern Sinai.

We may, in fact, have a firsthand account of that escape in an ancient couplet, ascribed in the text (probably improperly and legendarily) to Moses' sister Miriam (Exodus 15:20–21):

FIGURE 4. THE EXODUS FROM EGYPT

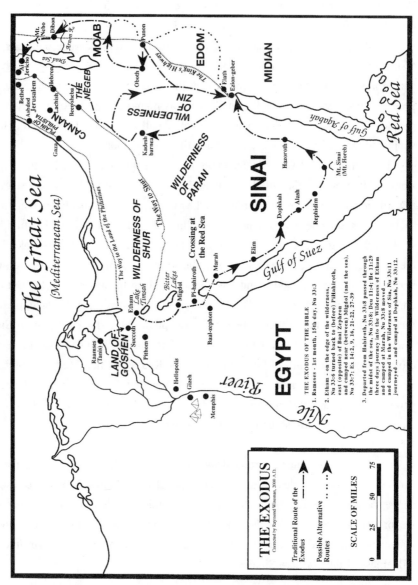

This map can be viewed at www.bible.ca; copyright, 1994 by Abingdon Press. Used by permission.

Then the prophet Miriam, Aaron's sister, took a tambourine in her hand; and all the women went out after her with tambourines and with dancing. And Miriam sang to them:
> Sing to the LORD (Yahweh)
>> for he has triumphed gloriously;
>> horse and rider he has thrown into the sea.

Given the ancient form of the poetic language of this couplet and given its unadulterated simplicity, most scholars are convinced that it may reach back to the event itself. Most important is the conviction that the escape is the work of Yahweh. It is Yahweh who has triumphed, and it is Yahweh who has thrown the Egyptian charioteers and their horses into the sea. The success of the escape clearly vindicated Moses and laid the foundation for the worship of the god whom Moses first met at Mount Sinai. The escape, of course, is history. The role of Yahweh in that event is interpretation and theological overlay. Beyond the scope of the biblical historian, that overlay rests in the interpretation of Moses and the belief of those who took part in the event and their successors throughout the history of Judaism.

THE JOURNEY TO SINAI
AND THE COVENANT WITH YAHWEH

Throughout Israelite history there persisted the memory that the wilderness experience was formative and that out of it came the understanding that this previously "mixed multitude" was now the people of Yahweh, not yet a nation to be sure, but surely a people with a self-identity. The name of that people "Israel" probably means "May God (El) Rule."

The wilderness was also a period of doubt—doubt about Moses, doubt about Yahweh, and doubt about whether the band of former slaves had gone from a situation that was bad to a situation that was even worse. Exodus 15:22–26; 16:2–3; 17:2–7; Numbers 11:4–6; 12:1–2; 14:2–3; 16:12–14; 20:2–13; and 21:4–5 are examples of times when the people murmured against Moses, and even against Yahweh. These stories must have some historical basis, as they surely cast the people in a negative light. They also argue against the heightened element of the miraculous in the Exodus stories in their present form. The issue is quite simple: why would people who had recently experienced the miracles described in the book of Exodus lapse so quickly into disbelief and begin to doubt both Moses and Yahweh?

Moses saw Yahweh's presence in those elements that enabled the people to survive, namely, food and water. Most especially, the manna and the quail, both familiar
phenomena in the Sinai wilderness, were viewed by Moses as gifts and signs of
Yahweh's presence and concern for the people (Exodus 16:1–36). Despite lack of food
and water and attacks from hostile tribes, Moses led the people to the foot of what
Exodus calls "the mountain of God" (Exodus 3:1; 24:13) and Numbers calls "the
mount(ain) of Yahweh" (Numbers 10:33). Although we can never know with certainty
the location of Mount Sinai, Jebel Musa (Arabic for "the mountain of Moses") in the
southern Sinai is a likely location.

According to Exodus 19:1, the journey from Egypt to Sinai took about three
months (or three new moons). It seems almost certain that it was Moses' intention
to take the people to the very mountain at which he believed he had received
Yahweh's command to deliver them from slavery. According to the story, Moses
ascended the mountain and, amid the traditional ancient Near Eastern imagery of
thunder and lightening that accompanies theophanies, received the laws that were to
bind Yahweh and the people into a contractual or covenantal relationship. We
cannot, of course, know what happened to Moses on the mountain, but we can be
relatively confident that he returned to the people with something like the Ten Commandments reported in Exodus 20:1–17 (and Deuteronomy 5:6–21). I say "something like the Ten Commandments" because most scholars are confident that the versions found in Exodus and Deuteronomy, which are slightly different, reflect later
clarification, elaboration, expansion, and commentary on what were initially probably very pithy statements of absolute or apodictic law.[10]

There is in Exodus 20:2 (and Deuteronomy 5:6) an important prologue to the
Decalogue, identifying the author of the commands that follow:

I am the LORD (Yahweh) your God, who brought you out of the land of Egypt, out
of the house of slavery.

The Ten Commandments then follow. Their original form was probably something
like this:

- You shall have no other gods before (or except) me.
- You shall not make any carved image of me.
- You shall not make wrongful use of the name of the LORD (Yahweh).
- Remember the Sabbath day, and keep it holy.

- Honor your father and your mother.
- You shall not murder.
- You shall not commit adultery.
- You shall not steal.
- You shall not bear false witness.
- You shall not covet your neighbor's house.

The Fourth and Fifth Commandments are positive commands in the second person singular. The others are all negative prohibitions, also in the second person singular. Basically what we have is a series of "do this" and "don't do that." By using the second person singular, it is clear that Moses was addressing each member of Israel's covenant community individually.

The commandments were initially what sociologists call an in-group ethic. They were intended to set limitations on the behavior of members of the community toward one another. The first three (or four) commandments deal with the relationship of the people to Yahweh. The remaining commandments govern the relationship of members of the group toward one another.

Let us look at the commandments briefly to clarify their meaning in their original historical context, the Exodus-Sinai experience:

1. The people were to worship only Yahweh, the author of their deliverance. Their loyalty was to be exclusively to Yahweh, what scholars call *henotheism*, the worship of one god without denying the existence of other gods for other people. This belief is different from *monotheism*, the conviction that there is only one god, a position that was adopted by the Israelites many centuries later.
2. The people were commanded not to make any carved images of their god, a practice that was almost universal in the ancient Near Eastern world of that period.
3. The people were enjoined not to use the divine name for purposes of conjuration, divination, or magic.
4. The seventh day of the week, Friday sundown until Saturday sundown, was to be a day free from work, a holy day during which the people would focus on Yahweh and on what he had done for them.
5. The word of one's parents was generally considered law and was not to be disobeyed under any circumstances.

6. This command was not a general order against all killing. It was a command against the premeditated murder of members of the in-group only. The Israelites found no difficulty whatsoever in killing their enemies.

7. Inasmuch as a woman was the property of her husband, adultery was a violation of the husband's property rights.

8. Members of the community were not to take from other members of the community property that was not theirs.

9. Members of the community should not be lying witnesses against other members of the community, especially inasmuch as the testimony of a witness could result in serious consequences for an accused offender.

10. Members of the community should not desire the house (i.e., property) of any other member of the community.

The law set forth in the Decalogue bound the people to one another and to Yahweh in a contractual or covenantal relationship that elucidated what it meant to say that Yahweh would henceforth be the god of Israel, and Israel would henceforth be the people of Yahweh.

The material that follows the Decalogue in the book of Exodus is represented as covenant law that was issued to the people by Yahweh through Moses immediately following the proclamation of the Ten Commandments. The matter is, however, far more complicated than that, and most of the material from the second half of Exodus and from Leviticus, Numbers, and Deuteronomy is later legal tradition that cannot be traced directly to Moses.

The stories of the plagues in Egypt (Exodus 7–11) and of the Passover festival (Exodus 12) likely put us in touch with ancient folklore and myth and, in the case of the Passover, with ancient pre-Israelite cultic ceremonies, a festival of unleavened bread and a festival of the sacrifice of the firstborn animal of the flocks. That said, the stories of the sojourn in Egypt, the escape through the sea of reeds, the wilderness tradition, and the Sinai covenant are likely, in their unadulterated form, based on accurate historical memory. Nevertheless, from the perspective of the biblical historian, the form in which these stories come to us leaves a great deal to be desired.

There is, of course, a final question that needs to be addressed in this section: Who was the author of the Ten Commandments? The text, of course, says Yahweh. A biblical scholar would likely answer Moses. What or whom it was that Moses was listening to, of course, falls beyond the realm of historical investigation. I suspect, however, that we should consider the likelihood that Moses' vision and/or audition was an "internal dialogue." Would that we had enough information to explore with some measure of objectivity the inner psychology of Moses!

IN THE WILDERNESS

Numbers is the fourth book of the Hebrew Bible, the fourth book of the Pentateuch (the five scrolls). The name of this book in the original Hebrew is taken from the opening words of the book "in the wilderness," a title that is actually more appropriate to the contents of the book. Numbers opens with Israel in the Sinai wilderness and covers the next forty years (a phrase that often means a generation rather than a specific number of years) of wandering until the people reached the east side of the Jordan River in the "plains of Moab," set to cross the river and enter the land of Canaan.

The book of Numbers is probably made up of two sources, the old epic tradition we have come to call the Yahwist or the J source, and the later priestly or P source with its strong interest in cultic matters, religious ritual, and genealogies. The book itself is easily divided into three parts:

(1) the period in the Sinai wilderness (Numbers 1:1–10:10);
(2) the trek through the wilderness to Transjordan (Numbers 11:11–22:1); and
(3) the time spent in Transjordan, on the "plains of Moab" (Numbers 22:2–36:13).

Although the story clearly has its eyes set forward to the conquest of Canaan, the period of the wilderness wanderings was certainly far more complicated. It is not clear that Moses or anyone else really knew where the newly established people of Yahweh would go once they had been brought together into the covenant community at Sinai. As we have seen, there was a great deal of discontent with Moses' leadership, and the people were not convinced that they were better off in the wilderness than they had been when they were pharaoh's slaves in Egypt.

There were presumably three possible choices, and on numerous occasions the people seem to have considered all three options: to remain in the forbidding Sinai wilderness, to go back to Egypt, or to move forward and try to establish themselves farther to the east.

The stories of the spies Joshua, Caleb, and others, sent forth from the oasis at Kadesh-Barnea to determine whether the people might enter Canaan from the south, echoes that uncertainty (Numbers 13). There was apparently a division of opinion as to whether the band could enter the land from the south. When they finally made an attempt to do so, they were repulsed by the Amalekites and the Canaanites who lived in the hill country in the southern region of the land of Canaan (Numbers 14:26–45).

The people continued to travel to the east around the southern end of the Dead Sea but were denied permission by the king of Edom to pass along the King's Highway through Edom (Numbers 20:14–21). The people tried once again to enter Canaan from the south but were challenged by the king of Arad (Numbers 21:1–3). Although the account suggests, perhaps wistfully, that the band of former slaves actually won this battle, they apparently did not continue into Canaan but rather retreated and set out once again to the east into Moab (Numbers 21:10–20).

It was there in the plains of Moab on the eastern shore of the Jordan River that Moses died and was buried (Deuteronomy 34:1–8), but, according to the story, only after he had anointed Joshua as his successor (Deuteronomy 34:9).

THE CONQUEST AND ENTRENCHMENT OF CANAAN

Joshua 1–12 tells the story of an impressive and decisive conquest of Canaan in three vital military operations:

(1) a campaign that gave Israel control of the central hill country, including Jericho and Ai (Joshua 7–9);
(2) a campaign that gave Israel control of the southern hill country, including Libnah, Lachish, Eglon, Hebron, and Debir (Joshua 10); and
(3) a campaign that gave Israel control of the northern hill country, including Hazor (Joshua 11).

According to this story, Joshua operated out of Gilgal as the military head of a united Israel and in a period of five years gained complete control over the land of Canaan. In his enthusiasm, the author of this account (generally referred to by scholars as the Deuteronomistic historian) simplified (and indeed distorted) the historical reality of the so-called conquest and entrenchment of Canaan.

There are, indeed, discrepancies in the accounts of the conquest. Joshua 10:36–37 reports that Joshua destroyed Hebron, a town associated with the patriarchs, whereas Judges 1:10 reports that it was the tribe of Judah that captured that city. Joshua 10:38–39 reports that Joshua captured Debir (or Kiriath-sepher), whereas Joshua 15:13–19 and Judges 1:11–15 both report that Othniel, the son of Kenaz, Caleb's younger brother, captured the city.[11]

Judges 1 presents a different and more realistic picture of the conquest of Canaan than does Joshua 1–12. Instead of reporting Joshua's total victory over Canaan in the course of a five-year period, Judges implies that there were independent and incomplete tribal victories. Scholars generally agree that the account in Judges 1, which indicates that Israel failed to complete the conquest of Canaan, is more reliable. Quite clearly, the conquest and entrenchment of Canaan was a far more complex process than what is reported in Joshua 1–12, which is a stylized, romanticized, and highly exaggerated account.

Indeed, the tribal occupation of Canaan apparently occurred over a relatively long period of time, not the five years of the book of Joshua, and under very different conditions for different regions of the land. It was only later, after the twelve tribes had united into the covenant community called Israel, that individual tribal traditions were subsumed and brought together in Joshua 1–12 into the single narrative of an all-Israelite conquest of the land under Joshua's leadership. The criterion of embarrassment favors the more realistic account in Judges 1, appropriately characterized as "Israel's Failure to Complete the Conquest of Canaan."[12]

Along with the textual evidence, archaeological evidence confirms this more complex picture of the conquest and entrenchment. Let it be clear at the outset that the role of archaeology is neither to confirm nor to undermine the Bible, although many individuals on both sides of the issue have used it in this way. Archaeology is the science of digging up the past and attempts, in the most objective way possible, to reconstruct the past based on archaeological data, used in conjunction with written records. In the case of one very famous story, archaeologists have shown that the famous wall of Jericho, which supposedly came tumbling down after the Israelites marched around the walled city three times and then blew their trumpets (Joshua 6), had actually been destroyed centuries earlier in about 1580 BCE, probably by Egyptians, more than three hundred years before Joshua's arrival in Canaan in about 1250 BCE. Jericho was probably reoccupied on a very small scale during the second half of the fifteenth century BCE, and destroyed once again in the second

half of the fourteenth century BCE, almost a century before Joshua's arrival. Archaeological evidence indicates that Jericho was in ruins at the time of Joshua and was
not reoccupied until much later, possibly in the early ninth century BCE.[13]

In addition, archaeological evidence indicates that the city of Ai, which Joshua
supposedly burned (Joshua 8:1–29), was also in ruins in Joshua's time, having been
destroyed in about 2400 BCE and remaining so from about 2400 to 1200 BCE, about
fifty years after Joshua's arrival in the land. In fact, the word Ai means in Hebrew
"the ruin." Several scholars have speculated that the account of its destruction in the
book of Joshua is an etiological legend, designed to explain the ruins at this site at
the time of Joshua's "conquest."

In all probability, the entrenchment of Canaan took place over many centuries
and was not completed until the time of King David in the tenth century BCE, more
than two hundred fifty years after Joshua's initial arrival in the land about 1250
BCE.[14] The initial occupation was not a conquest at all, but more probably a gradual
settlement in the sparsely settled hill country on unoccupied land between larger
Canaanite cities. It is quite possible that the Leah tribes (Reuben, Simeon, Levi,
Judah, Issachar, and Zebulun), roughly speaking, were already established in the land
before the arrival of the group that took part in the Exodus, roughly speaking the
Rachel tribes (Joseph and Benjamin), who were perhaps involved in a modest "invasion" from the plains of Moab, east of the Jordan River. The occupation of the land
was almost certainly both a combination of infiltration over a long period of time and
of limited warfare from some of the newcomers. Joshua, whose name is associated
with the whole of the conquest, was probably an Ephraimite tribal hero to whom
credit for the entire conquest was ascribed in the later version of the national epic, at
a time when the tribe of Joseph, likely one of the Exodus tribes, had grown in importance. Legend was apparently blended with history to enshrine Joshua, the designated
heir of Moses according to tradition, as the military hero of the conquest.

The relationship between the Hebrew tribes (roughly the Leah tribes?) that were
already established in the land of Canaan and the tribes of the Exodus (roughly the
Rachel tribes?) is not entirely clear. It does, however, appear that those already
established in Canaan joined forces with these latecomers whose forebears had come
out of Egypt and established at Sinai a covenantal relationship with Yahweh. Particularly important in this connection is the story in Joshua 24, which helps us to put
together many of the loose ends of the patriarchal stories, the Exodus, and the
accounts of the conquest.

THE ESTABLISHMENT
OF THE TRIBAL CONFEDERACY:
THE COVENANT AT SHECHEM

According to the account in Joshua 24:1–15, at a great convocation in Shechem, an important city in the central hill country, the following occurred:

₁Then Joshua gathered all the tribes of Israel to Shechem, and summoned the elders, the heads, the judges, and the officers of Israel; and they presented themselves before God. ₂And Joshua said to all the people, "Thus says the LORD (Yahweh), the God of Israel: Long ago your ancestors—Terah and his sons Abraham and Nahor—lived beyond the Euphrates and served other gods. ₃Then I took your father Abraham from beyond the River and led him through all the land of Canaan and made his offspring many. I gave him Isaac; ₄and to Isaac I gave Jacob and Esau. I gave Esau the hill country of Seir to possess, but Jacob and his children went down to Egypt. ₅Then I sent Moses and Aaron, and I plagued Egypt with what I did in its midst; and afterwards I brought you out. ₆When I brought your ancestors out of Egypt, you came to the sea; and the Egyptians pursued your ancestors with chariots and horsemen to the Red Sea (the Sea of Reeds). ₇When they cried out to the LORD (Yahweh), he put darkness between you and the Egyptians, and made the sea come upon them and cover them; and your eyes saw what I did to Egypt. Afterwards you lived in the wilderness a long time. ₈Then I brought you to the land of the Amorites; who lived on the other side of the Jordan; they fought with you, and I handed them over to you, and you took possession of their land, and I destroyed them before you. . . . ₁₃I gave you a land on which you had not labored, and towns that you had not built, and you live in them; you eat the fruit of vineyards and oliveyards that you did not plant.

₁₄Now therefore revere the LORD (Yahweh) and serve him in sincerity and in faithfulness; put away the gods your ancestors served beyond the River and in Egypt and serve the LORD (Yahweh). ₁₅Now if you are unwilling to serve the LORD (Yahweh), choose this day whom you will serve, whether the gods your ancestors served in the region beyond the River or the gods of the Amorites in whose land you are living; but as for me and my household, we will serve the LORD (Yahweh).

And the people replied (Joshua 24:18b): "Therefore we also will serve the LORD (Yahweh), for he is our God."

Shechem was an important Canaanite city when Joshua arrived on the scene in the mid-thirteenth century BCE. It was also an important religious center, and archaeologists have excavated its large and important temple of Baal Berith or El Berith (Lord or God of the Covenant). The name of this important Canaanite god of Shechem indicates clearly that Shechem was an important center of a tribal covenant community, even before the arrival of the descendants of the Exodus.

A close examination of the passage quoted above reveals a number of interesting facts:

- Joshua recited a primitive version of Israel's sacred history, beginning with the call of the patriarchs, focusing on the Exodus, and telling of the conquests in Transjordan and in the Canaanite hill country.
- Joshua made reference to the gods that the ancestors served beyond the river Euphrates and in Egypt, presumably not Yahweh.
- There is surprisingly no reference in this passage to the Sinai covenant.
- Joshua called upon the people to decide which god(s) they would serve: Yahweh, or the gods of the ancestors, or the gods of the Amorites (the Canaanites).
- The people affirmed that they would serve Yahweh, the god of the Exodus.

What should we make of this account? There seems to be an essential core of interesting information in the description of the covenant ceremony in Joshua 24. How do we determine when information is suddenly reliable, especially when we have dismissed so much other earlier evidence as myth or legend?

As we have already observed, information that runs counter to or that contradicts the received tradition generally has a greater claim to authenticity because it does not serve the purposes of the author(s). In this story, that "contradictory testimony" includes the information that the patriarchs worshiped "other gods," although, in the book of Genesis, Abraham, Isaac, and Jacob are said to have received calls and commissions from Yahweh. That important detail confirms the point we made in an earlier chapter, namely, that the patriarchal god was likely El Shaddai and that several other gods were also worshiped by the ancestors who preceded the Exodus tribes into the land of Canaan: El Elyon, El Olam, El Roi, El Berith, and so forth.

Joshua's demand is not simply whether the people will serve Yahweh, but whether they will set aside other earlier ancestral gods and serve Yahweh. Joshua's demand reinforces a point made earlier, namely, that Yahweh was a new god for these people, a god Moses first learned about in the Sinai wilderness from his father-in-law, and that it was Moses who had interpreted to the people that Yahweh was the author of their deliverance from slavery in Egypt.

Another story that makes better sense if this interpretation of the evidence is followed is the story of the Golden Calf in Exodus 32:1–6:

> 1When the people saw that Moses delayed to come down from the mountain (Sinai), the people gathered around Aaron, and said to him: "Come, make gods for us, who shall go before us; as for this Moses, the man who brought us up out of the land of Egypt, we do not know what has become of him." 2Aaron said to them, "Take off the gold rings that are on the ears of your wives, your sons, and your daughters, and bring them to me." 3So all the people took off the gold rings from their ears, and brought them to Aaron. 4He took the gold from them, formed it in a mold, and cast an image of a calf; and they said, "These are your gods, O Israel, who brought you up out of the land of Egypt!" 5When Aaron saw this, he built an altar before it; and Aaron made proclamation and said, "Tomorrow shall be a festival to the LORD (Yahweh)." 6They rose early the next morning, and burnt offerings and brought sacrifices of well-being; and the people sat down to eat and drink, and rose up to revel.

There is something clearly suspect with the details of this story. Having just experienced the miraculous crossing of the sea, with Moses missing for a period of time on the mountain and with the clear consent and participation of Moses' brother Aaron, the priest of Yahweh, the people forged a golden calf to worship. Then, in verse 6, Aaron proclaimed: "Tomorrow shall be a festival to Yahweh." The calf was a symbol of the fertility gods of Canaanite religion, certainly not a symbol of Yahweh.[15] What did the people think they were doing? And what did Aaron think he was doing? There can be little doubt that despite the tradition, Aaron was probably not a Levite priest of Yahweh. I doubt, for that matter, that Aaron was a priest at all. Just as later tradition made Moses the prototype of Israelite prophecy, so too that same later tradition made Aaron the prototype of the Israelite priesthood, with the two, prophet and priest, standing side by side from the beginning of Yahwist religion. The story makes little sense in its present form, but it does make sense if the people of the Exodus had been practicing a fertility religion during their wandering in the wilderness and maybe earlier, while they were in Egypt.

Let us also recall at this time something we mentioned in connection with patriarchal religion, namely, that Abraham was especially associated with holy trees in the area around Mamre, that Isaac was especially associated with watering places at Beersheba, and that Jacob was especially associated with stones at Bethel (see pp. 71–72). I referred to this information earlier as a probable recollection of animistic or polydaemonistic religion among the pre-Israelite ancestors. Mamre was in the territory of the tribe of Judah (a Leah tribe); Beersheba was in the territory of the tribe of Simeon (a Leah tribe); and Bethel was in the territory of the tribe of Ephraim (a Joseph and, therefore, a Rachel tribe). In addition, Shechem, the seat of the god El Berith, was in Manasseh (a Joseph and, therefore, a Rachel tribe). The Kenite god Yahweh likely came out of the religion associated with the holy mountain in the southern part of the Sinai Peninsula. What should we make of this data, especially as it all relates to the covenant at Shechem in Joshua 24?

I would venture to put this evidence together into the following hypothesis, which, I believe, best addresses the complex and often inconsistent evidence. At the covenant ceremony at Shechem, there was a conscious effort to bring together into a single covenant community with a single religious tradition both the Exodus tribes, probably the Rachel tribes (Joseph and Benjamin) and the pre-Israelite tribes already in the land, roughly the Leah tribes (Reuben, Simeon, Levi, Judah, Issachar, and Zebulun). The union of these two groups was contracted with Yahweh and Yahwism, the religion of Moses and the Exodus tribes. In joining these groups together, storytellers consciously linked individual tribal ancestors into a single family tree: Terah, the father of Abraham, the father of Isaac, the father of Jacob.

According to the tradition, Jacob experienced a name change and became known as Israel and subsequently fathered twelve sons, who, in turn, became the fathers of the twelve tribes:

- Joseph and Benjamin by Jacob/Israel's favorite wife, Rachel, roughly the Yahwist tribes of the Exodus;
- Reuben, Simeon, Levi, Judah, Issachar, and Zebulun by Jacob/Israel's first wife, Leah, Rachel's older sister, roughly the tribes already in the land who had been previously joined into a loose tribal confederation at Shechem, possibly under the god Baal Berith or El Berith.

The joining of these eight tribes may be the basis of the covenant (renewal) ceremony at Shechem as reported in Joshua 24. If there is some truth to this theory, then

- the tribes of Dan and Naphtali by Bilhah, the handmaid of Jacob/Israel's second and favorite wife, Rachel, and
- the tribes of Gad and Asher by Zilpah, the handmaid of Jacob/Israel's first wife, Leah,

may have been added later to the federation, or may simply be considered less important tribes in the Israelite confederation. (Review the genealogical table on p. 68.)[16]

The patriarchal story in Genesis is too neat, too narrowly focused on genealogy, and too structured to make sense as unadulterated history. The twelve sons of Jacob/Israel are the most transparent part of the legend. It is as if the beginnings of our own American history contained a story of Uncle Sam marrying Lady Liberty and bearing thirteen sons, whose names were Virginia, Massachusetts, New Hampshire, Maryland, Connecticut, Rhode Island, Delaware, North Carolina, South Carolina, New Jersey, New York, Pennsylvania, and Georgia.[17]

Indeed, when Americans tell the story of their own establishment in the land, the colonial period is generally told as a backdrop that seems to point, almost invariably and inevitably, to the Declaration of Independence and the American Revolution. Everything in the colonial period anticipates the establishment of the United States. The comparison with Israel's early history is not far-fetched.

What this reconstruction of the early history accomplishes is to bring together into a single hypothesis tradition from the book of Genesis (the primordial and patriarchal stories), tradition from the book of Exodus (Moses' apparent introduction to Yahweh by his father-in-law Jethro and the establishment of the Sinai covenant), tradition from the book of Numbers (the wandering in the wilderness), tradition from the book of Deuteronomy (the passage through Transjordan), and tradition from the book of Joshua (the conquest and entrenchment of Canaan and the covenant ceremony at Shechem).

The outline of the national epic in Joshua 24 was presumably recited at the time of the covenant (renewal)[18] ceremony at Shechem, an appropriate occasion to bring together in a meaningful way the two groups of tribes that were being joined together through that ceremony. The Leah tribes likely contributed elements of the ancestral history; the Rachel tribes contributed the story of the Exodus experience under Yahweh's divine guidance. The name of this covenant community under Yahweh was Israel.[19] Covenant renewal may have been celebrated annually at Shechem in succeeding years with the recitation of the national history in this abbreviated form.

A later and fuller account of that national epic in the form of the written Yahwist or J source, composed in the mid-tenth century BCE, probably during the reign of King Solomon, amplified, augmented, and enriched the simple outline of that earlier version of the national history by including other myths, legends, and stories from individual tribal traditions and reworking them into a unified whole.

That our texts attempt to subsume all of these ancestral gods under the divine Yahweh, the god of the Exodus, is understandable and is manifest from a reading of Joshua 24, which reports that Joshua gathered all of the tribes of Israel together (in about 1250 BCE), reminded them that "Terah and his sons Abraham and Nahor lived beyond the Euphrates *and served other gods* (italics mine)" (24:2), and demanded them to "choose this day whom you will serve, whether the gods your ancestors served in the region beyond the river or the gods of the Amorites in whose land you are living; but as for me and my house, we will serve the LORD (Yahweh)" (24:15). There is little doubt that Yahwism was not the religion of the people at the time of the ancestors.

THE PERIOD OF THE JUDGES

The period of the judges, roughly 1250–1000 BCE, was the era of the tribal federation, sometimes called by scholars the Israelite amphictyony, based on a term used by Greek city-states that united around a common religious sanctuary, especially the sanctuary at Delphi. During this period, Israel was not yet a nation; it was, however, a people whose identity was drawn from its perceived common history, its worship of Yahweh to the exclusion of other gods, and the covenant allegiance the tribes had established at the covenant ceremony at Shechem. The significance of the Israelite federation was primarily religious. There were, nevertheless, expectations of providing military support to another tribe if threatened from outside the federation.

A tribe is a group of families that believes its members are descended from a common ancestor, whose name the tribe generally carries as its own. It is, therefore, blood kinship that unites the members of a tribe, whether that kinship is, in fact, real or merely assumed. The Israelite tribes told stories, whether historically true or not, about ancestors from whom they claimed their common descent. The relationship between a tribe and neighboring tribes was also generally explained in terms of kinship, so stories usually linked contiguous tribes in a genealogical scheme, as we

FIGURE 5. ISRAEL IN CANAAN:
JOSHUA TO SAMUEL AND SAUL

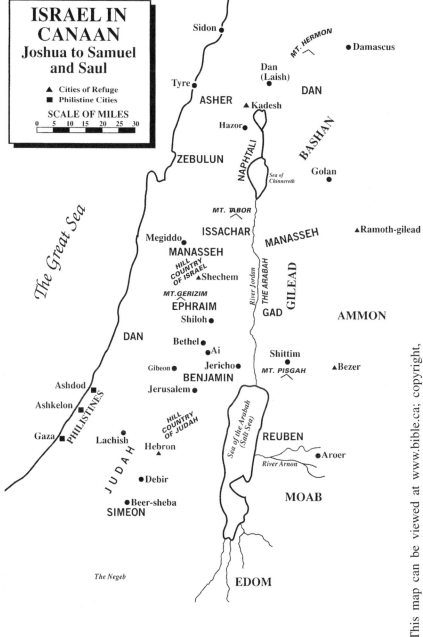

ISRAEL IN
CANAAN
Joshua to Samuel
and Saul

▲ Cities of Refuge
■ Philistine Cities

SCALE OF MILES
0   5   10   15   20   25   30

know from Israel's ancestral stories. As a general rule, however accurate individual family genealogies may have been, they became less accurate and more artificial once they were extended to include other tribes and other peoples.

Each tribe maintained its own organization based on kinship. The smallest unit, the *family*, consisted of the eldest male, his wife or wives, their unmarried children, their married sons and their wives and children, and the family's servants, all of whom generally lived together in the same household or complex of houses, or in close proximity. Several related families constituted the *clan*, which also lived in the same general area and which came together for religious festivals or special celebrations. The clan was ruled by the heads of the individual families. A group of such clans constituted the *tribe*, headed by a tribal chief.

Although tribal boundaries were not always well defined, each tribe had its own territory, which individual families generally cultivated as their own private land, although pasture land was usually held in common. Weak tribes were often absorbed into stronger ones, sometimes through intermarriage or adoption, through which individuals or groups acknowledged the ancestors of the tribe newly joined as their own ancestors. The number twelve in the case of the Israelite federation appears to have had some significance. Although tribes came and went, the number twelve seems to have been constant because it was likely symbolic (see footnote 16).

When a tribe became too large, it sometimes divided into two tribes, as in the case when Joseph divided into Ephraim and Manasseh. Marriage was generally limited to near kin, often first cousins, as we witness in the case of Israel's ancestors, who chose their sons' wives from close relatives, often first or second cousins.

Within this tribal structure there arose the office of "judge" or "ruler." The Hebrew word *šôpēṭ* is regularly and mistakenly translated into English as "judge," a word that conjures up in our minds imagines of men and women in black robes presiding over courts of law. The judges of ancient Israel were nothing of the sort. The word is better translated as "tribal ruler" and was applied to an individual who, in the eyes of the people, was chosen by Yahweh to maintain harmonious relations both within and among the tribes (Judges 2:16; 3:9; 6:34–35), both by settling legal disputes (Judges 3:10) and by defeating Israel's enemies through the necessary military action (Judges 3:7–11). The judges flourished in the period of the tribal confederacy, principally during the twelfth and eleventh centuries BCE; however, despite the impression created in the Bible, the judges did not follow one another in chronological succession as rulers over the entire twelve-tribe confederation.

I will examine the charismatic leadership of one judge, the only woman in the group of Israel's judges, because the story of her prowess is recorded in one of the oldest poems found anywhere in the Bible (datable to the twelfth century BCE, not long after the events reported), the so-called Song of Deborah in Judges 5:1–31:

1Then Deborah and Barak son of Adinoam sang on that day, saying:
2When locks are long in Israel,
when the people offer themselves willingly[20]—bless the LORD (Yahweh)!
3"Hear, O kings;
give ear, O princes;
to the LORD (Yahweh) I will sing,
I will make melody to the LORD (Yahweh), the God of Israel.

4"LORD (Yahweh), when you went out from Seir,
when you marched from the region of Edom,
the earth trembled,
and the heavens poured,
        the clouds indeed poured water.
5The mountains quaked before the LORD (Yahweh), the One of Sinai,
        before the LORD (Yahweh), the God of Israel.

6"In the days of Shamgar son of Anath,
in the days of Jael,
caravans ceased
and travelers kept to the byways.
7The peasantry prospered in Israel,
they grew fat on plunder,
because you arose, Deborah,
        arose as a mother in Israel.
8When new gods were chosen,
then war was in the gates.
Was shield or spear to be seen
among forty thousand in Israel?
9My heart goes out to the commanders of Israel
who offered themselves willingly among the people.
Bless the LORD (Yahweh).

10"Tell of it, you who ride on white donkeys,

    you who sit on rich carpets

    and you who walk by the way.

11"To the sounds of musicians at the watering places,

there they repeat the triumphs of the LORD (Yahweh),

    the triumphs of his peasantry in Israel.

Then down to the gates marched the people of the LORD (Yahweh).

12"Awake, awake, Deborah!

Awake, awake, utter a song!

Arise, Barak, lead away your captives,

O son of Abinoam.

13Then down marched the remnant of the noble;

the people of the LORD (Yahweh) marched down for him against the mighty.

14From Ephraim they set out into the valley,

following you, Benjamin, with your kin;

from Machir marched down the commanders,

and from Zebulun those who bear the marshall's staff;

15the chiefs of Issachar came with Deborah,

and Issachar faithful to Barak;

into the valley they rushed out at his heels.

Among the clans of Reuben there were great searchings of heart.

16Why did you tarry among the sheepfolds,

to hear the piping for the flocks?

Among the clans of Reuben there were great searchings of heart.

17Gilead stayed beyond the Jordan;

and Dan, why did he abide with the ships?

Asher sat still at the coast of the sea,

settling down by his landings.

18Zebulun is a people that scorned death;

Naphtali too, on the heights of the field.

19"The kings came, they fought;

then fought the kings of Canaan,

at Taanach, by the waters of Megiddo;

they got no spoils of silver.

20The stars fought from heaven,

from their courses they fought against Sisera.

21 The torrent Kishon swept them away,

The onrushing torrent, the torrent Kishon.

March on, my soul, with might!

22 "Then loud beat the horses' hoofs

with the galloping, galloping of his steeds.

23 "'Curse Meroz,' says the angel of the LORD (Yahweh),

curse bitterly its inhabitants

because they did not come to the help of the LORD (Yahweh),

to the help of the LORD (Yahweh) against the mighty.

24 "Most blessed of women be Jael,

the wife of Heber the Kenite,

of tent-dwelling women most blessed.

25 He asked water and she gave him milk,

she brought him curds in a lordly bowl.

26 She put her hand to the tent peg

and her right hand to the workmen's mallet;

she struck Sisera a blow,

she crushed his head,

she shattered and pierced his temple.

27 He sank, he fell,

he lay still at her feet;

at her feet he sank, he fell;

where he sank, there he fell dead.

28 "Out of the window she peered,

the mother of Sisera gazed through the lattice:

'Why is his chariot so long in coming?

Why tarry the hoofbeats of his chariots?'

29 Her wisest ladies make answer,

indeed, she answers the question herself:

30 'Are they not finding and dividing the spoil?—

A girl or two for every man;

spoil of dyed stuffs for Sisera,

spoil of dyed stuffs embroidered,
two pieces of dyed work embroidered for my neck as spoil?'

31"So perish all your enemies, O LORD (Yahweh)!
But may your friends be like the sun as it rises in its might."

Apart from the Song of Miram in Exodus 15:20–21, the Song of Deborah is the oldest piece of literature in the Hebrew Bible. It was likely composed for a post-victory celebration by someone close to the events described in the song and is datable to the mid-twelfth century BCE.

Victory songs from Egypt and Assyria from the fifteenth to the twelfth centuries BCE provide helpful information regarding the form and structure of such ancient hymns. The meter of this song displays the same patterns of repetitive parallelism found in ancient Ugaritic (Canaanite) poetry, betraying the archaic character of this gem of ancient Israelite poetry. Following its composition, the Song of Deborah was probably sung on subsequent occasions in pre-monarchal times when there was a similar call to battle.

Although virtually every major Old Testament scholar has written about the Song of Deborah, they have had difficulty in agreeing on details of this song, because of its archaic language, its poetic structure, obscurities in the text, and the uncertain meaning of some words. Complicating the matter even more, the song likely underwent changes in the course of oral performance over time, as well as at the hand of the Deuteronomistic historian, the author of the written text of Judges. Nevertheless, the meaning of the song is clear: it celebrates the victory of Israelites over Canaanites in a battle near Megiddo in the mid-twelfth century BCE.

Archaeological work at sites at Hazor, Taanach, and Megiddo provide a historical context for the song in the mid-twelfth century BCE, when these cities were all inhabited. Apparently, the involvement of peasants in the central hill country in attacking caravans provided Israelites in the area with a measure of prosperity. Although Yahweh had victoriously entered Canaan earlier (verses 4–6), defection from Yahwism to Canaanite religion may have come about with complacency and an unwillingness to take up Yahweh's cause (verse 8). Additionally, superior Canaanite and Philistine equipment, military leadership, and warfare threatened Israelite presence in the land.

Apparently Deborah, who is described in Judges 4:4–5 as "a prophetess," available for oracular consultation "under the palm of Deborah between Ramah and Bethel in the hill country of Ephraim," used the occasion of a meeting of tribal leaders, possibly at Mount Tabor, to rally leaders against the Canaanites. Consulted by Israelite leaders in the face of aggression, Deborah summoned Barak to serve as field commander of the Israelites in order to challenge Sisera, the commander of the forces of a coalition of northern Canaanite city-states. Success in the ensuing battle would determine control over the rich Esdraelon Valley between Megiddo and Taanach.

A partial picture of who did and who did not respond to Deborah's summons is provided in verses 14–18. Only ten tribes are listed: Ephraim, Benjamin, Manasseh (Machir), Zebulun, Issachar, and Naphtali, which responded to Deborah's call, and Reuben, Gad, Dan, and Asher, which did not. No mention is made of Simeon and Judah, or of Levi, which by this time had probably been scattered among the other tribes and had no land of its own.

Verses 19–22 describe the battle, which, the song claims, Israel won through Yahweh's intervention in the form of the cosmic elements of a cloudburst and flash-flood. The stars released nature's powers, which resulted in the flooding of the river Kishon, disabling the enemies' chariots and thereby enabling Israel's poorly equipped foot soldiers to gain the victory.

Jael, the wife of Heber the Kenite,[21] is credited with the treacherous murder of Sisera (verses 24–27). Her praise comes in the face of the fact that her violent act of murder violated basic principles of tribal hospitality. There is a somewhat anticlimatic ending to the song in the shift of scene to Sisera's mother, who awaits in vain the return of her son from battle (verses 28–30).

CONCLUSIONS

The material in this chapter covers the formative period of Israel's history: from its historical origins in the escape from Egypt and the establishment of the Sinai covenant, and through the wanderings in the wilderness and the conquest and entrenchment of Canaan, to the institution at Shechem of the tribal federation, and, finally, to the period of the judges. This chapter covers a period of almost three hundred years from 1290 BCE (the likely date of the Exodus) to circa 1000 BCE when there were initial efforts at establishing a monarchy in Israel, the subject of our next chapter.

This is a period not substantially different in many ways from the period in American history between Christopher Columbus's discovery of the New World in 1492 and the events of July 4, 1776, when the Second Continental Congress declared American independence from Great Britain—also a period of just under three hundred years. I draw this comparison to underscore how much can and did happen following the Exodus as history unfolded in a way that lead ultimately, but not inevitably, to the establishment of Israel as a monarchical state in about 1000 BCE, a far cry from Israel as a people united under Yahweh in a loose tribal confederation three hundred years earlier.

We obviously know much more about these three hundred years of Israelite history than we will ever know about the period of Israel's patriarchal ancestors, not to speak of the so-called primordial history, about which we know virtually nothing. There is, however, something central to the story, which we do not and cannot ever know.

The books of the Bible tell the story of Israel as a series of "acts of Yahweh" in the history of his people, not as the political, social, religious, and economic history of the people. Biblical scholarship does not and cannot deal with "acts of God," because this phrase belongs to the realm of the ancient interpretation of events in light of Moses' and the people's belief that their god Yahweh was a god who intervened in history on their behalf. As we have said before, the role of the historian is to examine the ancient evidence using the tools that any historian would use in studying and reconstructing the past. The historical approach neither affirms nor denies the existence of God or what role God may have played in that history or plays in any history, for that matter. The historian simply sets this question aside as a matter of principle and proceeds to examine evidence as objectively as possible, using the basic methodology and the rules of evidence introduced in the introduction, with the goal of writing a history, devoid of theological interpretation or bias.

To provide the reader with an analogy that I have frequently used with my students, imagine a jigsaw puzzle in which some of the pieces are missing. It is impossible to complete the puzzle, but it is certainly possible to see virtually the entire picture, even without the few missing pieces. Now consider the situation if we have a five-hundred-piece jigsaw puzzle, of which we have only two hundred pieces; the rest are lost. We will be able to connect many of the surviving pieces, but we will not have the entire picture. Yet it is tempting to try to fill in the missing areas and imagine what the picture would look like if we had all of the pieces. This is the challenge of biblical scholarship: to connect the evidence, the pieces of the puzzle that we do have, and then from that evidence to try to fill in as much of the rest of the picture as is reasonably possible. Different people will fill in the missing portions of the jigsaw puzzle differently, but presumably everyone will, in the process, draw clues from the evidence that we do have. If it appears that we have a picture from ancient Egypt, we would not fill in the missing sections of the puzzle with elements from modern America. Contextuality is essential to good history.

Applying this methodology of setting events in their own contexts, biblical scholars have established a reasonably accurate chronology for events covered in this chapter. The Exodus is probably best set in the transition between pharaoh Seti I, whose building campaign in the Nile Delta likely served as the period of the oppression of the Hebrew slaves, and the reign of his son and successor, Rameses II, the probable pharaoh of the Exodus. This transition took place in 1290 BCE, providing us, with some measure of confidence, likely the first firm date in Israel's history.

We have addressed the question of who was the author of the Exodus and of the Sinai covenant, particularly the Ten Commandments. From the perspective of biblical scholarship, there can be only one answer to that question: namely, Moses. Having said that, however, biblical scholars and psychologists of religion can and do address the issue of what may have motivated Moses to do what he did in the same way in which modern historians and psychologists would address the issue of what motivated Mahatma Gandhi and Martin Luther King Jr. to do what they did. There is no basic difference from the perspective of historical analysis.

A comparison of ancient Near Eastern texts reveals that there is a similarity between the legends of Sargon's birth and Moses' birth, and a study of law in the ancient Near East reveals a similarity between ancient legal codes, such as the Babylonian Code of Hammurabi from about 1760 BCE and the code of law (the Ten Commandments) that Moses delivered to the Israelites at the foot of Mount Sinai almost half a millennium later. This contextual approach to the subject enables us to understand Moses much better in his own historical, social, geographical, and religious context—a sine qua non of any serious historical investigation.

In the spirit of that method, we have also shown that Yahwism likely had its origin in the relationship between Moses and his father-in-law Jethro. It should not surprise the reader that Moses' religion is understood best in its own historical, social, geographical, and religious context: Moses lived in the Near East in the late fourteenth and early thirteenth centuries BCE. Like everyone, Moses was a product of his time and place. An objective reading of the evidence, especially examining discrepancies and inconsistencies in the text, led us to the conclusion that Yahweh was almost certainly a new god for Moses and for the Hebrew slaves and that it was Moses who advanced among the people the worship of Yahweh to the exclusion of other gods (henotheism, not monotheism).

The reader will observe that we have, in this chapter, tried to utilize evidence from previous chapters in our effort to fill in missing parts of the puzzle. Evidence about the religion of the ancestors in Genesis 12–50 makes more sense now in light of our theory that Yahweh was a new god for this people. Our study of the covenant ceremony at Shechem in Joshua 24 provided additional evidence to support this thesis. We are at every step filling in missing portions of the puzzle, and we are doing so by using as much of the existing data as possible to afford a consistent rational reconstruction of the past.

We trust that this reconstruction conforms in substantial measure to the elusive past that we are trying to recover. Unfortunately, we can never know that with the certainty of a mathematical science like physics or astronomy, because the doing of history is not a mathematical science. It does, however, use a tried-and-tested methodology, and biblical scholarship has used that methodology with considerable success. Hopefully after a particular thesis is advanced by one or more scholars, others will embrace or criticize both the methods and the thesis, and in the best of all worlds scholarship may move in the direction of developing a consensus on important issues.

We have identified an important principle of biblical scholarship in observing that when there are inconsistencies, discrepancies, or contradictions within a partic-ular book or among several books, it is usually the "harder" or "more embarrassing" reading that is likely to provide the more valuable data in our effort to reconstruct the past. The "easier" or "more orthodox" reading likely reflects changes in the tra-dition designed to bring it into conformity and harmony with the way in which people at a later time understood their history with the advantage of hindsight and a certain religious orthodoxy.

In this connection, the many references to the people's murmuring in the wilder-ness are likely authentic recollections of the uncertainty that accompanied those dif-ficult times and the serious challenges that Moses and the people faced. The fact that it was the tribe of Judah and not Joshua who captured Hebron, and that it was Oth-niel and not Joshua who captured Debir are examples of this principle at work.

The role of archaeology is critical because it is a relatively objective science. Archaeological evidence supports the picture in Judges 1 that the conquest and entrenchment of Canaan extended over a period of far more than the five years represented in Joshua 1–12, and, in addition, that there was something less than a full-scale military conquest. Archaeological evidence shows that both Jericho and Ai were unoccupied and in ruins at the time of Joshua's conquest. Accordingly, scholars must develop theses that take into account the unbiased evidence of archaeology.

We have learned to understand the genealogies of Genesis much better in their role as identifying political and social alliances rather than as accurate recollections of an ancient past. It is more important to understand how stories functioned in antiquity than it is to read them as if they were an unbiased and accurate account of what happened in the past. We cannot impose our own understanding of writing about the past on the ancient authors of the biblical texts, who seem to have had their own purposes in mind.

In the course of this chapter, we have examined in some detail two pieces of ancient poetry: the brief couplet the Song of Miriam, and the much longer Song of Deborah, both of which reflect the repetitive parallelism found in the form and structure of ancient Ugaritic (Canaanite) poetry, and both of which likely display evidence of being eyewitness accounts of important events. The simplicity of both songs is dazzling and stands in marked contrast to the ways in which modern readers often picture events from the ancient past.

A final word is in order regarding the methodology of biblical scholarship. Quoting a single verse out of context is useless; citing two or three seemingly related verses out of context is flawed methodology. Biblical scholarship tries to re-create the larger picture in broad strokes using all available evidence, both carefully and critically. All of the evidence needs to fit into the puzzle at some point, because it is, after all, one giant puzzle. It is, however, essential at all times to allow the evidence to lead the scholar to the best conclusions. Our challenge is that we sometimes think that we know so much about the Bible that we set our conclusions first and then look selectively for evidence to support those conclusions. That, of course, is not the method of good biblical scholarship. It is, however, often the method of unexamined and uninformed blind faith.

NOTES

1. The story of Sargon is available in Pritchard's *Ancient Near Eastern Texts*, an invaluable resource, containing in a single volume a plethora of ancient Near Eastern documents relating to the Old Testament: creation myths, flood stories, legal documents, and so on.

2. Johannes Lindblom, *Prophecy in Ancient Israel* (Philadelphia: Fortress Press, 1962), p. 34.

3. See, in this connection, Exodus 3:12: "He [God] said '*I will be* with you'"; Exodus 4:15: "*I will be* with your mouth"; Exodus 6:7: "*I will be* your God." What we may be witnessing here is the beginning of the transformation of this local Midianite deity into a god who *will act* in the history of the Hebrew slaves.

4. Specifically, why didn't the Egyptians use the opportunity of Moses' visit to pharaoh to arrest him for having killed the Egyptian taskmaster?

5. "The Israelites journeyed from Rameses to Succoth, about six hundred thousand men on foot, besides children. A mixed crowd also went up with them, and livestock in great numbers, both flocks and herds."

6. Exodus 1:15 makes it clear that two midwives, Shiphrah and Puah, served the women, hardly enough midwives if there were hundreds of thousands of women.

7. 2 Samuel 24:1–9 reports this census, although that text does not agree exactly with the six hundred thousand men in the account in Exodus and has instead eight hundred thousand from Israel and five hundred thousand from Judah. Scholars generally agree that these numbers in 2 Samuel are too high to correspond to historical reality at the time of David's reign.

8. As we have already observed, scholars refer to this argument as being based on the criterion of dissimilarity or embarrassment. That is, a detail that calls into question the reliability of the tradition has a greater claim to being historically reliable. The storyteller would, otherwise, have no motive in incorporating it into the account.

9. Exodus 13:17–18a is a particularly revealing, if not problematic, passage: "When Pharaoh let the people go, God did not lead them by way of the land of the Philistines, although that was nearer; for God thought, 'If the people face war, they may change their minds and return to Egypt.' So God led the people by the roundabout way of the wilderness toward the Red Sea (the sea of reeds)." Removing the theological overlay of God-talk from this passage, there is still some confusion about exactly where the people were headed and how they expected to get there. The reference to the "way of the land of the Philistines," although an obvious anachronism in this context, suggests that the people might have been headed directly to Canaan; but such a route would have bypassed Mount Sinai entirely and, hence, the contracting of the covenant. This verse also calls into question the position that

Moses intended from the outset to lead the people to the mountain of Yahweh, where he had received his call and commission.

10. Scholars have identified two types of law in the ancient Near East: (1) casuistic law, whose pattern is "if you do this, then that will happen to you"; and (2) apodictic law, which is unconditional and which is stated in the kind of pointed, curt, unequivocal language that we find here ("you shall"; "you shall not").

11. This is not the only example of assigning the victory of a minor individual to a more important heroic figure. The story of David's killing the giant Goliath (1 Samuel 17) was obviously taken over, romanticized, and exaggerated from the original version of the story, preserved in written form in 2 Samuel 21:19, which reports (probably correctly) that it was Elhanan, the son of Jaareoregim, the Bethlehemite, who killed Goliath. Once again, the criterion of dissimilarity or embarrassment enables the biblical scholar to distinguish likely fact from romanticized fiction.

12. The title given to this section in *The HarperCollins Study Bible*, p. 369.

13. T. A. Holland and Ehud Netzer, "Jericho," *The Anchor Bible Dictionary*, vol. 3 (New York: Doubleday, 1992), pp. 723–40.

14. The book of Joshua, our primary written source for the "conquest," was composed many centuries after the reported events, as is indicated by Joshua 8:28: "So Joshua burned Ai, and made it forever a heap of ruins, *as it is to this day*" (italics mine). Failing to meet the *time and place criterion*, the book of Joshua cannot be considered a historically accurate report of events that occurred centuries earlier than the time of its composition.

15. It is, of course, true that 1 Kings 12:25–29 reports that Solomon's son Jeroboam, the first king of the northern kingdom of Israel (ca. 922–901 BCE), following the civil war after Solomon's death (922 BCE), installed golden calf images of Yahweh at Dan and Bethel. Jeroboam's action was likely a syncretistic assimilation of Yahwism with the earlier and obviously still-viable Canaanite religion associated with the gods El and Baal. Both Aaron and Jeroboam were clearly violating Moses' commandment to make no images of Yahweh. It is relatively easy to imagine what Jeroboam may have had in mind in reacting against religious practices instituted in the south in Jerusalem by David and Solomon; it is incomprehensible what Aaron might have thought he was doing by building the golden calf just a few days after Moses initially delivered the Decalogue with a clear prohibition against making images of Yahweh.

16. The number twelve seems, for whatever reason, to have been ideal. Nevertheless, the Bible does not always agree on what constituted the twelve tribes. Sometimes, the Joseph tribe is counted as two tribes, for Joseph's two sons, Ephraim and Manasseh, making thirteen unless and until Levi is dropped from the list because of its priestly status. The Song of Deborah in Judges 5 enumerates ten tribes by reporting the Joseph tribes Ephraim and Masasseh (Machir) as two tribes, but omits Judah, Simeon, and Levi. The blessing of Moses (Deuteronomy 33) drops Simeon from the list, but separates Joseph into two tribes, Ephraim

and Manasseh. Apparently, the tribes of Israel were an ever-changing group, increasing or decreasing as circumstances warranted.

17. Or perhaps we could insert instead the names of the founders of the thirteen colonies: John Wheelwright for New Hampshire, Lord Baltimore for Maryland, Thomas Hooker for Connecticut, Roger Williams for Rhode Island, William Penn for Pennsylvania, and so on. But no one would pretend to make the claim that the founders were all brothers and that they, in turn, fathered the members of their colonies. Yet that is exactly the paradigm that we find in Genesis with regard to the ancestors. As we observed earlier, genealogies served a political and social function in the ancient Near East and were not intended to reflect historical memory.

18. I put the word "renewal" in parentheses, because scholars disagree on whether the Shechem covenant was, in fact, a renewal of the Sinai covenant, of which there is curiously no mention in Joshua 24. The closest we come to it is in verse 7b: "Afterwards you lived in the wilderness a long time." In addition, there is in Joshua 8:30–35 an account of a covenant in the Shechem Valley, although this story may actually be based on the events described in greater detail in chapter 24 but intentionally set earlier in Joshua's career. Shechem's importance for Israelite religion reaches back to Abraham, who, according to the reference in Genesis 12:6, stopped at Shechem on his journey to the land of Canaan and there received from Yahweh the promise of the land.

19. The earliest reference to Israel outside the Bible is in the Merneptah stele from circa 1223 BCE, a victory inscription in which Pharaoh Merneptah claimed to have suppressed conflict in Syria and Palestine. The inscription contains the line: "Israel is laid waste, his seed is not." The Egyptian text alludes to Israel as a people, not as a land, implying an early stage in Israel's evolution. Given the closeness in time to the arrival of the Rachel tribes in Canaan, the stele may have been referring to an earlier federation of the Leah tribes.

20. The Song of Deborah shows evidence of repetitive parallelism familiar from fourteenth century BCE Ugaritic (Canaanite) texts. Characteristically, this poetry is generally built of couplets, two lines which parallel each other by saying the same thing in somewhat different words. I have printed the Song of Deborah in a way that illustrates more clearly the poetic (parallel) features of the composition.

21. The Kenite connection goes back to the time of Moses, whose father-in-law Jethro, the priest of Yahweh, was a Kenite.

CHAPTER 4

THE PERIOD OF
THE UNITED KINGDOM

The Deuteronomistic History, extending over the books of Joshua, Judges, 1 and 2 Samuel, and 1 and 2 Kings, is our principal written source for a reconstruction of the history of the Israelite monarchy.[1] Based on the fact that the last event recorded in this history is Babylonian King Evil-merodach's release of King Jehoiachin of Judah from imprisonment in Babylonia in circa 561/560 BCE (2 Kings 25:27–30), scholars have concluded that the Deuteronomistic History in its final form was likely completed shortly after that date.

Some scholars have proposed that an earlier version of the Deuteronomistic History may have been written in the late seventh century BCE to support the religious reforms that King Josiah of Judah initiated in 621 BCE (2 Kings 22:8) and that a second and final edition of that work appeared during the Babylonian exile (586–538 BCE) to support the aspirations of those who had been exiled to Babylonia. The reference to the release of King Jehoiachin from prison extends hope in the midst of the exile that the Davidic dynasty might yet return to the throne in Jerusalem.

Be that as it may, the framework and theological viewpoint of the Deuteronomistic History is apparent. The history of the period from Joshua to Jehoiachin follows a clear pattern: when Israel obeys Yahweh's Torah,[2] the people prosper and experience welfare and peace; and when Israel turns aside from Yahweh's Torah, the people experience hardship and defeat.

This formula serves the entire period of history covered in these six books. For the period of the conquest and entrenchment of Canaan and the period of the tribal confederation and the judges, the author of the Deuteronomistic History was probably dependent on the oral traditions of individual tribes, which were woven into the books of Joshua and Judges. For the period of the monarchy(ies), the Deuteronomistic historian was likely dependent on oral traditions and on written court records, which were woven into the books of 1 and 2 Samuel and 1 and 2 Kings. In both instances, the author(s) of the Deuteronomistic History placed their own interpretative stamp on these oral and written sources.

For the periods of the United Kingdom and the divided kingdoms of Israel and Judah, the author(s) of the Deuteronomic History had access to valuable archival records, although the exact nature and content of these records remains unclear. 1 Kings 11:41 mentions "The Book of the Acts of [King] Solomon," an otherwise unknown work, which likely served as an important source of information for the first half of 1 Kings. 1 and 2 Kings also mention two other writings, the book of the Annals of the Kings of Israel and the book of the Annals of the Kings of Judah (eighteen times and fifteen times, respectively).[3] These books are also lost to us, but they appear to have been official court annals of the two kingdoms, modeled after Mesopotamian court annals, examples of which have, in fact, survived. The Israelite, Judean, and Mesopotamian annals seem to have contained information about military campaigns, building projects, and even court conspiracies.

Needless to say, the use of these early court records makes the Deuteronomistic History a valuable resource for scholars, although it is still important to read this history with a cautious and critical eye. The use of earlier sources means that we are not dependent solely on the testimony of a writer from the sixth century BCE, but that we likely also have indirect access to written information that is often centuries older and contemporaneous with the events reported. The problem remains that we do not always know what actually comes from the earlier annals and what has been filtered and interpreted through the eyes of the Deuteronomistic historian.

Scholars have long reflected on the manner in which Israel became a kingdom, apparently in imitation of virtually all of its neighbors. As we have already observed, the tribal federation that called itself Israel tended initially to reside in less populated regions of central Canaan, with several tribes established in the area for quite possibly a century or more before the Exodus. The places in which the Israelite tribes settled were determined largely by the military superiority of their better-established neighboring city-states, between which the Israelite tribes had settled. The fact that the Canaanite city-states never consolidated into a single nation is critical to an understanding of how Israel was able to survive on relatively unoccupied land between these stronger city-states.

There were probably two distinct but not unrelated factors that led to the eventual establishment of an Israelite state: (1) the threat of Philistine domination from the "sea people," who had arrived on the western coast of Canaan at about the same time that some of the Israelite tribes, primarily the tribes of the Exodus, were entering the central hill country by way of Transjordan; and (2) the threat of neighboring tribes, usually from the east, who regularly attacked Israelite tribes on land they had been relatively successful in occupying and cultivating over a period of several centuries.

EARLY ATTEMPTS AT KINGSHIP: GIDEON AND ABIMELECH

Events leading up to the establishment of the Israelite monarchy involved the two principal figures of Gideon and Abimelech.

The first of these, Gideon, is also known as Jerubbaal (meaning "let Baal contend" or "Baal makes [himself] great"), a name obviously associated with one of the principal deities of the indigenous Canaanites before the arrival of the Exodus tribe(s). At the time of Gideon's birth, his father, Joash the Abiezrite of Manasseh, apparently practiced the Canaanite fertility religion and therefore gave his son Jerubbaal a Baal name, a view further supported by the text of Judges 6:25–32. What is particularly interesting is that Joash (a shortened form of Jehoash, a Yahwist name meaning "Yahweh-fired") was, judging by his name, apparently an apostate from Yahwism. By contrast, Gideon, who was presumably given a Baal name by his father at birth, later became a zealous champion of Yahweh.

The story of Gideon in Judges 6:1–8:35 is obviously a composite story because there are two distinct accounts of Gideon's call to leadership (Judges 6:11–24 and Judges 6:25–32). The story of Gideon's emergence follows the usual theme of the Deuteronomistic historian, namely, that the Israelites had fallen away from the worship of Yahweh, who had therefore subjected them to plundering raids from neighboring tribes. Although the story of Gideon is laden with legendary material, he is significant because in the mid-twelfth century BCE, he was probably responsible for organizing a militia of men from his own tribe of Manasseh and from other northern tribes (specifically Asher, Zebulun, Naphtali, and later Ephraim) to end seven years of annual raids against the Israelites by camel-riding Midianites, Amalekites, and other "people of the east" (Judges 6:33–35). Annual raids at harvest time had put the Israelites on the defensive in a region that extended from an area east of the Jordan River to the plain of Jezreel-Esdraelon in the west and as far south as the coastal city of Gaza (Judges 6:1–6).

The story of Gideon and Joash reflects the ongoing struggle in the land of Canaan between the worship of Yahweh and the worship of Baal. Joash tended a sacred oak, an altar to Baal, and a sacred pole or *asherah*,[4] which Gideon is credited with destroying and replacing with an altar to Yahweh (Judges 6:25–32). Such stories, which meet the criterion of embarrassment, clearly cast a shadow of doubt on the initial success of Yahwism among many Israelites. In spite of Joshua's best effort a century earlier, the worship of Baal clearly persisted among the Israelites for several centuries.

Because of Gideon's leadership in delivering the people from the Midianite threat, the Israelites said to him, "Rule over us, you and your son and your grandson also; for you have delivered us out of the hand of Midian" (Judges 8:22). The implication is clear—the Israelites were offering Gideon dynastic kingship. Gideon is reported to have replied, "I will not rule over you, and my son will not rule over you; the LORD (Yahweh) will rule over you" (Judges 8:23). Although Gideon appears to have preferred theocracy to dynastic kingship, he likely served for a short time as king over at least a portion of the Israelite people.

Gideon had many wives and seventy sons, one of whom, Abimelech by Gideon's Shechemite concubine, was particularly important for the emergence of kingship in Israel. It is reported that as soon as Gideon died, the Israelites lapsed into the worship of the Baals, making Baal-berith, the pre-Israelite covenant god of Shechem, their god (Judges 8:33).

Abimelech means in Hebrew "My father is the king," which is an obvious reference to Gideon, who supposedly rejected this title. There is, therefore, some confusion as to whether Gideon was the absolute theocrat he is reputed to have been. Unlike his father, Gideon, Abimelech clearly wanted to be king and tried to persuade the men of Shechem to support him rather than the oligarchy of Gideon's seventy sons. In appealing to the Shechemites for support in his bid for the throne, Abimelech claimed kinship with them through his Shechemite mother (Judges 8:31; 9:1–3). With their political support and with seventy pieces of silver from the temple of Baal-berith at Shechem, Abimelech hired a band of outlaws to murder his brothers in order to eliminate all rivals to his power. The leading lords of Shechem and the mixed Canaanite and Israelite population of the area, who supported Abimelech's bid for the throne, then made him king by the oak of the pillar at Shechem (or by the oak that survives at the palisade in Shechem) (Judges 9:6). But Abimelech's youngest brother, Jotham, hid himself and survived (Judges 9:1–5) and is credited with having delivered a scathing fable against Abimelech and his supporters (Judges (9:7–21).

Judges 9:22 reports that Abimelech ruled as king of Israel for a period of three years. His downfall apparently began with dissension among the Shechemites (Judges 9:23), under the instigation of his younger half brother Jotham, and was probably sealed when a certain Gaal son of Ebed moved into Shechem with his family and won the confidence of the city's men (Judges 9:26). By ruthless action, Abimelech defeated the Shechemites and destroyed their city (Judges 9:45). Shortly thereafter, however, when he attempted to attack neighboring Thebez, a woman threw a millstone from the top of the city's wall onto Abimelech's head. Abimelech ordered a young man to kill him with his sword lest the people say that a woman had succeeded in killing Abimelech (Judges 9:50–57).

The stories of Gideon and Abimelech are essentially reliable, although obviously not in every detail, because they meet the criterion of embarrassment by showing the difficulties and disagreements involved in the establishment of the Israelite monarchy. Legendary elements are particularly clear in the Gideon story: for example, the account of the call by the angel of Yahweh in Judges 6:11–24 and the sign of the fleece in Judges 6:36–40. Archaeologists have shown that Shechem was destroyed in the mid-twelfth century BCE, objective evidence that coincides with the account of events surrounding Abimelech's razing of the city (Judges 9:45).

SAMUEL AND THE ESTABLISHMENT OF THE MONARCHY: SAUL

Israelite kingship was an almost inevitable outgrowth of the period of the judges. Charismatic leadership thrust individuals into the spotlight at various times during the period of the tribal federation, but clan and tribal loyalties had always been stronger than loyalty to any central military figure or political authority (Judges 5:15–17). Indeed, there was no central political or religious authority for the tribal federation, except for the invisible Yahweh to whom the tribes were bound by the covenant agreement. It is not entirely clear, however, how the tribes were bound to one another through this covenant. Tribes occasionally came to one another's assistance in times of military conflict, and tribal leaders likely met at Mount Tabor[5] or at Shechem for ceremonial functions, such as sacrifices at times of major agricultural festivals or at an annual covenant renewal ceremony. But there was apparently no central governing body of tribal leaders for the Israelite federation.

The emergence of Saul as a charismatic figure at the time of the Philistine threat was a major factor in the inauguration of Israelite kingship. Yet Saul's position was not substantially different from that of other leaders during the period of the judges. He was, in fact, more of a major judge than a king, and there was apparently no notion of hereditary kingship during Saul's reign.

1 Samuel 7–15 contains valuable information pertaining to the establishment of kingship in Israel. Although scholars disagree in their analysis of this material, most identify in this section two distinct strata of material: (1) an early pro-monarchical source (1 Samuel 9:1–10:16; 11:1–11, 15; 13–14); and (2) a later anti-monarchical source (1 Samuel 7:3–17; 8; 10:17–27; 11:12–13). Many scholars conclude that 1 Samuel 11:1–11, 14–15 preserves the most authentic account of Saul's accession to kingship. In any event, these very different traditions support the view of many scholars that the author(s) of the Deuteronomistic History used a number of different sources in composing their account of the history of Israel and Judah.

It appears that kingship was alien, perhaps even anathema, to most Israelites during the period of the judges. The view that Yahweh was Israel's king persisted, and, even more important, tribal allegiances were stronger than the allegiance of tribes to one another or to any central authority. Scholars are understandably interested in the economic, legal, military, and religious activities that contributed to the rise of kingship in Israel. The Deuteronomistic historian, on the other hand, is focused on the will of Yahweh regarding this matter.

At the time of the judges, Israel was a theocracy that was ruled by its heavenly king Yahweh, who, according to the Deuteronomistic historian, raised a host of tribal rulers with the charismatic qualities required to mobilize the military power that was required to deliver Israel from foreign enemies. The reasons for the emergence of the monarchy are complex and undoubtedly involve a number of factors, both internal and external, many of which will forever remain in doubt. The emergence of Israelite kingship, however, obviously had a great deal to do with pressure that Israel was experiencing at the hand of the Philistines. Furthermore, it is undeniable that Samuel played an important role in the decision that Israel would have a king in the person of Saul in order to deal with the Philistine threat.

An important aspect of kingship in many ancient Near Eastern societies is the belief in the deity as king (or the king as deity) and in some sort of genealogical relationship between the heavenly and earthly kings. It was commonly believed throughout the ancient Near East that the god or the high god of the pantheon was the king of the nation or city-state. In many ancient Near Eastern states, the earthly king was considered a descendant or a son of the (high) god and, therefore, himself divine. These god-kings were not only central symbols of their respective social systems, they were also responsible for religious welfare, justice, and the fertility of the land.

That Israel's king was understood, at least later, as the son of Yahweh is clear from many passages in the Old Testament: Psalm 2:7–8;[6] 89:26–27;[7] 2 Samuel 7:14a;[8] compare Isaiah 9:6,[9] but some scholars dispute the significance of these passages. The meaning of Psalm 45:6[10] is particularly problematic. Most consider Psalm 2:7, cited above, to express the more normative formula of Yahweh's *adoption* of Israel's king as his son on the occasion of the king's coronation.

Although passages in the Old Testament refer to Samuel variously as priest, prophet, seer, and judge, the role of legend more than historical memory is likely responsible for identifying him with three of these offices. Scholars are, however, virtually unanimous in identifying Samuel as a judge, a tribal ruler, one whose role was probably more juridical than military. Since virtually all accounts regarding the establishment of Saul's kingship involve Samuel in some way, it seems fairly certain that Samuel was instrumental in the transition to Israel's monarchy and the selection of Saul as Israel's first king.

In the choice of Saul or any king, it is apparent that the king had to be a man whose authority was already acknowledged within the tribal confederacy. The king also had to be a man who could orchestrate the transition from the tribal federation with Yahweh as its king to the new order of governance with a human king, and who could serve both the people and the nation as Yahweh's representative.

Scholars disagree, however, on the nature of Saul's kingship. Some see him as primarily a judge who served as a transitional figure between the pre-monarchic tribal federation and true nationhood under David. Others see Saul as a self-appointed ruler who attempted to extend his authority beyond his own tribe of Benjamin and to centralize power over as much of the tribal federation as possible. Still others view Saul as a chieftain who provided an important intermediate step between tribal society and Israelite statehood. And others view him as the founder of the Israelite state and its first monarch.

However we consider Saul, there is little doubt that he acceded to the throne with help from Samuel, primarily because of his military prowess in the Philistine crisis and as an immediate result of his rescue of the people from the Ammonite siege of Jabesh-gilead (1 Samuel 11:1–11). Saul's leadership was confirmed by the people who elected him as their king (1 Samuel 11:14–15) and likely reigned from circa 1022–circa 1000 BCE.[11]

Although the Bible devotes twenty-five chapters to a discussion of Saul's kingship, we learn virtually nothing about the ways in which he centralized his political power or administered the state, which actually covered a very modest area, primarily in the central hill country of portions of the tribes of Benjamin, Dan, Ephraim, Gad, and Manasseh. It did not include either Galilee or Judah. Saul's failure to establish a hereditary dynasty and Samuel's eventual rejection of Saul indicate the fragility of Israel's new kingship.

CONQUEST AND UNITY: DAVID

David was the youngest of eight sons of Jesse of Bethlehem. Although a descendant of Judah, according to genealogical lists, David's ancestry was also partially non-Israelite. He was Moabite via his paternal great-grandmother Ruth and Canaanite via Judah's wife Tamar, who was David's paternal great-great-great-great-great-great-great-great-grandmother (Ruth 4:18–22; see also Matthew 1:3–6).

Born of humble origins as a shepherd, David became a great military leader. There is a legendary account of David's selection as Israel's king by Samuel when he was a mere youth (1 Samuel 16:1–13), but this legendary tradition clearly has no historical merit. It is designed to show that Israel's future king was known to both Yahweh and his prophet Samuel, even when David was still a youth. The ascent of David to the throne was not the result of human efforts or of mere chance but was the result of divine intervention and the fulfillment of Yahweh's intention. A second and likely reliable account of David's emergence (1 Samuel 16:14–23) reports that David served as a musician and armor bearer in Saul's court, probably in Gibeah in Benjamin. A third account (1 Samuel 17:1–58) is a lengthy legendary story of David's encounter with the Philistine giant Goliath of Gath, a feat that is elsewhere attributed, probably correctly, based on the criterion of embarrassment, to Elhanan (2 Samuel 21:19). The plurality of stories concerning David's emergence as an important figure in Israel's history once again supports the view that the Deuteronomistic historian had access to several, sometimes even contradictory, sources.

The text of 1 Samuel reports that David was particularly close to two of Saul's children, his son Jonathan and his daughter Michal, who later became David's wife for the bride-price of a hundred Philistine foreskins (1 Samuel 18:20–29). The narrator indicates that Saul set the bride-price in the hope that David would fall to the Philistines in battle. It is evident that Saul had a definite jealousy and hatred for David, whom he apparently considered a serious rival to his throne and hoped to eliminate. For reasons that are also not entirely clear, Jonathan, Saul's presumed heir apparent to the throne, allied himself with David against his own father and, hence, against his own right of hereditary accession to his father's throne.

When Saul banished David from his kingdom, David offered himself as a mercenary to the Philistines, who seem to have feared treachery on his part. David collected a band of about four hundred outlaws, who became a formidable group of fighters (1 Samuel 22:1–2). David had an opportunity to kill Saul, possibly twice, but refused to do so (1 Samuel 24:7, 11; 26:1–25).[12]

Samuel eventually rejected Saul as king (1 Samuel 15:10–35) because in a battle against the Amalekites, Saul violated the ban on leaving any Amalekites alive. Consequently, Samuel selected David to be Saul's successor (1 Samuel 15:34–16:13). In a subsequent battle against the Philistines, Saul took his own life after Philistine archers had wounded him. Three of Saul's sons, Jonathan, Abinadab, and Malchishua, perished together with him in that battle.

Following the death of the king, the people of Hebron anointed David as king over the house of Judah (2 Samuel 2:1–4), while Abner, Saul's cousin and commander-in-chief, made Saul's son Ishbaal (whose name means "man of Baal") "king over Gilead, the Ashurites,[13] Jezreel, Ephraim, Benjamin, and over all Israel"[14] (2 Samuel 2: 8–9). The text tells us that Ishbaal reigned over Israel in his capital in Mahanaim in Gilead in Transjordan for a period of two years (2 Samuel 2:10) and that David reigned as "king in Hebron over the house of Judah" for "seven years and six months" (2 Samuel 2:11), evidence of the persistent rivalry between north and south, between Israel and Judah.

With the subsequent murder of Ishbaal by two members of the tribe of Benjamin who sought to gain favor with David (2 Samuel 4), David assumed power over the whole of Israel, the real beginning of the short-lived United Kingdom of Israel (2 Samuel 5:1–4). Shortly thereafter, David captured Jerusalem, moved his capital to that city, and reigned there for an additional thirty-three years, for a total reign of forty years, presumably from circa 1000 to circa 960 BCE.

The decision to capture Jerusalem, known earlier as Jebus, was apparently a strategic one. The city's central location between the northern tribes and the tribe of Judah to the south made it a more neutral capital than Hebron, which was clearly in David's home tribe of Judah. The ancient walled city of Jerusalem, which the tribes of Judah and Benjamin had both failed to conquer (Joshua 15:63; Judges 1:21), fell to David, although details of his victory are unclear (2 Samuel 5:6–9; 1 Chronicles 11:4–9).

David subsequently brought to Jerusalem the ark of the covenant of Yahweh, the sacred object that symbolized Yahweh's presence in ancient Israelite religion. The ark of Yahweh was apparently a chest built under Moses' command to contain the tablets of the Ten Commandments and to serve, as well, as the throne upon which the invisible Yahweh could be carried (Exodus 25:10–22; Numbers 7:89). It apparently served also as the place for the most reliable oracle-seeking. It played an important role in the desert wanderings (Numbers 10:33–36; 14:44), the crossing of the Jordan River (Joshua 3:2–6), and the subsequent conquest of Canaan (Joshua 6:6–7). The ark was eventually placed in the sanctuary of Shiloh under the care of a priestly family who may have claimed direct descent from Moses (1 Samuel 3:3). It was sometimes carried into battle, presumably as a talisman with magical power sufficient to guarantee victory for Israel, and was, on one such occasion, captured by the Philistines (1 Samuel 4:1–11).

After the Philistines returned the ark of Yahweh to Israel following outbreaks of plague in their cities, it was taken to Kiriath-jearim (1 Samuel 6:1–7:2), where it remained until David removed it, first to the house of Obed-Edom the Gittite (2 Samuel 6:10–11),[15] and thereafter to a specially created tent in Jerusalem (2 Samuel 6:17–19). Although David apparently intended to build a temple for the ark, he received instead from Yahweh (through the prophet Nathan) a promise that his house (i.e., dynasty) would rule in Jerusalem forever (2 Samuel 7:1–19).

David proved his shrewdness as a politician by the age of thirty-seven when he became the unchallenged ruler of the whole of Israel. David then turned his attention to waging war against neighboring Philistia, Moab, Ammon, Edom, Amalek, and Aram (Syria) (2 Samuel 8:1–14; 10:1–19), and he also concluded a treaty with the Phoenician king Hiram of Tyre. These military and political successes meant that David's empire extended from the mountains of Lebanon in the northwest to the borders of Egypt on the west, from the Mediterranean Sea to the Arabian Desert in the east. Only Phoenicia and a diminished Philistia blocked David from ruling over areas on the Mediterranean. He effectively controlled the area purportedly promised to Abraham in Genesis 15:18–21:

> On that day the LORD [Yahweh] made a covenant with Abram, saying, "To your descendants I give this land, from the river of Egypt to the great river, the river Euphrates, the land of the Kenites, the Kenizzities, the Kadmonites, the Hittites, the Perizzites, the Rephaim, the Amorites, the Canaanites, the Girgishites, and the Jebusites."[16]

This passage in Genesis is an example of what scholars refer to as *vaticinium ex eventu,* which is a prophecy *out of* or *as a result* of an event, or perhaps, more clearly, prediction after the fact. Stated succinctly, Yahweh promised to Abraham, presumably many centuries after the fact, the land that would become David's small empire.

His capital in Jerusalem, known officially as "the city of David" (2 Samuel 5:9), was also the "city of Yahweh." Yahweh's presence was now in the heart of Israel in a city that David himself had conquered. By moving the seat of Yahweh from the sanctuary of Shiloh in Benjamin to the royal city of Jerusalem, David further strengthened his own position. With the blessing of the prophet Nathan, David's dynasty had an everlasting covenant with Yahweh and David's heirs would sit on the throne forever (2 Samuel 7). David's plan to build a temple as a permanent house for Yahweh and the ark of the covenant, like the temples for the gods of Israel's neighbors, met with opposition from Nathan, who maintained that Yahweh had since the time of the Exodus always lived in a tent (2 Samuel 7:6).

Tradition has sometimes tended to romanticize David as the ideal king. He was evidently a significant military hero and the principal architect of the establishment of the Israelite state. It was David who consolidated the tribes into a single nation and expanded Israel's influence by creating a small empire that incorporated many of

Israel's neighbors. Many of the psalms have been ascribed to David, perhaps because of his reputation as a musician in Saul's court. Not insignificantly, Nathan's oracle, which established the basis for the special, perhaps unconditional, relationship between Yahweh and the house of David, gave rise in some circles to the belief centuries later that someone of Davidic lineage would in the indefinite future restore Israel to her prior greatness. Beyond the Old Testament, there were some who believed that a descendant of David would come in God's future time to establish his kingdom on earth, a view that became particularly popular in some Christian circles.

There was obviously a tendency to add to David's heroic stature: for example, the legendary account of Samuel's discovering and anointing the future king while David was still very young (1 Samuel 16:1–13), and the legendary account of the teenage David's killing the Philistine giant Goliath (1 Samuel 17).

Given this tendency, it is to the credit of the Deuteronomistic historian that many stories reflecting weaknesses in David's character survive in the text, especially from the court history in 2 Samuel 9–20 and 1 Kings 1–2. The criterion of dissimilarity or embarrassment assures the historical value of these stories. One of the best-known stories (2 Samuel 11) involves David's desire for Bathsheba, the wife of Uriah the Hittite, who was off to war at the time. When Bathsheba became pregnant by David, the king brought Uriah back from war in an attempt to conceal his act of adultery. The plan backfired when Uriah refused to sleep with his wife because of rules of purity that applied to soldiers in a time of holy war (Deuteronomy 23:9–14). David subsequently contrived Uriah's death in battle in a manner that would put the king beyond suspicion. The court prophet Nathan, however, apparently understood what had happened and confronted David and persuaded him to condemn himself for his sin against Yahweh (2 Samuel 12:1–15). Nathan's announcement that the child of this adulterous affair would die may be still one more example of *vaticinium ex eventu* (prophecy *out of* or *as a result of* an event, or, perhaps more clearly, prediction after the fact).

From the point of view of the Deuteronomistic historian, subsequent tragic events were viewed as consequences of David's indiscretion. David's firstborn son Amnon by David's wife Ahinoam raped his own virgin half sister Tamar by David's wife Maacah (2 Samuel 13:1–19). Two years later Tamar's full brother Absalom assassinated Amnon in revenge (2 Samuel 13:23–29) and then gained asylum for three years with his maternal grandfather, Talmai son of Ammihud, king of Geshur (2 Samuel 13:30–39).[17] David eventually restored Absalom from exile but initially would not agree to see his son (2 Samuel 14:1–24). Absalom subsequently rebelled against David and tried to usurp his father's throne (2 Samuel 15:1–12), but Absalom's army was defeated and David's nephew and commander Joab defeated and killed the renegade Absalom (2 Samuel 18:1–15).

Further intrigue followed toward the end of David's life when his sons engaged in still more treachery and intrigue over who would succeed him. Adonijah (meaning "Yahweh is my lord"), the son of Haggith, was now David's oldest son and, at least in his own mind, the heir apparent based on the principle of primogeniture. With support from David's nephew and commander Joab and from Abiathar, one of the king's high priests, Adonijah tried to set himself up as king, even while David lay on his deathbed. But the prophet Nathan, the high priest Zadok, Benaiah from David's private guard, and two unnamed officials conspired with David's wife Bathsheba to have her young son Solomon succeed his father as king, based presumably on a promise that David had previously made to Bathsheba (1 Kings 1:1–38). Solomon and Adonijah may have served as co-regents until David's death, at which time, Solomon, fearing Adonijah's threat to his throne, ordered the execution of both his brother and his brother's military commmander Joab and became the unchallenged heir to David's kingdom.

The court intrigues that lead to the accession of Solomon rather than his older brother Adonijah sound more like a Shakespearean tragedy than the Bible. Solomon's claim to the throne was apparently based more on David's love of Bathsheba and the political influence of Solomon's supporters than on Solomon's personal charisma or military prowess.[18]

CONSOLIDATION AND PEACE: SOLOMON

Information for the reign of Solomon, found in 1 Kings 3–11, is apparently based on a court record, known as the book of the Acts of Solomon (1 Kings 11:41), once again filtered through the theological viewpoint of the Deuteronomistic historian.

There is some question about Solomon's name. According to 2 Samuel 12:25, David named him Jedidiah, meaning "beloved of Yahweh," but there is no other reference to this name in the Bible. 1 Chronicles 22:9 suggests that the name šĕlōmōh means "peaceful" ("he shall be a man of šālôm [peace]"). Many scholars, however, suggest that the name means "replacement," because he was a replacement (from

FIGURE 6. THE KINGDOM OF DAVID AND SOLOMON

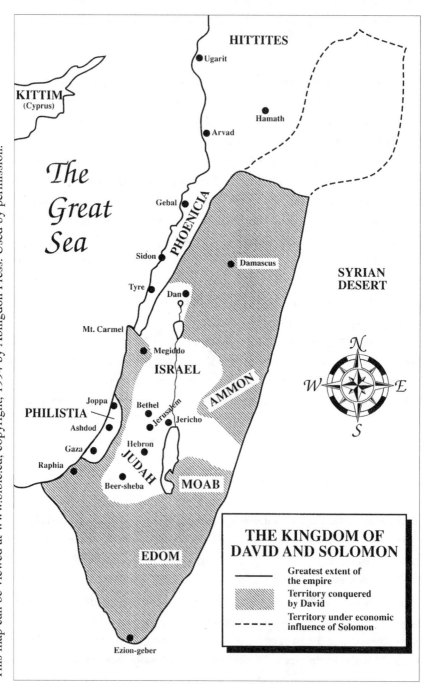

THE KINGDOM OF
DAVID AND SOLOMON

——	Greatest extent of the empire
▨	Territory conquered by David
- - -	Territory under economic influence of Solomon

Hebrew *šillem*, meaning "make compensation") for the lost child conceived through David and Bathsheba's adulterous relationship.

Irrespective of his name, Solomon's reign, which lasted from circa 960 BCE to circa 922 BCE, was a period of consolidation, building, and expansion. In a season of relative peace, Israel and Solomon were able to prosper due to Egypt's continued weakness and Mesopotamia's failure to emerge as a political threat until the next century. Moreover, David had already succeeded in either subjugating or binding by political and commercial alliances Israel's smaller neighboring territories. Solomon divided Israel into twelve administrative districts, which intentionally cut across tribal boundaries, in an effort to strengthen the king's central authority at the expense of the older tribal structure (1 Kings 4:7–19). Solomon developed or expanded trade routes connecting Africa, Asia, Arabia, and Asia Minor, and his fleet sailed south from Ezion-geber on the Gulf of Aqaba to Ophir on the coast of the Red Sea (1 Kings 9:26–28).

The record ascribes to Solomon enormous wealth: he had three hundred concubines and seven hundred wives, including Egyptian, Moabite, Ammonite, Edomite, Sidonian, and Hittite women, most of which marriages were likely arranged to secure political alliances (1 Kings 11:1–3). One of Solomon's wives was a daughter of Egypt's pharaoh.[19] To cement political arrangements, Solomon promoted or allowed the worship in Jerusalem of his wives' native gods (1 Kings 11:4–8).[20] His daily household food consumption was staggering (1 Kings 4:22–23: "thirty cors[21] of choice flour, and sixty cors of meal, ten fat oxen, and twenty pasture-fed cattle, one hundred sheep, besides deer, gazelles, roebucks, and fatted fowl").

Solomon's building program was extraordinarily ambitious and included chariot cities, storage cities, and other fortifications (1 Kings 9:15–19). We have not only the biblical testimony about Solomon's building campaign but extensive archaeological corroboration as well. Solomon devoted thirteen years to the building of his palace complex. A relatively detailed description of the palace appears in 1 Kings 7:1–12, which is almost certainly based on an old archival account from the book of the Acts of Solomon (1 Kings 11:41). The house was actually a complex of five buildings, including a separate house for Solomon's Egyptian queen.

YAHWEH GETS A HOUSE: THE JERUSALEM TEMPLE

Although much smaller than the royal palace, the crowning achievement of Solomon's building campaign was the construction of the temple of Yahweh, which took seven years to build (1 Kings 6:38). The Jerusalem temple had not only religious significance for the cult of Yahweh, but it had political significance as well. It afforded validity to the Israelite state and to Jerusalem, its capital, and was intimately associated with political rule. There can be no question that David understood that building the Temple of Yahweh would support and stabilize his rule, but Nathan stood in the way of the fulfillment of David's dream, so the task fell to David's son Solomon.

There is a temptation to impose on the temple a contemporary understanding of religious sites as places of worship, but the Jerusalem temple was not a place of public gathering and prayer. It was rather the earthly dwelling place, the palace or residence, of Israel's God Yahweh. No vestige of the Solomonic temple survives; so we have no archaeological evidence whatsoever for its structure and architecture. There is, however, a good deal of reliable information about Solomon's temple in 1 Kings 6–8 and 2 Chronicles 2–4, passages that were likely drawn from official records of the construction, perhaps contained in the book of the Acts of Solomon (1 Kings 11:41).[22]

The location of the temple, however, has never been questioned. Solomon's temple stood on the site in Jerusalem known today as the Dome of the Rock, a Muslim shrine built in 691 CE, atop the area in the old city known as the Temple Mount.

The description of the temple reveals, as we might expect, strong Canaanite and Phoenician influence, although no two temples of the period were exactly alike, just as no two modern churches are exactly alike. Each temple had its own idiosyncratic features. The basic plan of the building itself was a rectangle with interior dimensions estimated to have been about ninety feet long, thirty feet wide, and forty-five feet high, about as large as the structure could be, given the architectural conventions of the time.[23]

The interior space of the temple was divided into three sections. Entering the temple, the first area was called in Hebrew the '*ûlām*, the porch or entrance hall, and was about thirty feet wide and fifteen feet deep. It is not clear that this area functioned as anything more than the first space at the entrance to the temple, especially since it does not appear to have had exterior doors or a roof and may, therefore, have been an open-air space or a small transitional courtyard at the entrance to the temple proper.

The second area, the largest part of the temple, measured about sixty feet long by about thirty feet wide and about forty-five feet high and was called the *hêkāl*, the main room or the holy sanctuary. This was the area in which most cultic rituals took place. The interior furnishings of the temple were in this area; most specifically there was a small altar for incense directly in front of the inner sanctum, five lamp stands on each side of the room, and a small table for the "bread of the presence."[24] Entry into the *hêkāl* was through double-hung cypress doors hinged on olivewood doorposts.

The third and innermost area of the temple, a perfect cube about thirty feet on all sides, was the *děbîr*, the Holy of Holies, the inner sanctum and the most holy place in the temple. The word may be derived from the Hebrew verb *dbr*, meaning "to speak," implying that the *děbîr* was the place of oracles, the seat from which Yahweh spoke. Entry into the *děbîr* was through double-hung olivewood doors. The walls and the floors of both of these inner spaces, the sanctuary and the Holy of Holies, were covered with wood, and the floors of the *děbîr* were adorned with gold leaf (1 Kings 6:29–30). Inside the Holy of Holies were two large olivewood cherubim,[25] covered with gold (1 Kings 6:23–28), each about fifteen feet high and each with a wingspan of about fifteen feet, under which lay "the ark of the covenant of Yahweh" (1 Kings 6:19), the symbol of Yahweh's presence within the temple.

A number of small storage rooms extended over three stories along the two sides and the rear of the building, behind the Holy of Holies. Immediately outside the front entrance to the temple there were two freestanding bronze columns, called Jachin and Boaz, which seem to have functioned as gateposts at the entrance to the *'ûlām*.

Although Yahweh was a transcendent god, it was essential for the welfare of the state and the king that he be accessible and available for consultation. The temple afforded a sense of security that the divine presence was somehow within reach to afford protection to Israel and its people. Yahweh's presence in Jerusalem was particularly important during the period of transition from the tribal federation to the monarchy, as it represented Yahweh's approval of the new sociopolitical structure.

Typically, temples were understood to stand at the cosmic center of the universe, the place where heaven and earth converged, and, therefore, the place from which God's power reached out to his people through divinely approved earthly rep-

FIGURE 7. THE GROUNDFLOOR PLAN
OF SOLOMON'S TEMPLE

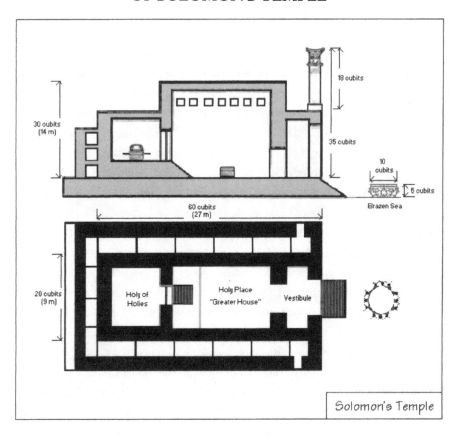

resentatives—priests, prophets, and, of course, the king. The rich furnishings of the temple befitted the residence of the divine king, represented by the tablets of stone contained in the ark of Yahweh, which served as the divine throne.[26] Psalm 48:1–3 proclaimed that the temple on its elevated platform replicated the mountain of Yahweh at Sinai and the heavenly mountain from which Yahweh protects his people:

> ₁Great is the LORD (Yahweh)
> and greatly to be praised in the city of our God.
> His holy mountain,
> ₂beautiful in elevation, is the joy of all the earth,
> Mount Zion, in the far north,

the city of the great King.

₃Within its citadels God has shown himself a sure defense.

For a brief moment in history, the Jerusalem temple served not only as the center of a small kingdom but also as the center of a small empire that extended into Syria and Transjordan. The ability of David to unite the Israelite tribes into a single nation and to acquire a small empire, and the ability of Solomon to consolidate his father's achievements received divine sanction and legitimization through the temple and its cult and ritual. It was believed that the presence of the temple would ensure peace and prosperity to the people and their king, as Solomon, the representative of Yahweh, ruled from the palace-temple complex in Jerusalem.

Solomon's programs came at a high cost. His efforts to eliminate the last vestiges of tribal independence were unpopular, as was the program of forced labor needed to accomplish his massive building campaigns (1 Kings 5:13–18). Resentment among the people eventually erupted in the form of a rebellion, led by Jeroboam of Ephraim, one of the northern tribes (1 King 11:26–40). The rebellion was endorsed by the prophet Ahijah, who was apparently associated with the old Israelite shrine at Shiloh and who provided theological justification for the division of Solomon's kingdom by expressing Yahweh's disapproval of Solomon's toleration and promotion of the worship of foreign gods in Israel and in Jerusalem. The groundwork had been laid for the division of the kingdom. On the occasion of Solomon's death in 922 BCE, Solomon's son Rehoboam succeeded his father as king in Jerusalem, but his kingdom extended over the territory of only two tribes, Judah and Benjamin, and became known as the Kingdom of Judah. Jeroboam, who had led the rebellion against Solomon's oppressive measures, became king of the ten breakaway tribes, and his kingdom was thereafter known as the Kingdom of Israel, with Samaria as its capital.

WRITING A NATIONAL EPIC: THE YAHWIST

Before moving on to the division of the kingdom upon the death of King Solomon, it is essential to visit one of the most important events of Solomon's reign, the creative literary work of the Yahwist. Whether part of Solomon's official program to strengthen the Davidic dynasty or the work of those in charge of the temple cult and ritual, those responsible for the writing of the Yahwist epic set forth in masterful prose, probably sometime during the reign of King Solomon, the story of the promise to the ancestors and the fulfillment of that promise in the establishment of the nation.

Based on oral traditions that had assumed their shape at many of the ancient tribal shrines, such as the confederation sanctuaries at Shiloh and Shechem, these traditions were gathered into a unified epic to accentuate and strengthen the establishment and the validity of the Israelite state. This historical and theological composition likely represented still one more effort to support the new nationalism of the Davidite monarchy.

Chapter 1 of this book set forth the case against the Mosaic authorship of the Pentateuch, leaving open the question of who were the actual authors of those five books. A chart on page 54 indicates the broad outline of the prevailing hypothesis that there are several distinguishable sources that make up our books of Genesis, Exodus, Leviticus, Numbers, and Deuteronomy. These sources do not survive intact. Rather they have been woven together into a single fabric by the latest editors of that work (the Priestly writers of about 400 BCE) and can be reconstructed only through the efforts of scholars using the tools of literary criticism. In that regard, it is important to be mindful of the fact that "J," or the Yahwist source, represents the earliest element in a scholarly hypothesis, a scientific theory, designed to explain evidence found in the Pentateuch and elsewhere. That said, we turn our attention now to the Yahwist, or the J source.

As mentioned earlier, it was in 1753 that the French medical doctor Jean Astruc first noticed that in Genesis 1–3 there were actually two creation stories that used different names for God: 'ĕlōhîm in Genesis 1:1–2:4a and yhwh in Genesis 2:4b–3:24. The second of these documents came to be called the Yahwist (J for Jahwist with a J, as much of the early work on this hypothesis appeared in German).

The principal criterion for attributing passages to J was initially the use of the divine name Yahweh, but scholars, initially and most particularly Johann Gottfried Eichhorn in 1780–83, subsequently noticed a number of stories in two different forms (what are called *doublets*), and they also began to understand the peculiar vocabulary, style, grammar, and theological outlook of this J material, especially as distinguishable from Priestly legislation (P), which proved to be the latest stratum of material.

In order to appreciate the distinction between the P and J versions of creation that led Jean Astruc to posit the existence of two different sources, it is appropriate to review, however briefly, some of the dissimilarities between the creation myth in Genesis 1:1–2:4a and the account in Genesis 2:4b–24.

Jean Astruc's initial observation was that there are two different names for God in what he concluded were two distinct creation myths; therefore, that is the obvious place to begin our investigation of the case for J. Specifically, the word *ĕlōhîm* (God) occurs thirty-five times in Genesis 1:1–2:4a[27] and never in Genesis 2:4b–24. Conversely, the combination *ĕlōhîm yahweh* (God Yahweh) occurs eleven times in Genesis 2:4b–24[28] and never in Genesis 1:1–2:4a.[29]

Another difference between the two creation myths is that the order of creation is significantly different:

Priestly account (Genesis 1:1–2:4a)	Yahwist account (Genesis 2:4b–24)
1. light (1:3–5)	a stream rose from the desert
2. the dome (1:6–8)	Yahweh formed a man from dust
3. (a) dry land and seas (1:9–10)	Yahweh planted a garden
(b) plants (1:11–12)	a river flowed from Eden
4. the heavenly lights (1:13–19)	Yahweh put the man in the garden
5. fish and birds (1:20–23)	Yahweh formed animals and birds
6. (a) terrestrial creatures (1:24–25)	Yahweh formed a woman from
(b) humankind (1:26–31)	one of the man's ribs
7. sabbath—*ĕlōhîm* rested (2:2)[30]	

In the Priestly account, there are eight distinct acts of creation folded into six days, with two acts of creation on the third day and two on the sixth day (see table above). The author has obviously compressed the eight acts into six days in order to institutionalize the Sabbath as a day of rest as part of God's plan from the very beginning of time. The Priestly writer has also followed a scheme for each of the days of creation: "God said. . . ."; the specific act of creation on that day, "And there was evening and there was morning day X."

The Yahwist myth is less structured, and there are important differences, even disagreements, between the two myths:

(1) the P myth of creation is essentially a cosmology, it addresses the creation of the entire universe, whereas the J myth is confined almost exclusively to events that unfold in the garden of Eden;

(2) in P, the primordial element is a watery chaos (Genesis 1:2); in J, a desert (Genesis 2:5);

(3) in P, man is the final act of creation after the animals (Genesis 1:26–27); in J, the man is created at the outset before the creation of the animals (Genesis 2:7), and the animals are created later as possible helpers and partners for the man (Genesis 2:18–20); and

(4) in P, God created male and female at the same time (Genesis 1:27); in J, the woman was created from the man's rib almost as an afterthought (Genesis 2:21–23).

Two ancient confessional affirmations of Israel's identity survive in the Old Testament: Deuteronomy 26:5–9 and Joshua 24:2–13. In chapter 3, we examined the second of these passages in our discussion of the conquest of Canaan and the covenant renewal ceremony at Shechem. The passage in Deuteronomy 26:5–9 is in many ways similar and may have been recited on the occasion of the presentation of the first fruits:

26:5A wandering Aramean was my ancestor; and he went down into Egypt, and lived there as an alien, few in number, and there he became a great nation, mighty and populous. 6When the Egyptians treated us harshly and afflicted us, by imposing hard labor on us, 7we cried to the LORD (Yahweh), the God of our ancestors; the LORD (Yahweh) heard our voice and saw our affliction, our toil, and our oppression. 8The LORD (Yahweh) brought us out of Egypt with a mighty hand and an outstretched arm, with a terrifying display of power, and with signs and wonders; 9and he brought us into this place and gave us this land, a land flowing with milk and honey.

These two mini-credos in Deuteronomy 26:5–9 and Joshua 24:2–13, both of which interestingly make no mention of the Sinai experience, otherwise afford the same basic outline of the Yahwist epic: (1) the promise to the ancestors, (2) the deliverance from Egypt, (3) the wandering in the wilderness, and (4) the entry into the land of Canaan. To these themes, the Yahwist apparently added three additional themes: (1) the creation myth and the primordial history as a background to the main story, (2) the development and expansion of the story of one patriarch (Abram, the "wandering Aramean" of Deuteronomy 26:5) into the three patriarchs of Joshua 24:2–4 and Genesis 12–50, and (3) the insertion of the Sinai covenant story.

Presumably these traditions were already developed in the oral traditions of individual tribes and at various cultic centers in the period before the Israelite monarchy. Borrowing and reshaping ancient Near Eastern traditions about creation and prehistory in material found in Genesis 2–11, the Yahwist restructured the mythical ancestral history in Genesis 12–50 as the period in which Yahweh promised Abraham that he would give to his descendants (Israel) a great nation (the kingdom of Israel), by promising to Abraham retrospectively the very boundaries of the kingdom of David and Solomon (Genesis 15:18–21).

The Yahwist story picks up in Exodus with the deliverance of the people from slavery under the leadership of Moses and the establishment of the covenant community at Mount Sinai with the giving of the Decalogue. The wanderings in the wilderness eventually lead up to the story of Moses' death in Transjordan, virtually on the eve of the entrance of the people into the promised land of Canaan.

As was indicated in chapter 1, there are a number of anachronisms that preclude the possibility that Moses could be the author of these books (pp. 50–53). Two passages, in particular, Exodus 15:17[31] and Genesis 36:31,[32] indicate that these written accounts date to the period after the establishment of the Israelite monarchy, after the capture of Jerusalem and its establishment as Israel's capital, and after the building of the sanctuary, Solomon's temple. A date for the writing of the Yahwist epic around 950–930 BCE, as still one more ingredient in the consolidation of power in the hands of the Davidite monarchy, makes the most sense of the evidence.

In recent decades, scholars have tried to penetrate behind the Yahwist's written account to the preliterary materials that served as the building blocks of J's version of the national epic. Most of these sources came presumably from oral traditions, whose original forms or literary patterns survive in our written texts. A study of Israel's ancient oral tradition necessary involves an analysis of the occasion and environment, the *Sitz im Leben* or the situation in life, the repeatable liturgical context that led to the formation of particular material during the period of oral transmission. Scholars are also able to compare material in the Yahwist document and elsewhere in the Old Testament with similar material in other ancient Near Eastern literature, which is now abundant because of archaeological discoveries over the last century.

The classification of these literary forms goes well beyond the books of the Yahwist and the other material in the Pentateuch. However, some of the forms that we have observed in the course of our study thus far include the following:

Poetic Forms:

the song (e.g., the Song of Miriam in Exodus 15:21; the Song of Moses in Exodus 15:2–18; the Song of Deborah in Judges 5:2–31);

the blessing (e.g., Noah's blessing of Shem in Genesis 9:25–27; the priestly blessing in Numbers 6:24–26); and

the fable (e.g., Jotham's fable in Judges 9:8–15).

Prose Forms:

the speech (e.g., Joshua's farewell address in Joshua 23:2–16; Joshua's address at Shechem in Joshua 24:2–28; Solomon's speech in 1 Kings 8:14–21);

the sermon (e.g., the Song of Moses in Deuteronomy 32:1–43);

the prayer (e.g., Joshua's prayer in Joshua 7:7–9; the prayer of Solomon in 1 Kings 8:22–53);

the Decalogue and other Mosaic law (e.g., Exodus 20:2–17; 34:14–26; Deuteronomy 5:6–21; 27:15–26);

the legend (e.g., etiological legends regarding place names, local phenomena, customs, etc.—the story of the birth of Ishmael and the naming of the well at Lahai-roi in Genesis 16:7–14; the story of Jacob's dream at Bethel in Genesis 28:10–17; the story of Jacob wrestling with God at Peniel in Genesis 32:22–32; the story of Joshua's defeat of five kings in Joshua 10:16–23);

the myth (e.g., the creation myths in Genesis 1:1–2:4a and 2:4b–3:24; the flood myths in Genesis 6:1–9:29).

This is by no means an exhaustive list, but it suggests the kinds of material that likely circulated during the period of oral transmission and that served as building blocks for the Yahwist in the composition of the national epic as well as for other writers subsequent to the Yahwist.

The Yahwist cast the national epic within the framework of the theme of promise and fulfillment, the promise made initially to the ancestors and fulfilled subsequently in the conquest and entrenchment of the land of Canaan. Because Israel's salvation history likely included an account of Israel's entry into the land of Canaan, some scholars have argued that elements of J must still exist in the book of Joshua.

The call of father Abraham in Genesis 12:1–3 seems to demand that:

> 12:1Now the LORD (Yahweh) said to Abram, "Go from your country and your kindred and your father's house to the land that I will show you. 2I will make of you a great nation, and I will bless you, and make your name great, so that you will be a blessing. 3I will bless those who bless you, and the one who curses you I will curse; and in you all the families of the earth shall be blessed."

CONCLUSIONS

This chapter has covered a formative period in the history of Israel, a little more than three hundred years during the transition from the period of the tribal federation, which began in about 1250 BCE, through the period of the united monarchy, which came to an end in 922 BCE. The move from federation to monarchy was not easy, because early loyalties were primarily to individual tribes and because the original federation of twelve tribes was essentially a theocracy with Yahweh as its only king and there was, therefore, no need for an earthly king. In fact, such a thought was anathema to many.

Circumstances leading to the establishment of the monarchy were largely the result of threats from neighboring enemies, who periodically attacked individual tribes. Although neighboring tribes of the Israelite federation often came to the aid of one another, there was apparently no clear understanding of any obligation to do so. There was no central leadership and certainly no central army.

The emergence of the monarchy is associated with Gideon, Abimelech, and Saul, but it was in actual fact with the ascent of David to the throne that a united monarchy seemed secure. Not only did David unite the Israelite tribes into a nation and establish Jerusalem as his capital, but he also succeeded in subjecting many of Israel's neighbors, who had posed threats at various times in the past. David's conquests were consolidated by his son and successor, Solomon, who ushered in Israel's golden age and who built in Jerusalem a palace for himself and a temple for Yahweh. It was also probably during Solomon's reign that the so-called Yahwist produced the national epic that scholars have come to know as the J source of the Pentateuch.

In writing the history of this three-hundred-year period, we have relied on a number of methods and principles of biblical scholarship, and it is helpful to summarize some of them here.

Dating Methods

In an effort to establish the dates of particular events, we have frequently had to pinpoint specific incidents and then calculate forward and backward to establish the dates of other events. For example, the release of King Jehoiachin from exile in Babylonia in 561/560 BCE was used to establish the likely date for the writing of the Deuteronomistic History. The dates for the reigns of Saul, David, and Solomon were established by reference to the division of the United Kingdom in 922 BCE and the approximate lengths of the reigns of kings as recorded by the Deuteronomistic historian. The conjecture about the Egyptian pharaoh whose daughter Solomon married was made on the basis of melding Israelite and Egyptian chronologies, both of which, quite frankly, pose serious challenges.

Ancient Sources

References to ancient written sources contemporaneous with reported events (a total of thirty-four references to the book of the Acts of Solomon, the book of the Annals of the Kings of Israel, and the book of the Annals of the Kings of Judah) in the writings of the Deuteronomistic historian meet the time and place criterion mentioned in the introduction, namely, that the closer in time and place a source or an author of a source is to an event, the more reliable that source is likely to be. In the case of these court annals, used by the Deuteronomistic historian, we are likely dealing with records initially composed by court historians who were very close in time and place to the events reported. Obviously, those ancient sources have been appropriated by the Deuteronomistic historian and reshaped and interpreted to meet his theological objectives. Nevertheless, for the first time in the history of Israel we have at least a secondary access to eyewitnesses, whose testimony constitutes sound historical evidence. These early court records make the Deuteronomistic History a valuable resource for scholars, particularly for the period of the monarchy(ies). In addition, in the account of details about the building of the temple in Jerusalem, we likely have access once again to official records, making it possible to reconstruct with some measure of certainty the architecture of the temple based on the accounts in 1 Kings and 2 Chronicles.

Names and Etymologies

In a number of instances, names and etymologies, even false etymologies, provide clues to people's identities and to the origins of some stories. For example, we have observed that a number of important figures had either Baal names or Yah(weh) names, providing insight into the complex and uncertain effort of Yahweh worshipers to supplant the indigenous Baal religion of the land of Canaan with the worship of the covenant god Yahweh. That struggle continued for many centuries. The worship of the Canaanite god Baal-berith (Baal or Lord of the Covenant) in Shechem provided us with an important clue about covenant associations at Shechem, even before the time of Joshua. It also provided us with clues about the intrigues involving Abimelech and his efforts to become king. In the Yahwist creation story in Genesis 2:4b–25, the creation of the man (*'ādām*) from the ground (*'adāmāh*), an interesting pun in Hebrew, likely affords the reason that the Yahwist recounted that man was created from the dust of the ground (Genesis 2:7). The creation of the woman from the man's rib also involves a pun in Hebrew (Genesis 2:23)

> This at last is bone of my bones
>> and flesh of my flesh;
> This one shall be called Woman (Hebrew *iššāh*),
>> for out of Man (Hebrew *iš*) this one was taken.[33]

Like the word *'ādām*, which actually means humankind, Eve's name *hawwāh* denotes "life." Just as Adam is the personification of humankind,[34] Eve is the personification of human life as that is perpetuated by woman (Genesis 3:20; 4:1). What we are witnessing here is one of the important tools of mythmaking.

Doublets or Multiple Accounts

In instances where we have doublets or multiple accounts of the same event, we are often able to see how stories have likely evolved, especially during the period of their oral transmission. We found two accounts of Gideon's call to leadership and three accounts of David's call to leadership. Each had its own purpose. Scholars have identified in 1 Samuel both a pro-monarchical source and an anti-monarchical source, providing thereby not only separate accounts of the emergence of the monarchy but also evidence of conflicting opinions as to whether Israel should have only Yahweh as its king or rather a human king, perhaps designated and protected by Yahweh. Two or more sources often enable scholars to provide a more balanced picture of important issues. We also observed that most stories in the Deuteronomistic History identify Samuel with Saul's ascent to the throne, indicating independent traditions in support of what were likely multiple independent witnesses.

Myths and Legends

It is only since the Enlightenment, and especially since the nineteenth century, that scholars have paid serious attention to the role of myth in the Bible. The literary movement known as Romanticism also focused attention on the role of creative imagination in humankind's earliest poetic expressions, including the Bible. The study of other ancient literatures revealed, as well, that biblical stories are not always the result of eyewitness testimony, but that they are sometimes best explained as part of the long process of ancient storytelling. Although scholars have not always agreed on a definition of "myth," the popular definition of myths as "stories about the gods" is a useful place to begin.

By contrast, legends are stories about wonderful events or extraordinary people, generally handed down in oral form for many generations and purporting to have a historical basis. There is a tendency for legends to heighten or exaggerate the events or people being described to the extent that these stories sometimes exceed the realm of verifiability, likelihood, or even possibility. We have legends about our own American heroes, like the story of George Washington cutting down the cherry tree or throwing the silver dollar across the river, designed to illustrate in imaginative stories our national father's honesty and physical prowess.

Both the Priestly and the Yahwist creation stories in Genesis 1 and 2 are examples of myths. The stories of Gideon's call by an angel, the sign of the fleece in the Gideon cycle, Saul's anointing of the child David as king, and David's slaying of Goliath are all examples of legends appearing to have a historical basis, but rather they are designed to heighten important events or people in Israel's history.

The Role of Archaeology

As mentioned in the introduction, archaeology provides external circumstantial evidence that sometimes supports and sometimes refutes biblical testimony. Archaeological evidence regarding the dates of the destruction of Jericho and Ai challenge the historical value of stories about the destruction of these cities in the book of Joshua and require us to look at those stories quite differently. Archaeological evidence regarding the destruction of Shechem in the mid-twelfth century confirms elements in the Gideon cycle. Archaeological evidence of temple architecture in excavations at Megiddo, Ai, Arad, Shechem, Beth-Shean, Hazor, and Tell Tainat provide important insights into the architecture of the Jerusalem temple.

Dissimilarity or Embarrassment

The criterion of dissimilarity or embarrassment helps considerably to clarify events surrounding Gideon and Abimelech and the earliest steps in the emergence of Israel's monarchy. It also provides important information that it was likely Elhanan and not young David who slew the Philistine giant Goliath. Likewise, this criterion casts considerable light on incidents during David's reign, assuring the historicity of David's scandalous affair with Bathsheba, the rebellion of Absalom, and the story of Amnon's incestuous affair with his half sister Tamar. Moreover, this criterion confirms Solomon's toleration and promotion of the worship of foreign gods in Jerusalem.

The Yahwist Epic

Perhaps the most important hypothesis raised in this chapter is the theory of the writing of the Yahwist or J epic, which was without doubt the single most important literary accomplishment in Israel up to the time of its composition in about 950–930 BCE. Although some scholars began in the 1970s to challenge the documentary hypothesis, and with that the writing of J, others have reaffirmed the classical view, often with modifications, such as looking at J as the work not of an individual but as the work of a "school." The debate on the scope and contents of the Yahwist document will obviously continue for many decades. Nevertheless, this discussion and even disagreement show both the vitality and the limitations of the historical method. It would be nice if scholars had more pieces of the jigsaw puzzle to work with, but we must continue to work with the evidence we have. We have no other choice.

Form Criticism

Form criticism, the study of oral tradition and the repeatable liturgical context in which many of our traditions first arose, is still a focus of a great deal of Old Testament scholarship. The discipline is still in its relative infancy, and there is always more to be done, especially as scholars work toward building a new consensus. It is essential to continue to hone our methodology to develop a better understanding of the building blocks that served as the foundation for the stories in the Pentateuch.

*   *   *

In many ways, this chapter has attempted to bring together material found in all of the previous chapters by folding into a single hypothesis the conclusions of previous chapters. The exercise of drawing more comprehensive conclusions is probably the single most important and certainly the most challenging work that historians can attempt. It is always easier and safer to look at micro-issues in detail, but the macro-picture should always be the objective of the historian—to see the big picture.

In that regard, there are always competing theories because equally qualified specialists can and often do interpret the same evidence differently and, therefore, draw very different conclusions. As we have already observed, biblical scholarship is not an exact science, even though the methodology is objective and scientific. What scholars always agree upon is the method, the historical method, and that is an essential element to keep in mind at every stage in our investigation.

NOTES

1. Or, one should perhaps say monarchies for the period after 922 BCE, following the civil war and the division of the kingdom of Israel into two kingdoms, Israel in the north and Judah in the south.

2. The reference to Yahweh's Torah is to the law book discovered during the renovation of the Jerusalem temple in 621 BCE during the reign of King Josiah.

3. The book of the Annals of the Kings of Israel is mentioned in 1 Kings 14:19; 15:31; 16:5, 14, 20, 27; 22:39; 2 Kings 1:18; 10:34; 13:8, 12; 14:15, 28; 15:11, 15, 21, 26, 31. The book of the Annals of the Kings of Judah is mentioned in 1 Kings 14:29; 15:7, 23; 22:45; 2 Kings 8:23; 12:19; 14:18; 15:6, 36; 16:19; 20:20; 21:17, 25; 23:28; 24:5.

4. The word *asherah* appears as both the name of the female consort of the Canaanite god El, and as her wooden pole or cult symbol.

5. Mount Tabor is referred to, although not by name, as a place of sacrifice in Deuteronomy 33:18–19.

6. "I will tell of the decree of the LORD (Yahweh): He said to me,

'You are my son;

today I have begotten you.

Ask of me, and I will make the nations your heritage,

and the ends of the earth your possession.'"

7. In the context of an oracle in which it is made clear that God established a covenant with David and his descendants to serve as kings of Israel (Psalm 89:19–37), we read in verses 26–27:

"He [David] shall cry to me,

'You are my Father, my God,

and the Rock of my salvation!'

I will make him the firstborn,

the highest of the kings of the earth."

8. "I [Yahweh] will be a father to him [David],

and he shall be a son to me."

9. In a passage proclaiming the divine birth or adoption of the king as Yahweh's son on the occasion of his coronation, we read:

For a child has been born to us,

a son given to us;

authority rests upon his shoulders;

and he is named Wonderful Counselor, Mighty God,

Everlasting Father, Prince of Peace.

The passage lists the coronation names of the new king in a manner similar to the coronation of Egyptian pharaohs on the occasion of their accession to the throne.

10. Alone in the entire Old Testament, this single verse within a psalm, apparently composed for a royal wedding, appears to call the king "God" and, therefore, appears to regard him as divine:

Your throne, O God, endures forever and ever.

Your royal scepter is a scepter of equity.

The following verse (Psalm 45:7) reflects the more normative view that Israel's king is the *anointed* of God: "Therefore God, your God, has anointed you with the oil of gladness beyond your companions."

11. The dating of the reigns of the first kings of Israel is challenging, and Saul's dates are particularly problematic. The reigns of David and Solomon are reported to have extended

for forty years each (2 Samuel 5:4 and 1 Kings 11:42). These chronological references belong to the framework of the Deuteronomistic historian and are, at best, round numbers, although forty years for both men is likely not far wrong. Most scholars date the end of Solomon's reign in 922 BCE, which provides a date of about 1000 BCE for the beginning of David's reign. The Deuteronomistic historian's note about the length of Saul's reign appears in the defective text of 1 Samuel 13:1 ("Saul was . . . years old when he began to reign; and he reigned . . . and two years over Israel."). It is not clear how old Saul was when he became king (the number is missing from the Hebrew text), and the length of his reign is also deficient: "X and two years," with X as the missing word. Assuming that "two" is part of the number of years of Saul's reign, the text likely reported twelve, twenty-two, or thirty-two years as the length of his reign. Twelve is too little time in which to fit all of Saul's military campaigns, and thirty-two is probably too great if we note that Saul's oldest son, Jonathan, had only a single son under the age of five at the time Saul and Jonathan fell at Gilboa. Inasmuch as people married and had children at a young age, at the time of his death Jonathan was likely not older than thirty, and Saul, therefore, not much older than fifty. Following this reasoning, we come up with twenty-two as the likeliest number for reconstructing the defective text and, accordingly, assign Saul's reign to circa 1022 BCE–circa 1000 BCE.

12. Because of the similarities of these stories, some scholars regard them as variant reports of a single incident.

13. Ashurites is the name generally given to the Assyrians, a claim that makes no sense whatsoever in this passage. Some have read this as a reference to the Asherites (the tribe of Asher), but they were far to the north and were never under the rule of either Saul or Ishbaal.

14. "Over all Israel" certainly does not refer to the whole of Israel and may simply be a summary of the areas previously mentioned. The areas over which Saul and Ishbaal ruled were very limited.

15. Obed-Edom, a non-Yahwistic name meaning "servant or worshiper of (the god) Edom," was from the Philistine city of Gath, suggesting that he may have been one of the Philistine brigands loyal to David and explaining why David was willing to entrust this valued trophy to a foreigner, who by now had presumably become a Yahwist.

16. If laid on a map of the contemporary Middle East, the empire of David and Solomon would cover basically most but not all of modern-day Israel (including the occupied West Bank, but not including Gaza), western Syria, and western Jordan.

17. The kingdom of Geshur lay just to the east of the Sea of Chinnereth (better known as the Sea of Galilee). Geshur, interestingly, was a semiautonomous kingdom of about 350 square kilometers within the territories that Israel had conquered. David apparently made an alliance with Geshur by marrying Maacah, the daughter of King Talmai.

18. In fact, Solomon may have been under adult age at the time of his accession (1 Kings 3:7: "And now, O LORD [Yahweh] my God, you have made your servant king in place of my

father David, although I am only a little child; I do not know how to go out or come in"), although some scholars have suggested that this language should be taken figuratively as a sign of the king's humility. Nonetheless, the text suggests that Solomon apparently assumed no role in his own accession, which meant that responsibility fell to his mother and his political supporters.

19. Although Egyptian chronology is problematic, especially during the twenty-first dynasty when there were kings ruling from Tanis and high priests ruling from Thebes, Pharaoh Psusennes II, whose reign covered the years from circa 959 to circa 945 BCE, appears to be the most likely candidate for Solomon's father-in-law.

20. 1 Kings 11:4 ("For when Solomon was old, his wives turned away his heart after other gods") seems to blame the king's lapse on senility, but Solomon's tolerance for other gods dates back quite early to his marriage to the Egyptian princess (1 Kings 3:1).

21. A cor was an ancient Israelite measure. As a dry measure, it was probably equivalent to about fourteen bushels; as a wet measure, to between thirty-five and sixty gallons.

22. Although there are no archaeological remains of Solomon's temple, archaeologists have discovered remains of Canaanite temples at Ai, Arad, Beth-Shean, Hazor, Megiddo, Shechem, and Tell Tainat, all of which afford us a better understanding of temple architecture of the period.

23. The measurements found in the Bible are, of course, not in feet, but in a unit called the "cubit," with 1 cubit equal to about 18 inches. The cubit was actually a measure of length extending from the elbow to the tip of the middle finger. Difficulty in converting cubits into feet arises because the cubit was different for different people: the Egyptian cubit was 20.64 inches, the Roman cubit 17.4 inches, and the English cubit 18 inches. The exact length of the cubit in ancient Israel is disputed, but 18 inches is sufficient for our purposes.

24. The bread of the presence consisted of twelve loaves of unleavened bread, representing the twelve tribes of Israel, and appears to have symbolized Yahweh's presence (Leviticus 24:5–9).

25. The cherub (singular) or cherubim (plural) were composite mythical creatures on which Yahweh was sometimes thought to ride (2 Samuel 22:11; Psalms 18:10; Ezekiel 1; 10). Their exact appearance is not entirely clear, except for the fact that they had wings. Although it is uncertain whether Israelite cherubim looked anything like their counterpart in ancient Near Eastern (particularly Assyrian) art, they certainly bore no resemblance to the round-faced infant cherubs familiar from Western art.

26. 1 Kings 8 describes the carrying of the ark of the covenant of Yahweh into the temple, commemorating Yahweh's arrival in his throne room and guaranteeing his presence henceforth among his people.

27. Genesis 1:1, 2, 3, 4 (twice), 5, 6, 7, 8, 9, 10 (twice), 11, 12, 14, 16, 17, 18, 20, 21 (twice), 22, 24, 25 (twice), 26, 27 (twice), 28 (twice), 29, 31; 2:2, 3 (twice).

28. Genesis 2:4b, 5, 7, 8, 9, 15, 16, 18, 19, 21, 22.

29. It is interesting to note that although the combination *ĕlōhîm yahweh* is the rule in Genesis 2:4b–3:24, it occurs in the Pentateuch in only one other place (Exodus 9:30). Scholars generally conclude that the original version of J's creation story consistently used the name *Yahweh* alone and that *ĕlōhîm* was likely added in Genesis 2:4b–3:24 by the Priestly editors under the influence of the account in Genesis 1:1–2:4a.

30. Scholars have long recognized that the Priestly account of creation in Genesis 1:1–2:4a corresponds to elements in the Babylonian creation myth *Enuma eliš*, both in a variety of details and in the order of the acts of creation. Inasmuch as P was composed some-time after the Babylonian exile (586–538 BCE) (see the chart on p. 54), the half century in Babylonia apparently served as the occasion during which Babylonian influence informed the writing of this later creation myth. It is impossible to doubt that the cosmogony of the *Enuma eliš* served as the foundation for the cosmogony in Genesis 1:1–2:4a.

31. "You brought them in and planted them on the mountain of your own possession, the place O LORD (Yahweh), that you made your abode, the sanctuary, O LORD (Yahweh), that your hands have established."

32. "These are the kings who reigned over the land of Edom, before any king reigned over the Israelites."

33. Our author uses a different word for man in this instance in order to be able to make the pun, not the word *'ādām* (meaning humankind), but the word *iš* (meaning a male being). The Hebrew pun works in English if we stress that the wo-*man* was made from the *man*. In the case of the man's (*'ādām*) being made from the dust of the ground (*'adāmāh*), the pun does not, of course, work in English and is missed by the reader without the benefit of an accompanying footnote to the text of Genesis. Although it stretches the meaning of the orig-inal text, it would be as if Genesis 2:7 said that *Adam* was made from mac*adam* (the material often used in the construction of roadways).

34. Although the Yahwist occasionally slips into using Adam as a personal name, it is not until Genesis 5:3–5 that it stands unmistakably for a particular individual.

CHAPTER 5

MEDIATORS BETWEEN
YAHWEH AND ISRAEL

Turning aside for the moment from an examination of the history of Israel, I intend in this chapter to focus on the phenomenon of prophecy in ancient Israel and on some of the major prophetic figures of the northern kingdom. That is not as much of a detour as it may seem, because Israel's prophets were deeply immersed in history and understood history as the arena in which Israel's God Yahweh revealed himself and his will.

As mentioned in the previous chapter, the United Kingdom lasted for a period of less than a hundred years through the reigns of only three kings, Saul, David, and Solomon. Upon Solomon's death in 922 BCE, Jeroboam, who had once been Solomon's taskmaster over all the forced labor of the house of Joseph (1 Kings 11:26–28), led ten of the twelve tribes in a revolt against Jerusalem and set up the independent Kingdom of Israel in the north with Samaria as its capital and with himself as its first king (1 Kings 12:1–24). A much-diminished Kingdom of Judah survived in the south with Jerusalem as its capital and with Solomon's son Rehoboam as its king. The house of David continued to rule in Jerusalem for another three hundred thirty-five years until the demise of Judah and Jerusalem in 587 BCE at the hands of the Babylonians. The northern kingdom fared less well, lasting for two hundred years, although with little political stability, until it fell to the Assyrians in 722/721 BCE.

To afford a framework for this and subsequent chapters, I am providing here a comprehensive chronology of the kings of Israel and Judah:

THE UNITED KINGDOM (1020–922 BCE)

Saul (1020–1000)[1]
David (1000–961)
Solomon (961–922)

THE DIVIDED KINGDOM

THE KINGDOM OF ISRAEL (922–721)

THE KINGDOM OF JUDAH (922–587)

The Davidic Dynasty (922–587)

Jeroboam I (922–901)

Rehoboam (922–915)
Abijah (Abijam) (915–913)

Nabad (901–900)
Baasha (900–877)
Elah (877–876)
Zimri (7 days, 876)

Asa (913–873)

Omri Dynasty (876–843/2)
Omri (876–869)
Ahab (869–850)
Ahaziah (850–849)
Jehoram (849–843/842)

Jehoshaphat (873–849)

Jehoram (849–843)

Jehu Dynasty (843/2–745)
Jehu (843/742–815)

Ahaziah (843–842)
Athaliah (queen, 842–837)

Jehoahaz (815–802)
J(eh)oash (802–786)
Jeroboam II (786–746)
Zechariah (6 months, 746–745)

Joash (837–800)
Amaziah (800–783)
Uzziah (Azariah) (783–742)
Jotham (regent, 750–742)

Shallum (1 month, 745)
Menahem (745–737)

Jotham (king, 742–735)

Pekahiah (737–736)
Pekah (736–732)   Jehoahaz (Ahaz) (735–715)
Hoshea (732–724)

FALL OF SAMARIA (722/721)

Hezekiah (715–687/686)
Manasseh (687/686–642)
Amon (642–640)
Josiah (640–609)
Jehoahaz II (Shallum) (3 months, 609)
Jehoiakim (Eliakim) (609–598/597)
Jehoiachin (Jeconiah) (3 months, 598/597)
Zedekiah (Mattaniah) (597–587/586)
FALL OF JERUSALEM (587/586)

THE PHENOMENON OF PROPHECY

Let me state unequivocally and emphatically at the outset that nothing could be clearer than that the prophets of Israel were *not* prognosticators, that they were *not* fortune-tellers, that they did *not* predict the future. Christianity is not alone in mis-understanding the original role of Israel's prophets, although most of us owe our personal misunderstanding of Israelite prophecy to Christianity because the New Testament regularly juxtaposes a passage from one of the prophets of the Old Testament with the presumed fulfillment of that prophecy in an event in the life and ministry of Jesus or in the life of the early Christian church.

The Deuteronomistic historian (the author of Joshua, Judges, 1 and 2 Samuel, and 1 and 2 Kings) and the Chronicler (the author of 1 and 2 Chronicles, Ezra, and Nehemiah) both advanced their belief in the efficacy of God's word and pointed to subsequent events in Israel's history as the fulfillment of earlier prophecies. Late Judaism from the time just before and during the period of Christian beginnings also adopted the practice of applying the words of Israel's prophets to contemporary events. We find ample examples of that interpretation of prophecy not only in the New Testament but in contemporary Jewish literature as well, and especially in the

Dead Sea Scrolls. Jews had long since forgotten or ignored the fact that although there may be a timelessness to some of the words of Israel's prophets, the prophets spoke primarily to situations contemporaneous with their own lives in a way that was often stinging, biting, and cutting. The focus of the prophets was primarily on the present moment. To the extent that the prophets spoke about the future, they did not predict the future. Rather they spoke about the near future because they were convinced that the future is a necessary consequence of the present. As with everything that we have considered in this volume, a study of prophecy in ancient Israel is about *contextuality*. How were the prophets and the phenomenon of prophecy understood not by later generations, but in their *original* contexts?

Men and women who belong to the prophetic type are people who speak for God or a god as if they were under divine guidance. They are religious teachers who either claim to be or are regarded as speaking under divine inspiration or direction. They are men and women who experience the divine in such a way that they believe that they have received revelations from the divine order. They listen to, they obey, and they then speak what they believe is the word of their god. They are appointed or self-appointed spokespersons for a pressing issue, often an issue of social injustice. What distinguishes the prophet from the mystic is that the prophet, after speaking to or listening to his or her god, feels obligated to communicate that word to others. This understanding of the role of the prophet is expressed well in Jeremiah 1:9:

> Then the LORD (Yahweh) put out his hand and touched my mouth; and the LORD (Yahweh) said to me, "Now I have my words in your mouth."

The prophet invariably points beyond himself or herself to the source of the authority whose word the prophet is delivering. As such, the prophet is always under a supernatural or superhuman constraint and serves as a mediator between the divine and humankind. In the Old Testament, the prophetic word, the oracle, often begins with the formula "Thus says the LORD (Yahweh)" and often concludes with the formula "an oracle of the LORD (Yahweh)," thus reminding the audience that the prophet is a messenger or a mediator speaking at the behest and on behalf of Yahweh.

In his classic study of prophecy in ancient Israel, Johannes Lindblom defines ecstasy as:

an abnormal state of consciousness in which one is so intensely absorbed by one single idea or one single feeling, or by a group of ideas or feelings, that the normal stream of psychical life is more or less arrested. The bodily senses cease to function; one becomes impervious to impressions from without; consciousness is exalted above the ordinary level of daily experience; unconscious mental impressions and ideas come to the surface in the form of visions and auditions. . . . Ecstasy in this sense merely indicates the presence of certain abnormal psycho-physical conditions, an alteration of the normal equilibrium, a shifting of the threshold of consciousness. Of course the worth of ecstasy depends entirely on the objective value of the dominating idea or feeling.[2]

Lindblom and others have pointed out that various external stimuli were often used by prophets to induce such mental rapture: intoxication with different kinds of hallucinogenic foods or drinks, fasting, isolation, self-flagellation, dancing, spinning, music, and so on. Dreams, prayer, and meditation are, in addition, virtually universal methods of communicating with the divine. Although full-blown ecstasy may not be a component in all prophecy, some form of psychical exaltation or inspiration is characteristic of all prophets. In addition, prophets almost always point to a single moment that serves as the occasion of the prophet's special call and commission by some higher power.

To underscore the timelessness, indeed the contemporaneousness, of the prophetic phenomenon and the special call and commission of the appointed mediator, I cite the following passage from the writings of Martin Luther King Jr.:

After a particularly strenuous day, I settled in bed at a late hour. My wife had already fallen asleep and I was about to doze off when the telephone rang. An angry voice said, "Listen, nigger, we've taken all we want from you. Before next week you'll be sorry you ever came to Montgomery." I hung up, but I could not sleep. It seemed that all of my fears had come down on me at once. I had reached the saturation point.

I got out of bed and began to walk the floor. Finally, I went to the kitchen and heated a pot of coffee. I was ready to give up. I tried to think of a way to move out of the picture without appearing to be a coward. In this state of exhaustion, when my courage had almost gone, I determined to take my problem to God. My head in my hands, I bowed over the kitchen table and prayed aloud. The words I spoke to God that midnight are still vivid in my memory. "I am here taking a stand for what I believe is right. But now I am afraid. The people are looking to me for leadership, and if I stand before them without strength and courage, they too will falter. I am at the end of my powers. I have nothing left. I've come to the point where I can't face it alone."

At that moment I experienced the presence of the Divine as I had never before experienced him. It seemed as though I could hear the quiet assurance of an inner voice, saying, "Stand up for righteousness, stand up for truth. God will be at your side forever." Almost at once my fears began to pass from me. My uncertainty disappeared. I was ready to face anything. The outer situation remained the same, but God had given me inner calm.[3]

This contemporary first-person description of Martin Luther King Jr.'s "call and commission" affords significant insight into the calls and commissions of Israel's prophets and of prophets in other religious traditions. The virtually universal phenomenon of the prophetic experience across time and cultures is evidence that this experience is deeply rooted in human nature, although it is obviously limited to the very few. We generally refer to this incursion of the divine spirit (*rûah*) into the human psyche as *inspiration* (from the Latin verb *inspirare*), meaning "to blow or to breathe into or upon." The word implies the sense that the feeling that we refer to as *inspiration*, even in the contemporary form of Dr. King's "inner voice," carries with it the sense that this voice, this power, originates from a power or force outside the individual.

Once again Lindblom affords us some insight into the nature of this experience when he says:

In the technical language of psychology it might be described rather differently, thus: the characteristic of inspiration in a general sense is that certain ideas, images, emotions, impulses from the subconscious, subliminal, unconscious, co-conscious self (whichever term may be used) arise in the mind so spontaneously and so independently of reflection and meditation, that the inspired person feels as though his ideas were coming not from himself, but from another realm, and are given him by a power other than himself. If the inspiration is of a religious nature, this "other power" is identified with the deity, and "the other realm" with the supernatural or heavenly world.[4]

Prophetic personalities often relate *visionary* or *auditory* experiences (*visions* or *auditions*) or sometimes both. Dr. King's account reflects an *audition*. Often such prophetic personalities speak of "seeing with the inner eye of the soul" or, as in the case of Martin Luther King, of "hearing through an inner voice," revealing that these experiences were not, in fact, caused or evoked by an exterior object or person. Unsure of the source of such experiences, some refer to them as hallucinations, others as imaginative experiences. Although the experiences themselves may be internal and imaginative, what were clearly objective and external were the historical circumstances that generally gave rise to prophecy in ancient Israel, and in the instance above, to the call and commission of Martin Luther King Jr.

Lindblom's definition of a prophet is helpful:

> A prophet may be characterized as *a person who, because he is conscious of having been specially chosen and called, feels forced to perform actions and proclaim ideas which, in a mental state of intense inspiration or real ecstasy, have been indicated to him in the form of divine revelations.*[5]

Prophecy in ancient Israel has its roots both in the phenomenon of prophecy in general and in ancient Near Eastern prophecy more specifically. Evidence of prophecy has been found in the Ebla texts from northern Syria as early as the third millennium BCE, in Ugaritic tablets near the Mediterranean coast of Syria from the second millennium BCE, in a corpus of old Aramaic inscriptions from about 800 BCE, in an Ammonite inscription from about 700 BCE, in Hittite texts from central Anatolia from the latter part of the mid-second millennium BCE, and in Mesopotamian texts from the region of Mari, Assyria, and Babylonia from the second and first millennia BCE.

Although not all of the evidence from these ancient sources is clear and unequivocal, and although we do not have from these sources the actual texts of prophetic oracles, the existence of the office of prophet is reasonably certain from very ancient times. Where there are examples of relatively clearer evidence, we find that although some prophetic oracles may have been unsolicited, it was often the case that a crisis prompted someone, perhaps a king, to make an inquiry from a deity, who generally responded with an oral or written message of assurance to the king. Apparently until the rise of Israelite prophecy, ancient Near Eastern prophetic oracles rarely admonished the king.

The word "prophet" most frequently represents in English the Hebrew word *nābî'*, a word that is likely not of Hebrew origin. The closest cognate is the Akkadian word *nabītu*, although the Mari word *nabû*, perhaps meaning "diviner," has also been proposed. The fact that the Hebrew word was borrowed from another language implies that the practice was not unique to Israel but that Israel apparently shared prophetic activity with and possibly learned about it from its neighbors.

1 Samuel 9:9 says: "Formerly in Israel, anyone who went to inquire of God would say, 'Come, let us go to the seer'; for the one who is now called a prophet (*nābî'*) was formerly called a seer (*rō'eh*)," a word found primarily in the books of Samuel and Chronicles. There are two other terms that are used occasionally in the Old Testament to describe such an individual: *ḥōzeh* (meaning "a visionary" or "a seer") and *'îš (ha) 'ĕlōhîm* (meaning "a man of God"). All of these terms imply that the prophet is a person who speaks in the name of Israel's God Yahweh.

EARLY PROPHECY IN ISRAEL

We must admit at the outset that we know nothing of the beginnings of prophecy in ancient Israel. Although the Pentateuch uses the word prophet for several individuals, including Abraham, Moses, Aaron, Miriam, and others, this use of the word is by retrospection. There were in this early period no individuals who functioned like an Elijah, an Amos, an Isaiah, or a Jeremiah. In the books of the so-called former prophets (Joshua, Judges, 1 and 2 Samuel, and 1 and 2 Kings), the word is used first in Judges of the "prophetess" Deborah, although it is not clear how Deborah functioned as a "prophetess," except that she is described in Judges 4:4–5 as sitting "under a palm of Deborah," to which the Israelites came for judgment.

Some scholars maintain that Samuel was the first of the prophets, but Samuel is also called judge and priest. Samuel was apparently a leader of the prophetic group known as "the sons of the prophets," which were apparently prophetic guilds that taught the practice of prophecy through the use of external stimuli, such as the slashing of one's self (1 Kings 20:35) to induce the state of prophetic ecstasy. We actually first encounter prophets in 1 Samuel 10:5–8, where it is reported that Saul met "a band of prophets coming down from the shrine with harp, tambourine, flute, and lyre playing in front of them." They are described as being "in a prophetic frenzy," and Saul is described as also falling into prophetic ecstasy on meeting them and of being "turned into a different person." This ancient phenomenon of prophetic ecstasy was apparently contagious, just as it is still contagious today in Pentecostal churches in the United States.

THE MIRACLE WORKER: ELISHA

The ministry of Elisha, Elijah's designated successor, covered half a century from about 850 to 800 BCE and the reigns of four kings of Israel: Jehoram, Jehu, Jehoahaz, and Joash. The name Elisha means "My God is salvation." One of the most interesting stories in the Elisha cycle tells of the prophet asking for a musician to play a stringed instrument in order to induce the prophetic state (2 Kings 3:15), a not uncommon feature of early prophecy.

Elisha functions in the tradition primarily as a miracle worker. Following the ascension of Elijah into heaven in the fiery whirlwind (2 Kings 2:1–12), Elisha parted the waters of the Jordan (2 Kings 2:13–14), just as Moses had parted the waters of the sea of reeds (Exodus 14:1–25) and as Yahweh had parted the waters of the Jordan when the people prepared to enter the promised land (Joshua 3:1–17). Elisha also sweetened a spring of bitter water (2 Kings 2:19–22), just as Moses had done before him at Marah (Exodus 15:23–25). Elisha multiplied the oil for the poor widow (2 Kings 4:1–7), just as Elijah had previously done (1 Kings 17:8–16); and restored life to the Shunammite woman's dead son (2 Kings 4:8–37), just as Elijah had previously done (1 Kings 17:17–24). He rendered harmless a pot of poisonous stew (2 Kings 4:38–41), multiplied a few loaves of bread (2 Kings 4:42–44), healed Namaan of leprosy (2 Kings 5:1–19), and made an iron ax head float for the man who had lost it in the water (2 Kings 6:1–7). These stories indicate the uncontrolled and imitative power of legend in the development of oral tradition.

Interestingly, many of the miracle stories associated with Elisha parallel stories associated earlier with Moses and Elijah. Moreover, many of the miracle stories associated with Elijah and Elisha in the books of 1 and 2 Kings serve as the basis for some of the miracle stories associated with Jesus in the New Testament.

ONE VOICE AGAINST FOUR HUNDRED: MICAIAH

There is in 1 Kings 22 a story of another prophet, Micaiah (meaning perhaps "who is like Yah[weh]"), who appears in an interesting narrative about oracular inquiries by the kings of Israel and Judah, Ahab and Jehoshaphat, respectively. The two kings discussed a treaty between them for the purpose of reacquiring from the Syrians the city of Ramoth-Gilead in Transjordan (1 Kings 22:3–4), which King Omri of Israel had earlier ceded to Syria but which had not been returned as promised.

Before going to battle against the Syrians, however, Jehoshaphat recommended asking about Yahweh's will in the matter by inquiring of Ahab's four hundred court prophets, who with one voice extended Yahweh's approval to the mission (22:6). Suspicious of their quick and unqualified acquiescence, Jehoshaphat asked if there were no other prophets who might be consulted regarding the matter. Ahab replied that there was still one more prophet who might be asked, Micaiah son of Imlah, but that he was reluctant to ask Micaiah because he always prophesied unfavorably against the king.

When consulted, Micaiah initially told the kings to go to war against Syria at Ramoth-Gilead and win the victory. But Ahab pressed Micaiah and admonished him to tell the truth and not simply echo what the kings wanted to hear, to which Micaiah replied, "I saw all Israel scattered on the mountains, like sheep that have no shepherd" (22:17). The story in 1 Kings ends with the victory of the Syrians over Israel and Judah and the death of King Ahab. Although it is difficult to use this story in 1 Kings 22 for a historical reconstruction of the incident, the story does afford interesting insight into the question of prophecy: how does one distinguish between true and false prophets and how does one know who is, in fact, delivering an oracle from Yahweh, and who is not?

What is important about Micaiah is not that he accurately predicted that Israel and Judah would lose the battle against Syria for Ramoth-Gilead. What is important is that he opposed the two kings and the four hundred mercenary prophets in Ahab's court and spoke not what the kings wanted to hear, but what he believed was the word of Yahweh. Like Elijah before him, Micaiah no longer blindly supported the political establishment, represented in the story by the four hundred court prophets, who told Jehoshaphat and Ahab exactly what they wanted to hear.

The concept of Yahweh as a god of history meant that the prophets spoke about historical events, including in this case the upcoming battle with the Syrians. The significance of the story about Micaiah is clear—honest people read history differently, especially when it comes to times of war. People often disagree on what is and what is not a just war and what the outcome of going to war might be. Opposing the establishment is not always popular, but history remembers those who, in their wisdom, foresight, and vision, know when it is time to oppose a decision to go to war. People remember the Micaiahs and their contribution to history, even if only with a few verses in the Deuteronomistic History.

YAHWEH IS PREPARING TO DESTROY ISRAEL: AMOS

Amos is the earliest of the prophetic books and has its origin in events in the mid-eighth century BCE. It is also the first prophetic book to contain examples of the prophetic oracle. The title or superscription of the book (Amos 1:1) places the prophet during the reigns of King Uzziah of Judah (783–742 BCE) and King Jeroboam II of Israel (786–746 BCE). Information elsewhere in the book indicates that Amos was originally a native of the southern kingdom of Judah but that he went to the northern kingdom of Israel to proclaim the word of Yahweh, probably during the last decade of Jeroboam's reign, likely about 750 BCE.

The reigns of both Uzziah and Jeroboam were quite long and were relatively peaceful and prosperous, with no serious threats to the two small kingdoms from their more powerful neighbors in Egypt and Mesopotamia. However, toward the end of the reigns of these two kings, a serious threat loomed on the horizon in the form of the aggressive King Tiglath-Pileser III of Assyria (745–727 BCE), who was determined to incorporate the three smaller western states of Syria, Israel, and Judah into his empire. Although Tiglath-Pileser succeeded in conquering Syria (732 BCE), the conquest of Israel was actually achieved a decade later in 722/721 BCE by King Sargon II (721–705 BCE), at which time the history of the northern kingdom came to an end, probably some thirty or so years after Amos had prophesied against the northern kingdom.

The book of Amos is a collection of Amos's oracles and also of stories and traditions about the prophet. It is likely that the material that eventually found its way into this book was collected by disciples or followers of the prophet, perhaps after his death. It is obvious that our current book underwent later editing, probably during the period of the Babylonian exile (586–539 BCE). The original ending of the book was almost certainly Amos 9:8a: "The eyes of the Lord GOD (Yahweh) are upon the sinful kingdom, and I will utterly destroy it from the face of the earth." The continuation of this verse in 9:8b "except that I will not utterly destroy the house of Jacob" is quite evidently a latter addition and part of a sixth-century BCE editorial ending that provides an important insight into the way in which books of the Bible were edited (and updated) by later scribes.

The call and commission of Amos are reported not by Amos, but in the third person by a later writer, perhaps a disciple of the prophet. We read in 7:10–15:

7:10Then Amaziah, the priest of Bethel, sent to King Jeroboam of Israel, saying, "Amos has conspired against you in the very center of the house of Israel; the land is not able to bear all his words. 11For thus Amos has said,

'Jeroboam shall die by the sword,

and Israel must go into exile away from his land.'"

12And Amaziah said to Amos, "O seer, go, flee away to the land of Judah, earn your bread there, and prophesy there; 13but never again prophesy at Bethel, for it is the king's sanctuary, and it is a temple of the kingdom."

14Then Amos answered Amaziah, "I am no prophet, nor a prophet's son; but I am a herdsman, and a dresser of sycamore trees, 15and the LORD (Yahweh) took me from following the flock, and the LORD (Yahweh) said to me, 'Go, prophesy to my people Israel.'"

The situation described in these few verses is very clear. Amaziah was evidently the priest at the royal sanctuary at Bethel, a major religious center that had been associated earlier with the patriarch Jacob (see above, pp. 71–72). Amos had apparently gone to Bethel from his native Judah, perhaps for a pilgrimage festival, and was challenged by Amaziah, who accused the prophet of conspiracy against the king because of his accusations against Israel. Amaziah speaks to Amos dismissively, calling him a "seer" or "a visionary" (ḥōzeh), and tells him to go back to Judah from whence he came and to prophesy there for hire. Amos replies that he is not a professional prophet, neither is he a member of one of the prophetic guilds, but that he is a simple herdsman and a pincher of sycamore fruit and that he is in Bethel on the order of Yahweh to prophesy against the people of Israel.

This passage is followed by what may be Amos's earliest oracle, a condemnation of Amaziah and an announcement of the impending destruction of Israel at the hand of Assyria (7:16–17):

7:16Now therefore hear the word of the LORD (Yahweh).

You say, "Do not prophesy against Israel,

and do not preach against the house of Isaac.'

17Therefore thus says the LORD (Yahweh):

'Your wife shall become a prostitute in the city,

and your sons and your daughters shall fall by the sword,

and your land shall be parceled out by line;

you yourself shall die in an unclean land,

and Israel shall surely go into exile away from its land."

Amos's message is direct and addresses clearly and unequivocally circumstances contemporaneous with the time of its delivery. The prophet introduces his oracles as words of Yahweh with the common formulas "Hear the word of Yahweh," "Hear this word that Yahweh has spoken," and "Thus says Yahweh." Amos's oracles are built on the principle of Hebrew poetry, the unit of which was the couplet in which the same idea is expressed slightly differently in two consecutive lines. Amos introduces his initial oracle in response to Amaziah's muttering command: "Do not prophesy against Israel" and "Do not preach against the house of Isaac" (7:16) by telling the priest what Yahweh has to say.

Amos's oracle (7:17) is five simple lines in poetic parallelism:

your wife shall become a prostitute in the city,
your sons and daughters shall fall by the sword,
your land shall be parceled out by line,
you yourself shall die in an unclean land, and
Israel shall surely go into exile away from its land.

The message is clear and uncompromising: Israel will be totally destroyed and its people will perish or be sent into exile, while the land will be carved up by the conquerors (presumably the Assyrians).

Turning to the beginning of the book, obviously not the words of the prophet himself, we read in the superscription the curious phrase "the *words* of Amos, . . . which he *saw*." Interestingly, the prophet is represented as having *seen*, not as having *heard*, the *words* of Yahweh. The very nature of the vision/audition is such that the prophet is represented as having *seen* the prophetic *words* of Yahweh (so too Isaiah 2:1: "The *word* that Isaiah son of Amoz *saw* concerning Judah and Jerusalem").

The brief statement in verse 2 summarizes the theme of the book: The words of Yahweh, as spoken by (or through) the Judean (southern) prophet, roar like a lion toward the north to signal the destruction of the land of (northern) Israel. Notice once again the simplicity of the parallelism in the two poetic couplets:

The LORD (Yahweh) roars from Zion,
        and utters his voice from Jerusalem;
the pastures of the shepherds wither,
        and the top of Carmel dries up.

Element by element is repeated in the strict poetic parallelism that characterizes the form in which Amos delivers his simple but poignant oracles against the northern kingdom.

This introduction to the book is followed in 1:3–2:16 by a series of oracles against the nations, culminating in an oracle against Israel. The indictment begins with an oracle against Israel's longtime adversary Syria, explaining the reasons for the impending destruction of that neighboring enemy (1:3–5). The delivery of this oracle by Amos in the midst of the religious festival at Bethel is certain to have attracted a large crowd as the prophet spoke out against a hated rival. The oracle against Syria was followed by oracles against Gaza, an old Philistine foe (1:6–8); against Tyre, a longtime Israelite ally (1:9–10); against Edom, the nation fathered by Jacob-Israel's twin brother, Esau (1:11–12); against the Ammonites, a rival neighbor to the east (1:13–15); against Moab, another rival neighbor to the east (2:1–3); and against Judah, the southern kingdom of the former United Kingdom of Israel (2:4–5). Finally the longest and most biting indictment of all is directed against the northern kingdom of Israel (2:6–16). By now the prophet had presumably attracted a crowd around him as he moved closer and closer, preparing for his (or Yahweh's) attack against the home audience gathered for the pilgrimage festival.

Amos's (or should we say Yahweh's?) most bitter criticism is reserved for Israel herself, Yahweh's chosen people (3:2):

> You only have I known of all the families of the earth;
> therefore I will punish you for all your iniquities.

One by one, the prophet lays out indictments against the nation for its multifold sins: oppression of the needy, violence and robbery against their kinsmen, greed, selfishness, rejection of their prophets, trampling of the poor, affliction of the righteous, and so on. In spite of multiple warnings in the form of destruction, pestilence, killing young Israelites, and capturing the people's horses, the people of Israel continue to reject Yahweh. What will it take for them to understand that Yahweh is tired of their faithlessness? Yahweh no longer wants anything more to do with their empty prayers and their meaningless sacrificial offerings (5:21–24):

> 5:21I hate, I despise your festivals,
> and I take no delight in your solemn assemblies.
> 22Even though you offer me your burnt offerings and grain offerings,

I will not accept them;

and the offerings of well-being of your fatted animals

I will not look upon.

₂₃Take way from me the noise of your songs;

I will not listen to the melody of your harps.

₂₄But let justice roll down like waters,

and righteousness like an ever-flowing stream.

In other words, you are now gathered here at Bethel for this great pilgrimage festival, but Yahweh will have nothing to do with the festival or with you. If you want to know what is expected from you, that is very simple: not your prayers, not your offerings, not your songs, not your music, but rather Yahweh requires the covenant demands of justice and righteousness toward one another.

The geography of this section is particularly interesting—Amos has moved diagonally to make an "X" with Israel as the bull's eye. It is Israel that will suffer most seriously from Yahweh's indictment.

Finally, in a series of five visions, the first four of which are introduced by the formula "This is what the Lord GOD (Yahweh) showed me," Amos adds further to the indictment against Israel. Amos *saw* the following:

(1) A locust plague about to consume the crop at the time of the latter growth, the crop for the people (7:1–3). The prophet pleaded with Yahweh, who changed his mind and decided not to destroy the people.

(2) A supernatural shower of fire (7:4–6). This cosmic fire brought a severe drought to the land. Once again the prophet pleaded with Yahweh, who again changed his mind and decided not to destroy the people.

(3) A man with a plumb line in his hand standing beside a wall built with a plumb line (7:7–9). The man with the plumb line was measuring the deviation of the wall, just as Yahweh was measuring the deviation of his people from the straight line of covenant righteousness that he expected from them.

(4) A basket of summer fruit (8:1–3). The word in Hebrew for "summer fruit," *qayitz*, reminds the prophet of the Hebrew word for "end," *qētz*, an apparent pun that signals that Israel's end is near.

(5) A vision of Yahweh destroying the people in the sanctuary. There will be no escape, not in the heights of Mount Carmel nor in the depths of Sheol, the underworld (9:1–4).

The first four visions are probably examples of what Lindblom calls symbolic perceptions, observations of real objects in the material world, which the prophet believed came as signs from the hand of Yahweh and which reveal a deeper religious significance.[6] In other words, Amos literally saw a swarm of locusts, a drought, a man with a plumb line, and a basket of summer fruit. What is more important, however, is the *meaning* that Amos saw in these otherwise everyday natural events; he saw them as messages from Yahweh about Israel's waywardness and impending destruction.

Amos 6:8 states the case clearly:

The Lord GOD (Yahweh) has sworn by himself
(says the LORD [Yahweh], the God of hosts):
I abhor the pride of Jacob
and hate his strongholds;
and I will deliver up the city [Samaria]
and all that is in it.

It is no wonder that the prophet's final words in 9:8a are "The eyes of the Lord GOD (Yahweh) are upon a sinful kingdom, and I will destroy it from the face of the earth."

There remains in our study of Amos one important unanswered question: Why did the oracles of Amos find their way into a distinctive *book*, when none of the words of his prophetic predecessors did? Surely Nathan, Elijah, Elisha, Micaiah, and others made an impression on Israelite religion, but the record of the activities of those earlier prophets are contained only in the much later writings of the Deuteronomistic historian, where we have only fragments of their preaching reported secondhand.

Scholars can, of course, only speculate about why Amos was the first prophet whose spoken oracles found their way into a distinctive collection. We have in the book of Amos a compilation of many of the prophet's very own words, probably preserved quite faithfully, and couched in narrative material that for the first time preserved for future generations a reasonably accurate glance into a single individual and his place in Israel's religious history.

I would venture to speculate that there might be two reasons for this decision to write the words of Amos into a distinct book. First, Amos consciously distinguished himself from his predecessors because he was not a professional prophet and he had not been trained in one of the prophetic guilds or professional academies. Neither was Amos a mercenary prophet, a prophet for hire in the royal court. In his own mind, Amos was doing what Yahweh had always intended his prophets to do, but Amos discharged that function with a faithfulness and simplicity that had not been previously seen in Israel. Second, and no less important, the message of Amos's oracles was validated in relatively short order through the destruction of Samaria and the fall of the northern kingdom in 722/721 BCE, relatively soon after Amos had delivered his scathing indictment against the nations.

Just a generation after Amos spoke at the sanctuary at Bethel, there were apparently still some individuals, perhaps followers or disciples of the prophet, who remembered his oracles and enough about the man to assemble into a book the material that we find in Amos 1:1–9:8a. As I remarked above, the material in Amos 9:8b–15 clearly refers to a much later period of history.

There are two possible explanations for those final verses of the book:

—except that I will not utterly destroy the house of Jacob,
says the LORD (Yahweh).
9For lo, I will command,
and shake the house of Israel among all the nations
as one shakes with a sieve,
but no pebble shall fall to the ground.
10All the sinners of my people shall die by the sword,
who say, "Evil shall not overtake or meet us."

11On that day I will raise up the booth of David that is fallen
and repair its breaches and raise up its ruins,
and rebuild it as in the days of old;
12in order that they may possess the remnants of Edom
and all the nations who are called by my name,
says the LORD (Yahweh) who does this.
13The time is surely coming, says the LORD (Yahweh),
when the one who plows shall overtake the one who reaps,
and the treader of grapes the one who sows the seed;
the mountains shall drip sweet wine,
and all the hills shall flow with it.
14I will restore the fortunes of my people Israel,
and they shall rebuild the ruined cities and inhabit them;
they shall plant vineyards and drink their wine,
and they shall make gardens and eat their fruit.

₁₅I will plant them upon their land,

and they shall never again be plucked up out of the land that I have given them,

says the LORD (Yahweh) their God.

Either the prophet himself had a very long-range view of history and could see in detail events two hundred years into the future, or those final verses are an addition to the original book by a much later writer. There can be no doubt that the latter explanation is more reasonable. The former requires an understanding of prophecy for which there is no basis, and it requires the implausible belief that people can see with detail centuries into the future, a position that most biblical scholars and I reject outright.

Unlike the earlier chapters of Amos, verse 9:8b reflects the fact that not all of Israel was destroyed, because the southern kingdom of Judah, in fact, survived the Assyrian assault of 722/721 BCE and later fell to the Babylonian Empire one hundred thirty-five years afterward in 587 BCE. In addition, whereas the oracles of Amos consistently pronounce Yahweh's judgment against the people as a whole, Amos 9:9–10 reserves that judgment for sinners only. Finally, Amos 9:11–15 assumes a historical situation totally different from the rest of the book. These verses presuppose the period of the Babylonian exile (586–539 BCE), when the southern kingdom of Judah (the booth of David) had already fallen (587/586 BCE) and Yahweh was about to restore the Davidic kingdom and rebuild its cities (9:11). These final seven-plus verses of the book of Amos could not have been written much earlier than 540 BCE, more than two hundred years after Amos prophesied against Israel in about 750 BCE. They obviously come from the hand of a later editor of the book, a scribe who thought it was important for Amos to speak meaningfully to the new circumstances of a subsequent generation and who, therefore, added these verses to the text.

GO MARRY AN ADULTERESS: HOSEA

Hosea's career followed closely upon that of Amos. Both prophesied in the northern kingdom of Israel during the latter years of the reign of King Jeroboam II (786–746 BCE), although Hosea's activity apparently extended into the reign of King Hoshea (732–724 BCE) (Hosea 13:10–11; cf. also 2 Kings 17:4). Some of Hosea's teachings, specifically Hosea 5:8–14, seem to reflect the period of the war that northern

Israel and Syria waged against the southern kingdom of Judah to force Judah into their anti-Assyrian alliance (735–733 BCE). Hosea 13:16 appears to anticipate but not confirm the fall of Samaria to the Assyrians in 721 BCE. In the course of the three decades from 750 to 721 BCE, Hosea may have seen seven kings of northern Israel come and go in a series of court intrigues and murders that included Jeroboam II, Zechariah, Shallum, Menahem, Pekahiah, Pekah, and Hoshea.

The title or superscription of the book (Hosea 1:1) places Hosea's prophetic activity during the reigns of kings Uzziah (783–742 BCE), Jotham (742–735 BCE), Ahaz (735–715), and Hezekiah (715–687/686 BCE) of Judah; and of King Jeroboam II (786–746 BCE) of Israel. But the verse's list of the kings of northern Israel is clearly incomplete, as the reigns of Ahaz and Hezekiah of Judah take us more than three decades beyond the reign of Jeroboam of Israel. This superscription, like the superscriptions to other prophetic books (such as Isaiah 1:1; Joel 1:1; Amos 1:1; Micah 1:1; Zephaniah 1:1; and Zechariah 1:1) is likely the work of editors from the exilic or post-exilic period.

This minor detail of chronology is perhaps the least of the challenges of the book of Hosea. With the exception of the book of Job, Hosea is probably the most difficult book of the Old Testament to understand. The text and language of the book are problematic, making the meaning obscure in many instances and almost unreadable in some places. The style of the book is also difficult, including several problematic shifts of speakers between the first and the third persons. There are rarely clear indications of the individual units in Hosea, and the book abounds in linguistic idiosyncrasies. The reasons for these problems are not entirely clear, so it is uncertain whether they existed at the earliest stage in the composition of the book or are the result of subsequent editing.

It is possible that some of the difficulties in the book of Hosea may be attributable to our lack of familiarity with the dialect of Hebrew that was spoken in northern Israel and in which the book may initially have been written. With that in mind, some scholars have suggested looking at Hosea in light of epigraphic evidence, especially texts from the excavations at Ugarit, in the hope that such evidence might assist in clarifying some of the book's more difficult passages and more obscure vocabulary. That said, we can either throw up our hands in despair and move on to another topic or we can do our best and try to understand what is most clear about the prophet Hosea and the book. I prefer to make an effort at the latter, riddled with challenges as that course may be.

We have very little biographical information about the prophet, and what we do have is confusing and often obscure. The name Hosea is an abbreviated form of Hoshaiah, which means in Hebrew "Yahweh has saved" or "Yahweh has delivered." The book opens with a third-person account of Hosea's call and of serious misfortunes with his family (Hosea 1:2–6, 8–9), events that were clearly integral to the prophet's call and commission. The story opens with Yahweh's command to Hosea to marry a whore and to have children of whoredom, because the land of Israel has committed great whoredom by its unfaithfulness to Yahweh. We are told that Hosea's wife Gomer, the daughter of Ziblaim, bore the prophet three children.

Hosea gave the children symbolic names, suggesting that he regarded them as living oracles, carrying in their names messages from Yahweh. Yahweh commanded Hosea to name his first son Jezreel, meaning "God sows" or "God will sow." Jezreel was also the name of the place in central Israel associated with the power politics and bloody violence of some of Israel's most ruthless kings. Jezreel's name was a reminder of the place where the Jehu dynasty had quite recently in 745 BCE met its bloody end and may, therefore, have served Hosea as a sign of the impending destruction of Israel.

Yahweh commanded Hosea to name his second child, a daughter, *lō'ruhāmâ* (meaning, "not pitied") because Yahweh would no longer have pity on the house of Israel and would no longer forgive the people. Yahweh commanded Hosea to name his third child, a son, *lō' 'ammî* (meaning "not my people") because the people of Israel were no longer Yahweh's people, and Yahweh was no longer their God. The covenant bond between the people and their God was effectively broken, null and void.

There is apparently a doublet to this story, an autobiographical account of Hosea's call in Hosea 3:1–3, in which Hosea is directed to love a woman who has a lover and is an adulteress. This marriage will serve as a symbolic acting out of Yahweh's relationship with his whorish and adulteress wife Israel. In this version of the story, Hosea's wife has no name, and there is no mention of any children.

It is possible, but by no means clear, that a follower or disciple of the prophet drew the two accounts together (perhaps he was the author of the first account) and joined them with the oracle of judgment against Israel because of Gomer's faithlessness and because of the couple's subsequent reconciliation (Hosea 2:2–15). Some scholars have gone as far as to suggest that Gomer was actually a temple prostitute in the Canaanite religion, as there are allusions to sexual rites in Canaanite religion for the purpose of securing the fertility of the land. This is still one more issue in the book of Hosea that cannot be clearly resolved.

The details of the story are both confused and confusing, and scholars have understandably disagreed over virtually every detail in the book. Although it is not certain, it appears that Hosea decided to take back his adulterous wife after she had abandoned her family or had been thrown out.[7] If so, Hosea apparently bought her back in a slave market (3:2), the payment of a price implying that Gomer was at that time someone else's legal possession. According to the prophet himself, people called him "a fool" and "mad" for forgiving his wife and accepting her back into his household (9:7).

During the course of his prophetic activity, Hosea focused attention on two elements that were particularly important during this period: (1) the continuing struggle between Yahweh and Baal; and (2) royal politics of the northern kingdom, especially during the downward spiral and political intrigues following the death of Jeroboam II in 746 BCE.

If my interpretation of this problematic book is correct (and I am by no means certain that it is), then the message of Hosea may be that Yahweh's love for his people Israel is so great that he was not able simply to reject her and toss her aside, even though she was so consistently unfaithful and deserved to be abandoned. According to Hosea 11:8–9:

> 11:8How can I give you up, Ephraim?
> How can I hand you over, O Israel?
> How can I make you like Admah?
> How can I treat you like Zeboiim?[8]
> My heart recoils within me;
> my compassion grows warm and tender.
> 9I will not execute my fierce anger;
> I will not again destroy Ephraim;
> for I am God and no mortal,
> the Holy One in your midst,
> and I will not come in wrath.

Hosea's own personal relationship with Gomer may have served him as the key to the message of Yahweh's unrequited and unquestioning love for Israel.

The clue to this interpretation of the book comes in 2:16–23, and most especially in verses 19–23:

2:19And I will take you for my wife forever; I will take you for my wife in right-eousness and in justice, in steadfast love, and in mercy. 20I will take you for my wife in faithfulness; and you shall know the LORD (Yahweh).

21On that day I will answer, says the LORD (Yahweh),

I will answer the heavens

and they shall answer the earth;

22and the earth shall answer the grain, the wine, and the oil,

and they shall answer Jezreel;

23and I will sow him for myself in the land.

And I will have pity on Lo-ruhamah [Not-Pitied],

and I will say to Lo-ammi [Not-My-People], "You are my people";

and he shall say, "You are my God."

In verse 23, the names of the three children are all transformed from living oracles of threat into living oracles of promise. Although Yahweh was the aggrieved hus-band of a faithless wife, his steadfast love was far greater than his anger; and like Hosea, Yahweh was prepared to make a new beginning. Yahweh will sow (Jezreel means "God sows") his people in the land. He will have pity on Not-Pitied, and will say to Not-My-People, you are my people, to which they will respond, "You are my God."

The people have been forgiven and redeemed by Yahweh's unconditional love. The covenant has been restored.

CONCLUSIONS

In this chapter I have examined the phenomenon of prophecy, especially as it mani-fested itself in northern Israel until the fall of the northern kingdom in 722/721 BCE.

The chronology at the beginning of this chapter is based primarily on the Deuteronomistic History, which provides the historical setting for the kings and the prophets of both Israel and Judah. As indicated previously, the reliability of this out-line of history is based on the fact that the Deuteronomistic historian(s) had access to the book of the Acts of Solomon, the book of the Annals of the Kings of Israel, and the book of the Annals of the Kings of Judah, meeting thereby the time and place criterion that the closer in time and place a source or an author is to an event, the more reliable that source is likely to be. Biblical scholarship has refined this chronology over a long period of time, and the table of kings at the beginning of this chapter reflects a broad consensus among scholars.

Beyond the appeal to historical contextuality in everything under examination, I have also tried to introduce another form of contextuality in this chapter in order better to understand the prophets of ancient Israel. Most specifically I have looked at the phenomenon of prophecy and the psychology of prophecy, and I have stressed the roots of Israelite prophecy in both the universal phenomenon of *homines religiosi* and the specific phenomenon of ancient Near Eastern prophecy. As I have consistently observed, ancient Israelite religion is most clearly understood as one phenomenon within the larger context of ancient Near Eastern religions.

Certainly one of the most important observations made in this chapter has to do with the claim that prophets spoke not about the future but about the present and that they invariably addressed circumstances contemporaneous with their own times. To the extent that they spoke about the future at all, it was because Israel's prophets understood that the future was a necessary consequence of the present, and because of the way in which Yahweh, as a god of history, worked out and would continue to work out in history his will with his chosen people Israel.

Although we looked at dream interpretation and the sacred lots Urim and Thummim as early techniques for ascertaining the will of Yahweh, prophecy alone emerged in Israelite religion as the means *par excellence* for ascertaining the divine will.

The earliest prophets of Israel are difficult to understand, because our information about them comes solely from the Deuteronomistic History. Our knowledge of ancient Israelite prophecy begins with a handful of elusive figures who emerge from that Deuteronomistic History: Nathan, Elijah, Elisha, and Micaiah. We have no prophetic books written by contemporaries or disciples of these prophets, and it is not clear what oral or written sources the Deuteronomistic historian(s) may have used in telling their stories.

Perhaps court records from the reign of David concerning Nathan were available to later historians, although there is no mention of such records in the Old Testament. To be sure, Nathan's close relationship to the House of David seems clear, as was his judgment of the king in the scandalous Bathsheba incident and the incident regarding Naboth's vineyard, two stories whose historicity is assured by the criterion of dissimilarity or embarrassment.

The tradition about Elijah is obviously a blend of both history and legend, and it is not always easy to know where the one ends and the other begins. Yet it seems clear that Elijah's contribution to Israelite religion was based primarily on his challenge to Ahab and especially Jezebel at a time when the future of Yahwism in northern Israel was in doubt. Historical context once again proves critical to an understanding of this elusive and somewhat mysterious figure. Elijah clearly added something to the earlier concept of Yahweh as a god of history by incorporating into Yahweh's portfolio of activities the functions of Baal as a fertility god. Without that essential development, the struggle between Yahweh and Baal would likely have persisted much longer, and the outcome of that conflict might have been very different.

I have said little in this chapter about Elisha's role as a prophet, as the tradition about Elisha is especially problematic. Elisha clearly survived in Elijah's shadow, and the stories about him mirror many of the stories about Moses and Elijah to a degree that they have little to no value as history. As I stated earlier, the stories of the Elijah and Elisha cycles contributed significantly to the development of the miracle stories of Jesus in the New Testament, posing the question of the historical value of many of Jesus' miracle stories. Miracle falls outside the realm of historical investigation, but biblical scholarship does have a great deal to say about the function of legendary material and miracle stories in religious traditions. Such stories clearly function in a way that heightens the authority of figures who have been clothed in these imaginative oral and literary traditions.

Like Elijah, the prophet Micaiah established his reputation on the basis of his challenge to King Ahab in his case over a relatively inconsequential battle between Israel and Judah, on the one side, and Syria, on the other side. Micaiah was remembered because he challenged the authority of the mercenary court prophets and refused to placate the king. Like Elijah before him, Micaiah contributed to the development of prophecy as a function independent of the royal court.

Written prophecy in northern Israel began with the book of Amos. Although Amos was from the southern kingdom of Judah, he prophesied in the north at the royal sanctuary at Bethel against Israel and the house of Jeroboam and announced that because of their iniquities the people of Israel would be delivered into the hands of the Assyrians. The realization of Amos's vision of that destruction came just a few decades after his ministry and may have resulted in the decision of people contemporaneous with the period of Amos's prophetic activity to collect some of his oracles and some information about the prophet into a book. The proximity of the writing of that book to the events and the message described in it provide us with a highly reliable source for reconstructing the mission and message of Amos.

An important detail in our analysis of the book of Amos was the conclusion that the final verses of the book of Amos came not from Amos himself, but from the pen of a southern editor of the book fully two hundred years after Amos's activity in the northern kingdom. The criterion applied to dating these verses is quite simple: material is best understood in its own historical context, and the context of Amos 8:8b–15 is clearly the mid-sixth century BCE and not the mid-eighth century BCE, the period of Amos's activity against the northern kingdom. Biblical scholarship functions within the limits of historical reason and demands rational explanations for the evidence. Placing Amos 8:8b–15 within the context of Amos's prophetic activity would demand from the historian a suspension of the rules of the historical method and would require a supernatural rather than a natural view of the world. Biblical scholarship does not allow for historical leaps of faith in the handling of such unequivocal and unambiguous evidence.

The book of Hosea is more problematic for reasons that are not entirely clear. The book itself is particularly difficult to understand, and the oracles of the prophet are not organized in a way that is as clear as in the case of Amos. Nevertheless, it is evident that Hosea introduced into Israelite religion the concept of marriage as a metaphor for understanding the covenant relationship between Yahweh and Israel.

Unlike Amos, who was a prophet of doom and destruction, Hosea was a prophet of hope and love. It is noteworthy that those who later gathered these books into the canon of sacred scriptures had the wisdom to include both writings in their collection. Indeed, the collection is richer because of its diversity and complexity. The writings of the prophets reflect not only the historical circumstances to which they spoke (contextuality) but the personal history and the personality of each prophet as well.

There are two negative conclusions that surface in this chapter, and it is essential to note them, as they are foundational principles of conservative Christianity, namely, the inerrancy of scripture and the matter of predictive prophecy. Both of these principles are seriously compromised by evidence set forth in this chapter.

NOTES

1. All dates in this chronology are approximate, and all dates are BCE.
2. Johannes Lindblom, *Prophecy in Ancient Israel* (Philadelphia: Fortress Press, 1962), pp. 4–5.

3. Martin Luther King Jr., "Our God Is Able," in *Strength to Love* (Philadelphia: Fortress Press, 1963), pp. 113–14.

4. Lindblom, *Prophecy in Ancient Israel*, p. 34. See also James Bissett Pratt, *The Religious Consciousness: A Psychological Study* (New York: Macmillan, 1946), p. 45ff.

5. Lindblom, *Prophecy in Ancient Israel*, p. 46.

6. Ibid., pp. 137–41.

7. Some scholars have argued that Hosea took a second wife, who was also a harlot, but this interpretation of the text seems improbable.

8. Admah and Zeboiim were cities of the plain near Sodom, although their destruction is not reported in the account of the destruction of Sodom and Gomorrah in Genesis 19.

CHAPTER 6

THE NORTHERN KINGDOM'S EPIC

THE ELOHIST

In chapter 1, I presented evidence for and against Mosaic authorship of the Pentateuch and concluded that most scholars are convinced that Moses could not have been the author of the whole or of even a portion of the Pentateuch. I outlined on page 54 the regnant hypothesis that there are, in fact, four different strata of material in the Pentateuch—J (the Yahwist), E (the Elohist), D (Deuteronomy), and P (the Priestly redaction)—and indicated that I would resume a discussion of the four-document hypothesis and its individual components at appropriate places in this volume.

In chapter 4, it was fitting to discuss the first of these documents, the Yahwish epic (pp. 135–41), because it was apparently in the context of the period of the United Kingdom, specifically during the reign of King Solomon, that the J document was perhaps written, at least in part, to consolidate and solidify the legitimacy of the Davidic monarchy with its seat in Jerusalem. It is appropriate to discuss at this time the second of the sources of the Pentateuch, the document referred to as E, or the Elohist epic.

THE WRITING OF THE ELOHIST EPIC

Following the division of the United Kingdom in 922 BCE, it was evident to those in the north that the religious heritage of Israel should be preserved in an Ephraimite or northern version of the national history. In order to tell the story of the early history from a northern point of view, someone composed the so-called Elohist epic or the E narrative in the mid-ninth century BCE, although some scholars have suggested a date as late as the peaceful and prosperous reign of King Jeroboam II (786–746 BCE).

Underlying both the J and the E epics were common oral traditions, most of which almost certainly originated in tribal memories. It was the Yahwist or J, likely writing in Jerusalem about 950 BCE during the reign of King Solomon, who created the first written version of the national epic, possibly to strengthen the Davidic dynasty and to confirm the legitimacy of Jerusalem as the capital of the United Kingdom. Favoring the Davidic or southern point of view, the Yahwist epic was unsuited to the political situation in northern Israel following the separation of the ten northern tribes from Davidic rule when in 922 BCE Jeroboam I broke with Solomon's son Rehoboam following Solomon's death.

The patriarchal narratives in Genesis contain three sets of doublets, a word that indicates that there are two parallel or related narrative versions of the same story:

Genesis 12:10–20 = 20:1–18;
Genesis 16:4–14 = 21:8–21; and
Genesis 26:26–33 = 21:22–32, 34.

An examination of some details in each of these three doublets discloses interesting similarities and differences:

1. All three versions of this story are essentially the same: (1) a patriarch and his wife are in a foreign land; (2) because he fears that his wife's beauty will endanger him, the patriarch represents himself as his wife's brother; (3) the ruse is discovered by the foreign ruler.[1] Yet there are also subtle differences as indicted in this table:

Genesis 12:10–20	Genesis 20:1–18
Abram and Sarai in Egypt	Abraham and Sarah in Gerar
wife/sister motif with pharaoh	wife/sister motif with Abimelech
Yahweh (12:17)	Elohim (20:3, 6, 11, 13, 17)
	Yahweh (20:18)[2]
	Elohim came to Abimelech in a dream (20:3, 6)
	Abraham is described as a prophet (20:7)

2. Abraham's decision to have a child (Ishmael) with his wife Sarah's slave-girl Hagar leads to strife between the two women. Again some similarities and differences are evident in the following table:

Genesis 16:4–14	Genesis 21:8–21
Abram and Sarai	Abraham and Sarah
Yahweh (16:5, 7, 9, 10, 11, 13)	Elohim (21:12, 17 [3x], 19, 20)
Angel of Yahweh (16:7, 9, 10)	Angel of Elohim (21:17)
El-roi (God Who Sees) (16:13)	
the well at Beerlahairoi (16:14)	the well at Beersheba (21:14, 19)

3. Isaac (in Genesis 26) and Abraham (in Genesis 21) make a covenant at Beersheba with Abimelech of Gerar. Once again, similarities and differences are evident in the following table:

Genesis 26:26–33[3]	Genesis 21:22–32, 34[4]
Isaac's covenant with Abimelech	Abraham's covenant with Abimelech
Phicol commands Abimelech's army	Phicol commands Abimelech's army
Yahweh (26:28, 29)	Elohim (21:22, 23)
Beersheba (well of the oath)	Beersheba (well of the oath)

In each instance the version on the left is identified by scholars as being from the Yahwist or J source, and the version on the right as being from the Elohist or E source. Although E is closely related to J, a careful comparison of these three doublets discloses, nevertheless, some of the distinctive characteristics of the J and E traditions, because scholars are able in the case of such doublets to examine the two versions side by side.

In these doublets, E typically uses the generic word for god Elohim instead of the personal name Yahweh, which we find in J, especially in stories from the pre-Mosaic period. In the examples above, Elohim appears thirteen times in E material, and Yahweh appears nine times in J material. The difference between J and E with regard to the use of different words for God does not apply after Exodus 3:13–14, when the divine name Yahweh is introduced by the Elohist for the first time within the context of Moses' call and commission.

In addition, there is in E a focus on dreams as a vehicle of revelation (Genesis 20:3, 6; 31:10, 11, 24; 37:5, 6, 9, 10; 40:5 [3x], 8, 9 [2x], 16; 41:7, 8, 11 [2x], 12, 15

[2x], 17, 22, 25, 26, 32). Moreover, E refers to Abraham as a prophet (Genesis 20:7). Using information found in these three doublets as a starting point, a number of other passages have been assigned by scholars to E, covering every major theme in the Pentateuch: the promise to the patriarchs, the story of Moses and the Exodus from Egypt, the covenant at Mount Sinai, the wanderings in the wilderness, the oracles of Baalam, and the end of Moses' life. Although Elohist material survives only in fragmentary form, the identification of coherent E stories indicates that the Elohist material was not simply a supplement to or an editorial correction of the Yahwist source, but that E was evidently at one time a separate and distinct written document.

In addition to the details noted above, the Elohist version of the national epic shows a clear northern bias by emphasizing the importance of Joseph and his son Ephraim (Genesis 48:17–20). It also shows special interest in northern shrines such as Bethel (Genesis 28:12, 17–18, 20–21a, 22; 35:1–8) and Shechem (Genesis 33:18b–20). In J, it is Judah and not Reuben who is the leader among the sons of Israel (Genesis 49:3–4, 8–12; cf. 1 Chronicles 5:1), whereas in E, Reuben's position as firstborn is underscored by his attempt to save Joseph when the other brothers wanted to kill him (Genesis 37:21–24) and by his offer to Jacob of the lives of his two sons if he failed to return Benjamin from Egypt (Genesis 42:37). The status of Reuben as Jacob's firstborn son and the position of primacy he holds within various genealogies suggest that Reuben must at one time have been an important tribe. In addition, the Elohist (and D) use the name Horeb (Exodus 3:1; 17:6; 33:6; see also Deuteronomy 1:2, 6, 19; 4:10, 15; 5:2; 9:8; 18:16; 29:1), whereas the Yahwist (and P) refers to the holy mountain as Mount Sinai.

That E wrote after the beginning of the prophetic movement is clear. It is the Elohist who calls Abraham a prophet (Genesis 20:7) and Miriam a prophetess (Exodus 15:20). The Elohist also regards Moses as a prophet, although not explicitly in name. Moreover, in Numbers 11:16–17, 24–30, the seventy elders receive from Yahweh the spirit of prophecy.

The Elohist has no creation story and no account of the primordial history, or at least none survive. Unless early traditions that were originally in E were suppressed in the later redaction of J and E following the fall of the northern kingdom, it appears that E apparently began his epic with the call of Abraham in Genesis 15:2b–3a, 5, 13–16. The Elohist focuses on four ancestors: Abraham, Jacob, Joseph, and Moses, all of whom are represented either explicitly or implicitly as prophets who received revelations from God.

According to the four-document hypothesis (see the table on p. 54), the Elohist document survives in only fragmentary form, because following the fall of northern Israel in 722/721, the Elohist document was reshaped and edited by Judean or southern editors, who understandably favored their own Yahwist version of the national epic. Accordingly, apart from a few relatively coherent passages, most of E survives only in fragmentary form within the framework of J, or as JE.

Although there have been many challenges to the four-document hypothesis in the past century, and particularly challenges to E, it appears that the foundation of the documentary hypothesis is still relatively secure.

CONCLUSIONS

The purpose of this chapter has been to provide information about the second building block of the four-document hypothesis (the Elohist epic or E) within the historical context of the northern kingdom in the ninth (or eighth) century BCE. The documentary hypothesis is exactly that, a reasoned hypothesis based on an analysis of the text of the Pentateuch once it is clear that Moses was not its author.

The work of determining what material in the Pentateuch belongs to what source is not easy, but scholars have worked over the text with the finest of fine-tooth combs for more than a century in an effort to understand better the complicated history of the transmission of the material that eventually came together in the Pentateuch over a period of many centuries. Obviously the more complicated the actual process of composition, the more difficult it is to identify and categorize the relevant data and to develop arguments for a single hypothesis that will lead ultimately to a scholarly consensus. Yet, whatever their differences, I think it is safe to say that most scholars agree with the broad strokes of the four-document hypothesis.

Although the identification of the sources of the Pentateuch may have begun with Dr. Astruc's identification of different names for God, it is evident that the documentary hypothesis has moved well beyond that initial observation. The importance of doublets to the documentary hypothesis cannot be overstated, as it is especially important to be able to analyze carefully and critically two or sometime even three versions of the same story and thereby to identify stylistic differences, geographical biases, and other motifs and subtleties that appear in the doublets (or triplets) and that can then be identified subsequently in other passages elsewhere in the Pentateuch.

It is also very important to note in this chapter both the similarities and the differences between the doublets and the importance of this information for understanding the development of oral tradition. Assuming that we have in these doublets in Genesis different versions of the same stories, we have observed that in the course of the transmission of these stories, the oral tradition has played quite freely with details in the stories, even to the extent of changing the names of the principal characters. What relevance does this observation have to our understanding of the reliability of the many stories that come down to us from the oral tradition in only a single version with no way of checking the story against variant parallel versions?

Once again, the issue is what biblical scholars can determine within the limits of historical reason. The fact that there are still many questions about the creation of the Pentateuch does not mean that our methodology is flawed. It means that there is not as much indisputable evidence as scholars might like to have and that there is more than one way to interpret the data that we do have. The method of investigation is sound, however uncertain the specific conclusions of individual scholars. To put it simply: there are many things that we will never know about the past, but we must continue to do our best with the evidence that we have.

NOTES

1. In addition to the doublet identified here, there is actually a third version of this story in Genesis 26:6–11, a Yahwist or J story, involving Isaac, Rebekah, and once again Abimelech of Gerar.

2. The Samaritan Pentateuch and the Septuagint Greek both read Elohim, *probably correctly*, in verse 18. The Masoretic text, *probably incorrectly*, reads Yahweh. See chapter 13 for a fuller discussion of the difficulties involved in establishing the text of the Old Testament.

3. It is interesting that the only traditions about Isaac as a grown man appear in Genesis 26:1–33 (J) and that they all involve dealings with Abimelech of Gerar. These stories about Isaac appear to be variants or duplicates of traditions about Abraham and Abimelech in Genesis 20:1–18 and Genesis 21:22–32, 34, both of which are Elohist (E) traditions.

4. The reference in Genesis 21:33 to Yahweh El Olam is generally regarded as part of the J source.

CHAPTER 7

MEDIATORS BETWEEN YAHWEH AND JUDAH

W hile the political history of northern Israel was tumultuous during almost its entire two-hundred-year history following the civil war, the southern Kingdom of Judah enjoyed relative political stability during the three hundred thirty-five year reign of the house of David in Jerusalem from 922–587/586 BCE.

It is not surprising that most of the prophets whose writings survive in the Old Testament were from the Davidic kingdom, inasmuch as it was in the south that most of the books of the Hebrew Bible were either written or edited in the period following the Babylonian exile. Of the written prophets, only the writings of Amos (ca. 750 BCE) and Hosea (ca. 745 BCE) survive from the northern kingdom. Stories about Micaiah, Elijah, and Elisha lived on only in the Deuteronomistic History, a southern document; and technically Amos was actually a southerner who delivered his indictment against Israel in the northern kingdom.

Judah produced far more in the way of written prophets than did northern Israel:

Eighth Century BCE
>   Isaiah of Jerusalem [Isaiah 1–39] (ca. 742–701 or 688 BCE)
>   Micah (ca. 722–701 BCE)
Seventh Century BCE
>   Zephaniah (ca. 628–622 BCE)
>   Jeremiah (ca. 626–587 BCE)

    Nahum (ca. 612 BCE)

    Habakkuk (ca. 605 BCE)

Sixth Century BCE

    Ezekiel (ca. 593–573 BCE)

    Obadiah (after 587 BCE)

    Second Isaiah [Isaiah 40–55] (ca. 540 BCE)

    Haggai (ca. 520–515 BCE)

    Zechariah [Zechariah 1–8] (ca. 520–515 BCE)

    Third Isaiah [Isaiah 56–66] (ca. 520–515 BCE)

Fifth Century BCE

    Joel (ca. 500–350 BCE)

    Malachi (ca. 500–450 BCE)

    Second Zechariah [Zechariah 9–14] (over several decades culminating in the late fifth century BCE)

It has never been my intention to write a comprehensive introduction to the Old Testament, so I shall not discuss all of these prophets. This work is rather an introduction to biblical scholarship, and chapter 5 and this chapter are dedicated primarily to the phenomenon of prophecy in the northern and southern kingdoms of Israel and Judah.

Accordingly, I shall focus on only four of the prophets from the southern kingdom, one from each century in which prophecy flourished (the eighth, seventh, sixth, and fifth centuries BCE), in order to provide some overview of the history of Judah and of the phenomenon of prophecy in the southern kingdom. I have chosen to focus on Isaiah of Jerusalem (ca. 742–701 BCE), Jeremiah (ca. 626–587 BCE), Deutero-Isaiah (ca. 540 BCE), and Malachi (ca. 500–450 BCE), because each of these prophets and their books involves important matters of interest regarding methodology in biblical scholarship, which is the principal focus of this study. That said, I shall not pretend to provide a comprehensive treatment of even these few prophets. I shall provide instead some overview of each of the four prophets and their books and then focus on particular issues of method to highlight important matters regarding biblical scholarship.

HOLY, HOLY, HOLY IS YAHWEH OF HOSTS: ISAIAH OF JERUSALEM

Our book of Isaiah is actually a composite work that reflects the ministries of probably three different prophets: Isaiah (or Isaiah of Jerusalem for reasons of clarity), who was active in Jerusalem in the second half of the eighth century BCE; Second Isaiah or Deutero-Isaiah, an anonymous prophet who lived in Babylon during the Babylonian exile (586–539 BCE) and whose teachings were appended to those of Isaiah of Jerusalem in ancient times; and Third Isaiah or Trito-Isaiah, an anonymous prophet (or prophets) who lived in Judah following the return from exile in 539 BCE, prophesied there circa 520–515 BCE, and whose writings were appended in ancient times to those of Isaiah of Jerusalem and Second Isaiah.

Historical allusions in these three "books" make it evident that the ministries of these three (or more) men covered the late eighth century BCE, the mid-sixth century BCE, and the late sixth century BCE, respectively. The grouping of these three "books" onto a single scroll has little if anything to do with the content of their teachings but was rather dictated by the amount of material that could be contained on a parchment scroll, which was typically about twenty-four feet long. It is this same practice that resulted in the traditional grouping of the teachings of twelve different prophets (Hosea, Joel, Amos, Obadiah, Jonah, Micah, Nahum, Habakkuk, Zephaniah, Haggai, Zechariah, and Malachi) onto a single scroll, resulting in their being called the twelve minor prophets. In fact, the difference between the so-called major and minor prophets has nothing to do with their importance or the value of their messages and everything to do with whether their teachings were contained on separate scrolls (as in the cases of Isaiah, Jeremiah, and Ezekiel)[1] or were collected with the teachings of others onto a single scroll (as in the case of the minor prophets).

According to the superscription of the book (1:1), Isaiah, the son of Amoz,[2] prophesied to Judah and Jerusalem during the reigns of Uzziah (ca. 783–742 BCE), Jotham (ca. 742–735 BCE), Ahaz (ca. 735–715 BCE), and Hezekiah (ca. 715–687/686 BCE), kings of Judah. Isaiah 6 reports that the prophet's call and commission occurred in the year that King Uzziah died (742 BCE). Although the end point of the prophet's ministry is less clear, he prophesied at least until 701 BCE, and perhaps as late as 688 BCE.

The datable oracles of Isaiah fall into three distinct periods:

(1) circa 735–732 BCE, the period of the Syro-Ephraimite war against Judah (Isaiah 6–11, see especially Isaiah 7:1–2);

(2) circa 720–710 BCE, the period of efforts of the western alliance to ward off the threats of the Assyrian king Sargon II (see, for example, Isaiah 20:1–6); and

(3) circa 705–701 BCE, the period of Hezekiah's rebellion against the Assyrian king Sennacherib (Isaiah 28–33).

Some scholars think that Isaiah's ministry may have extended into the period of 689/688 BCE, when Hezekiah may again have rebelled against the Assyrian king Sennacherib, but that is less clear.

There is, nevertheless, even in chapters 1–39, material that clearly does not come from the period of Isaiah of Jerusalem. This later material provides us with clues regarding the complicated process by which our biblical books were put together by later editors:

(1) Apart from the song attributed to Hezekiah on the occasion of his recovery from his sickness in Isaiah 38:9–20, the historical appendix in chapters 36–39 was apparently lifted from 2 Kings 18:13 and 18:17–20:19, material in the Deuteronomistic History, which was written after the religious reform of King Josiah, more than a century after the beginning of the prophetic activity of Isaiah of Jerusalem.

(2) Isaiah 34 (a passage pronouncing judgment on the nations) and Isaiah 35 (a passage proclaiming hope for the return of the redeemed to Zion) are more like material from the Third Isaiah and the Second Isaiah, respectively, than like material from Isaiah of Jerusalem.

(3) Isaiah 24–27 (the so-called Isaian Apocalypse) contains a number of themes that were popular in later apocalyptic writings and should probably be assigned to a period a century or more after the ministry of Isaiah of Jerusalem.

(4) Isaiah 12 (a series of very brief psalms or songs of praise for Yahweh's deliverance) appears to have been added by the compiler of Isaiah 1–11 to round off this collection of early oracles and narrative material.

(5) Isaiah 33 (a late prophetic liturgy) appears to have been added by a compiler of Isaiah 28–32 to round off a series of late prophetic oracles.

If the identification and relative dating of these components in Isaiah 1–39 and, indeed, in the entire book of Isaiah is essentially correct, we can then readily see that the process by which the book of Isaiah was put together over a long period of time was, without a doubt, very complicated.

Isaiah's Call and Commission

Isaiah of Jerusalem describes his own call and commission (Isaiah 6:1–8):

> 6:1In the year that King Uzziah died, I saw the Lord sitting on a throne, high and lofty; and the hem of his robe filled the temple. 2Seraphs were in attendance above him; each had six wings: with two they covered their faces, and with two they covered their feet, and with two they flew. 3And one called to another and said:
> "Holy, holy, holy is the LORD (Yahweh) of hosts;
> the whole earth is full of his glory."
> 4The pivots on the thresholds shook at the voices of those who called, and the house filled with smoke. 5And I said: "Woe is me! I am lost, for I am a man of unclean lips, and I live among a people of unclean lips; yet my eyes have seen the King, the LORD (Yahweh) of hosts!"
> 6Then one of the seraphs flew to me, holding a live coal that had been taken from the altar with a pair of tongs. 7The seraph touched my mouth with it and said: "Now that this has touched your lips, your guilt has departed and your sin is blotted out." 8Then I heard the voice of the Lord saying, "Whom shall I send, and who will go for us?" And I said, "Here am I; send me!"

The account of the vision/audition, call, and commission of Isaiah is cloaked in ancient Near Eastern mythology, yet there is little reason to question what it is that Isaiah believed he saw and heard. The people of Israel believed that the Jerusalem temple was a microcosm of the heavenly temple and that Yahweh was truly present and enthroned in his house on Mount Zion, just as he was present and enthroned in heaven.

Isaiah must have been a young priest at the time of his vision/audition, as only priests entered the Jerusalem temple, and his ministry lasted for a period of forty or fifty years. In his vision Isaiah is transported from the earthly temple into the heavenly temple, where he "sees" Yahweh sitting upon his throne clothed in a magnificent robe, which is so enormous that its bottom border fills the temple. Yahweh is attended by two seraphs, probably winged cobras (cf. Numbers 21:8; Deuteronomy

8:15; Isaiah 14:29; 30:6; 1 Enoch 20:7; 61:10), figures familiar from Israelite cylinder seals, Egyptian art, and Syro-Phoenician thrones. These grotesque figures had their wings extended to protect the holy being, Yahweh. To safeguard themselves from Yahweh's glorious presence, the six-winged seraphs covered their faces with one pair of wings, their feet (a euphemism for their nakedness) with a second pair of wings; with a third pair of wings they flew. The seraphs' cry that Yahweh is the most holy of all filled the Jerusalem temple, and Yahweh's glory, his visible radiance, filled the whole earth.

The young priest was probably attendant at or participating in an important ritual in the Jerusalem temple, possibly an annual enthronement ceremony to coincide with and mark the beginning of the New Year. The renewal of Yahweh's enthronement would, it was believed, guarantee his presence in Israel during the ensuing year. The shaking of the thresholds is probably poetic language to emphasize the sanctity of the occasion, while the smoke that filled the temple may have been incense that helped to set the mood for this most solemn of occasions.

Whatever the specifics of the event, the young Isaiah was obviously overwhelmed by the occasion, perhaps his first such celebration in the temple, so much so that he was overpowered by his own sense of worthlessness: he describes himself as being lost because he is "a man of unclean lips," living "among a people of unclean lips" (6:5). Isaiah has now beheld "the King, the LORD (Yahweh) of hosts," a situation that would ordinarily result in the death of any mortal person (Exodus 33:20; Judges 13:22).

Isaiah was prepared for his prophetic ministry when one of the seraphs took a live coal from the altar with a pair on tongs and with it touched Isaiah's mouth, symbolizing thereby the purification of Isaiah's unclean lips. His mouth was now able to speak the holy word of Yahweh. At that point Yahweh himself spoke and asked Isaiah, "Whom shall I send, and who will go for us?" The plural "us" presumably reflects the belief that Yahweh is surrounded by his Heavenly Council. Isaiah accepted Yahweh's call and commission and answered in humility, "Here am I; send me."

However we try to explain the details of this theophany, however we attempt to understand what it was that transformed this young man into a prophet, there is little doubt in the minds of most biblical scholars that we have in these few verses the prophet's own description of what he assumed to have happened to him that fateful day when he believed he had been called and commissioned in the temple as a messenger of Yahweh.

In the context of this call, Isaiah understood that he had received Yahweh's first message, and he subsequently delivered his first oracle, a message so painful that the prophet asked how long it must continue (Isaiah 6:9–13):

> 6:9And he [Yahweh] said, "Go and say to this people:
> 'Keep listening, but do not comprehend;
> keep looking, but do not understand.'
> 10Make the mind of this people dull,
> and stop their ears,
> and shut their eyes,
> so that they may not look with their eyes,
> and listen with their ears,
> and comprehend with their minds,
> and turn and be healed."
> 11Then I said, "How long, O Lord?" And he said:
> "Until cities lie waste without inhabitant,
> and houses without people,
> and the land is utterly desolate;
> 12until the LORD (Yahweh) sends everyone far away,
> and vast is the emptiness in the midst of the land.
> 13Even if a tenth part remain in it,
> it will be burned again,
> like a terebinth or an oak,
> whose stump remains standing when it is felled."
> The holy seed is its stump.

Isaiah's message must be seen against the background of the history of the southern kingdom. The reign of Uzziah had brought substantial economic and military power to Judah. Perhaps the only bad news during Uzziah's forty-year reign was that the king contracted leprosy in about 750 BCE and that Assyrian imperialism began to lurk on the horizon. The message that Yahweh delivered to the prophet will not lead to their repentance (6:10). It will lead only to a further blinding, deafening, and hardening of the hearts of the people, as Yahweh prepares them for their inevitable destruction (6:10–13; cf. Isaiah 29:9–16).

Isaiah clearly understood that Yahweh's destruction of Judah would come at the hands of the Assyrians, and possibly during his own lifetime. In that respect the prophet was mistaken. Judah's end came, in fact, more than one hundred fifty years later, and not at the hands of the Assyrians, but at the hands of the Babylonians, who in Isaiah's lifetime were not yet a threat. Although this important detail was long since forgotten, succeeding generations saw the fulfillment of Isaiah's earliest prophetic oracle in the events of the fall of Judah and Jerusalem in 587/586 BCE.

The Syro-Ephraimite Alliance

Isaiah 8:16 ("Bind up the testimony, seal the teaching among my disciples") indicates that Isaiah and his disciples created the "memoir" contained in Isaiah 7:1–8:18 to serve as a record of the coalition formed by Syria and northern Israel to bring Judah into their alliance for the purpose of opposing the Assyrian threat. We have in these verses a firsthand account written by the prophet's disciples at a time very close to the events described.

As always, the background history is essential for a proper understanding of the words of the prophets. The crisis referred to in these two chapters of Isaiah occurred in 733/732 BCE. During the period of King Uzziah's illness, his son Jotham served as regent for eight years from 750 to 742 BCE before becoming king of Judah upon his father's death in 742 BCE. Seven years later, in 735 BCE, Jotham's son Ahaz succeeded his father on the throne of Judah. It was in 738 BCE, during Jotham's reign, that both King Rezin of Syria (the exact dates of his reign are unknown) and King Menahem of Israel (745–737 BCE) agreed to pay tribute to Assyria's king Tiglath-Pileser III to keep him at bay and thereby maintain their independence (2 Kings 15:19–20).

Just three years later, however, in 735 BCE, early in King Ahaz's reign, a league formed by King Rezin of Syria and one of Menahem's successors, King Pekah of Israel (736–732 BCE), tried to secure the cooperation of the young and inexperienced Ahaz in a coalition of western states to oppose Assyrian aggression. When Ahaz expressed unwillingness to join the western coalition against Assyria, Rezin of Syria and Pekah of Israel waged war against Judah from 735 to 732 BCE with the hope of replacing Ahaz with a non-Davidic puppet king, the son of Tabeel.[3]

One additional detail is important to a proper understanding of the events in this story. A few years after his call and commission as a prophet, Isaiah's wife gave birth to a son, whom Isaiah named Shear-jashub, meaning "a remnant shall return." Like Hosea before him, Isaiah gave his firstborn son a symbolic name as a living oracle, a visible sign of the prophet's message that Judah faced imminent destruction and that only a small remnant of the people would return, that is, would "turn to God" or "repent" (Isaiah 6:10). This history serves as the immediate background to what is described in Isaiah 7:1–8:18.

At the time of Syria and Israel's attack on Judah, we are told, Yahweh sent Isaiah, along with his sign-son Shear-jashub ("a remnant shall return"), out to meet King Ahaz "at the end of the conduit of the upper pool on the highway to the Fuller's Field" (Isaiah 7:3), an unidentified spot near Jerusalem, where three decades later messengers from King Sennacherib of Assyria demanded of Ahaz's son King Hezekiah the surrender of Jerusalem (2 Kings 18:17–18; Isaiah 36:1–2). Ahaz was terrified that invading armies were occupying his land and apparently offered his own son as a burnt offering (2 Kings 16:3), part of the worship of the god Molech in the Valley of Hinnom just outside Jerusalem (Leviticus 18:21; 20:2–5; 2 Kings 23:10; Jeremiah 32:35; see also Isaiah 57:9; Jeremiah 7:31; 19:5).[4]

Young King Ahaz was apparently still equivocating about what to do when Isaiah confronted him and assured him that because Yahweh had promised King David that his dynasty would sit on the throne in Jerusalem forever, the kings of Syria and Israel could not possibly prevail against the Judean king. Isaiah's message to Ahaz was simple: "Take heed, be quiet, do not fear, and do not let your heart be faint because of these two smoldering stumps of firebrands," Rezin of Syria and Pekah of Israel (Isaiah 7:4). Isaiah apparently thought that these two "smoldering stumps of firebrands" were already burning out, that the coalition of Syria and Israel was no longer a serious threat. But Ahaz was not so sure and continued to equivo-cate and to consult his political advisers.

Isaiah apparently offered Ahaz a sign in the symbolic naming of another child (7:10–17):

> 7:10Again the LORD (Yahweh) spoke to Ahaz saying, 11"Ask a sign of the LORD (Yahweh) your God; let it be deep as Sheol or high as heaven." 12But Ahaz said, "I will not ask, and I will not put the LORD (Yahweh) to the test." 13Then Isaiah said: "Hear then, O house of David! Is it too little for you to weary mortals, that you weary my God also? 14Therefore the LORD (Yahweh) himself will give you a sign. Look, the young woman is with child and shall bear a son, and shall name him Immanuel. 15He shall eat curds and honey by the time he knows how to refuse the evil and choose the good. 16For before the child knows how to refuse the evil and choose the good, the land before whose two kings you are in dread will be deserted. 17The LORD (Yahweh) will bring on you and on your people and on your ancestral

house such days as have not come since the day that Ephraim departed from Judah—the king of Assyria.

In the name of Yahweh, Isaiah offered King Ahaz a sign, with no limits, as evidence to support the prophet's demand that the king should resist the ultimatum of the western alliance of Syria and Israel to join them in their resistance of Assyria.

When Ahaz refused for whatever reason to ask for a sign, Isaiah told the king that Yahweh would give him a sign anyway. The sign would be in the form of the birth of a child born to a young woman, who would name him Immanuel, meaning "God is with us," a name that signified that Yahweh would protect Judah and Jerusalem from Syria and northern Israel's impending threat. By the time the child is able to distinguish good from evil, those who were threatening Judah would be destroyed.

Isaiah's confrontation with Ahaz occurred circa 735 BCE. The prophet obviously saw what was happening because the Assyrians laid siege to the Syrian capital of Damascus just three years later in 732 BCE and to the northern Israelite capital of Samaria in 722/721 BCE. Isaiah was right: the threat to Judah was removed within just a few years of the pregnant young woman's delivery of her child.

But who was this young woman, and who was this child? In verse 14, Isaiah uses the definite article, "*The* young woman," implying that he is referring to a particular young woman already known to the king. Scholars lean to the theory that the young woman was Ahaz's pregnant wife and that the child was, therefore, the king's son and successor, Hezekiah. How does the imminent birth of this child relate to the threat of the Syro-Ephraimite coalition? The prophet was apparently telling the king, who was equivocating in his trust of the prophet (and therefore Yahweh), that the Immanuel child would in the foreseeable future govern on the basis of trust in Yahweh (see Isaiah 9:1–7, an oracle that was probably delivered on the occasion of the coronation of a new Judean king, probably Hezekiah).

At this point, I would like to show how religious belief sometimes inappropriately influences the decisions of biblical scholars. Many translations of the Bible render Isaiah 7:14 as "Behold, *a virgin shall conceive* and bear a son, etc." instead of as "Look, *the young woman is with child* and shall bear a son, etc." A footnote to the text of the New Revised Standard Version indicates that the Septuagint Greek translation of Isaiah 7:14 identifies the future mother not as a "young woman," but as a "virgin."[5] In fact, that footnote is certainly there because the Authorized Version (the King James Bible) and many subsequent versions have translated this passage in Isaiah 7:14 thus:

> Therefore the Lord himself shall give you a sign; Behold, a virgin shall conceive, and bear a son, and shall call his name Immanuel.

The passage in Isaiah 7:14 has been understood by Christians since the time of the writing of the Gospel of Matthew (see Matthew 1:22–23) as a prophetic prediction of the birth of Jesus of Nazareth more than seven hundred years after Isaiah spoke these words to Ahaz. The author of the Gospel of Matthew was obviously not familiar with the Hebrew text of Isaiah but was using instead the Greek (mis)translation of this passage, when he wrote:

> Look, the virgin shall conceive and bear a son, and they shall name him Emmanuel (Matthew 1:23).

As we have already seen, the setting for this passage in Isaiah 7 was political events in the southern kingdom of Judah in 735–732 BCE. Isaiah offered Ahaz a sign that "the young woman (Hebrew *'almâ*) was pregnant and about to give birth to a son; she would give him the name Immanuel." Although there is some doubt who the young woman and the child were, it is clear that the passage does not and cannot refer to the virgin Mary and Jesus. For the sign to have had meaning for Ahaz, the young woman must have been known to both the prophet and the king, and the birth of the child must have been no more than a few months away, and certainly not seven hundred years in the future.

The meaning of Isaiah 7:14 is eminently clear to scholars who have studied the text in the original Hebrew. Jesus' birth to Mary would obviously have had no significance whatever to the prophet and the king in circa 735 BCE.

Obviously the translators of the King James Bible in 1611 assumed the legitimacy of the connection between Isaiah 7:14 and Matthew 1:23, because the translation of this passage in the King James Version of Isaiah (and in most subsequent conservative Christian translations) was informed by the (mis)translation in the third century BCE Septuagint and the use of this passage from Isaiah in the Gospel of Matthew.

It is one thing to note that the translators of the King James Bible (perhaps unknowingly) mistranslated this text in Isaiah 7:14 four hundred years ago. It is quite another matter when modern scholars, who can read Hebrew and understand the issues, continue to perpetuate the error for theological reasons. Contemporary conservative Christian translations knowingly and intentionally ignore the best intentions of modern biblical scholarship by continuing to perpetrate the error that Isaiah was referring to Mary and Jesus.

The following table illustrates the ways in which various translations of the Bible have rendered into English the critical Hebrew word *'almâ*:[6]

Bible Translation	Date	Character	Translation of *'almâ*
Douay-Rheims Bible	1609	translated from Vulgate	virgin
King James Version	1611	authorized Protestant	virgin
Revised Standard Version	1946	revision of KJV	young woman
Jerusalem Bible	1966	Roman Catholic	maiden
New International Version	1978	evangelical Christian	virgin
Anchor Bible Commentary	2000	nondenominational	young woman

The study of the phenomenon of prophecy, lexicography, Hebrew grammar, the meaning of the words in related foreign languages, and so on have all made it eminently clear what this passage in Isaiah does and does not say.

I have taken the time and effort to look very closely at the Syro-Ehpraimite war of 735–732 BCE and the material in Isaiah 7–8 for two reasons:

(1) It is important to understand how biblical scholarship examines the ancient texts in detail with contextuality as a fundamental principle. The material in Isaiah 7–8 makes sense against the background of the time and place in which Isaiah and Ahaz actually lived. This study exhibits what biblical scholarship is at its very best and that religious belief and personal bias cannot and should not play a role in what is essentially a scientific discipline.

(2) It is important to understand that there are people who pose as biblical scholars but who do not work with the accepted canons of historical criticism and who allow their personal religious beliefs to influence their scholarship. The role of biblical scholarship is neither to criticize nor to promote religious belief. Biblical scholarship must be neutral.[7]

THE TRANSITION FROM JUDGMENT
TO SALVATION: JEREMIAH

The superscription of the book (Jeremiah 1:1–3) states:

1:1The words of Jeremiah son of Hilkiah, of the priests who were in Anathoth in the land of Benjamin, 2to whom the word of the LORD (Yahweh) came in the days of King Josiah (ca. 640–609 BCE) son of Amon of Judah, in the thirteenth year of his reign. 3It came also in the days of Jehoiakim (ca. 609–598/597 BCE) son of Josiah of Judah and until the end of the eleventh year of King Zekekiah (ca. 597–587/586 BCE) son of Josiah, until the captivity of Jerusalem in the fifth month.

Like Isaiah before him, Jeremiah's prophetic activity spanned a period of four decades (ca. 627–587 BCE).

Jeremiah's Call and Commission

Jeremiah, which means "Yahweh exalts," describes his call and commission in 1:4–10:

4Now the word of the LORD (Yahweh) came to me saying,

5"Before I formed you in the womb I knew you,

and before you were born I consecrated you;

I appointed you a prophet to the nations."

6Then I said, "Ah, Lord GOD (Yahweh)! Truly I do not know how to speak, for I am only a boy." 7But the LORD (Yahweh) said to me,

"Do not say, 'I am only a boy';

for you shall go to all to whom I send you,

and you shall speak whatever I command you.

8Do not be afraid of them,

for I am with you to deliver you," says the LORD (Yahweh).

9Then the LORD (Yahweh) put out his hand and touched my mouth; and the LORD (Yahweh) said to me,

"Now I have put my words in your mouth.

10See, today I appoint you over nations and over kingdoms,

to pluck up and to pull down,

to destroy and to overthrow,

to build and to plant."

The call of the prophet contains the traditional form of the encounter with Yahweh (v. 4), the commission (v. 5), the objection of the prophet (v. 6), followed by the reassurance of Yahweh (v. 7–8). The parallels with the call and commission of Moses are striking (Exodus 3:1–4:17), and Isaiah 6 contains most of the same elements.

In the case of Jeremiah, we are told that he was destined by Yahweh to be a prophet even before his birth. The experience of the divine call was so overpowering to young Jeremiah that it appeared to him that he had been set apart by Yahweh for his mission as part of a divine plan that reached back to a time even before he was born. Unlike those who came before him, Jeremiah understood that he had been called to be a prophet to the nations and not only to Israel and Judah. For Jeremiah, Yahweh's word reaches well beyond the land of Judah.

Touching Jeremiah's mouth and placing the divine words in his mouth recalls both what Deuteronomy 18:18 says about Moses, "I will put my words in the mouth of the prophet," and what Isaiah 6:6 says about the seraphs touching Isaiah's mouth with a live coal to prepare the prophet to speak the word of Yahweh. In each of these cases, the prophet sees himself as the passive agent or mediator, the mouthpiece of the divine word.

Jeremiah's Early Message

The story of the call and commission of Jeremiah is followed by an account of two visions set in a question and answer style that is similar to what we found previously in the visions in Amos 7:7–9; 8:1–3. And like four of Amos's visions, Jeremiah's two visions seem to be examples of symbolic perceptions, observations of real objects in the material world, which the prophet believes come from the hand of Yahweh and reveal a deeper religious significance (see above pp. 169–70):

1. Jeremiah 1:11–12. The branch of an almond tree (Hebrew *shāqēd*). The almond tree suggests to Jeremiah the Hebrew word *shôqēd*, meaning "watching," because this vision serves Jeremiah as a sign that Yahweh is "watching over his word to perform it," suggesting to Jeremiah that Yahweh will carry out the terms of the message contained in his prophetic word.

2. Jeremiah 1:13–14. A boiling pot tilted away from the north. Perhaps Jeremiah is sitting in his home, where his wife is preparing dinner. The prophet sees a pot cooking on the fire and facing from the north and tilting slightly

toward the south, a warning that "out of the north disaster shall break out on all the inhabitants of the land [of Judah]." Some biblical scholars think that at this point in his ministry (ca. 627 BCE) Jeremiah may have been referring to a threat from the Scythians (Jeremiah 4:29; 5:15–17; 6:22–26; 60:41–42),[8] although the Scythians never actually attacked Judah. Destruction from the north ultimately came at the hands of the Babylonians some forty years later.

Jeremiah understood that, through the events of history, Yahweh was imploring his faithless children to return to him: "Return, O faithless children, I will heal your faithlessness" (Jeremiah 3:22). The cry to "return" is a call for repentance in order to repair the covenant relationship, which the people have broken.

Jeremiah asks the people still one more time, reminding them of Joshua's call to choose Yahweh, to remove the abominations, the idols and the cult associated with idol worship that had been set up in the temple of Yahweh in Jerusalem (Jeremiah 7:30) and in the hills of the countryside (Jeremiah 13:27; see also 16:18).

There was, of course, nothing new in Jeremiah's message that destruction was about to come to the nation. He certainly understood that he was part of a long tradition of prophets who had preceded him. Although the details of Israel's faithlessness to the covenant with Yahweh were no different in Jeremiah's time from circumstances that prophets before him had addressed, there is nothing stale or old in Jeremiah's message, because the sins of the nation were real and vivid. Indeed, there is no more bitter indictment of the nation than the words in Jeremiah 5:1:

> Run to and fro through the streets of Jerusalem,
> look around and take note!
> Search its squares and see if you can find one person
> who acts justly
> and seeks truth—
> so that I may pardon Jerusalem.

Jeremiah knew that prophets before him had tried to call Israel back to Yahweh. He also believed that Yahweh's patience with the wayward people was dwindling. Yet he still held out hope for the nation if only the people would listen to him (Jeremiah 4:1–2):

4:1If you return, O Israel, says the LORD (Yahweh),
if you return to me,
if you remove your abominations from my presence
and do not waver,
2and if you swear, "As the LORD (Yahweh) lives!"
in truth, in justice, and in uprightness,
then nations shall be blessed by him, and by him shall they boast.

Nevertheless, Jeremiah knew that it would be almost impossible for Israel to change after so long (Jeremiah 13:23):

13:23Can Ethiopians change their skin
or leopards their spots?
Then also you can do good
who are accustomed to do evil.

Although Isaiah before him believed that Yahweh would ultimately spare Jerusalem, Jeremiah (and Micah 3:9–12 a century before him) believed that Yahweh's judgment would be unsparing and would include even Jerusalem and the temple (Jeremiah 7:12–15):

7:12Go now to my place that was in Shiloh, where I made my name dwell at first, and see what I did to it for the wickedness of my people Israel. 13And now, because you have done all these things, says the LORD (Yahweh), and when I spoke to you persistently, you did not listen, and when I called you, you did not answer, 14therefore I will do to the house that is called by my name [the Jerusalem temple], in which you trust, and to the place that I gave to you and to your ancestors [Jerusalem], just as I did to Shiloh. 15And I will cast you out of my sight, just as I cast out all your kinfolk, all the offspring of Ephraim [the northern kingdom of Israel, which had fallen to the Assyrians in 722/721 BCE].

People around Jeremiah, including so-called prophets of peace and prosperity, opposed him constantly (Jeremiah 23:16–17):

23:16Thus says the LORD (Yahweh) of hosts: Do not listen to the words of the prophets who prophesy to you; they are deluding you. They speak visions of their own minds, not from the mouth of the LORD (Yahweh). 17They keep saying to those who despise the word of the LORD (Yahweh), "It shall be well with you"; and to those who stubbornly follow their own hearts, they say, "No calamity shall come upon you."

Jeremiah 28 tells the story of one such prophet of good fortune, Hananiah of Gibeon, who, "at the beginning of the reign of King Zedekiah of Judah, in the fifth month of the fourth year" (594/593 BCE), told Jeremiah in the Jerusalem temple, "in the presence of the priests, and all the people," that within two years Yahweh would "break the yoke" of King Nebuchadnezzar of Babylon and would return the temple treasury that had been looted, together with the exiled King Jeconiah [Jehoiakim] and the exiles who had been sent to Babylon in 597 BCE.[9]

The Babylonian king Nebuchadnezzar began his siege of Jerusalem in 588 BCE. Although the city held out for two years, it ultimately fell to the Babylonians in 587/586 BCE. The Temple of Yahweh was burned, and a significant portion of the population was deported to Babylonia. The fall of Jerusalem also marked the end of the house of David, which had occupied the throne of Judah for more than four hundred years. It seemed to anyone with any vision that Israel's and Judah's history had come to an end. Many of the better families of Jerusalem fled to Egypt, taking Jeremiah and his secretary Baruch with them, in spite of Jeremiah's pleas for them to remain in Judah. There in Egypt the people of Israel took up the worship of Ishtar, the Queen of Heaven (Jeremiah 7:17–18; 44:17–19),[10] and Jeremiah once again took up the cause of Yahweh in his vision of a New Covenant.

The New Covenant

Jeremiah 30–33, the so-called Book of Consolation or Book of the Future, is material that Jeremiah or Baruch added to the book during the time of their exile in Egypt. This material comes from the period of the Babylonian exile and offers a vision of hope beyond the apparently irreversible national disaster.

The catastrophe that prophets had warned about for centuries had finally arrived, but Jeremiah met the challenge in a unique and imaginative way. When the earthly Zion, the city of Jerusalem, had fallen, Jeremiah in exile in Egypt looked to the future and developed a new image to deal with the loss of the nation and the holy city of David.

Jeremiah is often called the prophet of individualism, because he moved beyond the concept of collective responsibility to one of personal or individual responsibility. Jeremiah modified the concept of Israel's covenant with Yahweh, which had heretofore been a contract between Yahweh and the people of Israel.

In a symbolic act, a sign that the people would eventually return to the land, during the siege of Jerusalem in 588 BCE the prophet bought a field offered to him by his cousin (Jeremiah 32:1–15). Jeremiah believed that Yahweh would restore the people and return them to the land (Jeremiah 30:1–3):

> 30:1The word that came to Jeremiah from the LORD (Yahweh): 2Thus says the LORD (Yahweh), the God of Israel: Write in a book all the words that I have spoken to you. 3For the days are surely coming, says the LORD (Yahweh), when I will restore the fortunes of my people, Israel and Judah, says the LORD (Yahweh), and I will bring them back to the land that I gave to their ancestors and they shall take possession of it.

Jeremiah's vision of the new community is expressed in his vision of a New Covenant (Jeremiah 31:31–34):

> 31:31The days are surely coming, says the LORD (Yahweh), when I will make a new covenant with the house of Israel and the house of Judah. 32It will not be like the covenant that I made with their ancestors when I took them by the hand to bring them out of the land of Egypt—a covenant that they broke, though I was their husband, says the LORD (Yahweh). 33But this is the covenant that I will make with the house of Israel after those days, says the LORD (Yahweh): I will put my law within them, and I will write it on their hearts; and I will be their God, and they shall be my people. 34No longer shall they teach one another, or say to each other, "Know the LORD (Yahweh)," for they shall all know me, from the least of them to the greatest, says the LORD (Yahweh); for I will forgive their iniquity, and remember their sin no more.

This oracle is unusual in that it is in prose rather than in poetry. It promises Israel a new beginning, a New Covenant. The old covenant, the Mosaic covenant, had been broken, but this New Covenant will afford a new beginning that will be based on an inward transformation of the people's hearts that will enable them to know God personally.

The restoration that Jeremiah promised was something far better than the recovery of the land. It implied a spiritual renewal, a change of heart among the people. The Torah, which had previously been written on tablets of stone, would now be written in the hearts of the people. Jeremiah was demanding a thoroughgoing conversion of the people's inner being that would involve Yahweh's full and final pardon of the people's iniquity and sin (31:34).

The Writing of the Book of Jeremiah

Jeremiah 36, probably written by Jeremiah's scribe Baruch, reports that in the fourth year of the reign of King Jehoiakim (ca. 605 BCE),[11] Jeremiah received a command from Yahweh to "Take a scroll and write on it all the words that I (Yahweh) have spoken to you against Israel and Judah and all the nations, from the day I spoke to you, from the days of Josiah until today" (36:2). Jeremiah apparently hoped that the early oracles, which had heretofore been preserved within his own memory and within the memory of his disciples, would persuade the people to return to Yahweh, who would "forgive their iniquity and their sin" (36:3). Jeremiah dictated to his secretary Baruch "all the words of the LORD (Yahweh) that he had spoken to him" (36:4).

It is not exactly clear what constituted the contents of this original scroll, which presumably contained the oracles of Jeremiah from 627 to 605 BCE, the twenty-two years since his call and commission. Biblical scholars have attempted to determine how the book of Jeremiah was put together, based both on its contents and on the clues contained in chapter 36. It is possible that this first book corresponded in size and content to Jeremiah 2–12, less 9:23–26; 10:1–16; and 12:7–17, which are probably later additions.

Jeremiah had been forbidden to enter the temple precincts at that time, so Baruch was directed to go in his place to read Jeremiah's words to the people, who had assembled in the temple area for a public fast day (Jeremiah 36:9–10). Report of Baruch's reading of Jeremiah's oracles reached the royal palace, and Jeremiah and Baruch were advised to hide as the words must have sounded treasonous with Judah now under the threat of an attack by the Babylonians. As the words of Jeremiah were read to King Jehoiakim, the king cut off three or four columns of the scroll at a time and threw them into the fire in his winter palace until the entire scroll had been destroyed (36:20–25). Jehoiakim ordered the arrest of Jeremiah and Baruch, but they had already hidden (36:26).

Following King Jehoiakim's burning of the first scroll, Jeremiah dictated to Baruch a second scroll containing "all the words of the scroll that King Jehoiakim

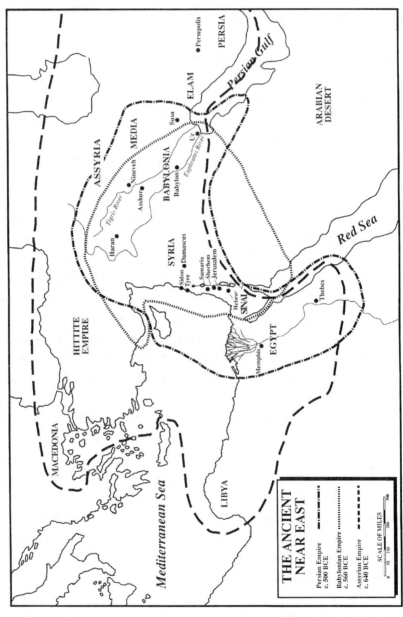

FIGURE 9. THE ANCIENT NEAR EAST

This map can be viewed at www.bible.ca; copyright, 1994 by Abingdon Press. Used by permission.

of Judah had burned in the fire; and many similar words were added to them" (36:32), possibly chapters 1 and 14–20. If this assessment is correct, the second scroll of Jeremiah 36:32, which dates from the winter of 604 BCE, was basically chapters 1–20, except for a few later additions.

To this material the later oracles found in chapters 21–29 were apparently added, and, as we have already seen, chapters 30–33, the Book of Consolation or Book of the Future, was added. The remainder of the book, chapters 34–52, was likely composed at several points later in Jeremiah's life, either by Jeremiah himself, by his secretary Baruch, or in some instances by a post-exilic prophet.[12]

An important clue to the composition of the book of Jeremiah is evident in the Septuagint version (the Greek translation created between 250 and 150 BCE in Alexandria, Egypt). The Greek text of Jeremiah is only 88 percent as long as the standard Hebrew text (the Masoretic text) and organizes some of the material differently, in particular "the oracles against the nations" in Jeremiah 46:1–51:58. Manuscripts of Jeremiah found among the Dead Sea Scrolls indicate that the Septuagint Greek is apparently based on a Hebrew text of Jeremiah that is actually more ancient than our standard Masoretic text. The Septuagint version is, therefore, obviously an earlier version of the book of Jeremiah than that found in our Hebrew Bibles. Apparently a later editor of the book added material to an earlier edition (represented in the Dead Sea Scrolls and in the Septuagint) to produce our canonical Hebrew version of the text of Jeremiah.

What is obvious from this discussion is that the book of Jeremiah and presumably other books of the Bible as well were put together in several stages. In the case of Jeremiah, we have written evidence within the book itself to attest to and to explain the process in some detail. We have, as well, the internal evidence within the book in the form of oracles that can sometimes be dated to specific events in Israel's history. It the case of other books of the Bible, we usually have only the internal evidence with which to work, but we can use the example of the book of Jeremiah as a clue to the process of the writing and editing of biblical manuscripts.

A NEW EXODUS: DEUTERO-ISAIAH

The unimaginable tragedy of the fall of both the northern and southern kingdoms brought a dramatic change in Israelite religion from a theme of judgment to a theme of hope and deliverance. That positive shift was picked up by Jeremiah in his message of the New Covenant and again by the prophet known as Second Isaiah or Deutero-Isaiah.

There is widespread agreement among biblical scholars that Isaiah of Jerusalem is not responsible for the material in the book of Isaiah beginning in chapter 40. This judgment is based on a number of facts:

(1) The material in Isaiah chapters 1–39 presupposes a historical situation totally different from what we find beginning in chapter 40. Chapters 1–39 assume a situation in which the Assyrian Empire is the threatening power, people are still living in Judah and Jerusalem under the rule of Davidic kings, and the Jerusalem temple is still standing. Beginning in chapter 40, the situation is totally different: Babylonia is the political power of the age, Jerusalem and the cities in Judah have been destroyed, the temple lies in ruins, and people are exiled in Babylon. In fact, the prophet tells the people in 48:20 to "Go out from Babylon."

(2) The man who will conquer Babylon is named in two passages (44:28 and 45:1) as Cyrus of Persia, and he is clearly alluded to again in 41:25. Cyrus, who is called in Isaiah 45:1 Yahweh's anointed, the one who will redeem Israel, became king of Persia in 559 BCE and captured Babylon in 539 BCE, probably very shortly after the writing of Deutero-Isaiah.

(3) In other words, there is a gap of about two hundred years between the time of Isaiah of Jerusalem and the writing of the Second Isaiah, which occurred sometime between the emergence of Cyrus in 559 BCE and the fall of Babylon in 539 BCE, and probably sometime closer to the latter date.

(4) The vocabulary, the literary style, and the poetic structure of Isaiah of Jerusalem and of the Deutero-Isaiah are entirely different. Whereas the material concerning Isaiah of Jerusalem is essentially in the form of brief prophetic oracles, the Second Isaiah writes rich, flowing extended poetry in which his message appears and reappears. We find double imperatives as a common feature of Second Isaiah: "Comfort, O comfort" (40:1) and "Rouse yourself, rouse yourself!" (51:17), a device not found in the oracles of Isaiah of Jerusalem. In addition, there are also in Deutero-Isaiah a number of extended rhetorical questions in 40:12–14; 41:2; 45:21; 50:1–2, and parallel imperatives in 44:23 and 51:1–9, literary devices not found in the brief but charged oracles of Isaiah of Jerusalem.

(5) There is, as well, a totally different theological emphasis beginning in chapter 40. Instead of the threats and rebukes of Isaiah of Jerusalem, Second Isaiah offers the people comfort (40:1) and "speaks tenderly" to Jerusalem (40:2). The mood of Second Isaiah is one of exultant joy. In addition, the name of Yahweh is emphasized in a series of effusive epithets and appositional clauses in 42:5 and 43:1, 3; and Yahweh affirms his own distinctive nature in 41:4 and 43:11.

The opening scene of Deutero-Isaiah is set in heaven, where Yahweh's Heavenly Council is assembled. The prophet stands in the midst of the solemn assembly, where Yahweh directs him to comfort the people, to speak tenderly to Jerusalem, to tell the people that the time of their punishment has ended, that their prison term in exile has, in fact, been double-time for the nation's sins. There will be a new beginning. As a matter of fact, the prophet envisions a New Exodus (40:3–5):

40:3A voice cries out:
"In the wilderness prepare the way of the LORD (Yahweh),
make straight in the desert a highway for our God.
4Every valley shall be lifted up,
and every mountain and hill be made low;
the uneven ground shall become level,
and the rough places a plain.
5Then the glory of the LORD (Yahweh) shall be revealed,
and all people shall see it together,
for the mouth of the LORD (Yahweh) has spoken."

Yahweh is preparing to return from Babylon, where he too has been in exile, to his home in Jerusalem and will lead his people on their journey home as a shepherd leads his flock (40:11). The prophet envisions a great return to Israel as the people presumably walk in a stately procession across the desert, where the road has been straightened and the ground leveled to provide an easy return to Judah and Jerusalem in anticipation of Yahweh's and the people's return. Just as the people of Israel originally entered the Promised Land after crossing the sea, this time they will enter by walking across a desert, the way that has been prepared by order of Yahweh himself.

Just as the Exodus from Egypt was the decisive event in Israel's past history, the moment of Israel's beginning, so too with this new beginning the prophet portrays an imminent return from exile in Babylonia by employing imagery drawn from the Exodus and the wilderness traditions. The return to the Promised Land will mark a new beginning in the nation's history. Like the Exodus from Egypt, this too is a time of national redemption.

Second Isaiah was able to read the signs of the times. The Babylonian Empire was about to fall into the hands of Cyrus of Persia, dating the prophet's poems to the period just before 540 BCE, fully two hundred years after the call and commission of Isaiah of Jerusalem. It is evident that the material that begins in chapter 40 was written in a different time and in a different place than the oracles of Isaiah of Jerusalem.

The Elevated Theology of Deutero-Isaiah

The experiences of the destruction of both the northern kingdom of Israel and the southern kingdom of Judah and of the half century in exile in Babylonia brought significant changes to Israelite religion. Among those changes was the insightful theology of Deutero-Isaiah. Among the themes that the prophet developed are:

Absolute Monotheism. Most important and most original is the unequivocal declaration that Yahweh only is God and that all other gods are nothing. Although since the time of Moses the people of Israel had been required to worship only Yahweh, never before had anyone proclaimed so explicitly that there was no god but Yahweh (44:6; 44:8; 45:5–6; and 45:21).

44:6Thus says the LORD (Yahweh), the King of Israel,
and his Redeemer, the LORD (Yahweh) of hosts:
I am the first and I am the last;
besides me there is no God.

44:8Do not fear, or be afraid;
have I not told you from of old and declared it?
You are my witnesses!
Is there any god besides me?
There is no other rock; I know not one.

45:5I am the LORD (Yahweh), and there is no other;
besides me there is no god.

I arm you, though you do not know me,

₆so that they may know, from the rising of the sun

and from the west, that there is no one besides me;

I am the LORD (Yahweh), and there is no other.

₄₅:₂₁Declare and present your case;

let them take counsel together!

Who told this long ago?

Who declared it of old?

Was it not I, the LORD (Yahweh)?

There is no other god besides me,

a righteous God and a Savior;

there is no one besides me.

The Vanity of Idolatry. Deutero-Isaiah declared unequivocally that idol worship is simply the worship of objects that are nothing more than creations of human artisans (40:18–20; 44:9–20).

₄₀:₁₈To whom then will you liken God,

or what likeness compare with him?

₁₉An idol?—A workman casts it,

and a goldsmith overlays it with gold,

and casts for it silver chains.

₂₀As a gift one chooses mulberry wood

—wood that will not rot—

then seeks out a skilled artisan

to set up an image that will not topple.

₄₄:₉All who make idols are nothing, and the things they delight in do not profit; their witnesses neither see nor know. And so they will be put to shame. ₁₀Who would fashion a god or cast an image that can do no good? ₁₁Look, all its devotees shall be put to shame; the artisans too are merely human. Let them all assemble, let them stand up; they shall be terrified, they shall all be put to shame.

₁₂The ironsmith fashions it and works it over the coals, shaping it with hammers, and forging it with his strong arm; he becomes hungry and his strength fails, he drinks no water and is faint. ₁₃The carpenter stretches a line, marks it out with a stylus, fashions it with planes, and marks it with a compass; he makes it in human form, with human beauty, to be set up in a shrine. ₁₄He cuts down cedars or chooses a holm tree or an oak and lets it grow strong among the trees of the forest. He plants a cedar and the rain nourishes it. ₁₅Then it can be used as fuel. Part of it he takes and warms himself; he kindles a fire and bakes bread. Then he makes a god and worships it, makes it a carved image and bows down before it. ₁₆Half of it he burns in the fire; over this half he roasts meat, eats it and is satisfied. He also warms himself and says, "Ah, I am warm, I can feel the fire!" ₁₇The rest of it he makes into a god, his idol, bows down to it and worships it; he prays to it and says, "Save me, for you are my god!"

₁₈They do not know, nor do they comprehend; for their eyes are shut, so that they cannot see, and their minds as well, so that they cannot understand. ₁₉No one considers, nor is there knowledge or discernment to say, "Half of it I burned in the fire; I also baked bread on its coals, I roasted meat and have eaten. Now shall I make the rest of it an abomination? Shall I fall down before a block of wood?" ₂₀He feeds on ashes; a deluded mind has led him astray, and he cannot save himself or say, "Is not this thing in my right hand a fraud?"

Yahweh Is the Creator. Yahweh, the God and Redeemer of Israel, is the creator and lord of the universe (40:12–14).

₄₀:₁₂Who has measured the waters in the hollow of his hand
and marked off the heavens with a span,
enclosed the dust of the earth in a measure,
and weighed the mountains in scales
and the hills in a balance?
₁₃Who has directed the spirit of the LORD (Yahweh),
or as his counselor has instructed him?
₁₄Whom did he consult for his enlightenment,
and who taught him the path of justice?
Who taught him knowledge,
and showed him the way of understanding?

Yahweh Is Lord. Because Yahweh is the Lord of all history, he is also the god of other people (41:2, 4).

₄₁:₂Who has roused a victor from the east [i.e., Cyrus of Persia],
summoned him to his service?

He delivers up nations to him,
and tramples kings under foot;
he makes them like dust with his sword,
like driven stubble with his bow.

41:4Who has performed and done this,
calling the generations from the beginning?
I, the LORD (Yahweh), am first,
and will be with the last.

The exalted Yahweh of Deutero-Isaiah is a far cry from the Yahweh of Moses, a (Kenite?) tribal deity, who adopted the Hebrew slaves in Egypt as his own people and entered into a covenant relationship with them at Mount Sinai following their escape from Egypt. Seven hundred fifty years had transpired between Moses and Deutero-Isaiah, and the concept of Yahweh had grown as a consequence of new and challenging circumstances that Israel had faced in the course of her history. The destruction of the nation was an enormous challenge, and visionary prophets like Jeremiah and Deutero-Isaiah rose to the occasion.

Deutero-Isaiah faced squarely the greatest challenge of all, which was how to explain Israel's exile and suffering. His answer was twofold: that Israel's suffering had been both disciplinary (i.e., it had served as punishment for her sins), and it had been expiatory (i.e., it had made amends, reparation, and atonement for the nation's sins). This theme was developed by Deutero-Isaiah most poignantly in the Servant Poems.

The Servant Poems

The so-called Servant Poems represent one of the most important and, at the same time, most problematic portions of Second Isaiah. We find these poems in four different places in the book:

1. Isaiah 42:1–4

42:1Here is my servant, whom I uphold,
my chosen in whom my soul delights;
I have put my spirit upon him;
he will bring forth justice to the nations.

2He will not cry or lift up his voice,
or make it heard in the street;
3a bruised reed he will not break,
and a dimly burning wick he will not quench;
he will faithfully bring forth justice.
4He will not grow faint or be crushed
until he has established justice in the earth;
and the coastlands wait for his teaching.

The identification of the servant poses problems from the outset. Indeed, no one familiar with the literature on the subject would venture to claim to know definitively the identity of the servant of these four poems.[13]

In the opening words of this first poem, it is presumably Yahweh who is speaking and who identifies the servant as "my chosen in whom my soul delights." Earlier, in 41:8–10, Second Isaiah uses the phrase "my servant" to refer to Jacob Israel, leading some scholars to identify the servant with the nation Israel. Elsewhere in the Old Testament "my chosen" is used to refer to David, Israel, Zion, the Israelites, and (in Haggai 2:23) Zerubbabel, the governor of Jerusalem during the Persian occupation. Isaiah 42:1 reports that Yahweh has put his spirit upon the servant, an act usually identified with either a king or a prophet.

This first poem speaks three times of bringing forth or establishing "justice," thereby making justice the principal emphasis of this poem. The poem reports that Yahweh put his spirit upon his servant so that he might bring justice to the nations. Generally it is the king who is credited with bringing forth justice.

And so, in this first poem a figure is introduced who is in character both prophetic and kingly and who has been sent by Yahweh to bring a message to the entire world.

2. Isaiah 49:1–6

49:1Listen to me, O coastlands,
pay attention you peoples from far away!
The LORD (Yahweh) called me before I was born,
while I was in my mother's womb he named me.
2He made my mouth like a sharp sword,
in the shadow of his hand he hid me;

he made me a polished arrow,

in his quiver he hid me away.

₃And he said to me "You are my servant,

Israel, in whom I will be glorified."

₄But I said, "I have labored in vain,

I have spent my strength for nothing and vanity;

yet surely my cause is with the LORD (Yahweh),

and my reward with my God."

₅And now the LORD (Yahweh) says,

who formed me in the womb to be his servant,

to bring Jacob back to him,

and that Israel might be gathered to him,

for I am honored in the sight of the LORD (Yahweh),

and my God has become my strength—

₆he says,

"It is too light a thing that you should be my servant

to raise up the tribes of Jacob

and to restore the survivors of Israel;

I will give you as a light to the nations,

that my salvation may reach to the end of the earth."

In the first song, the servant was spoken of in the third person, but here the servant is now speaking to the world in the first person. Verse 1 is reminiscent of the call of Jeremiah (1:5), who likewise claimed that he was called as a prophet even before he was formed in his mother's womb;[14] the name of the servant, however, is not given here or anywhere in these poems.

In verse 3, Deutero-Isaiah seems once again to identify the servant with Israel,[15] but the meaning of the passage is not entirely clear. The verse could mean that the servant is the *true* Israel, in whom or in which Yahweh will be glorified. Such a reading suggests that Yahweh had called and prepared the servant as the true Israel, the core around which the whole of Israel would grow, in whom Yahweh (and Israel) would be glorified, and whose purpose it would be to bring light and salvation to the nations.

The sword and the arrow of verse 2 suggest a military figure, someone hard and driving. Verse 2 also suggests that Yahweh protected his servant and hid him in secret until the time appointed for his service. In verse 4, the servant seems to think that his service has been in vain, yet he sees that he has lived his life under the rule of Yahweh and that his reward will, therefore, be with Yahweh.

Verse 5 poses a major problem if the servant is Israel, inasmuch as the servant's role is "to bring Jacob (Israel) back" to Yahweh, "and to restore the survivors of Israel." What would that mean if Israel is the servant? The passage would, however, have a great deal of meaning if a portion of Israel, the "true Israel," is the servant. Indeed, in verse 6, the servant has a mission not only to Israel, but "to the nations" so that Yahweh's "salvation may reach to the end of the earth."

3. Isaiah 50:4–9

50:4The Lord GOD (Yahweh) has given me the tongue of a teacher,

that I may know how to sustain the weary with a word.

Morning by morning he wakens—

wakens my ear

to listen as those who are taught.

5The Lord GOD (Yahweh) has opened my ear,

and I was not rebellious,

I did not turn backward.

6I gave my back to those who struck me,

and my cheeks to those who pulled out the beard;

I did not hide my face from insult and spitting.

7The Lord GOD (Yahweh) helps me;

therefore I have not been disgraced;

therefore I have set my face like flint,

and I know that I shall not be put to shame;

8he who vindicates me is near.

Who will contend with me?

Let us stand up together.

Who are my adversaries?

Let them confront me.

9It is the Lord GOD (Yahweh) who helps me;

who will declare me guilty?

All of them will wear out like a garment;

the moth will eat them up.

Once again, as in the second poem, the servant is the speaker. Is the prophet himself the servant? The servant is, in any case, a teacher and has met with opposition to his mission. In this poem, the theme of suffering is introduced for the first time. But the Lord Yahweh helps the servant, and those who oppress him will wear out and be removed. It appears that the suffering of the servant has involved him in some sort of controversy, but it did not destroy his confidence and strength to be able to remain faithful to Yahweh.

4. Isaiah 52:13–53:12

52:13See, my servant shall prosper;
he shall be exalted and lifted up,
and shall be very high.
14Just as there were many who were astonished at him,
—so marred was his appearance, beyond human semblance,
and his form beyond that of mortals—
15so he shall startle many nations;
kings shall shut their mouths because of him;
for that which had not been told them they shall see,
and that which they had not heard they shall contemplate.
53:1Who has believed what we have heard?
And to whom has the arm of the LORD (Yahweh) been revealed?
2For he grew up before him like a young plant,
and like a root out of dry ground;
he had no form or majesty that we should look at him,
nothing in his appearance that we should desire him.
3He was despised and rejected by others;
a man of suffering and acquainted with infirmity;
and as one from whom others hide their faces
he was despised, and we held him of no account.

4Surely he has borne our infirmities
and carried our diseases;
yet we accounted him stricken,
struck down by God and afflicted.
5But he was wounded for our transgressions,
crushed for our iniquities,

upon him was the punishment that made us whole,

and by his bruises we are healed.

₆All we like sheep have gone astray;

we have all turned to our own way,

and the LORD (Yahweh) has laid on him

the iniquity of us all.

₇He was oppressed, and he was afflicted,

yet he did not open his mouth;

like a lamb that is led to the slaughter,

and like a sheep that before its shearers is silent,

so he did not open his mouth.

₈By a perversion of justice he was taken away.

Who could have imagined his future?

For he was cut off from the land of the living,

stricken for the transgressions of my people.

₉They made his grave with the wicked,

and his tomb with the rich,

although he had done no violence,

and there was no deceit in his mouth.

₁₀Yet it was the will of the LORD (Yahweh) to crush him with pain.

When you make his life an offering for sin,

he shall see his offspring, and shall prolong his days;

through him the will of the LORD (Yahweh) shall prosper.

₁₁Out of his anguish he shall see light;

he shall find satisfaction through his knowledge.

The righteous one, my servant, shall make many righteous,

and he shall bear their iniquities.

₁₂Therefore, I will allot him a portion with the great,

and he shall divide the spoil with the strong;

because he poured out himself to death,

and was numbered with the transgressors;

yet he bore the sin of many,

and made intercession for the transgressors.

Once again, as in the first song, the servant is spoken of in the third person. Although the speaker is not identified, it is clearly Yahweh who is the speaker of the opening and closing verses. This song speaks of the rejection, affliction, oppression, sacrifice, death, and exaltation of the servant. The triumph of the servant comes in his suffering and death. In verses 4–6, the people realize that the servant has borne their sins because he himself was sinless. In verses 10–12, we read that it was Yahweh's purpose to crush the servant with pain and to cause him to suffer. It was Yahweh's purpose to use the servant's undeserved suffering to vindicate the people's sin.

The suffering of the servant was not in vain, because others have been released from pain as a result of the servant's suffering and will be made righteous. The prophet claims that the innocent suffering of one individual results in the rescuing of others from their need to suffer for their sin. As someone who has suffered unjustly, the servant bears the pain and suffering that is due to others. The prophet introduces a revolutionary idea—that the unjust suffering of one man can bring salvation and deliverance to others and unjust suffering is ultimately redemptive.

The early Christian community (see Acts 8:32–35) identified the servant in this poem with Jesus:

> 8:32Now the passage of the scripture that he [a court official of the queen of the Ethiopians] was reading was this:
>
> "Like a sheep he was led to the slaughter,
> and like a lamb silent before its shearer,
> so he does not open his mouth.
> 33In his humiliation justice was denied him.
> Who can describe his generation?
> For his life is taken away from the earth.
> 34The [Ethiopian] eunuch asked [the apostle] Philip, "About whom, may I ask, does the prophet say this? About himself, or about someone else?" 35Then Philip began to speak, and starting with this scripture,[16] he proclaimed to him the good news about Jesus.

These four poems, and especially the third and the fourth songs, are particularly well known in Christian circles, because they were appropriated by early Christian preachers and writers to enable them to find meaning in Jesus' suffering, crucifixion, and death. That these poems were known and consciously used in the formation of the preaching of the early Christian community is beyond question. The theme of sacrifice and expiation is clear in the servant poems. Early Christianity picked up on this important theme six centuries later and made a religion out of it.

This was, of course, not the intention of the original author of these poems, whoever he was. Deutero-Isaiah would have understood the servant within the context of his own time in history, the sixth century BCE. Within that context, the servant appears to have been those who suffered unjustly in the Babylonian exile. It was their undeserved suffering that redeemed the nation and made possible the return to Judah and Jerusalem from the death of the Babylonian exile.

The identification of the servant with Jesus is defended by no reputable scholar today except in fundamentalist circles, where religious bias rather than objective scholarship often dictates the conclusions. The kind of predictive prophecy demanded by such an identification of Jesus as the servant appears nowhere in the Old Testament.

The key to an understanding of what the writer had in mind may be found in Isaiah 49:3:

And he (Yahweh) said to me, "You are my servant,
Israel, in whom I will be delighted."

Elsewhere in the poetry of the Deutero-Isaiah, there are references to Israel as the servant (Isaiah 41:8–10; 43:8–13; 44:1–2; 44:21; 45:4). All of these passages suggest that in some sense the author understood that Israel was Yahweh's servant. Yet, as we have also seen, Isaiah 49:5 makes it clear that it is the role of the servant "to bring Jacob back to him, and that Israel might be gathered to him," implying that the servant is actually not Israel. Isaiah 49:3 may provide the solution to the dilemma if we understand that passage to mean something like: "You are my servant, (the true) Israel in which I will be delighted."

Might the servant be those who suffered in exile unjustly at a time when punishment was generally regarded as corporate, and not individual? And might the unjust suffering of the righteous not have been redemptive for the rest of the nation? Deutero-Isaiah seems to have introduced into Israelite religion the concept that undeserved suffering on the part of the servant (the righteous who had been unjustly taken into exile in Babylonia?) would lead the entire nation from defeat to victory.

Followers of Jesus, in the aftermath of his apparently unexpected and unexplained death, took this theme of redemptive suffering from Second Isaiah and made of it a new religion. Until the birth of Christianity, Jewish thought probably did not associate the suffering servant of Second Isaiah with the Messiah of Israel. It is interesting to note that Luke 24:46 makes it clear that it was *following* Jesus' death that Christians came to believe that it was "the risen Christ" who first "opened their minds to understand the scriptures."

The origin of the poems is not clear. Neither is it clear why they are scattered throughout Deutero-Isaiah. It appears that the four poems are a unit, or should at least be looked at together. The language of the songs is quite similar to the rest of the material in Deutero-Isaiah, yet the relationship of the two is not entirely clear, because the tone of the poems is subdued when compared to the tone of exultant joy found elsewhere in the book.

Are the poems an integral part of the book? Were they written earlier and incorporated into the book by the prophet or a later editor? Were they written later than the prophecy and incorporated into the book by the prophet or a later editor? We can probably never know the answers to these questions, but we can be relatively certain that the poems are integral to the book and its message.

Whatever their origin and meaning there is no question of the subsequent importance of the songs to Christianity.

YAHWEH IS ABOUT TO SEND A MESSENGER: MALACHI

Although the book of Malachi is the final book of the Hebrew Bible (the Old Testament), it was certainly not the last book to be written. Malachi's criticism of the temple priesthood (Malachi 1:6–2:9) makes it clear that the prophet preached sometime after the dedication of the second temple in 516/515 BCE, during the period when the people of Israel were ruled by a Persian governor (Malachi 1:8).

The book of Malachi contains six of the prophet's oracles:

1. Malachi 1:2–5. This oracle against Edom (the descendants of Jacob/Israel's twin brother, Esau) proclaims Yahweh's sovereignty even "beyond the borders of Israel" (1:5).
2. Malachi 1:6–2:9. This indictment against the priesthood of the Jerusalem temple for their shortcoming condemns current practices. It had been more

than seventy years since the destruction of Solomon's temple in 586 BCE, and temple ritual was no longer familiar to the people. Malachi charged the people and the priests with dishonoring Yahweh by offering polluted food on the altar of the temple (1:7) and by offering sacrifices of blind, lame, and sickly animals (1:8). The people and the priests were going through the motions of temple ritual, but their hearts were not in it (1:13).

3. Malachi 2:10–16. This indictment against the people for their behavior toward one another indicates that Jewish men were divorcing their Jewish wives in order to marry foreign women. Indeed, Malachi contains the most serious condemnation of divorce to be found anywhere in the Bible: "For I hate divorce, says the LORD (Yahweh), the God of Israel" (2:16).

4. Malachi 2:17–3:5. This indictment against those who complain to Yahweh because the wicked prosper contains these observations: "All who do evil are good in the sight of the LORD (Yahweh)"; and "Where is the God of justice?" (2:17). This oracle also contains the promise that Yahweh will send a messenger, who will purify the Levitical priesthood (3:1–4).

5. Malachi 3:6–12. If the people return to Yahweh (i.e., repent of their evil ways and tithe), Yahweh will return to the people.

6. Malachi 3:13–4:3. On the day of judgment, Yahweh will save the faithful, whose good deeds are recorded in the "book of remembrance" (3:16–17).

In spite of his loud protests, Malachi does not measure up to the greatest of the prophets of previous generations. He lacks the focus on covenant justice so evident in Amos, the passionate understanding of Yahweh's love for his people so vivid in Hosea, the richness and poetic imagery of Isaiah, and the clear vision of the future in Jeremiah and the Deutero-Isaiah. For Malachi, if only Israel gives a tenth (tithe) of its produce to Yahweh, then Yahweh will pour out his blessings on the nation (3:6–12)—a mere shadow of the golden age of Israelite prophecy!

Malachi is perhaps best remembered by Christians because of the concluding verses of the book (4:5–6), which announce that Yahweh will send the prophet Elijah "before the great and terrible day of the LORD (Yahweh) comes" (4:5). The New Testament's gospel tradition identified Malachi's promised return of Elijah before "the terrible day of Yahweh" with the coming of John the Baptist, who served for Christians as the precursor of Jesus of Nazareth (see Matthew 11:13; 17:9–13; Mark 1:2–4 [which quotes Malachi 3:1, along with Isaiah 40:3 and Exodus 23:20];

6:14–15; Luke 1:17). Once again, we see in this instance an example of the New Testament's reading meaning into Old Testament passages that had a very different meaning in their original historical contexts. Whatever else he may have meant, Malachi was not announcing that Elijah (in the person of John the Baptist) would return to herald the arrival of Jesus of Nazareth as Messiah.

CONCLUSIONS

This chapter builds on material in chapter 5, by examining the phenomenon of prophecy in the southern kingdom of Judah following the division of the United Kingdom in 922 BCE.

Once again the chronology of the Deuteronomistic History (Joshua, Judges, 1 and 2 Samuel, and 1 and 2 Kings) provides the requisite historical setting for our study of the prophets and kings of Judah. In using this historical narrative, it is appropriate to recall that the Deuteronomistic History is substantially reliable history largely because the author(s) had access to the book of the Acts of Solomon, the book of the Annals of the Kings of Israel, and the book of the Annals of the Kings of Judah, thereby meeting the time and place criterion that the closer in time and place a source is to an event, the more reliable that source is likely to be. Nevertheless, it is essential to note that the Deuteronomistic History is at the same time a "theologically motivated history."

The study of mediators between Yahweh and Judah has led us to study in some detail the prophetic ministries of four of a possible fifteen prophets: Isaiah of Jerusalem, Jeremiah, the so-called Deutero-Isaiah, and Malachi from the eighth, seventh, sixth, and fifth centuries BCE, respectively.

Particularly important in this chapter has been what I have called the principle of contextuality, meaning that Judah's prophets are best understood in their own historical, cultural, and religious contexts. Most specifically this principle has led to the observation that individual prophetic oracles can often be dated within the context of an individual prophet's ministry by linking allusions in the oracles to known historical events or circumstances, especially as known either from the Deuteronomistic History and/or from the official records of Israel's and Judah's neighbors.

In the case of Isaiah of Jerusalem, the application of this principle led to a number of important conclusions: (1) that the book of Isaiah actually reflects the work of more than one prophet, Isaiah of Jerusalem (chapters 1–39), the so-called Deutero-Isaiah (chapters 40–55), and the so-called Trito-Isaiah (chapters 56–66). Even after this division of the book was acknowledged, the composition of each portion of the book indicates clearly that there are several layers to the material regarding each of the three prophets, indicating the pens of later individuals who subsequently collected, edited, and added to earlier material. Even in chapters 1–39, the material concerning Isaiah of Jerusalem, scholars have identified no fewer than five instances of material that does not come from the period of the prophet (see pp. 190–91).

As we saw in chapter 5, the work of Johannes Lindblom on prophecy provides important insights for understanding the calls and commissions of the prophets, most specifically in this chapter the calls and commissions of Isaiah of Jerusalem and Jeremiah, and to a lesser extent the call and commission of Second Isaiah.[17] In the case of Isaiah and Jeremiah, we seem to have firsthand accounts of their calls and commissions (Isaiah 6:1–8; Jeremiah 1:4–10), and of their earliest messages (Isaiah 6:9–13; Jeremiah 1:11–19). There is no reasonable justification for questioning the authenticity of these personal accounts; nevertheless, in looking at the narrative accounts of the calls and commissions of Isaiah and Jeremiah, we perceive the degree to which the psychology of prophecy and the use of poetic conventions, including the contextual setting in ancient Near Eastern mythology, have played an important role in the prophets' accounts of their calls. Specifically, the calls and commissions of Isaiah and Jeremiah follow the traditional form of the prophetic call, which we find expressed also in the call and commission of Moses in Exodus 3:1–4:7: (1) the initial encounter with Yahweh, (2) the commission, (3) the objection of the prophet that he is unworthy or otherwise unsuited to the task, and (4) Yahweh's reassurance to the prophet and the prophet's reluctant acquiescence.

In the case of Isaiah, his call seems to have come to him in the temple when, as a young priest, he was attending and participating in an important cultic event, perhaps the celebration of the New Year, involving an annual reenthronement of Yahweh as king. The setting of Jeremiah's call is less specific, but the overwhelming power of the experience convinced the prophet that Yahweh had set him apart from a time prior to his conception in his mother's womb.

Second-Isaiah's vision appears to have transported him into the presence of Yahweh and the Heavenly Council, where the anonymous prophet heard a voice from someone in Yahweh's council declare the timeless endurance of the word of Yahweh ("the word of our God will stand forever" [Isaiah 40:8b]), especially as compared to the transitory quality of human existence ("All people are grass, their constancy is like the flower of the field" [Isaiah 40:6b]).

Not only are the narrative accounts of the prophets' calls poetic in character, their oracles too conform almost always to the literary form of Hebrew poetry, namely, that two lines form a couplet in which the second line either repeats the substance of or stands in antithesis to the first line, what scholars label synthetic parallelism and antithetical parallelism, respectively, as illustrated by these two examples from Deutero-Isaiah:

> A voice cries out:
> "In the wilderness prepare the way of the LORD (Yahweh)
>   make straight in the desert a highway for our God" (Isaiah 40:3).

> The grass withers, the flower fades;
> but the word of our God will stand forever (Isaiah 40:8).

The use of poetic imagery sometimes makes it difficult for readers to understand the meaning of every passage, because we often do not have immediate access to the particular circumstances in which each oracle was delivered or to the shades in meaning of every Hebrew word and every poetic nuance. Poetry is by its very nature often imprecise; it uses the language of metaphor and symbolism, and it is generally more evocative than descriptive.

In the case of Isaiah 7, scholars have observed that the setting for the material in this chapter was political events in Judah in 735–732 BCE. Following the principle that the prophets addressed circumstances in their own times, we set aside and dismissed in our discussion of this material the notion of some fundamentalist scholars who read the Old Testament prophets as "predictive prophecy," requiring a long-term view of what an individual prophet might have been speaking or writing about. In Isaiah 7 and 53, Jeremiah 31–33, and Malachi 4, we disallowed the belief common among many Christians that these prophets were speaking about events in the life and ministry of Jesus of Nazareth and the early Christian church. Biblical scholars have maintained consistently that the prophets of Israel spoke not about the long-term future but about events contemporaneous with their own times. To the extent that prophets addressed the future, it was because they were convinced that the immediate future is the necessary consequence of decisions in the present, something that Martin Luther King Jr. also understood very well.

Like Amos, who came before him, Jeremiah's earliest "visions" reflect examples of what Johannes Lindblom and others have referred to as "symbolic perceptions," the observation of real objects in the material world, which the prophet believed came from the hand of Yahweh and which revealed deeper religious significance.

Jeremiah also calls attention to a particularly interesting challenge: How is it possible to distinguish between true prophets and false prophets (e.g., Hananiah of Gibeon in Jeremiah 28)? Deuteronomy suggests that false prophets speak in the names of gods other than Yahweh, speak falsely in the name of Yahweh, prophesy peace and prosperity instead of judgment against the nation, or make predictions that do not come to pass (18:15–22). The issue is, of course, far more complicated, as decisions about who are true and who are false prophets are often made with the advantage of hindsight and from the perspective of those whose religious views ultimately prevail. It is, of course, the victors who usually write the history. Was Martin Luther King Jr. a true or a false prophet, or no prophet at all? The answer to that question ultimately depends on who is answering the question, and on when in time the answer is given. Biblical prophecy is no different.

We have seen that the book of Jeremiah affords important insight into the process of writing, adding to, and editing a book. With the help of details provided in Jeremiah 36, scholars have speculated about how the book of Jeremiah was put together, which chapters are from the earliest period of the prophet's career, which reflect later periods in his ministry, and so on. In the case of Jeremiah, scholars have also identified later additions to the book by applying the principle of contextuality and identifying the historical circumstances underlying a particular passage. In spite of the importance of this method, the available evidence does not always allow biblical scholars to draw assured conclusions. Equally competent scholars can sometimes draw very different conclusions from the same evidence, even when they are using the same methodology, because they are often working with limited evidence that may lend itself to different interpretations. Assured conclusions are rare in the study of history, and more especially in the study of ancient history.

Our discussion of Deutero-Isaiah identified data and criteria that have enabled scholars to conclude that Isaiah of Jerusalem is not the author of material beyond Isaiah chapter 39. Those data and criteria include: (1) the historical backgrounds of various parts of the book of Isaiah are often quite different, separated sometimes by two or more centuries; (2) different sections of the book have distinct vocabulary, literary styles, and poetic structures; and (3) there are often distinct theological emphases in different parts of what appears to be the same book.

The Servant Poems of Deutero-Isaiah pose an especially interesting challenge. Although bona fide scholars are unanimous in agreeing that Jesus of Nazareth was not the servant anticipated by the prophet (the criterion of contextuality), they are not agreed on whom the author had in mind when he spoke of the servant. In the pages above, we identified the servant as a core of righteous individuals within the community in exile in Babylonia, but scholars differ significantly on the identity of this important figure. Yet there is no disagreement among competent scholars as to how to go about identifying who it was that the prophet had in mind. The problem is not a disagreement in method; it is a disagreement on how to interpret the very limited data. Neither is it clear whether the Servant Poems were written before or after the rest of the material in Deutero-Isaiah or whether the poems are by the same author as the rest of the material in Isaiah 40–55 or by a different author.

The most important lesson to be learned in studying the prophets of Israel and Judah is to understand clearly what prophecy is and what prophecy is not. In this regard, understanding the historical context of each prophet is a sine qua non of understanding the ministry and the message of each and every prophet. Moreover, to preserve the integrity of the historical method, it is essential to avoid bringing religious bias into the discussion, as it is not and cannot be a factor in drawing sound scholarly conclusions.

NOTES

1. Although the Isaiah scroll actually contains the prophecies of three or more individuals, Deutero-Isaiah and Trito-Isaiah are not identified in their respective writings. Consequently, it came to be believed, quite erroneously, that Isaiah of Jerusalem was the author or, more accurately, the source of the prophetic utterances in the entire book. Isaiah is, accordingly, considered one of the major prophets.

2. Not to be confused with the prophet Amos.

3. The Hebrew form of the name Tabeel means "God is good." But who was this man? An Assyrian document lists Tubail or (It)tobaal as king of Tyre in Phoenicia immediately following King Rezin of Syria and King Menahem of Israel. It is possible that Tyre was part of the coalition of western states and that the son of the Tyrian king was offered the throne of Judah in exchange for his support in the western coalition.

4. The sacrificing of children as burnt offerings to Molech may be of Phoenician origin. Deuteronomy 12:31 explains that the sacrificial burning of children was a practice of the indigenous population of the land of Canaan, which Israelites obviously continued to practice along with their worship of Yahweh. References to the practice in various books of the Bible suggest that Israelites engaged in this form of worship from at least circa 735 BCE to circa 575 BCE, and probably much longer.

5. Jewish scholars living in Alexandria, Egypt, between 250 and 150 BCE translated the Hebrew Bible into Greek for the benefit of Jews whose families had been living in Egypt for several centuries. These Jews no longer understood their scriptures in the original Hebrew, hence the need for the Greek translation.

6. In addition to the translations listed in the chart, the Web site www.biblegateway.com lists numerous additional, presumably evangelical-approved, translations, which yield the following results: *New American Standard Bible* (NASB): "a virgin"; *The Message* (MSG): "a girl who is presently a virgin"; *Amplified Bible* (AMP): "the young woman who is unmarried and a virgin"; *New Living Translation* (NLT): "the virgin"; *English Standard Version* (ESV): "the virgin"; *Contemporary English Version* (CEV): "a virgin"; *New King James Version* (NKJV): "the virgin"; *21st Century King James Version* (KJ21): "a virgin"; *American Standard Version* (ASV): "a virgin"; *Young's Literal Translation* (YLT): "the Virgin"; *Darby Translation* (DARBY): "the virgin"; *New International Version—UK* (NIV-UK): "the virgin." A footnote to the CEV, in an effort to be scholarly, clearly betrays its prejudice: "In this context the difficult Hebrew word did not imply a virgin birth. However, in the Greek translation made about 200 (B.C.) and used by many early Christians, the word parthenos had a double meaning. While the translator [of the Septuagint] took it to mean 'young woman,' Matthew understood it to mean 'virgin' and quoted the passage (Matthew 1:23) because it was the appropriate description of Mary, the mother of Jesus." It is evident that in each and every one of these instances, the translation is colored by evangelical orthodox bias, not by scholarly philological study. This table first appeared in Arthur J. Bellinzoni, *The Future of Christianity: Can It Survive?* (Amherst, NY: Prometheus Books, 2006), p. 97.

7. This exercise helps to illustrate what biblical scholarship is and what biblical scholarship is not. The 2005 effort of the Kansas school board to secure the teaching of intelligent design alongside Darwinian evolution parallels the occasional conflict between mainstream biblical scholarship and evangelical biblical scholarship.

8. Herodotus reports that the Scythians, who were centered in what is today northwestern Iran, mastered fighting on horseback, which is why some scholars have interpreted these passages as referring to a threat from the Scythians. Jeremiah nowhere names the impending enemy.

9. The issues involved in distinguishing between true and false prophets were substantial. In addition to this passage in Jeremiah 28 regarding Jeremiah and Hananiah, 1 Kings 13:11–32

deals with the issue of true and false prophecy, as does the story of Micaiah in 1 Kings 22 (see above pp. 163–64). Deuteronomy 18:15–22 offers ways of distinguishing between true and false prophets. False prophets speak in the names of other gods, speak falsely in the name of Yahweh, prophesy peace and prosperity instead of judgment against the nation, or make predictions that do not come to pass. The issue is obviously far more complicated as Isaiah obviously qualified as a true prophet, even though he apparently believed that Jerusalem and the Davidic dynasty would be spared, presumably on the basis of Nathan's promise to King David that his family would sit upon the throne in Jerusalem forever (Isaiah 14:32; 37:32–35).

10. The Queen of Heaven, Ishtar, was an Assyro-Babylonian goddess in the Akkadian pantheon and was associated with war, sexuality, and fertility, as well as with the planet Venus. The Bible preserves the name Ishtar only in the personal name Esther.

11. Jehoiakim was the son of the great reformer King Josiah, who had been executed in 609 BCE at Megiddo following a battle with Egypt's Pharaoh Necho (2 Kings 23:28–30).

12. The collection of oracles of judgment against Babylon in Jeremiah 50:1–51:58 speak of the destruction of Babylon and of the return of the Jews from exile in Babylon and are clearly from the period following the return from exile sometime after 538 BCE. It is likely that the editor of this collection of oracles against Babylon also composed the narrative in Jeremiah 51:59–64 for the specific purpose of attributing these oracles to Jeremiah. Chapter 52 was taken from 2 Kings 24:18–25:30 and incorporated here in order to provide important historical information about King Zedekiah, the fall of Jerusalem to Nebuchadnezzar, and the deportation to Babylonia of forty-six hundred residents of Jerusalem and Judea. The mention in Jeremiah of the release of King Jehoiachin of Judah from prison in 560 BCE (Jeremiah 52:31–34) is unequivocal evidence that these final verses were added to the book sometime after that date, which is some sixty-seven years after the call and commission of Jeremiah in 626 BCE.

13. Bernard Duhm, *Das Buch Jesaja, übersetzt und erklärt*, 4th ed. (Göttingen: Vanderhoeck & Ruprecht, 1922) was the first scholar to identify the four Servant Poems. Duhm identified the servant as an unknown teacher of the law who lived shortly before the time of Deutero-Isaiah. For more than a century, there has been no consensus among scholars regarding the identification of the servant.

14. Paul says something similar in Galatians 1:15–17 about his own call and commission.

15. The word "Israel" in verse 3 is regarded by many scholars as a gloss, a later addition to the text, as its presence here seems to be inconsistent with verses 5–6.

16. Acts 8:32–33 is quoting Isaiah 53:7cde–8abc. The minor differences between the two texts are the result of the fact that Isaiah is translated into English from the original Hebrew, whereas Acts is translated into English from a Greek translation (the Septuagint) of the original Hebrew.

17. There is nothing in the book of Malachi that might be considered an account of the prophet's call and commission.

CHAPTER 8

THE REFORM OF KING JOSIAH, DEUTERONOMY, AND THE DEUTERONOMISTIC HISTORY

I t is here, following our examination of prophecy in the southern kingdom of Judah, that it seems appropriate to consider the third literary component of the Pentateuch, the D material or the book of Deuteronomy (see p. 54).

THE BOOK OF DEUTERONOMY

The book of Deuteronomy consists essentially of three speeches (Deuteronomy 1:6–4:40; 5–26, 28; and 29:2–30:20) and two poems (Deuteronomy 32 and 33), all of which are represented as having been delivered to the Israelites by Moses on the plains of Moab shortly before his death and the entrance of the people of Israel into the promised land of Canaan. In fact, the book of Deuteronomy purports to be Moses' guide for the people of Israel as to what they must do to live successfully in the new land that they are about to occupy.

Scholars are virtually unanimous in agreeing that the large middle section of the book (chapters 5–26 and 28) was the law book that was found in the Jerusalem temple in the eighteenth year of the reign of King Josiah (622/621 BCE) and that served subsequently as the basis for the religious reform described in 2 Kings 22:1–13:

₁Josiah was eight years old when he began to reign; he reigned thirty-one years [640–609 BCE] in Jerusalem. His mother's name was Jedidah, daughter of Adaiah of Bozkath. ₂He did what was right in the sight of the LORD (Yahweh), and walked in all the way of his father David; he did not turn aside to the right or to the left.

₃In the eighteenth year of King Josiah (622/621 BCE), the king sent Shaphan son of Azaliah, son of Meshullam, the secretary, to the house of the LORD (Yahweh) saying, ₄"Go up to the high priest Hilkiah, and have him count the entire sum of the money that has been brought into the house of the LORD (Yahweh), which the keepers of the threshold have collected from the people; ₅let it be given into the hand of the workers, who have the oversight of the house of the LORD (Yahweh); let them give it to the workers who are at the house of the LORD (Yahweh), repairing the house, ₆that is, to the carpenters, to the builders, to the masons; and let them use it to buy timber and quarried stone to repair the house. ₇But no accounting shall be asked from them for the money that is delivered into their hand, for they deal honestly."

₈The high priest Hilkiah said to Shaphan the secretary, "I have found the book of the law in the house of the LORD (Yahweh)." When Hilkiah gave the book to Shaphan, he read it. ₉Then Shaphan the secretary came to the king, and reported to the king, "Your servants have emptied out the money that was found in the house, and have delivered it into the hand of the workers who have oversight of the house of the LORD (Yahweh)." ₁₀Shaphan the secretary informed the king, "The priest Hilkiah has given me the book." Shaphan then read it aloud to the king.

₁₁When the king heard the words of the book of the law, he tore his clothes. ₁₂Then the king commanded the priest Hilkiah, Ahikam son of Shaphan, Achbor son of Micaiah, Shaphan the secretary, and the king's servant Asaiah, saying, ₁₃"Go inquire of the LORD (Yahweh) for me, for the people, and for all Judah, concerning the words of this book that has been found; for great is the wrath of the LORD (Yahweh) that is kindled against us, because our ancestors did not obey the words of this book, to do according to all that is written concerning us."

After the authenticity of "the book of the law" was confirmed by the prophetess Huldah (2 Kings 22:14–17), King Josiah "brought all the priests out of the towns of Judah, and defiled the high places" of Judah and "the high places that were east of Jerusalem" and confined legitimate worship of Yahweh exclusively to the Jerusalem temple (2 Kings 23:8, 13). Centralization of the cult in Jerusalem is a major theme of Deuteronomy 5–26, thereby linking the material in 2 Kings with Deuteronomy. Other more specific connections between 2 Kings and Deuteronomy include:

(1) In response to commands in the newly discovered book of the law, Josiah purified the worship of Yahweh from the contamination of corrupting elements and destroyed the Asherah[1] and the houses of prostitution in the temple precincts:

2 Kings 23:6	Deuteronomy 16:21–22
6He brought out the image of Asherah from the house of the Lord, outside Jerusalem, to the Wadi Kidron, burned it at the Wadi Kidron, beat it to dust and threw the dust of it upon the graves of the common people.	21You shall not plant any tree as a sacred pole beside the altar that you make for the LORD (Yahweh) your God; 22nor shall you set up a stone pillar—things that the LORD (Yahweh) your God hates.

2 Kings 23:7	Deuteronomy 23:17–18
7He broke down the houses of the male temple prostitutes that were in the house of the LORD (Yahweh), where the women did weaving for Asherah.	17None of the daughters of Israel shall be a temple prostitute; none of the sons of Israel shall be a temple prostitute. 18You shall not bring the fee of a prostitute or the wages of a male prostitute into the house of the LORD (Yahweh) your God in payment for any vow, for both of these are abhorrent to the LORD (Yahweh) your God.

(2) Josiah's opposition to idolatry was directed against the same forms of idolatry that are denounced in Deuteronomy:

2 Kings 23:5, 11	Deuteronomy 17:2–3
5He deposed the idolatrous priests whom the kings of Judah had ordained to make offerings in the high places at the cities of Judah and around Jerusalem; those also who made offerings to Baal, to the sun, the moon, the constellations,	2If there is found among you, in one of your towns that the LORD (Yahweh) is giving you, a man or a woman who does what is evil in the sight of the LORD (Yahweh) your God, and transgresses his covenant 3by going

and all the host of the heavens.
11He removed the horses that the kings
of Judah had dedicated to the sun, at the
entrance to the house of the LORD
(Yahweh), by the chamber of the
eunuch Nathan-melech, which was
in the precincts; then he burned the
chariots of the sun with fire.

to serve other gods and worshiping
them—whether the sun or the moon
or any of the host of heaven, which
I have forbidden. . . .

2 Kings 23:10, 13

Deuteronomy 12:31

10He defiled Topheth, which is in the
valley of Ben-hinnom, so that no one
would make a son or a daughter pass
through fire as an offering for Molech.
13The king defiled the high places that
were east of Jerusalem, to the south of
the Mount of Destruction, which King
Solomon of Israel had built for Astarte
the abomination of the Sidonians, for
Chemosh the abomination of Moab,
and for Milcom the abomination of the
Ammonites.

31You must not do the same for the
LORD (Yahweh) your God,
because every abhorrent thing
that the LORD (Yahweh) hates,
they have done for their gods.
They would even burn their
sons and their daughters in
the fire to their gods.

(3) The Passover that was celebrated in Josiah's day in Jerusalem is described
    as being unique; Deuteronomy forbids the celebration of the Passover any-
    where except in Jerusalem:

2 Kings 23:21–23

Deuteronomy 16:5–6

21The King commanded all the
people, "Keep the Passover to the LORD
(Yahweh) your God as prescribed in this
book of the covenant." 22No such
Passover had been kept since the days
of the judges who judged Israel, or during
all the days of the kings of Israel or of the

5You are not permitted to offer the
Passover sacrifice within any of
your towns that the LORD (Yahweh)
your God is giving you. 6But at
the place that the LORD (Yahweh)
your God will choose as a dwelling
for his name, only there shall you

Kings of Judah; 23but in the eighteenth year of King Josiah this Passover was kept to the LORD (Yahweh) in Jerusalem.

offer the Passover sacrifice, in the evening at sunset, the time of day when you departed from Egypt.

(4) Josiah abolished all superstitious practices for determining the divine will:

2 Kings 23:24

Deuteronomy 18:10–11

Moreover Josiah put away the mediums, wizards, teraphim, idols, and all the abominations that were seen in the land of Judah and in Jerusalem, so that he established the words of the law that were written in the book that the priest Hilkiah had found in the house of the LORD (Yahweh).

10No one shall be found among you who makes a son or a daughter pass through fire, or who practices divination, or is a soothsayer, or an augur, or a sorcerer, 11or one who casts spells, or who consults ghosts or spirits, or who seeks oracles from the dead.

In each instance cited above, the demands of Deuteronomy 12–26 correspond to the actions of King Josiah as reported in the account of Josiah's reform in 2 Kings 23.

The prophet Zephaniah had protested loudly against the paganism associated with the Yahweh cult (Zephaniah 1:4–6), probably at a time early in the reign of King Josiah (640–609 BCE) and certainly before the reforms were fully implemented. As a result of Zephaniah's protests, the discovery of the book of the law, and certainly as a result of Josiah's sweeping reform, the Jerusalem temple was purged of all foreign influences, and the paganism in Judah and Jerusalem was abolished. By focusing all worship of Yahweh in the Jerusalem temple, the official priesthood could now supervise cultic practices and keep them free from defilement by such pagan influences as Canaanite Baal worship, the astral cult of Assyrian religion, and the worship of other foreign deities such as the Moabite god Chemosh and the Ammonite god Milcom.

THE ORIGINS OF DEUTERONOMY

The origins of the Deuteronomic law code are not entirely clear, but the fact that it does not specifically identify Jerusalem as the central sanctuary in which all legitimate worship of Yahweh must be concentrated implies that the core of the book of

Deuteronomy may have had its origin in the northern kingdom of Israel, perhaps in the judicial rulings of Levites, who were teaching and preaching priests.[2] The core of the book of Deuteronomy may have inspired the earlier religious reform of King Hezekiah (715–687/586 BCE) and appears to have served also as the basis for the subsequent writing of the Deuteronomistic History (the books of Joshua, Judges, 1 and 2 Samuel, and 1 and 2 Kings).

If the Deuteronomic law code originated among the Levitical priests in the northern kingdom, it was likely later edited and preserved in the south during the two centuries following the fall of the northern kingdom of Israel (722/721 BCE) and the beginning of the restoration of Judah (ca. 535 BCE) following the Babylonian exile (687/686–540 BCE). It is likely that a body of reformers created an updated written version of the code of law in the latter years of the reform under King Hezekiah (ca. 715–687/686 BCE). Those reformers would not have created new legislation; they would rather have put a new spirit into an older law code whose purpose it was to interpret and implement for the people the Mosaic legacy of covenantal law.

Following Hezekiah's death in 687/686 BCE, he was succeeded by his son Manasseh, the archvillain of Judah's history in the mind of the Deuteronomistic historian(s), because he reacted strongly against his father's religious reforms and reinstituted practices that compromised the worship of Yahweh (2 Kings 21:2–16).

The Deuteronomistic historian(s) regarded Manasseh's long reign (687/686–642 BCE) as the embodiment of evil, the darkest period in Judah's four-hundred-year history, as shown in 2 Kings 21:3–6:

> 3For he rebuilt the high places that his father Hezekiah had destroyed; he erected altars for Baal, made a sacred pole [Asherah], as King Ahab of Israel had done, worshiped all the host of heaven, and served them. 4He built altars in the house of the LORD (Yahweh), of which the LORD (Yahweh) had said, "In Jerusalem I will put my name." 5He built altars for all the host of heaven in the two courts of the house of the LORD (Yahweh). 6He made his son pass through fire; he practiced soothsaying and augury, and dealt with mediums and with wizards.

Much of Manasseh's program was apparently enacted out of deference to Assyria, as it was Manasseh's policy to appease rather than confront this major Mesopotamian political and military power.

Apparently the book of the law was set aside following Hezekiah's death (687/686 BCE) and was forgotten and buried in some deep recess of the temple, only to be rediscovered decades later in the eighteenth year of the reign of King Josiah. It was likely this book of law from the time of Hezekiah that Hilkiah the priest discovered during the renovation of the Jerusalem temple in 622/621 BCE, about sixty-five years after it was presumably hidden and then forgotten.

Although Deuteronomy exhibits more coherence than the earlier sources of the Pentateuch, both J and E, it too underwent a lengthy process of composition. Final editing of the book likely took place during the period of the Babylonian exile. This so-called D document serves as the third component in the four-source hypothesis (see the chart on p. 54).

THE DEUTERONOMISTIC HISTORY

The book of Deuteronomy serves as a theological preface or introduction to the books of Joshua, Judges, 1 and 2 Samuel, and 1 and 2 Kings, the so-called Deuteronomistic History. The first edition of this historical work probably comes from the period of Josiah's reform, although the author(s) clearly had access to existing sources, such as:

(1) a collection of oral and written stories, lists, and poetic fragments of varying antiquity from the time of Joshua;

(2) various oral and written tribal stories of local leaders and of crises concerning twelve leaders or "judges": Othniel, Ehud, Shamgar, Deborah, Gideon, Tola, Jair, Jephthah, Ibzan, Elon, Abdon, and Samson;

(3) the ark narrative;

(4) a cycle of stories about Saul;

(5) the story of David's rise to power;

(6) the story of Absalom's revolt;

(7) the book of the Acts of Solomon;

(8) the book of the Annals of the Kings of Israel, and

(9) the book of the Annals of the Kings of Judah.

As a component of Josiah's reform, the so-called Deuteronomistic historian(s) apparently gathered available oral and written sources to compile a history of the nation from the time following Moses' death to the then present time (the final decades of the seventh century BCE). The history was subsequently updated and edited, with the final version coming from the period of the Babylonian exile, and the last recorded event of the history being the release from prison of King Jehoiachin of Judah in about 560 BCE (2 Kings 25:27–30). There is no mention in the Deuteronomistic History of the emergence of Cyrus of Persia or of the fall of Babylonia in 539 BCE, suggesting that the Deuteronomistic History in its final form was likely completed around 550 BCE.

If scholars are correct in hypothesizing that the Deuteronomistic History appeared in two or more editions, then we have in this instance still one more example of the revising and updating of an earlier writer's work, a feature common in ancient Israelite literature.

In their recounting of the history of Israel and Judah, the Deuteronomistic historian(s) had two matters with which to work: (1) the history of the nation(s), and (2) the will of Yahweh. As they wove these two elements into a single fabric, the historians exercised certain principles in their interpretation of the national history:

(1) the demand for unconditional obedience to Israel's covenant with Yahweh; more specifically, did the people and did the kings put their trust in Yahweh?;

(2) the efficiency of the prophetic word—(a) the prophet says something; (b) it comes to pass; (c) the prophet's words are recalled by the people; and

(3) the relationship between the Davidic dynasty and the will of Yahweh—did the kings follow faithfully the ways of David, not the David of history, but a David idealized by the Deuteronomistic historian(s)?

The first of these principles centers Israel in Moses, while the second centers Israel in the teachings of the prophets and the third centers Israel and its kings in David.

For the Deuteronomistic historian(s), the history of Israel and Judah is the story of the unraveling of the will and the word of Yahweh as the nation spiraled downward and declined from the moment of the crossing of the Jordan into the land of Canaan, through the destruction of the northern kingdom of Israel in 722/721 BCE by the Assyrian Empire, to the demise of the southern kingdom of Judah in 587/586 BCE at the hands of the Babylonian Empire and the ensuing deportation to Babylon. Looking back on the history of the nation over almost seven hundred years, the author(s) could see how the nation had suffered and failed because of its faithlessness to the demands of the covenant with Yahweh, its failure to heed the words of prophets whom Yahweh had sent to warn the people, and the failure of Israel's and Judah's kings to walk in the ways of the idealized King David whom Yahweh had anointed. In their minds, that faithlessness explained the decline and fall of the empire of King David.

CONCLUSIONS

There is general agreement among scholars that the book of the law that Hilkiah the priest discovered in the Jerusalem temple during the reign of King Josiah was the core of our present book of Deuteronomy. The correspondence between the demands set forth in Deuteronomy 12–26 and the decisive action that Josiah took in response to the discovery of the scroll in the temple in 622/621 BCE, as reported in 2 Kings 23, leaves no doubt in this regard.

The exact origin and history of the book of the law is another matter, but evidence points to an origin among the Levitical priests of the northern kingdom more than a hundred years earlier. Following the fall of the northern kingdom of Israel in 722/721 BCE, the book apparently found its way to the southern kingdom of Judah where it was edited and updated and where it may have served as the inspiration for the religious reform of King Hezekiah of Judah (715–687/686 BCE).

When Manasseh succeeded his father as king of Judah (687/686–642), he reinstituted religious practices that compromised the worship of Yahweh and the reforms of Hezekiah. Accordingly, it was apparently during Manasseh's reign that someone in the temple precincts hid the scroll of the book of the law in a remote storage room of the temple, where it remained until its discovery by Hilkiah more than six decades later in 622/621, when it served once again as the basis of a religious reform, this time under the sponsorship of King Josiah. This reconstruction of the book's history best addresses the evidence available to us.

Sometime later, this Deuteronomic law book (D) was apparently attached to the end of the combined JE version of the national epic as the third component in what would eventually become our Pentateuch (see p. 54). Unlike the first two sources, the Yahwist (J) and the Elohist (E) and the subsequent Priestly source (P), the Deuteronomic law (D) was not integrated throughout the other sources but remained relatively intact at the end of the national epic in the form of our present book of Deuteronomy.

The Deuteronomic law served also as the theological basis for the writing of the Deuteronomistic History (the books of Joshua, Judges, 1 and 2 Samuel, and 1 and 2 Kings). Scholars have identified the operative theological principles for the writing of the history, which the Deuteronomistic historian(s) put together from primary oral and written sources, including court annals that were available to them. Their objective was to compile a written record of the nation over a period of almost seven hundred years from the time of the entrance into the land of Canaan in about 1250 BCE until the destruction of the southern kingdom in 587/586 BCE and the subsequent release from prison of King Jehoiachin of Judah in about 560 BCE.

The proximity of the Deuteronomistic historian's early sources to many of the events described gives us confidence in the reliability of a good deal of the basic material. There is, however, still earlier legendary material such as the Elijah and Elisha cycles and the theological layer of interpretation of that earlier oral and written material that scholars must penetrate in order to distinguish those relatively reliable primary sources from the Deuteronomistic historian's interpretation of that material.

Like the Isaiah scroll and the Jeremiah scroll, the book of Deuteronomy and the six-book Deuteronomistic History underwent frequent revising, editing, and updating of earlier writers' works before the final editions of these books were produced, probably in Jerusalem during the period of reconstruction following the Babylonian exile, a major watershed event in the national history.

Once again, we have observed that biblical scholars often come to a consensus in their reconstruction of the past, although they sometimes disagree with respect to how to read and interpret the same data. The dilemma lies not in a flawed methodology, but in the limited information that is often available to scholars and in the need to make considered judgments within the limits of historical reason.

NOTES

1. According to Ugaritic tradition, the goddess Asherah was the female consort of the god El, but she served as the consort of Baal in Canaanite tradition. The word Asherah also refers to a cult object associated with and perhaps representing the goddess. This cult object was likely in the form of a pole carved from wood, or in some case it may have been a living tree.

2. Additional evidence of the likely origin of the Deuteronomic law code in the northern kingdom may be found in its consistent use of the name Horeb for the holy mountain. As was mentioned above (see p. 184), the northern Elohist version of the national epic and Deuteronomy both use the name Horeb, whereas the Yahwist and P, both southern documents, refer to the holy mountain as Sinai.

CHAPTER 9

THE RESTORATION AND
THE PRIESTLY SYNTHESIS

Few people are as important to the history of Israel and the survival of Judaism as Cyrus the Great, the son of Cambyses I and founder of the Persian Empire. Our knowledge of Cyrus comes primarily from Herodotus,[1] the Babylonian Chronicles,[2] the Cyrus cylinder,[3] and the Old Testament. He is referred to in the Hebrew Bible as "king of Persia" (2 Chronicles 36:22–23; Ezra 1:1, 2, 8; 3:7; 4:3, 5; Daniel 10:1); as "the Persian" (Daniel 6:28); and as "the king of Babylon (Ezra 5:13). Deutero-Isaiah calls him "the anointed of Yahweh" (Isaiah 45:1), who will redeem Israel, set the exiles free, and restore Jerusalem and the temple (Isaiah 44:28; 45:13).

Although Herodotus's stories of Cyrus's childhood are little more than fanciful legends, the account of Cyrus's rise to power in his conflict with Astyages, the last king of the ancient Iranian kingdom of Media, is the first well-documented event in Archaemenid history. Our sources generally agree about Cyrus's victories against the Medes (550 BCE) and Lydia (550–547 BCE), his successful campaign east and northeast of the Iranian plateau (546–540 BCE), and his victory over Babylon (539/538 BCE).

Although Cyrus II came to the Persian throne in 559 BCE, it was twenty years later in 539/538 BCE that he conquered Babylon and the Babylonian Empire and allowed the exiles who had been deported to Babylon decades earlier to return to their homes. Among the repatriated exiles were Jews[4] who had been deported to

Babylon two generations earlier in 597 BCE and in even greater number in 587/586 BCE, the year that Jerusalem finally fell to the Babylonians.

Ezra 1:1–4 purports to quote from Cyrus's famous decree, presumably the version proclaimed in Jewish communities in Babylon at the time the decree was initially issued:[5]

> [1]In the first year of King Cyrus of Persia,[6] in order that the word of the LORD (Yahweh) by the mouth of Jeremiah might be accomplished, the LORD (Yahweh) stirred up the spirit of King Cyrus of Persia so that he sent a herald throughout all his kingdom, and also in a written edict declared: [2]"Thus says King Cyrus of Persia: The LORD (Yahweh), the God of heaven, has given me all the kingdoms of the earth, and he has charged me to build him a house at Jerusalem in Judah. [3]Any of those among you who are of his people—may their God be with them!—are now permitted to go up to Jerusalem in Judah, and rebuild the house of the LORD (Yahweh), the God of Israel—he is God who is in Jerusalem; [4]and let all survivors, in whatever place they reside, be assisted by the people of their place with silver and gold, with goods and with animals, besides freewill offerings for the house of God in Jerusalem."[7]

It is surprising, indeed inconceivable, to read in the words quoted here as the Edict of Cyrus that Yahweh gave the Persian king victory over all the kingdoms of the earth and charged him to rebuild the Jerusalem temple (Ezra 1:2). As a Persian, Cyrus would not have worshiped Yahweh, however benevolent he was toward the exiles, and he certainly would not have attributed his victory over the Babylonians to the Israelite god. Rather, the decree in the form in which we have it in Ezra and in 2 Chronicles reflects either the Chronicler's own interpretation of the edict or the language of a Jewish secretary who may have been charged to publish Cyrus's decree among the Jews. Although represented as a direct quote, the edict simply could not have come from Cyrus in this form.

THE CHRONICLER

The story of the events that transpired in Jerusalem following the people's return from the Babylonian exile is reported in Ezra and Nehemiah, two of the four books that scholars refer to as the Chronicler's History or, more simply, the Chronicler. The books of 1 and 2 Chronicles, Ezra, and Nehemiah comprise the Chronicler,[8] a term commonly applied to a school of historical interpreters who wrote during the post-exilic period.

The date of composition of 1 and 2 Chronicles is related to the question of whether 1 and 2 Chronicles was written first and Ezra-Nehemiah subsequently, or whether Chronicles-Nehemiah is a single composition written at one time. Some scholars believe that 1 and 2 Chronicles, which is a single manuscript in the Hebrew Bible, was composed by an ecclesiastical official in Jerusalem, perhaps as early as 520–515 BCE, about the time of the building of the second temple and just a couple of decades after the last event mentioned in 2 Chronicles 36:22–23, namely, the issuing of the decree of Cyrus (about 539/538 BCE). This work may have been edited and enlarged at various times thereafter until it reached its final form, 1 and 2 Chronicles and Ezra-Nehemiah, sometime about 400 BCE.

If, on the other hand, we are dealing with a single literary composition Chronicles-Nehemiah by one author, then the date of composition of the composite work is likely sometime about 400 BCE, based on known dates of the rule of Darius II (423–405 BCE) (mentioned in Ezra 4:5, 24; 6:14; and Nehemiah 12:22). In addition, the Davidic genealogy in 1 Chronicles 3:10–24 traces seven generations from Jehoiachin (Jeconiah) (598/597 BCE), which on the basis of about twenty-five years per generation would bring the birth of Elioenai's eldest son, Hodaviah, to about 420 BCE and of his youngest son, Anani, to about 405 BCE (1 Chronicles 3:24). If this genealogy is original to 1 Chronicles,[9] then a date of about 400 BCE is probable for the composite writing Chronicles-Nehemiah. If the Davidic genealogy was added by a later editor, then the completed version of the entire work, Chronicles-Nehemiah, can be dated to about 400 BCE, presuming the earlier date of 520–515 BCE for 1 and 2 Chronicles, and the date of 400 BCE for the edited 1 and 2 Chronicles and the writing of Ezra-Nehemiah. I assume the simpler theory, namely, the unity of Chronicles-Ezra-Nehemiah and, therefore, a date of composition of circa 400 BCE for the completed document.

In composing his history, the Chronicler apparently made use of earlier written material, including:

(1) the Deuteronomistic History (specifically material found in 1 and 2 Samuel and 1 and 2 Kings, which the Chronicler reworked to suit his particular theological bias);

(2) early sources either not known to or not otherwise included in the Deuteronomistic History but known to the Chronicler;

(3) a memoir of Ezra the priest, which provided material for Ezra 7–10 and Nehemiah 8–9;

(4) a memoir of Nehemiah the governor, which was edited to form Nehemiah 1–7; 11:1–2; 12:31–43; 13:4–31); and

(5) several purportedly original documents in Aramaic[10] that are incorporated into the text of Ezra, including:

a letter from Rehum, the Persian royal deputy of the province "Beyond the River" (including Samaria and Judea), Shimshai the scribe, and others to King Artaxerses regarding the repair of the walls of Jerusalem (Ezra 4:11–16);

a reply from Artaxerses to Rehum, Shemshai, and their associates authorizing them to stop the building activity in Jerusalem (Ezra 4:17d–22);

a letter from Tattenai, the Persian governor of the province "Beyond the River," Shethar-bozenai, and his associates to King Darius I informing the king of building activities in Jerusalem and asking whether the work was authorized (Ezra 5:7b–17);

a reply from Darius to Tattenai, Shethar-bozenai, and their associates in the form of a decree of Darius authorizing the rebuilding of the temple in Jerusalem (Ezra 6:6–12).[11]

The work of the Chronicler is, accordingly, a rewriting, a reediting, or a reinterpretation of Israel's history from Adam to about 400 BCE, with a focus on the Jerusalem temple, where priests and most especially Levites played an indispensable role in overseeing the nation's liturgy. In his writing of the national history, the Chronicler focused most especially on the continuity of the true worship of Yahweh in Jerusalem and in the Jerusalem temple.

As an example of the way in which earlier history was reinterpreted, the Chronicler was not particularly interested in David as a political leader, because by the time the Chronicler wrote, Israel was no longer a nation-state. David is portrayed rather as the king who organized Israel as a worshiping community in Jerusalem (Israel's religious capital rather than its political capital), who instituted instrumental music in the temple, and who assigned responsibility for the oversight of the temple to Levite priests. Accordingly, the Chronicler painted David in a way that reflected the interests of post-exilic priestly Judaism.

What is particularly interesting in this regard is that it was not David but rather David's son Solomon who actually built the temple to Yahweh in Jerusalem. The Chronicler glosses over this technicality by implying in 1 Chronicles 29:19 that it was, in fact, David who conceived of the temple according to a plan ordained by Yahweh ("Grant to my son Solomon that with single mind he may keep your [Yahweh's] commandments, your decrees, and your statutes, performing all of them, and that he [Solomon] may build the temple for which I [David] have made provision" [see also 1 Chronicles 17]).[12]

Beginning with the reign of David and down to the time of the Babylonian exile, the Chronicler reports the history of Israel in ecclesiastical terms. Following the civil war of 922/921 BCE, the northern kingdom of Israel separated from Judah and Jerusalem and subsequently fell to the Assyrians in 722/721 BCE, the Chronicler reports, because King Jeroboam I of northern Israel had departed from the true Davidic community of worship in Jerusalem. Yahweh had, accordingly, punished northern Israel for Jeroboam's rebellion against the legitimate Davidic dynasty in Jerusalem. The southern kingdom of Judah subsequently fell to the Babylonians in 587/586 BCE because Yahweh was punishing it for its corruption, its faithlessness, and its sinfulness.

It is at this point, the fall of Jerusalem in 587/586 BCE and the subsequent onset of the restoration of Jerusalem at the hand of King Cyrus of Persia in 539/538 BCE, that the Chronicler picks up the account with the events found in Ezra-Nehemiah. The Edict of Cyrus enabled the Jews to return to Judah and Jerusalem. Soon after their return, Jews began to agitate to rebuild the temple, a project that was completed in 516/515 BCE. Ezra the priest subsequently came from Babylonia with the Mosaic Law and initiated a major religious reform in order to establish and maintain the identity of the Jewish community. According to the chronology of the Chronicler, next came Nehemiah, also from Babylon, to serve as governor of the Persian district of Jerusalem, to supervise the rebuilding of the city walls, and to institute religious and social reforms.[13] In the eyes of the Chronicler, Israel returned from the Babylonian exile not as a nation-state, but as a religious community, the kind of religious community that Yahweh had always intended Israel to be.

The return from exile and the rebuilding of Jerusalem and the temple posed enormous challenges to the Jews (Ezra 4:1–5). Exiles returned from Babylon slowly, and many who had remained in Judah and Jerusalem during the exile resented the returning exiles, whom the Chronicler claimed were the true Israel. Survivors of the earlier Assyrian deportation, who survived in what remained of the northern kingdom of Israel, the so-called Samaritans, were initially willing to cooperate in the rebuilding of the temple with Zerubbabel,[14] a returning exile and the grandson of the exiled Judean king Jehoiachin, who was himself a descendant of King David and one of the last kings of Judah. Cyrus II had appointed Zerubbabel as his governor in Jerusalem, and Jeshua (or Joshua, as he is called in Haggai and Zechariah) served as high priest.

Apparently under the inspiration of two prophets, Haggai and Zechariah (Ezra 5:1–5), and under the Davidic leadership of Zerubbabel and the high priest Jeshua, the Jews started to rebuild the temple. Despite efforts on the part of some to stop the project and the suspension of work on the temple during the reigns of Cyrus II and Cambyses III, the rebuilding of the temple was finally completed in 516/515 BCE. Zerubbabel disappeared from the scene for unknown reasons, leaving the high priest Jeshua and his successors as the undisputed leaders of the Jerusalem community. From this time forth, Israel was to be a temple-centered community, ruled by priests as originally prescribed by David, according to rules laid down by the Chronicler.

We have no information about the seventy-year period between 516/515 BCE and 445 BCE, except for mention of the disintegration of Hebrew religion and worship. Nehemiah, who was a Jew in the Persian court in Babylon, persuaded King Artaxerses to appoint him governor with the specific assignment of rebuilding the walls of Jerusalem. Nehemiah is reported to have arrived from Babylon in 445 BCE, when he began to reorganize the religious scene in Jerusalem. The rebuilding, or more likely the repair of the city wall, was completed in fifty-two days "with the help of our God" (Nehemiah 6:15–16).[15] Ezra, an exile of a Zadokite high-priestly family and a scribe skilled in the law (Ezra 7:1–6), subsequently assumed leadership in Jerusalem and read "the book of the Torah of Moses" (Nehemiah 8:1) to the people,[16] presumably the Pentateuch itself, the final Priestly redaction in the centuries-long process of composing the Pentateuch.[17]

During this period of restoration, Jerusalem remained part of the Persian Empire, but the Persians were far more benevolent than the Assyrians and the Babylonians before them. The Assyrians had essentially decimated northern Israel in 722/721 BCE, and the Babylonians had done much the same to Judah in 587/586 BCE. Under the Persians, the Jews apparently had complete religious liberty, although they had no political independence. This development led the Jews to look toward the establishment in Jerusalem of a theocracy within the Persian Empire, a nation ruled not by a Davidic king, but by Yahweh alone. Although Israel and Judah no longer existed politically, Israel continued to exist as the people of God.

The post-exilic restoration resulted in the development in Jerusalem of a hierarchy of priests. Responsibility for preserving Yahweh's chosen people was effectively handed over to this priestly hierarchy. From the period of Persian rule, there emerged Chronicles, which served as a history of Israel from Adam until Cyrus, and Ezra-Nehemiah, which continued the history after Cyrus until about 400 BCE, the presumed date of composition of this history.

During this period of restoration, the Chronicler applied the doctrine of retribution in this reworking of the national history. When Israel is obedient to the will of Yahweh, she is rewarded; when disobedient, she is punished. If, for some reason, the historical data do not conform to the principle, then the historical data are wrong, not the principle. Therefore, history, the vehicle through which Yahweh carries out his purposes for his people Israel, was reworked, rewritten, and even changed to satisfy the principle of divine retribution. In any event, history is understood by the Chronicler consistently as a series of things that Yahweh has done for Israel and humankind and it is not a recounting of events that humankind and Israel have done. The Chronicler was not so much a historian of Israel's past as he was an interpreter of Israel's past.

THE PRIESTLY CODE (P)

The period of the final years of the Babylonian exile and the time of the restoration in Jerusalem were evidently times of great literary activity, primarily in priestly circles. Out of this consolidation of power by the priests, out of a priestly synthesis toward the end of and in the aftermath of the Babylonian exile, there emerged the Priestly Code of the Pentateuch, P. Some scholars think P was originally a separate document that came to serve as the framework for the national history as reported previously in the J and E sources, of the southern and northern kingdoms, respectively. Others view P simply as the framework that the priestly editors created in their final redaction of the earlier version of the national history, found in the JE document (see above p. 54).

As has been mentioned previously, the French physician Jean Astruc observed in 1753 that, when referring to the deity, some narratives in Genesis use the generic word Elohim, meaning god or a divine being, whereas other narratives use the personal name of Israel's God Yahweh. Astruc's discovery served as a useful starting point in the identification of the multiple sources of Genesis and the rest of the Pentateuch. Although our purposes here allow for only a brief treatment of the documentary hypothesis in order to illustrate both the methods and the results of biblical scholarship on the subject, it seems suitable at this point to identify some of the characteristics of the Priestly source (P) beyond the simple use of Elohim instead of the divine name Yahweh, which is characteristic of J:

(1) In addition to the word Elohim for Israel's god, P uses the name El Shaddai (Genesis 17:1; 28:3; 35:11; 48:3; see also Exodus 6:3, where the name El Shaddai is restricted to the patriarchal period).[18]

(2) Typical of P are the numerous genealogies or family trees (see Genesis 1:1–2:4a [see especially the use of "these are the generations" in 2:4a at the conclusion of P's creation story, as if it were just one more genealogical list]; 5:1–28, 30–32; 6:9–10; 10:1–7, 20, 22–23, 31–32; 11:10–27, 31–32; 25:12–17, 19–20; 36:1–37:2a; and Numbers 3:1–4).

(3) P uses the name Paddan-aram (Genesis 25:20; 28:2, 5, 6, 7) as the ancestral home of the patriarchs, whereas J uses Aram-naharaim = "the city of Nahor" in Haran (Genesis 24:10; see also Genesis 11:31).

(4) P regularly uses the expression "be fruitful and multiply" (Genesis 1:22, 28; 8:17; 9:1, 7).[19]

In other words, the identification of the several sources of the Pentateuch has become something of a science with scholars assigning individual verses or even parts of a verse in the Pentateuch to one of the sources. Among those portions of the Pentateuch that scholars generally assign to P are:

(1) the creation story in which the law of the Sabbath is, in effect, written into the divine act of creation (Genesis 1:1–2:4a);

(2) the story of Noah, in which humankind is permitted for the first time to eat meat, but meat without blood, and which introduces the covenant of the rainbow (Genesis 6:9–22; 7:6, 11, 13–16a, 17a, 18–21; 7:24–8:2a, 8:3b–5, 13a, 14–19; 9:1–17);

(3) the Abraham cycle, with the institution of the covenant of circumcision

(Genesis 11:31–32; 12:4b–5; 13:6, 11b–12a; 16:1a, 3, 15–16; 17:1–27; 19:29);

(4) the Mosaic covenant, in which the law of the Passover is instituted (Exodus 12:1–20, 28, 40–51); and

(5) apart from the law book Deuteronomy, all law in the Pentateuch is represented in the Priestly Code as having been set forth by Moses at Mount Sinai (Exodus 25–31; 35–40; Leviticus 1–17; see also Numbers 1–10).

By 397 BCE and perhaps earlier, this Priestly tradition (P) was fitted into existing written traditions, JE and Deuteronomy, to serve as the framework of the Pentateuch. Accordingly, it was the post-exilic priests who created the Pentateuch. It is they who composed the Torah in the form in which we have it today. The purpose of this Priestly reconstruction of history was to maintain the unity and integrity of Israel as a people at a time when Israel no longer existed as a nation-state, as was the situation both during and following the Babylonian exile.

The priests' method was to rework older tradition, the material that existed previously as J, E, and D, and to put it into their own framework (P) in order to afford unified meaning to the whole. The theme of this final work was essentially that Yahweh God was trying to establish a society through which he could work out his purpose in history. Fulfilling this intention could be accomplished only through the observance of the Law, the Torah.

In the aftermath of the destruction of the state and the exile of the people to Babylon, cult and ritual became the focus of the new society. Everyday life was regarded as a religious affair, because virtually everything in everyday life was put under the Torah, which was understood as the word of Israel's God. The Priestly tradition sought to describe a utopia that lay within the realm of human possibility.

As a result of the work of the post-exilic priests, the cult became the people's central responsibility to Yahweh. This development made the written Torah the heart and soul of post-exilic Israel. Subjugation of the people to the Torah was viewed not as an imposition on the people of something that they did not like and did not want. Observance of God's Torah was rather understood as a great joy.

Religion served as the central focus of the people's lives, as every aspect of their existence was infused with a religious significance. Action in every sphere of life seemed to be covered in the Law. In rewriting the old traditions of Israel, the priests created a national history as seen through the eyes of the post-exilic remnant based in Judah and Jerusalem, with the temple and the priesthood at the center of their existence.

The priestly method accomplished what it was attempting to do: it succeeded in maintaining a holy people, separate from the rest of the world and devoted to their God Yahweh. The result is that for twenty-five hundred years following the destruction of the nation-state, Jews succeeded in maintaining their identity as a people without political unity or a land of their own. Only with the establishment of modern Israel in 1948 has there once again been a political and national focus for Jews. It is safe to say that twentieth-century Zionism, which brought about the re-creation of Israel, would not have been possible without the priestly effort of the post-exilic period. The survival of Israel in exile for twenty-five hundred years in spite of persecutions wherever Jews went is surely the crowning success of the Priestly movement of the sixth and fifth centuries BCE.

CONCLUSIONS

Watershed events often define a people. They provide occasions to reflect on the past and to look toward a new understanding of the future. Such watershed events have afforded meaning and understanding to Americans over the centuries:

> October 12, 1492 (Columbus's discovery of the New World);
> July 4, 1776 (signing of the Declaration of Independence);
> April 12, 1861 (beginning of the Civil War with the attack on Fort Sumter);
> December 7, 1941 (Japanese attack on Pearl Harbor); and
> September 11, 2001 (terrorist attacks on the World Trade Center and the Pentagon).

Many of these dates appear to focus on single moments in American history, although these specific dates usually mark the beginning of an important transitional period with a future that is still unknown at the time of the original event. The events themselves are often perceived retrospectively by subsequent generations as containing the seeds of the future; but that insight is, of course, generally the result of hindsight.

The ancient Israelites had several such watershed events, as well, although we cannot assign specific dates to any of them. Our records are not adequately detailed or sufficiently reliable to enable us to set these events in a precise historical frame-work: the Exodus, circa 1290 BCE; the establishment of the United Kingdom, circa 1000 BCE; the civil war, 922/921 BCE; the fall of Samaria, 722/721 BCE; the fall of Jerusalem, 587/586 BCE; the Edict of Cyrus, 539/538 BCE. These events in Israel's national history afforded new beginnings or challenging detours that enabled or sometimes even required Israel to understand more clearly and somewhat differ-ently the meaning of her national existence and her relationship to her God Yahweh.

Biblical scholars have sometimes found it difficult to unravel these important events themselves from the meaning attached to them by subsequent generations. That difficulty invariably poses a challenge to those involved with the writing of his-tory, especially ancient history. What follows an important event often determines how that event is understood and how it is remembered by subsequent generations. In fact, especially at such times, the future often brings a substantial rewriting of the past in ways that complicate or even thwart the best efforts of historians. With this chapter, we have such a watershed event, the Edict of Cyrus in 539/538 BCE, with all that this event meant to the subsequent history of Israel.

Although our biblical sources for this period, 1 and 2 Chronicles and Ezra-Nehemiah, were written relatively close in time to many of the events that they report, especially the events of the restoration in Jerusalem, these sources are not without their challenges. The Chronicler reports events from Adam to Cyrus in 1 and 2 Chronicles, using several sources available to him. We likely have access to one of those sources, the Deuteronomistic History found in Joshua, Judges, 1 and 2 Samuel, and 1 and 2 Kings, so we are able to see how the Chronicler used his sources to advance his personal theological agenda. We do not, however, have direct access to many of the Chronicler's sources: early sources unknown to the Deutero-nomistic historian, the memoir of Ezra, the memoir of Nehemiah, and other written documents (some of them in Aramaic)—written sources to which the Chronicler apparently had access but which we know only as the Chronicler used them.

There are, however, some ways to check our biblical sources. We have Herodotus of Halicarnassus's *History of the Persian Wars*, the Babylonian Chron-icle, and the Cyrus cylinder seal, all of which lend some greater objectivity to our study of the period, although their value is understandably also somewhat limited. They provide glimpses into the time, but they do not provide us with more than a fraction of the information that we need in order to write a comprehensive history of the period. Archaeology too is of limited value in assisting scholars in the reconstruction of the history of the period of the restoration. The existence of residences and holy places in areas of modern Jerusalem where archaeologists might find evidence of the city walls and perhaps even of the second temple makes "digging up the past" essentially impossible. With all of its limitations, the Old Testament remains our single most important source for most of what we are trying to reconstruct in the course of this chapter.

The existence of the text of the Edict of Cyrus in both Hebrew and Aramaic confirm the likely authenticity of our texts. Yet scholars disagree on whether it was Ezra or Nehemiah who appeared in Jerusalem first, because of perceived discrepancies in the text of Ezra-Nehemiah. Scholars also disagree on the date of Ezra's reading of "the Torah of Moses" alluded to in Nehemiah 8:1, because it is not clear whether Ezra 7:1 is referring to Artaxerses I or Artaxerses II. That single difference means a discrepancy of some fifty years.

Although Ezra-Nehemiah makes reference or allusion to some two dozen or more sources, the order and arrangement of this material pose serious challenges to biblical scholars in their effort to write a chronological narrative of exactly what transpired in the aftermath of the Edict of Cyrus. Even in antiquity the sequence of events was an issue for the author of 1 Esdras, which was likely compiled in the second century BCE from the Greek Septuagint of 2 Chronicles, Ezra, and Nehemiah; and for Josephus (*Antiquities*, 11.1–5), who, writing toward the end of the first century CE, seems to follow the chronological order in 1 Esdras.[20]

This chapter also provides the final piece in the solution to the question of the sources of the Pentateuch with discussion of the creation of P and its incorporation into the Pentateuch as the framework for the other sources: J, E (or JE), and D. Over the last century or more, scholars have identified verse by verse in the Pentateuch what was written by the authors of J, E, D, and P, although there is understandably not complete unanimity about this matter however much scholars' conclusions may agree.

Reconstructing the past is not an easy exercise, and it is certainly not an exact science. What is involved is collecting, studying, and analyzing all of the evidence without bias or prior preconception. Most scholars are able to accomplish that, but equally competent scholars can and often do afford different reconstructions of the past based on an examination of the same evidence. The reason is clear—the data are usually insufficient and limited in what they tell us. We are required to reconstruct an entire jigsaw puzzle with only the very limited number of pieces of the puzzle available to us.

Yet even within the limits of historical reason, it is relatively easy to see the significance of Cyrus's decree to allow the Jewish exiles to go home to Judah and Jerusalem. It is relatively easy to see how the priests used this opportunity as a means of securing more power for themselves at a time when there was essentially a political vacuum in Jerusalem following the demise of the nation-state. It is relatively easy to see how the Chronicler rewrote history to justify the events that were unfolding in Jerusalem during the period of reconstruction, and it is relative easy to understand how and why the priests rewrote the national history in the form of the Pentateuch to prepare from the earliest stages of the national epic for the challenging events that subsequently unfolded in the sixth and fifth centuries BCE.

NOTES

1. Herodotus of Halicarnassus (484 BCE–ca. 425 BCE), a Dorian Greek historian, is generally regarded as "the father of history." His most famous work, *History of the Persian Wars* (ca. 445 BCE), is a collection of "inquiries" (Greek *historia*) about peoples and places that he encountered during his travels around the eastern Mediterranean and in Mesopotamia. Herodotus is our principal source for Median and Persian history, as well as an invaluable resource for information about ancient Egypt, Mesopotamia, and Scythia.

2. See James B. Pritchard's *Ancient Near Eastern Texts Relating to the Old Testament*, 2nd ed. (Princeton, NJ: Princeton University Press, 1955), pp. 301–15.

3. Ibid., pp. 315–16.

4. The word "Jews" is used to refer to the people of Israel in the period following the Babylonian exile, when they no longer had a nation-state of their own. It is a short form of the word "Judean," meaning literally an inhabitant of Judea. The word "Hebrews" is used properly of the people in the formative period before the occupation of the land of Canaan and the establishment of the monarchy under Saul, David, and Solomon. The term "Israelites" is most properly used of the people during the period of the monarchy; they are the people of Israel. The words are sometimes used interchangeably.

5. The book of Ezra actually provides two accounts of Cyrus's decree, the version in Ezra 1:1–4 in Hebrew, and an Aramaic version quoted in Ezra 6:3–5. The two are similar, and both are likely original. Both the Hebrew and Aramaic versions of the edict emphasize Cyrus's benevolent behavior toward the Jews in allowing them to return to Jerusalem. External evidence for this policy is afforded in Pritchard's *Ancient Near Eastern Texts*, pp. 315–16, which contains the text of the so-called Cyrus cylinder. This inscription reports similar acts of amnesty toward people of other countries and their gods, following Cyrus's con-

quest of Babylon: "(As to the region) from . . . as far as Ashur and Susa, Agade, Eshnunna, the towns Zamban, Me-Turnu, Der as well as the region of the Gutians, I returned to (these) sacred cities on the other side of the Tigris, the sanctuaries of which have been ruins for a long time, the images which (used) to live therein and established for them permanent sanctuaries. I (also) gathered all their (former) inhabitants and returned (to them) their habitations."

6. The reference to "the first year of King Cyrus of Persia" in Ezra 1:1 refers, of course, to the first year of Persian hegemony over the Jews (539/538 BCE), not the first year of Cyrus's reign as king of Persia, which was twenty years earlier in 559 BCE.

7. The words of Ezra 1:1–3a are virtually identical to the text of 2 Chronicles 36:22–23. Both passages view Cyrus of Persia as the fulfillment of Jeremiah 25:11, which foresaw a seventy-year subjection of Judah to Babylon; and of Jeremiah 29:10, which promised that Judah would be restored to the land after seventy years.

8. The unity of Chronicles-Nehemiah has been questioned in recent decades, and there are now three main scholarly positions on the issue: (1) those who affirm the unity of Chronicles-Nehemiah in whole or in major part; (2) those who claim that Chronicles and Ezra-Nehemiah are separate works by separate authors; and (3) those who believe that Chronicles and Ezra-Nehemiah are separate works but by the same author. Before Jerome translated the Old Testament into Latin in what is known as the Vulgate, Ezra and Nehemiah were treated as one book in the ancient Hebrew and Greek (Septuagint) manuscripts. It was apparently Jerome (ca. 340 to 343 CE–420 CE) who, at the end of the fourth century CE, split Ezra-Nehemiah into two books, Ezra and Nehemiah.

9. Those who argue for the earlier date of 1 and 2 Chronicles (i.e., about 520–515 BCE) are, accordingly, required to regard this genealogy in 1 Chronicles 3:10–24, for no other reason, as a later addition to the original work.

10. During the period from circa 600 BCE to circa 700 CE, Aramaic served as the principal language of both literature and communication throughout much of the Near East. The appearance of these documents in their original Aramaic in the text of Ezra attests to the importance of Aramaic as the *lingua franca*.

11. Jacob M. Myers, Ezra-Nehemiah, in *The Anchor Bible* (Garden City, NY: Doubleday, 1965), pp. xlviii–lii, identifies in the text of Ezra-Nehemiah no fewer than twenty-six sources used in the composition of Ezra-Nehemiah.

12. 1 Chronicles 28:2–3 likely affords the Chronicler's interpretation of why David did not build the temple: 2Then King David rose to his feet and said: "Hear me my brothers and my people, I had planned to build a house of rest for the ark of the covenant of the LORD (Yahweh), for the footstool of our God; and I made preparations for building. 3But God said to me, 'You shall not build a house for my name, for you are a warrior and have shed blood.'"

13. Many scholars maintain that Ezra came to Jerusalem later than Nehemiah. According to Nehemiah 7:4, Nehemiah found Jerusalem deserted when he arrived, whereas

according to Ezra 9:9; 10:1, Ezra found the wall rebuilt and the city populated. In addition, Nehemiah is represented in Nehemiah 3:1, 20–21 as a contemporary of the high priest Eliashib, whereas according to Ezra 10:6, Ezra was a contemporary of Eliashib's son or grandson Jehohanan (or Johanan).

14. Interestingly, Zerubbabel is a Babylonian name, Zer-babili (meaning perhaps "shoot of Babylon"), implying that the Jews, and in particular the Judean royal family, were well assimilated in Babylon. Actually, the first governor appointed by Cyrus was Sheshbazzar (or Sin-ab-uṣur, meaning "may [the moon-god] Sin protect the father"), also a Judean prince, perhaps Zerubbabel's uncle, although the relationship is not clear. Little is known of him or of his term as governor.

15. Josephus (*Antiquities* 11.5.8) reports that it took two years and four months to repair the city walls, which some scholars think is a more probable time frame for such an enormous task. Archaeology has unfortunately been of little help in reconstructing the history of the rebuilding of the city walls and the temple during this period of restoration, as the site involved is covered with residences and religious structures and therefore not suitable for archaeological investigation.

16. The chronology of the Judean restoration is extremely complicated, and historians do not agree on the time of Ezra's arrival in Jerusalem, dated by some as early as 458 BCE if King Artaxerxes of Persia in Ezra 7:1 is a reference to Artaxerxes I, and by others as late as 398 BCE if the reference is to Artaxerxes II.

17. Once again, scholars differ on this issue. Some claim Ezra read the Holiness Code (Leviticus 17–24), or the Priestly Code, or Ezekiel's plan of restoration (Ezekiel 40–48). The Chronicler appears to believe that "the book of the Torah of Moses" was the completed Pentateuch, a view that seems most probable.

18. See also the ancient list of names in Numbers 1:5–15 for mention of Shaddai as a component in personal names: Zurishaddai = "Shaddai is my rock" (Numbers 1:6; see also Numbers 2:12; 7:36, 41; 10:19), and Ammishaddai = "my kinsman is Shaddai" (Numbers 1:12; see also Numbers 7:66, 71; 10:25).

19. Scholars have long recognized that the vocabulary of P is quite different from the vocabulary of J, E, and D and, therefore, often provide lists of words and idioms that are characteristic of P. For example, S. R. Driver, *The Book of Genesis,* 12th ed. (Edinburgh: T & T Clark, 1926; reprinted 1954), pp. vii–ix, which provides a long list of words and phrases that are characteristic of P.

20. Modern scholars have sometimes tried to reorder the events in Ezra-Nehemiah, the most important contribution to that effort being the work of Charles C. Torrey, *The Chronicler's History of Israel: Chronicles-Ezra-Nehemiah Restored to Its Original Form* (New Haven, CT: Yale University Press, 1954), p. xix; and *Ezra Studies* (Chicago: Chicago University Press, 1910), pp. 255–58.

CHAPTER 10

ISRAEL'S WISDOM LITERATURE

T he period following the Babylonian exile brought significant changes in Israelite history and religion. Some exiles returned from Babylon to Jerusalem to rebuild the city walls and the temple and to reestablish temple worship. Others remained in Babylon, Egypt, and elsewhere, effectively marking the beginning of Diaspora Judaism or Judaism of the dispersion, a Judaism that exists apart from the land of Israel and apart from the Jerusalem-centered temple cult.

The post-exilic period also marked the end of the prophetic movement and the period of revealed religion and prophetic inspiration. It was believed that the period of revelation and inspiration now lay primarily in the past and was effectively over. One cause of this shift was the writing of most of Israel's great literature, and the growing reliance on these written books as the primary sources of religious authority.

Judaism became increasingly a religion of the Torah, the written law, as codified first and foremost in the Pentateuch, and as subsequently interpreted in the now written words of Israel's great prophets primarily of the eighth, seventh, and sixth centuries BCE. This shift to the written word implied that Israelite religion was evolving from a living religion to a religion of the book. It is this shift that gave rise to Judaism, as we have come to understand it over the last two thousand plus years.

Essentially the acts of God were now viewed principally as events in the past rather than as ongoing. Israel's God was now only minimally active in history, and his acts on behalf of his people were understood to have occurred for the most part in the past. The writings of the great histories, the Deuteronomistic History (Joshua, Judges, 1 and 2 Samuel, and 1 and 2 Kings) and the Chronicler (1 and 2 Chronicles, Ezra, and Nehemiah), as well as the completion of the Pentateuch (Genesis, Exodus, Leviticus, Numbers, and Deuteronomy), reflect the increased focus on Israel's past, beginning essentially with the call of the patriarchs and leading up to the restoration of Jerusalem following the Babylonian exile.

THE WISDOM MOVEMENT
IN THE ANCIENT NEAR EAST

One interesting development of post-exilic Judaism is the wisdom movement that had its roots in the pre-exilic age but flourished in the post-exilic period. Most of the wisdom literature of the Hebrew Bible is, in its final form, post-exilic. Unlike the revealed religion that was most characteristic of earlier Israelite religion and of Israel's great prophets, the wisdom movement reflects the practical skill learned from ancient Near Eastern teachers and sages who dealt in large measure with the routine problems of everyday life.

Wisdom (or *ḥokmāh*) refers to exceptional talent, ability, expertise, and aptitude achieved by instruction and practice. In that respect Israel's wisdom literature is part of a larger pan-Semitic movement and is similar to what we find among Israel's neighbors, such as the Edomites and the Canaanites, and the older cultures of Phoenicia, Mesopotamia, and Egypt. This international wisdom movement dealt with basic issues such as kindness, fidelity, truthfulness, honesty, and family loyalty. Israel's wisdom literature is much more secular in tone than the corpus of books in the Law and the Prophets, yet Israel's wisdom was, nevertheless, essentially religious, even if not markedly so and even if not distinctively Yahwistic.

The Old Testament affords evidence that the Israelites acknowledged the existence of "wise men and women" or "sages" not only among their own people but in neighboring nations as well: in Egypt (Genesis 41:8, 39; Exodus 7:11; Isaiah 19:11–12); in Phoenicia (Ezekiel 28:1–6; Zechariah 9:2); in Canaan (Judges 5:29); in Edom (Obadiah 8); and in Babylon (Jeremiah 50:35; 51:57; Daniel 2:12–13; 4:6, 18; 5:8, 15).

Ancient Near Eastern wisdom, including Hebrew wisdom, may have had its origin in both familial and tribal settings, as well as in more formal schools of instruction. The author of Ecclesiastes is described as a teacher and a wise man, who "taught the people knowledge" (Ecclesiastes 12:9), while the author of the Wisdom of Sirach refers to his "house of instruction," perhaps a "school" (Sirach 51:23). Isaiah 29:14 and Jeremiah 8:8–9; 9:23; 18:18 all imply that wise men were a recognizable group in Israelite society, although the meaning of these passages may not be self-evident.

The most remarkable feature of Israelite wisdom literature is the absence of elements that are generally considered basic to Israelite religion: the promise to the patriarchs, the exodus from Egypt, the covenant at Sinai, the conquest and entrenchment of Canaan, and the focus on Israel's history of salvation.[1] To state the situation positively, wisdom was apparently an international movement in which Israel shared. Hence Israel's wisdom was not narrowly Israelite in its outlook.

Israel's wisdom literature consists of the following writings:

Proverbs: a compendium or series of compilations of folk wisdom, moral maxims, didactic essays, and brief excursions into theology, ascribed by tradition to Solomon, but likely edited in the post-exilic period, probably in the sixth or fifth century BCE;

Ecclesiastes: the notebook of an agnostic philosopher, ascribed loosely to Solomon (Ecclesiastes 1:1, 12; 2:9), but likely written between 300 and 200 BCE;

Job: a dramatic dialogue concerning the justice of God and the meaning and cause of human suffering, probably from the late sixth or fifth century BCE;

Some psalms and some passages in the prophets of similar tone (e.g., Psalms 34:11–22; 37; 49; 78; Isaiah 28:23–29);

Ecclesiasticus or The Wisdom of Jesus the Son of Sirach (commonly referred to as Sirach): a book of proverbs and essays aimed at a synthesis of traditional Mosaic religion and ancient Near Eastern and Israelite wisdom, written originally in Hebrew about 180 BCE and subsequently translated into Greek by the author's grandson;

The Wisdom of Solomon: a book written originally in Greek between 50 BCE and 50 CE by a Hellenized Jew in order to awaken enthusiasm among apathetic and apostate Jews of the Diaspora;

Baruch: represented as a letter ascribed falsely to Jeremiah's friend and secretary Baruch, this composite work was written in Hebrew probably in Palestine between 200 and 60 BCE;

Tobit: a romantic tale designed to comfort pious individuals when calamities befall them, this book is a theodicy or effort to vindicate God's justice, probably written between 225 and 175 BCE;

4 Maccabees: an extended philosophical sermon extolling the supremacy of "religious reason" over passion and the compatibility of reason with Mosaic law. This book was almost certainly composed in the Jewish-Hellenistic Diaspora, perhaps in Alexandria or Antioch, possibly between about 50 and 120 CE;

Pirke Aboth or The Sayings of the Fathers: a collection of a few hundred aphorisms, proverbs, and ethical sayings from rabbis learned in the Jewish law, written about 200 CE and preserved in the rabbinical tradition known as the Mishnah; and

Parables of Jesus: found in the gospels of Matthew, Mark, and Luke, from the late first century CE.

Of all these writings only Proverbs, Ecclesiastes, and Job are included in the canon of the Hebrew Bible. The other books are found in the collections known as the Apocrypha and the Pseudepigrapha and are late extra-canonical writings primarily from the period between the writing of the books of the Old Testament and the New Testament. The proverbs of Jesus come, of course, from the New Testament. Our focus in this chapter will be on the three canonical books: Proverbs, Ecclesiastes, and Job.

PROVERBS

Of all of the wisdom literature produced in Israelite circles, the book of Proverbs appears to be most closely related to the wisdom literature of the broader ancient Near East. Unfortunately, the relationship of Israelite wisdom literature to the wisdom literature of the Phoenecians, the Canaanites, the Edomites, and other "peoples of the East" is somewhat unclear, because so little survives of their wisdom literature, except for possible traces that may continue to exist in Proverbs 30:1–4 and

31:1–8.[2] Egypt and Mesopotamia have, however, left a more extensive cache of wisdom literature related to the book of Proverbs.

From Egypt there comes a didactic type of writing that assumes the literary form of "instructions" from a king or an important official to his son, similar in its couplet form to some of the precepts found in the book of Proverbs. There are, for example, the following Egyptian wisdom writings, accompanied by a few excerpts from each:

The Instruction of the Vizier Ptah-Hotep to his son, from about 2450 BCE[3]

51Then he [the Mayor and Vizier Ptah-Hotep] said to his son:

Let not thy heart be puffed-up because of thy knowledge;

be not confident because thou art a wise man.

Take counsel with the ignorant as well as the wise.

The (full) limits of skill cannot be attained,

and there is no skilled man equipped to his (full) advantage.

Good speech is more hidden than the emerald,

but it may be found with maidservants at the grindstones.

The Instruction for King Meri-ka-Re to his son and successor, from the end of the twenty-second century BCE[4]

25The contentious man is a disturbance to citizens:

he produces two factions among the youth.

If thou findest that the citizens adhere to him . . . ,

denounce him in the presence of the court, and remove [him].

He is also a traitor. A talker is an *exciter*[5] of a city.

Divert the multitude and suppress its heat . . .

In addition, there are *The Instruction of King Amen-em-het* to his son and successor, from before 1960 BCE;[6] *The Instruction of Prince Hor-dedef*, a scribe of the temple of Nefer- . . . -Re-teri to his son, from about the twenty-seventh century BCE;[7] *The Instruction of Ani*, frequently mentioned as one of the traditional wise men of Egypt, to his son, from the eleventh to the eighth century BCE;[8] *The Instruction of Amen-em-Opet*, son of Ka-nakht, for his son, from about the seventh to the sixth century BCE;[9] and *The Instructions of 'Onchsheshonqy*, from about the fifth century BCE.[10]

Also a component of Egyptian wisdom literature, but quite different from the genre of the Instructions cited above are the following works: *The Divine Attributes of Pharaoh*, which identifies some of the divine elements found in a pharaoh, from about 1840–1790 BCE;[11] *In Praise of Learned Scribes*, dealing with the prestige and privileges of the secretarial profession, probably from Thebes, from about 1300 BCE;[12] *The Satire on the Trades* (also known as *The Proverbs of Duauf* or *The Instructions of Duauf*), a copybook for schoolboys extolling the scribal profession and detailing the misery of nonscribal activity, originally from about 2150–1750 BCE;[13] and *The Protests of the Eloquent Peasant*, a text dealing with the theme of social justice, from the twenty-first century BCE.[14]

From Mesopotamia there also come several works that bear resemblance to the book of Proverbs in both form and content:

Several Akkadian proverbs and counsels, from about 1800–1600 BCE[15]

[II]As long as a man does not exert himself, he will gain nothing.
Whoso has neither king nor queen, who is then his lord?
[III.B. Sm 61 (3)]The gift of the king (produces) the good work of the carpenter.
[(5)]Friendship is of a day, slavery is perpetual.
[(6)]Where servants are there is quarrel,
Where cosmeticians are there is slander.
[(7)]A (plain) citizen in another city becomes a thief.

Aramaic proverbs and precepts in the form of *The Words of Ahiqar*[16]

[viii.111]I have lifted sand, and I have carried salt;
but there is naught that is heavier than [*rage*].
I have lifted bruised straw, and I have taken up bran;
but there is naught which is lighter than a sojourner.
War troubles calm waters between good *friends*.
If a man be small and grow great, his words soar above him.
For the opening of his mouth is an *utte*[*ra*]*nce* of gods,
and if he be beloved of gods they will put something good in his mouth to say.

Having examined several Egyptian and Mesopotamian wisdom writings, we discover that these writings bear formal resemblances to the Old Testament book of

Proverbs in the manner of: the literary feature of the teachings of a father to a son, the listing of sometimes unrelated brief aphorisms of a generally secular nature, and the recurrence of couplets in the form of poetic parallelism.

We turn now to the canonical collection of the book of Proverbs, where we find the following distinct literary units:

Book 1: The proverbs of Solomon, the son of David, king of Israel (1:1–9:18)

Book 2: The proverbs of Solomon (10:1–22:16)

Book 3: The words of the wise (22:17–24:22)

Book 4: More sayings of the wise (24:23–34)

Book 5: Other proverbs of Solomon that the officials of King Hezekiah of Judah copied (25:1–29:27)

Book 6: The words of Agur, son of Jakeh (30:1–33)

Book 7: The words of King Lemuel (31:1–9)

Book 8: Ode to a capable wife (31:10–31)

The Old Testament book of Proverbs is composed primarily of two-line sayings in the typical form of Hebrew parallelism, likely spoken and taught in wisdom schools in Israel from the period before the exile down to the time the book was put together, probably in the sixth century BCE or later. Like the Egyptian instructions, the teachings in Proverbs are represented as the words of a father to a son, perhaps a euphemism for the instructions of a teacher to a pupil (e.g., Proverbs 1:8, 10, 15; 2:1; 3:1, 11, 21; 4:1, 10, 20; 5:1, 7, 20; 6:1, 3, 20; 7:1, 24; 8:32; 23:15, 19, 26; 24:13, 21; 27:11). Nineteen of the twenty-five references listed here are in book 1 (1:1–9:18) and five are in book 3 (22:17–24:22) in the outline above, indicating perhaps a special proclivity of the authors of those two "books" of the composite book of Proverbs.

Book 1

The first section of Proverbs (1:1–9:18), which carries the superscription "The proverbs of Solomon son of David, king of Israel," is a collection of various proverbs with little unity except that they are all concerned with aspects of daily life. Although these proverbs accept traditional Yahwism, they do so quite superficially.

The theme of book 1, and perhaps of the entire collection of eight books, is stated in Proverbs 1:7:

The fear of the LORD (Yahweh) is the beginning of knowledge;
fools despise wisdom and instruction.

The "fear" expressed here goes far deeper than the ordinary understanding of that word. It implies the obedience and the submission to Yahweh that served as the foundation of all Israelite religion and morality. Yet the maxims often reflect the very practical consideration that people's actions invariably result in certain consequences and that wise persons will invariably be mindful of the likely costs of their action before doing something, as seen in Proverbs 1:8–19.

> 1:8Hear, my child, your father's instruction,
> and do not reject your mother's teaching;
> 9for they are a fair garland for your head,
>   and pendants for your neck.
> 10My child, if sinners entice you, do not consent.
> 11If they say, "Come with us, let us lie in wait for blood;
>   let us wantonly ambush the innocent;
> 12like Sheol let us swallow them alive and whole,
> like those who go down to the Pit.
> 13We shall find all kinds of costly things;
> we shall fill our houses with booty.
> 14Throw in your lot among us;
> we will all have one purse"—
> 15my child, do not walk in their way,
>   keep your foot from their paths;
> 16for their feet run to evil,
> and they hurry to shed blood.
> 17For in vain is the net baited
> while the bird is looking on;
> 18yet they lie in wait—to kill themselves!
> and set an ambush—for their own lives!
> 19Such is the end of all who are greedy for gain;
> it takes away the life of its possessors.

This first advisory discourse in the book of Proverbs is set in the same literary form as the Egyptian instructions,[17] as the child is admonished to listen to the advice of the father and mother to avoid bad company. The thrust of this parental advice in

1:8–19 is well expressed in summary form in the contemporary saying: "Crime doesn't pay." This discourse follows the form of ancient Near Eastern and ancient Hebrew poetry, most specifically the synonymous parallelism we have already observed in earlier Israelite poetry such as the Song of Miriam (Exodus 15:20–21) and the Song of Deborah (Judges 5) and in most of the prophetic literature.

We find similar admonitions in Proverbs 6:16–19:

6:16There are six things that the LORD (Yahweh) hates,

seven that are an abomination to him:

17haughty eyes, a lying tongue,

and hands that shed innocent blood,

18a heart that devises wicked plans,

feet that hurry to run to evil,

19a lying witness who testifies falsely,

and one who sows discord in a family.

This passage suggests that there are several things that Yahweh hates (verse 16):

five bodily organs (verses 17–18):

    haughty eyes

    a lying tongue

    hands that shed innocent blood

    a heart that devises wicked plans

    feet that hurry to run to evil

and two types of people (verse 19):

    a lying witness who testifies falsely

    one who sows discord in the family.

The purpose of these proverbs is to call the listener's attention to right ethical behavior, even with regard to issues to which the Torah does not speak directly. The teacher appeals rather to the listener's conscience and good sense. By identifying specific bodily parts that can serve as the source of evildoing, the teacher presents an ancient version of the contemporary "Speak no evil, see no evil, hear no evil." The evil deeds of the five bodily organs ultimately bring about the kinds of strife identified in verse 19.

This epigram displays the common poetic element of synonymous parallelism, and its form is reminiscent of the form of a passage in the Ugaritic myth of *Baal and Anath* iii. 17–21:[18]

> For two [kinds of] banquets Baal hates,
> Three the Rider of the Clouds:
> A banquet of shamelessness,
> A banquet of baseness,[19]
> And a banquet of handmaids' *lewdness* [conjectural reading].

Within this first section of the book of Proverbs there are several passages in which Wisdom is personified as a woman (1:20–33; 3:13–18; 4:5–9; 7:4–5; 8:1–36; and 9:1–6). She appears at first as a prophet or a street preacher, crying out to the people (1:20–23). A reference to Wisdom as holding longlife in her right hand and riches and honor in her left hand (3:16) has led some scholars to see the Egyptian goddess Maat as the source for female wisdom in Proverbs. The most fully developed personification of the female wisdom is in 8:1–36, in which it is said that Yahweh acquired, conceived, or possessed wisdom before the creation of the universe (8:22–29). In 3:19–20 and 8:22–13, in language that is equally extraordinary, it is by wisdom that Yahweh established the earth.

Book 2

The second section of Proverbs (10:1–22:16), which carries the superscription "The proverbs of Solomon," contains material in 10:1–15:33 that is in antithetical parallelism, in which the second line in the parallel structure contrasts or opposes the first line. For example, Proverbs 10:1–5:

> ₁A wise child makes a glad father,
> but a foolish child is a mother's grief.
>
> ₂Treasures gained by wickedness do not profit,
> but righteousness delivers from death.
>
> ₃The LORD (Yahweh) does not let the righteous go hungry,
> but he thwarts the craving of the wicked.

₄A slack hand causes poverty,
but the hand of the diligent makes rich.

₅A child who gathers in summer is prudent,
but a child who sleeps in harvest brings shame.

Unlike the material in book 1, the proverbs in book 2 are not only in the form of antithetical parallelism rather than synthetic parallelism, but each is a freestanding couplet, unlike the longer units that we find in chapters 1–9. Once again, although this second collection of miscellaneous proverbs is attributed to King Solomon, this attribution is more honorific than historical. In fact, "a proverb of Solomon" may be nothing more than a conventional designation for a two-line proverb in poetic synonymous or antithetical parallelism. The term "a proverb of Solomon" apparently has nothing to do with authorship.

In the material in Proverbs 16:1–22:16, still in book 2, there is a shift back to synonymous parallelism in which the second line restates the substance of the first. Many of these proverbs, such as 16:8, 10, 12, and 15 reflect an emphasis on issue of the king's court and appear to have as their setting the situation in and around the royal court in Jerusalem.

₁₆:₈Better is a little with righteousness
than large income with injustice.

₁₆:₁₀Inspired decisions are on the lips of a king;
his mouth does not sin in judgment.

₁₆:₁₂It is an abomination to kings to do evil,
for the throne is established by righteousness.

₁₆:₁₅In the light of a king's face there is life,
and his favor is like the clouds that bring the spring rain.

Book 3

The third section of Proverbs (22:17–24:22), which carries the superscription "The words of the wise," appears to be dependent upon the popular Egyptian wisdom text known as *The Instruction of Amen-em-Opet*.[20] Many of the proverbs in book 3, such as 23:1–3, 6–8, 19–21, seem particularly appropriate for the education of young civil servants for roles in court life.

> 23:1When you sit down to eat with a ruler,
> observe carefully what is before you,
> 2and put a knife to your throat
> if you have a big appetite.
> 3Do not desire the ruler's delicacies,
> for they are deceptive food.
>
> 23:6Do not eat the bread of the stingy;
> do not desire their delicacies;
> 7for like a hair in the throat, so they are.
> "Eat and drink!" they say to you;
> but they do not mean it.
> 8You will vomit up the little you have eaten,
> and you will waste their pleasant words.
>
> 23:19Hear, my child, and be wise,
> and direct your mind in the way.
> 20Do not be among wine-bibbers,
> or among gluttonous eaters of meat;
> 21for the drunkard and the glutton will come to poverty,
> and drowsiness will clothe them with rags.

In addition to issues of court life, many of the proverbs in this section deal with typical wisdom themes such as family relationships and issues involving the poor. Although this section seems largely dependent on its Egyptian source, the material has been thoroughly reworked and reordered to suit the author's Yahwistic theology. There is quite evidently an illusion to the thirty sections or "chapters" of the Egyptian *Instruction of Amen-em-Opet* xxvii.7–8 ("See thou these thirty chapters: They entertain; they instruct") in the words of Proverbs 22:20–21:

> Have I not written for you thirty sayings
> of admonition and knowledge
> to show you what is right and true,
> so that you may give a true answer to those who sent you?

In examining parallels between the two books, scholars often compare such passages as:

The Instruction of Amen-em-Opet iii.7–11   Proverbs 22:17–18a

Give thy ears, hear what is said,	Incline your ear and hear my words,
Give thy heart to understand them.	and apply your mind to my teaching;
To put them in thy heart is worthwhile, . . .	for it will be pleasant if you keep them within you, . . .

The Instruction of Amen-em-Opet xiv.16–17 Proverbs 23:8

The mouthful of bread (too) great thou Swallowest and vomitest up,	You will vomit up the little you have eaten,
And art emptied of thy good.	and you will waste your pleasant words.

The full degree of the interrelationship of the two writings is evident in the following table:[21]

Proverbs	Amen-em-opet	Subject
22:17–18	3:9–11, 16	Appeal to hear
22:19	1:7	Purpose of instruction
22:20	27:7–8	Thirty sayings
22:21	1:5–6	Learning a worthy response
22:22	4:4–5	Do not rob a wretch
22:24	11:13–14	Avoid friendship with violent people
22:25	13:8–9	Lest a trap ruin you
22:28	7:12–13	Do not remove landmarks
22:29	27:16–17	Skillful scribes will be courtiers
23:1–3	23:13–18	Eat cautiously before an official
23:4–5	9:14–10:5	Wealth flies away like an eagle/geese
23:6–7	14:5–10	Do not eat a stingy person's food
23:8	14:17–18	Vomiting results
23:9	22:11–12	Do not speak before just anyone
23:10–11	7:12–15; 8:9–10	Do not remove landmarks of widows
24:11	11:6–7	Rescue the condemned

Book 4

The fourth section of Proverbs (24:23–34) carries the superscription "These are also sayings of the wise," which is clearly intended to link this independent collection of twelve verses of proverbs to what immediately precedes. Examples of these proverbs are seen in 24:23b–26:

> 24:23bPartiality in judging is not good.
> 24Whoever says to the wicked, "You are innocent,"
> will be cursed by peoples,
> abhorred by nations;
> 25but those who rebuke the wicked will have delight,
> and a good blessing will come upon them.
> 26One who gives an honest answer
>   gives a kiss on the lips.

Book 5

The fifth section of Proverbs (25:1–29:27), which carries the superscription "These are other proverbs of Solomon that the officials of King Hezekiah of Judah copied," implies that there was a scribal establishment under the patronage of King Hezekiah of Judah (ca. 715–687 BCE), whose religious reformation likely served as an occasion for ordering the collection and the copying of literature of the past as well as the creation of new literature. Hezekiah was apparently responsible for directing the collection and synthesizing of historical, prophetic, and wisdom literature from northern Israel and southern Judah.

This section is composed of two discrete units: Proverbs 25–27 and Proverbs 28–29. The literary style of 25–27 reflects authorship by a highly educated and skilled writer who was exceedingly skilled with language and the art of Hebrew poetry. Proverbs 28–29 reverts to the basic independent antithetical proverb found in chapters 10–16, an element in the first part of book 2.

Examples of passages from each discrete unit of book 5 include 25:11–14; 28:1–2, 6, 12):

> 25:11A word fitly spoken
> is like apples of gold in a setting of silver.

₁₂Like a gold ring or an ornament of gold
is a wise rebuke to a listening ear.
₁₃Like the cold of snow in the time of harvest
are faithful messengers to those who send them;
they refresh the spirit of their masters.
₁₄Like clouds and wind without rain
is one who boasts of a gift never given.

₂₈:₁The wicked flee when no one pursues,
but the righteous are as bold as a lion.
₂When the land rebels it has many rulers;
but with an intelligent ruler there is lasting order.

₂₈:₆Better to be poor and walk in integrity
than to be crooked in one's ways even though rich.

₂₈:₁₂When the righteous triumph, there is great glory,
but when the wicked prevail, people go into hiding.

Book 6

The sixth section of Proverbs (30:1–33), which carries the superscription "The words of Agur son of Jakeh, An oracle," contains a series of short independent units.

As was mentioned above, the meaning of the opening verse of this section is disputed. The New Revised Standard Version (30:1) reads:

₃₀:₁The words of Agur son of Jakeh. An oracle.[22]
Thus says the man: I am weary, O God,
I am weary, O God. How can I prevail?

The phrase "an oracle" is usually the sign of a prophetic message, but there is none here. Several scholars read the word instead as a place name, Massa, referring to an Ishmaelite people and territory of northern Arabia (see also 31:1).[23] The Hebrew words translated as "I am weary, O God" (30:1) are also problematic. R. B. Y. Scott says that the words are not Hebrew but Aramaic and should be translated "There is no God! There is no God, and I can [not know anything]."[24] This verse evidently raises the questions of a skeptic, who seems to be wrestling with the problem of whether man can ever know God.

The HarperCollins Study Bible states convincingly in the footnote to Proverbs 30:1 (p. 982): "The context supplies a sense of distance from a transcendent God, not doctrinal atheism." In this passage we are clearly close to the skepticism found in both Ecclesiastes and Job. If, indeed, Scott is correct in emending the text to suggest that the author of book 6 was from northern Arabia, it would make sense that the skepticism of this proverb is so very close to some of the questioning found in the book of Job, which may have originally come from the same general geographic area.

Book 7

The seventh section of the book of Proverbs (31:1–9) contains "the words of King Lemuel. An oracle that his mother taught him"[25] appears in the form of a poem (31:3–5) that deals with the abuse of alcohol:

> 31:3Do not give your strength to women,
> your ways to those who destroy kings.
> 4It is not for kings, O Lemuel,
> it is not for kings to drink wine,
> or for rulers to desire strong drink;
> 5or else they will drink and forget
> what has been decreed,
> and will pervert the rights of all the afflicted.

Book 8

This eighth and final section of Proverbs (31:10–31) is an acrostic poem, meaning that its twenty-four couplets begin with the twenty-four letters of the Hebrew alphabet in order (א, ב, ג, ד, etc.). This poem (31:10–14) affords a glimpse of the ideal housewife:

> 31:10A capable wife who can find?
> She is far more precious than jewels.
> 11The heart of her husband trusts in her,
> and he will have no lack of gain.
> 12She does him good, and not harm,

all the days of her life.

13She seeks wool and flax,

and works with willing hands.

14She is like the ships of the merchant,

she brings her food from far away.

It seems evident that the eight sections of the book of Proverbs had independent authorships and independent histories before they were brought together into a single book in the post-exilic period, perhaps by the author of book 1. Our book of Proverbs is, in fact, a patchwork quilt of several ancient books, which have been sewn together in such a way that the original sources are still eminently clear. Nevertheless, there is a consistency to the final effort in that the several parts are all anthropocentric. Their purpose is to deal with the human dilemma in a manner that we would consider far more secular than in any other book of the Old Testament that we have looked at thus far in our study.

ECCLESIASTES

Just as the wisdom that is found in the book of Proverbs had antecedents in ancient Near Eastern wisdom literature (most specifically in Egyptian, Mesopotamian, and Edomite literature), so too do we find antecedents to the book of Ecclesiastes in Egyptian and Akkadian literature.

The Egyptian text known as *The Song of the Harper* was found in the tomb of Inherkhawy, the chief of the workers at the cemetery at Thebes. The text comes from circa 1300 BCE and, like the book of Ecclesiastes, seems to have as its theme carpe diem, or "seize the day." The text, sung originally to the accompaniment of a harp, calls upon its listeners to succumb to worldly pleasures:

Let thy desire flourish,

In order to let thy heart forget the beatifications [funerary rites] for thee.

Follow thy desire, as long as thou shalt live.

Put myrrh upon thy head and clothing of fine linen upon thee,

Being anointed with genuine marvels of the god's property.

Set an increase to thy good things;

Let not thy heart flag.

Follow thy desire and thy good.

Fulfill thy needs upon earth, after the command of thy heart,

Until there come for thee that day of mourning.[26]

A Mesopotamian psalm of lament known as *I Will Praise the Lord of Wisdom*, probably from about 1100 BCE, expresses similar motifs of pessimism, skepticism, and doubt in verse II.1 and II.39:

II.1I have arrived, I have passed beyond life's span.

I look about me: evil upon evil!

My affliction increases, right I cannot find.

I implored the god, but he did not turn his countenance;

I prayed to my goddess, but she did not turn her head.

II.39He who was living yesterday has died today:

Instantly he is made gloomy, suddenly is he crushed.

One moment he sings a happy song,

And in an instant he will moan like a mourner.

Like day and night their mood changes,

When they are hungry they resemble corpses,

When they are sated they rival their god;

In good luck they speak of ascending to heaven,

When they are afflicted they grumble about going down to the underworld.[27]

The book of Ecclesiastes is called in Hebrew *Qoheleth*, which probably means "someone who addresses or teaches a congregation or an assembly," or more simply "a preacher" or "a teacher." The author writes that he has been "king over Israel in Jerusalem" (Ecclesiastes 1:12), and the superscription of the book (1:1) refers to him as "the son of David, king in Jerusalem," unmistakably identifying him as King Solomon (see also 2:4–11). Few scholars maintain that Solomon is actually the author of Ecclesiastes, and most suggest that the book is written rather "in the name of Solomon," the patron of Israelite wisdom and wisdom literature.

Ecclesiastes is the most unusual and the most unorthodox book in the entire Bible. In fact, its presence in the canon of sacred scriptures is, at best, puzzling. Ecclesiastes diverges radically from the mainstream of Israel's revealed religion and implies that God is both unknown and unknowable to humankind. The book's acceptance into the canon was ultimately due to belief in its Solomonic authorship and to the orthodox epilogue (12:9–14) that was undoubtedly added to the unorthodox book by a later author in order to make Ecclesiastes more palatable to religious Jews.

The theme of Ecclesiastes is stated in several passages, sometimes in slightly different ways, but the message is always the same—everything is vanity and a chasing after wind.[28] The word translated into English as "vanity" (Hebrew: *hebel*) literally means "emptiness" or "breath," something fleeting, transitory, and devoid of substance. The expression "vanity of vanities" is the equivalent of the superlative form of the Hebrew adjective, hence suggesting that everything under the sun is devoid of any substance or worth whatsoever. In other words, Qoheleth maintains that everything within the realm of human experience is totally empty and devoid of meaning.

The author examines the full range of human experience (accomplishments, pleasure, work, wisdom, knowledge, skill, riches, laughter, reputation, righteousness, youth, birth, and so forth) and reiterates throughout the book that it matters not what one looks at, the result is always the same: utter meaninglessness. The totality of human experience is completely futile, totally devoid of any ultimate meaning or significance.

Qoheleth's metaphysical position is summarized in the recurrent phrase "Vanity of vanities! All is Vanity." And upon this metaphysical position the author develops an ethical inquiry of his own.

Human life specifically is meaningless, as seen in 1:3–11:

1:3What do people gain from all the toil
at which they toil under the sun?
4A generation goes, and a generation comes,
but the earth remains forever.
5The sun rises and the sun goes down,
and hurries to the place where it rises.
6The wind blows to the south,
and goes around to the north;
round and round goes the wind,
and on its circuits the wind returns.
7All streams run to the sea,
but the sea is not full;
to the place where the streams flow,
there they continue to flow.

8All things are wearisome;

more than one can express;

the eye is not satisfied with seeing,

or the ear filled with hearing.

9What has been is what will be,

and what has been done is what will be done;

there is nothing new under the sun.

10Is there a thing of which it is said,

"See, this is new"?

It has already been,

in the ages before us.

11The people of long ago are not remembered,

nor will there be any remembrance

of people yet to come

by those who come after them.

Wisdom itself is likewise meaningless, as seen in 1:12–18:

1:12I, the Teacher, when king over Israel in Jerusalem, 13applied my mind to seek and to search out by wisdom all that is done under heaven; it is an unhappy business that God has given to human beings to be busy with. 14I saw all the deeds that are done under the sun; and see, all is vanity and a chasing after wind.

15What is crooked cannot be made straight,

and what is lacking cannot be counted.

16I said to myself, "I have acquired great wisdom, surpassing all who were over Jerusalem before me; and my mind has had great experience of wisdom and knowledge." 17And I applied my mind to know wisdom and to know madness and folly. I perceived that this also is but a chasing after wind.

18For in much wisdom is much vexation,

and those who increase knowledge increase sorrow.

It appears, as in 2:24–26, that there is nothing better for man to do than to enjoy himself during his brief lifetime:

2:24There is nothing better for mortals than to eat and drink, and find enjoyment in their toil. This also, I saw, is from the hand of God; 25for apart from him who can eat or who can have enjoyment? 26For to the one who pleases him God gives wisdom and knowledge and joy; but to the sinner he gives the work of gathering and heaping, only to give to one who pleases God. This also is vanity and a chasing after wind.

Qoheleth encourages the young man to delight in his youth. In other words, enjoy life while you can, because it is passing quickly and will soon be over. Qoheleth's conclusion is essentially negative on all of the major issues. His positive conclusion, if there is one, is to make the best of life. You're here anyway, so you may as well enjoy yourself as much as you can. This negative outlook is contradicted by the conclusion in Ecclesiastes 12:13 ("The end of the matter: all has been heard. Fear God and keep his commandments; for that is the whole duty of everyone"). The glaring contradiction between the unorthodox body of the book and its orthodox conclusion serves as clear evidence that a later editor has added the concluding verses to soften the author's agnostic skepticism.

However much people may wish, they cannot change the inevitable. There is a definite fatalism or determinism to the author's thought, as seen in 3:1–8:

3:1For everything there is a season, and a time for every matter under heaven:
2a time to be born, and a time to die;
a time to plant, and a time to pluck up what is planted;
3a time to kill, and a time to heal;
a time to break down, and a time to build up;
4a time to weep, and a time to laugh;
a time to mourn, and a time to dance;
5a time to throw away stones, and a time to gather stones together;
a time to embrace, and a time to refrain from embracing;
6a time to seek, and a time to lose;
a time to keep, and a time to throw away;
7a time to tear, and a time to sew;
a time to keep silence, and a time to speak;
8a time to love, and a time to hate;
a time for war, and a time for peace.

Qoheleth concludes that the important matters of the universe are impenetrable, enigmatic, and inscrutable. People can never know the things they most want to know, and so they must learn when to suspend judgment. Humankind must learn to accept the limitations of what it means to be human. This is, in itself, an act of reverence (7:23–24):

> 7:23All this I have tested by wisdom; I said, "I will be wise," but it was far from me.
> 24That which is, is far off, and deep, very deep; who can find it out?

Qoheleth was an agnostic teacher, a man who admitted that he was without knowledge of the things that matter most in life.

Some scholars have argued for a date in the third century BCE for the writing of Ecclesiastes, because the book appears to reflect elements of Greek philosophical thought. It was only after Alexander the Great's conquest of the Near East in the late fourth century BCE that Jews came under the influence of such skeptical thinking and began to ask questions about the meaning of human existence. Ecclesiastes is an attempt by such a Hellenized independent-thinking Jew to try to understand rationally and philosophically the meaning of life. It was most unusual for a Jew of this period to step back and think about matters of reality in and of themselves. The author of the book was an intellectual, a rationalist, a teacher of wisdom, and a skeptic.

Yet, as we saw at the outset of this section, Egyptian and Mesopotamian wise men undertook the same kind of examination almost a millennium earlier. The existence of such literature much earlier than the Hellenistic period may mean that Qoheleth was not necessarily under the influence of Greek philosophical thought, but merely a serious student of the wisdom movement of the greater ancient Near East. Dating the book may be particularly difficult because its message is both universal and timeless. In fact, it is the timelessness of Qoheleth's message that makes this modest book so appealing, especially to our own skeptical age.

JOB

The book of Job has affinities to several ancient Near Eastern writings. An Egyptian text from the end of the third millennium BCE known as *A Dispute over Suicide* is an account of a poignant dialogue between a suicidal man, who finds his life insufferable, and his own soul.[29] A Mesopotamian writing, *I Will Praise the Lord of Wisdom*, from which we quoted above in connection with the book of Ecclesiastes and which can be dated to circa 1100 BCE, describes the sufferings of a man who blames the god Marduk, the Lord of wisdom, for his misfortune.[30] A Babylonian text, *A Dialogue about Human Misery*, an acrostic poem also from about 1000 BCE, is sometimes known as "The Babylonian Ecclesiastes" or "The Babylonian Theodicy."[31] The story begs the intervention of the god Ninurta and the goddess Ishtar to remedy its author's misery and contains this couplet that is reminiscent of both Job and Ecclesiastes:

> [256]The mind of the god, like the center of the heavens, is remote;
> His knowledge is difficult, men cannot understand it.

The Words of Ahiqar, a fifth-century Aramaic text from the Jewish military colony of Elephantine in Egypt, tells the story of a scribe who lived in Assyria in the seventh century BCE and who, like Job, unjustly suffered misfortunes but who, like Job, was subsequently restored to a position of honor.[32]

The origin of the book of Job is debated, and it is by no means evident that the story originated among the Israelites because Job is identified as a man from the land of Uz (Job 1:1). The name Job is known from ancient Egyptian texts (an Egyptian execration text from about 2000 BCE and Amarna letter #256 from about 1350 BCE), from Mesopotamian texts (Akkadian documents from Mari and Alalakh from the early second millennium BCE), and from a Canaanite text (a list of personnel from the palace in Ugarit).[33] Job was apparently a relatively common western Semitic name in the second millennium BCE. The mention in Ezekiel 14:14, 20 of Noah, Daniel (or Danel), and Job as righteous men, who were presumably renowned in the ancient Near East, implies that Job was thought to have lived in the distant past, perhaps in patriarchal or even pre-patriarchal times.

Locating Job's homeland of Uz is challenging. On the one hand, in Genesis 10:23 (see also 1 Chronicles 1:17), Uz is the son of Aram and the grandson of Shem. In Genesis 22:20–21, Uz is the son of Abraham's brother Nahor, whose descendants Genesis 24:10 places in Aram-naharaim, the city of Nahor. Inasmuch as the names in these genealogies are probably also tribal designations, meaning that they are also geographical terms, both of these traditions appear to locate Uz in northwest Mesopotamia.

On the other hand, Genesis 36:28 identifies Uz as one of the Horites, who lived in the land of Edom. Likewise Lamentations 4:21 identifies Uz with Edom, and Jeremiah 25:20 appears to locate Uz in the desert east of Israel, probably also in Edom.

Although the book of Job is somewhat vague about the location of Job's homeland of Uz, the author apparently had in mind the area of Edom or northern Arabia.

Job's three friends, Eliphaz the Temanite, Bildad the Shuhite, and Zophar the Naamathite (Job 2:11), were apparently all from the region of Edom or northern Arabia. Eliphaz appears in the Edomite genealogy in Genesis 36:4, 10 as the son of Esau and Adah; his place of origin is listed as Teman, a district and secondarily a tribe of Edom (Genesis 36:11, 15, 42; 1 Chronicles 1:53; see also Amos 1:12; Obadiah 9; Ezekiel 25:13; Jeremiah 49:7). Eliphaz is identified as a Shuhite, that is, from Shuah, referred to in Genesis 25:2 as a son of Abraham and Keturah (see also Genesis 38:2, 12), who, like all of the sons of Abraham and Keturah, is of either Arabian or Syrian origin. Zophar was from Naamah, which is the name for several different places: a town in Judah (Joshua 15:41); a place in Nejd in central Arabia; and a Sabean clan in the vicinity of Tema (Job 6:19), an oasis city in northern Arabia. The common denominator in all of these variables is northern Arabia, suggesting that Job's three friends came from the area of the northern Arabian Peninsula. Thus, Job's homeland of Uz was also likely in Edom or northern Arabia rather than in northwest Mesopotamia.

Does the homeland of the principal characters of the book of Job in Edom or northern Arabia suggest that the story of Job may also have been of non-Israelite origin? Almost certainly yes! It appears quite evident that the book of Job not only has strong affinities to several ancient Near Eastern writings in Egypt and Mesopotamia, but it may be that the story itself is of Edomite or Arabian origin and was subsequently appropriated by an Israelite writer.

Support for a theory of non-Israelite origin for the book of Job may be found in the fact that Job is textually the most problematical book in the entire Hebrew Bible. The Hebrew text of Job is in many places unclear or incomprehensible. In addition, the book presents daunting philological and linguistic challenges. It has more *hapax legomena* (words that appear in the Bible, and hence in ancient Hebrew literature, only once) than any other biblical book, and Job has many additional words that rarely appear elsewhere in the Bible. The language of the book of Job is seemingly Hebrew, but there are so many peculiarities in the text that some scholars have suggested that the language of the book of Job may have been influenced by some other Semitic dialect, such as Edomite, Arabic, or Aramaic. Some have even suggested that the book was written initially in another language and subsequently translated poorly into Hebrew.[34]

Dating the book is also challenging inasmuch as it is difficult to know what material constituted the original book, the prose narrative or the cycles of poetic dialogue (see the outline below). A date in the sixth or fifth century BCE seems most likely, but with little internal evidence on which to make the case, scholars are reluctant to overdraw their conclusions.

There are few books in the entire Bible that are so formally structured as the book of Job, so an outline is helpful to an understanding of the book:

(1) Narrative Prologue Describing Job's Misfortune (1:1–2:13)
(2) Job's Objections (3:1–26)
(3) Three Cycles of Dialogue between Job and His Three Friends (4:1–28:28)
      A. The First Cycle (4:1–14:22)
            1. Eliphaz and Job (4:1–7:21)
            2. Bildad and Job (8:1–10:22)
            3. Zophar and Job (11:1–14:22)
      B. The Second Cycle (15:1–21:34)
            1. Eliphaz and Job (15:1–17:16)
            2. Bildad and Job (18:1–19:29)
            3. Zophar and Job (20:1–21:34)
      C. The Third Cycle (22:1–28:28)
            1. Eliphaz and Job (22:1–24:17)
            2. Bildad and Job (25:1–6; 26:1–27:12)
            3. Zophar and Job (24:18–25; 27:13–23; 28:1–28)—uncertain?
(4) Job's Final Speech (29:1–31:40)
(5) Elihu's Speeches (32:1–37:24)
(6) Yahweh's Speeches from the Whirlwind and Job's Submissions (38:1–42:6)
(7) Narrative Epilogue Describing the Restoration of Job (42:1–17)

Although Proverbs, Ecclesiastes, and Job are all built primarily on the formal structure of poetic couplets that we have seen elsewhere in Israelite poetry and in the poetry of the ancient Near East, the book of Job is otherwise very different from both Proverbs and Ecclesiastes. Job deals with the contradictions between the religious claims of the Deuteronomistic view of history and human experience as seen through the eyes of the book's protagonist. Religious orthodoxy taught that good was rewarded and evil punished; Job's personal experience dictates otherwise.

Ecclesiastes looked at some of the same problems as the book of Job and found them insoluble by wisdom or by human reason. Job looked at these problems and settled on a kind of religious agnosticism or agnostic religiosity: the world rests in the unknowable hand of divine providence.

A prose narrative in sections 1 and 7 in the outline above frames the body of the book, which contains three cycles of poetic dialogue between Job and his three friends, found primarily in sections 3 and 4, and a dialogue between Yahweh and Job in a series of four speeches in section 6. The speeches of Elihu in section 5 interrupt the flow of the book and are regarded by most scholars as a later addition.

The prologue to Job introduces a man named Job, who was famous for his blamelessness, his uprightness, and his piety (1:2). Job was a very wealthy man with a large and happy family, consisting of his wife and their ten children (1:2–3). One day at a meeting of the heavenly council, Yahweh asked the Accuser (the Satan)[35] about Job, and the Accuser answered that if Job were stripped of his earthly possessions, he would curse God to his face (1:6–11). Yahweh accepted the Accuser's challenge and gave him permission to test Job (1:12). The Accuser initially took away Job's wealth (1:13–17) and then his children (1:18–19), but Job did not curse Yahweh. Instead, he stood firm in his faith and blessed the name of Yahweh (1:20–21). Yahweh then allowed the Accuser to afflict Job with a loathsome and painful skin disease (2:1–8), but Job continued to bless Yahweh in spite of pleas from his wife that he simply curse Yahweh and die (2:9). Still Job did not curse Yahweh or sin with his lips (2:10). This first section ends with the arrival of three of Job's friends who, having learned of Job's plight, came to visit him (2:11–13).

Job then cursed his own life and the day he was born (3:3, 11):

3:3"Let the day perish in which I was born,
and the night that said, 'A man child is conceived.'"
3:11Why did I not die at birth,
come forth from the womb and expire?

There follows then the main body of the book, the dialogue between Job and his three friends (4:1–28:28). The form of this section is three cycles of six speeches each: a speech by each of the three friends, followed by a response by Job to each friend (Eliphaz and Job, Bildad and Job, and Zophar and Job in each cycle). The third cycle is corrupted, as Zophar's final speech is missing; parts of it may possibly be preserved in portions of Job's speeches (see the outline above), although that is by no means clear.

One by one the friends confront Job with their claims that he must have sinned, and one by one Job answers their orthodox claims. In effect, their accusation is that Job's suffering, in and of itself, proves that Job has sinned in the face of God. In his final speech immediately following the dialogue section, Job reaffirms his innocence (27:1–6):

27:1Job again took up his discourse and said:
2"As God lives, who has taken away my right,
and the Almighty (Shaddai), who has made my soul bitter,
3as long as my breath is in me
and the spirit of God is in my nostrils,
4my lips will not speak falsehood,
and my tongue will not utter deceit.
5Far be it from me to say that you are right;
until I die I will not put away my integrity from me.
6I hold fast my righteousness, and will not let it go;
my heart does not reproach me for any of my days."

Job knows that he has done nothing to merit the degree of suffering that he is currently experiencing. Nevertheless, in his final speech in section 4 in 31:5–12, Job even goes as far as to make a negative confession for sins that he may have committed but has since forgotten:

31:5If I have walked with falsehood,
and my foot has hurried to deceit—
6let me be weighed in a just balance,
and let God know my integrity!—
7if my step has turned aside from the way,
and my heart has followed my eyes,
and if any spot has clung to my hands;
8then let me sow and another eat;
and let what grows for me be rooted out.
9If my heart has been enticed by a woman,
and I have lain in wait at my neighbor's door;
10then let my wife grind for another,

and let other men kneel over her.

11For that would be a heinous crime;

that would be a criminal offense;

12for that would be a fire consuming down to Abaddon,[36]

and it would burn to the root all my harvest.

Effectively ignoring everything that his friends have said to him, Job reflects on the totality of his life and affirms that he is now ready to meet God on equal terms, and he finally challenges God to meet him and answer him. Job writes his defense and signs his signature to it, convinced that he is right and that God is wrong. Job's defiance finally rises to the level of blasphemy when Job says that if God will not meet him, then he is prepared to meet God (31:35–37):

31:35Oh that I had [some]one to hear me!

(Here is my signature! Let the Almighty [Shaddai] answer me!)

Oh, that I had the indictment written by my adversary!

36Surely I would carry it on my shoulder;

I would bind it on me like a crown;

37I would give him an account of all my steps;

like a prince I would approach him.

In fact, Job ultimately appeals to a Redeemer, a vindicator, a god beyond God before whom he might appeal his case, because Job is convinced that it is he and not God who would in the end be justified and prevail in any impartial court of final appeals (19:23–27):

19:23O that my words were written down!

O that they were inscribed in a book!

24O that with an iron pen and with lead

they were engraved on a rock forever!

25For I know that my Redeemer lives,

and that at the last he will stand upon the earth;

26and after my skin has been thus destroyed,

then in my flesh I shall see God,

27whom I shall see on my side,

and my eyes shall behold, and not another.

My heart faints within me!

Elihu's speeches follow in section 5, once again reiterating the orthodox position of Eliphaz, Bildad, and Zophar. This material is likely a later addition to the book by an orthodox editor who apparently thought that the traditional orthodox case had not been adequately presented by Job's three friends. These speeches of Elihu add nothing to the book and actually interrupt its flow and its unity.

The book reaches its climax in section 6 in two speeches of Yahweh to Job from the whirlwind (38:1–40:2 and 40:6–41:34), in which Yahweh reveals his majesty to Job:

> 38:3Gird up your loins like a man,
>
> I will question you, and you shall declare to me.
>
> 4Where were you when I laid the foundation of the earth?
>
> Tell me, if you have understanding.
>
> 5Who determined its measurements—surely you know!
>
> Or who stretched the line upon it?
>
> 6On what were its bases sunk,
>
> or who laid its cornerstone
>
> 7when the morning stars sang together
>
> and all the heavenly beings shouted for joy?

Job 38:3–39:30 reflects ancient Near Eastern cosmology, which comes in the form of a series of questions from Yahweh to Job about Job's role in the formation and order of the universe. Yahweh never answers the questions that Job posed to him earlier but instead asks questions of Job, who thereupon confesses his own inadequacy and remains silent (40:3–5):

> 40:3Then Job answered the LORD (Yahweh):
>
> 4See I am of small account; what shall I answer you?
>
> I lay my hand on my mouth.
>
> 5I have spoken once, and I will not answer;
>
> twice, but will proceed no further.

Yahweh attacks Job once again with a second barrage of questions and statements that overwhelm him (40:8–9):

> 40:8Will you even put me in the wrong?
>
> Will you condemn me that you may be justified?

9Have you an arm like God,

and can you thunder with a voice like his?

Job acknowledges Yahweh's omnipotence and his own ignorance and repents unqualifiedly (42:1–6):

42:1 Then Job answered the LORD (Yahweh):

2 "I know that you can do all things,

And that no purpose of yours can be thwarted.

3 'Who is this that hides counsel without knowledge?'

Therefore I have uttered what I did not understand,

things too wonderful for me, which I did not know.

4 'Hear, and I will speak;

I will question you, and you declare to me.'

5 I had heard of you by the hearing of the ear,

but now my eye sees you;

6 Therefore I despise myself,

and repent in dust and ashes."

As Yahweh's questions to Job reveal, Job is obviously overwhelmed by the order and the majesty of the universe, which reduce Job's own questions to insignificance. He is now willing and able to live with a form of religious agnosticism. Although Job still does not have satisfactory answers to his question, he realizes that he never will. The questions that Yahweh (i.e., the universe) asks of Job are far greater than anything that Job might want to ask of Yahweh (i.e., the universe).

The book concludes, quite unsatisfactorily, with a narrative epilogue (42:7–17) in which Yahweh first rebukes Eliphaz, Bildad, and Zophar for having spoken falsely of Yahweh (42:7–9) and then restores Job's fortune doubly (42:10–12). Job's wife then bears him ten more children (42:13–16) before Job dies one hundred forty years later (42:17). In fact, this Deuteronomistic conclusion contradicts the main thesis of the book.

Scholars have long debated the integrity of the book of Job and most agree that the narrative prologue and epilogue are by an author different from the author of the poetic dialogues. First of all, the dialogues function with no knowledge of the wager between the Accuser and Yahweh. In the form in which the book comes down to us, it appears that Yahweh is almost malevolent to have succumbed to such a challenge from the Accuser at the expense of a righteous human being. Second, the prologue is concerned with the question of human piety, whereas the dialogue addresses the issue of a clearly unjustified human tragedy. Third, in the prologue we find a gentle and patient Job, whereas in the body of the dialogues Job is righteously and justifiably indignant and confrontational. Fourth, there is the matter of the names of god: he is called Yahweh in the prose narrative, both in the prologue (section 1)[37] and in the epilogue (section 7),[38] as well as in the narrative portion of the speeches of Yahweh in section 6;[39] and he is called El,[40] Eloah,[41] and Shaddai[42] in the poetry, with the single exception of 12:9 (which has Yahweh), likely a later editorial addition to the dialogue.

How did this material all come together? Obviously we do not have a definitive answer to this question. We do, however, know that a tale of a righteous sufferer was prevalent throughout the ancient Near Eastern world, perhaps in a form much like what we have in the narrative prologue and epilogue of our current book of Job. This material may reflect the earliest Israelite form of the story. It may be that a very different author, perhaps originally an Edomite, subsequently wrote the brilliant poetic dialogue and framed it with the earlier prose narrative tale.

The book of Job raises a number of important existential questions: Why do the righteous suffer and the wicked prosper? Why is it that human pain and suffering apparently bear no relationship to a person's life? Is God just in his dealings with people, or does he act arbitrarily in people's lives and sometimes in two parts of the same man's life? Why does God refuse to answer the pleas of an innocent man?

The orthodox answer to these questions is expressed over and over again by Job's three friends, and again by Elihu. The justice of God is axiomatic: good is rewarded, and evil is punished. Not only do the friends all presume that Job has sinned, but it can be established that Job has sinned and his suffering is proof positive. This Deuteronomistic answer to Job proves, however, to be unsatisfactory and outright mistaken.

Job rebuts this position in each of his speeches in response to his friends. The abstract dogma of the friends is existentially untrue for Job. His own experience teaches him as much, and his own personal integrity demands that Job reject the authoritarian advancement of the Deuteronomistic formula in the form of his friends. Job is convinced that sometime or somewhere he will be vindicated, even if it is long after he is dead.

The answer of the author of the book of Job is made clear in the climax in section 6. Job's questions are certainly legitimate, but neither Yahweh nor the author of the book offers any rational or intellectual answer to Job's dilemma. Yahweh never answers Job's existential questions; instead he asks Job other very different questions about the majesty of the cosmos, questions that Job cannot, of course, answer.

Nevertheless it is eminently clear from the book that Job's suffering is neither proportionate to his sin, nor is it evidence of Yahweh's hostility toward Job. It is also clear that Job cannot set the terms of the debate. Job cannot ring a bell and expect Yahweh to come running with an answer acceptable to the suffering Job. The concept of God as a cosmic bellhop is wrong. Job's God (and certainly the God of his three or four friends) was too small. The book makes it clear, in fact, that the denial of a false concept of God honors God and indirectly affirms certain truths about God. In the end, the book of Job makes it clear that it is not possible to answer the most important questions of human existence. Job must leave room for mystery in his effort to understand himself in his relationship to God and to the universe.

CONCLUSIONS

This chapter raises several important issues involving the methodology of biblical scholarship.

In the books of Proverbs and Job, and to a lesser extent in Ecclesiastes, the text is primarily in the form of ancient Israelite poetry. We witness once again, but more pointedly in this chapter, that not only Israelite poetry but also the poetry of Egypt, Mesopotamia, Canaan, Edom, and Arabia was built on the simple couplet, two lines either in synonymous parallelism in which the second line of the couplet repeats or reinforces basic elements from the first line, or in antithetical parallelism in which the second line stands in contrast or opposition to the first line. This principle of the simple two-line couplet is the building block of ancient Near Eastern poetry, apparently as early as the third millennium BCE. In this chapter, wherever it has been possible, ancient Near Eastern wisdom literature is printed in a manner that illustrates this characteristic of that simple poetic feature.

As with many books of the Bible, foreign influences are especially evident in Israel's wisdom literature. Most important are influences on Proverbs, Ecclesiastes, and Job from Egyptian and Mesopotamian literature. The reason for this influence is eminently clear. Ancient Near Eastern wisdom literature spread across national borders and religious boundaries in ways in which many other kinds of ideas did not. Because the insights from wisdom literature reflect what might be considered almost universal truths and because wisdom literature is generally more secular than religious, foreign influence is especially evident in Israel's wisdom books. There are, in fact, references in the Old Testament to the important role of sages in Egypt, Phoenicia, Canaan, Edom, and Babylon. It was obviously much easier for Israelite literature to acknowledge an openness to foreign wisdom, whereas the borrowing of religious ideas was generally viewed as anathema, even if only centuries after the fact. Unfortunately, little wisdom literature survives from Phoenicia, Canaan, and Edom, the nations in which the Old Testament acknowledges that there were sages, but there is a fair amount of wisdom literature that survives from Egypt and Mesopotamia, allowing us to make meaningful comparisons and to draw important conclusions.

The influence of Egypt's wisdom is particularly evident. The Egyptian instructions from as early as the third millennium BCE reflect the feature of teaching from a father to his son, a formula that appears frequently in the book of Proverbs. In both Egypt and Israel, the formula of father-son likely carried over into wisdom schools as instruction from a teacher to his students. Likewise some scholars have maintained that the personification of Wisdom as a female figure in the book of Proverbs may be rooted in the Egyptian goddess Maat, who is sometimes depicted as holding symbols of life and wealth in her hands (cf. Proverbs 3:16). It is also apparent that Proverbs 22:17–24:22 used both the form and the content of the Egyptian *Instruction of Amen-em-Opet*.

It is unmistakable in all three canonical books of Israelite wisdom literature (Proverbs, Ecclesiastes, and Job) that many biblical books were put together from earlier existing written material. The evidence is clearest in the book of Proverbs, whose eight sections (or eight "books") clearly reflect the preexistence of each book as a distinct literary collection of ancient wisdom, probably from different teachers in different schools, both in Israel and elsewhere (e.g., Massa in Edom or northern Arabia in Proverbs 30 and 31). The several sources or units of the book of Proverbs appear to have survived virtually intact, and it is easy to see where one book ends and another begins.

The situation with the book of Job is somewhat more complicated, but there are in the book certainly at least three distinct units, and maybe more: the narrative prologue and epilogue, the poetic dialogue between Job and his three friends, and the speeches of Elihu. It is less evident in the book of Job than in the book of Proverbs how these separate pieces were put together, but it is relatively easy to distinguish these discrete elements for what they are. In the case of Ecclesiastes, it is obvious that a later author added to the original book a more acceptable ending (12:9–14), whose orthodoxy blatantly contradicts the more skeptical conclusions reached in the main body of the book.

All three of the canonical wisdom books, Proverbs, Ecclesiastes, and Job are attributed to Solomon, although virtually no reputable scholar would argue for Solomonic authorship for any of these books. Instead it appears that Israelites regularly attributed the inspiration for wisdom to King Solomon, in much the way in which they attributed the musical psalms to King David. The phrase "a proverb of Solomon" appears to be nothing more than a conventional term for the two-line proverb in Israel's wisdom literature, whether in poetic synonymous or antithetical parallelism. Attribution of wisdom literature to Solomon is apparently a literary convention rather than an indication of actual authorship.

One important, if minor, detail that we have seen in this chapter is the effort of some scholars to suggest ways of emending the traditional Hebrew text when its meaning is either not clear, or is otherwise problematic. Two examples in this chapter appear in Proverbs 30:1 and 31:1 in the case of a Hebrew word that in both instances is usually translated as "an oracle," a translation that makes no sense in the context of these two verses. An oracle is usually a word of Yahweh delivered by a prophet of Yahweh in the conventional poetic form, but neither of these two chapters contains a prophetic oracle. With a simple emendation of the Hebrew text, it is possible to read that Proverbs 30 comes from Agur a son of Jakeh from Massa, and that Proverbs 31 comes from Lemuel, an otherwise unknown king of Massa. This minor emendation of the Hebrew text makes good sense. It is evident that changes were made when scribes copied ancient manuscripts, changes that were sometimes intentional and sometimes accidental. We will discuss the matter of the transmission of the books of the Old Testament more fully in the final chapter of this book.

Likewise, we have seen, especially in the case of the book of Job, that there are sometimes serious textual and linguistic problems because of unusual vocabulary, with some words appearing only once (*hapax legomena*) in the entire Old Testament, making it especially difficult for scholars to understand the meaning of some passages. In such instances, scholars generally search for cognate words in closely related languages, such as Babylonian-Assyrian, Canaanite, Moabite, Edomite, Aramaic, Ethiopic, and Arabic, in order to uncover the meaning of obscure words.

In discussing the nature of ancient Near Eastern wisdom literature, it was noted that the literature is not only pan-Semitic, but that it is not religious in the traditional understanding of that word. Indeed, wisdom literature is more secular, even if it sometimes has a religious veneer. For example, it is notable that there is rarely mention in Israel's wisdom literature of the major events of Israel's salvation history: the call of the patriarchs, the exodus from Egypt, the conquest and entrenchment of Canaan, among the many themes that are otherwise central to Israelite religion.

In that regard, it is important to note also that there is sometimes even a skeptical or an agnostic quality to Israel's wisdom literature. Proverbs makes superficial reference to Israel's God when it claims in several instances "The fear of the LORD (Yahweh) is the beginning of knowledge." The phrase is almost formulaic. The book of Job is more blatant in raising questions regarding God's justice, a subject that is generally referred to by scholars as theodicy. Job clearly attacks the traditional view of God as the impartial dispenser of justice and suggests something quite different about God. Job and his friends knew of God only through "the hearing of the ear" (Job 42:5), the tradition that had been passed down for generations both orally and in written books. This concept of God was, at best, limited, and, at worst, outright wrong. Job is eventually able to confront God face-to-face, an opportunity generally denied to the rest of humankind. Hence, what does Job's message mean to those who can only *read* the book of Job and not otherwise encounter God in their own experience through visions or auditions? Are people now encouraged to raise their own questions about God, or are they expected simply to follow the example of the submissive Job without the benefit of a personal theophany? The book provides no clear answer to those burning questions.

Ecclesiastes is the most agnostic of the books of Israel's wisdom literature, and yet it found its way into the canon of the Old Testament, although apparently with considerable dissent from some rabbis in the first century CE. What significance should we attach to the fact that the rabbis eventually chose to include in their canon of sacred writings this "marginal" writing? Was the orthodox ending that was added to the original book really sufficient to soften the book's blatant agnosticism? Is the totality of life really meaningless? Is the totality of human experience completely futile? Are the most important problems of human life frighteningly enigmatic and altogether inscrutable? This is, at least on one level, an important component of the teaching of Israel's wisdom literature, especially in the book of Ecclesiastes.

Particularly problematic in our study of the wisdom literature has been the effort of scholars to date the composition of the various wisdom books. Sometimes biblical books contain clear clues about their dates of composition, positive allusions to specific historical events, such as the fall of Jerusalem or the publication of the Edict of Cyrus. The wisdom literature, given its very nature, generally does not afford such clues. The antecedents of Israelite wisdom in third and second millennium BCE Egyptian and Mesopotamian documents allows for the possibility of assigning a relatively early date for many of these teachings, at least in their earliest form. Most scholars, however, date the composition of the three canonical wisdom books to the period just before or just after the Babylonian exile, and in the case of Ecclesiastes perhaps a bit later to the Hellenistic period. These dates are unfortunately somewhat speculative, because the evidence in this regard is rather slim. We need in these instances to understand not only the value of biblical scholarship but also its limitations.

NOTES

1. The Wisdom of Solomon (especially chapters 10–19) appears to be an obvious exception to this remark. In these chapters, Wisdom works in Israel's history as a providential power, at least for the period from Adam to Moses. The focus in the chapters is, however, essentially on Wisdom rather than on Israel's history of salvation.

2. With a slight emendation of the Masoretic text (from Hebrew *hammassā'* [meaning "the solemn word" or "the oracle"] to *hammassā'ī* [meaning "of Massa"], Proverbs 30:1–4 would read "The words of Agur ben Yakeh of Massa' . . ." See R. B. Y. Scott, *Proverbs · Ecclesiastes*, The Anchor Bible (Garden City, NY: Doubleday, 1965), pp. 175–76. According to Genesis 25:13–14, Massa was an Ishmaelite people of northern Arabia. Likewise, following the same reasoning, Lemuel in Proverbs 31:1 was apparently a king of Massa. Most scholars identify southern Edom or the area of northern Arabia as the most likely setting for the book of Job (see below, pp. 279–80).

3. James B. Pritchard, *Ancient Near Eastern Texts Relating to the Old Testament with Supplement* (Princeton, NJ: Princeton University Press, 1969), pp. 412–14.

4. Ibid., pp. 414–18.

5. The use of italics in texts quoted from Pritchard's *Ancient Near Eastern Texts* indicates an uncertain translation of a particular word.

6. Ibid., pp. 418–19.

7. Ibid., pp. 419–20.

8. Ibid., pp. 420–21.

9. Ibid., pp. 421–25.

10. Edited by S. R. K. Glanville, ed., *Catalogue of Demotic Papyri in the British Museum*, vol. 2, 1955. The *Instructions of 'Onchsheshonqy* closely resembles the book of Proverbs. The resemblance between the two "lies in the bringing together of a very large number (about five hundred fifty) of short sayings, precepts, and adages like those of Proverbs—practical, moral, and to some extent religious, in a rather haphazardly arranged collection." The citation is from R. B. Y. Scott, *Proverbs · Ecclesiastes*, p. xlv.

11. Pritchard, *Ancient Near Eastern Texts*, p. 431.

12. Ibid., pp. 431–32.

13. Ibid., pp. 432–34.

14. Ibid., pp. 407–10.

15. Ibid., pp. 425–27.

16. Ibid., pp. 427–30.

17. This is also the customary form of Assyrian and Babylonian wisdom books and is evident, as well, in other Jewish wisdom literature: Ecclesiastes 12:12; Tobit 4:5, 12, 20; Sirach 2:1; 3:1.

18. Pritchard, *Ancient Near Eastern Texts*, p. 132.

19. The text actually says "A banquet banquet of baseness." The repetition of the word "banquet" is obviously due to erroneous dittography.

20. Pritchard, *Ancient Near Eastern Texts*, pp. 421–25.

21. James L. Crenshaw, "Proverbs, Book of," in *The Anchor Bible Dictionary* (New York: Doubleday, 1992), p. 516.

22. See footnote 2 above.

23. See, for example, R. B. Y. Scott, *Proverbs · Ecclesiastes*, pp. 175–76.

24. Ibid., p. 176.

25. Or "the words of King Lemuel of Massa that his mother taught him." See footnote 2 and the discussion of book 6 (Proverbs 30:1) immediately above.

26. Pritchard, *Ancient Near Eastern Texts*, p. 467.

27. Ibid., pp. 434–37.

28. Ecclesiastes 1:2, 14; 2:1, 11, 15, 17, 19, 21, 23, 26; 3:19; 4:4, 7, 8, 16; 5:7, 10; 6:2, 4, 9, 11; 7:6; 8:10, 14; 11:8, 10; 12:8.

29. Pritchard, *Ancient Near Eastern Texts*, pp. 405–407.

30. Ibid., pp. 434–37.

31. Ibid., pp. 438–40.

32. Ibid., pp. 427–30.

33. Marvin H. Pope, *Job*, The Anchor Bible (Garden City, NY: Doubleday,1965), pp. 5–6.

34. There is an excellent discussion of these issues in ibid., pp. xxxix–xlv.

35. The noun śāṭān is related to the verb śātan, meaning "to accuse" or "to slander" or

"to be an adversary" (Victor C. Hamilton, "Satan," in *The Anchor Bible Dictionary*, vol. 5 [New York: Doubleday, 1992], p. 958). The noun occurs fourteen times in the book of Job, always with the definite article, meaning "the Accuser," with the nuance that he is either "an adversary" or "a slanderer," depending on whether the accusation is deserved or undeserved. In the case of the righteous man Job, of course, it is clear that the accusation is undeserved, so he is actually more than "an adversary"; he is "a slanderer." In the book of Job, "the Accuser" is clearly not the diabolical Satan, the named lord of the underworld. He is not yet the ruler of some primordial realm; neither is he able to act without Yahweh's full consent. Yehèzkel Kaufmann has stated that "biblical religion was unable to reconcile itself with the idea that there was a power in the universe that defied the authority of God and that could serve as an antigod, the symbol and the source of evil" (*The Religion of Israel*, translated into English by Moshe Greenberg [Chicago: University of Chicago Press, 1960], p. 65). The belief in such an antigod emerged much later than the book of Job and is found in some of the intertestamental literature (e.g., in Jubilees 23:29 and in The Assumption of Moses 10:1, both of which date to about 168 BCE. Satan is mentioned by name in the New Testament thirty-five times. In Job, "the Accuser" appears along with other "heavenly beings" (1:6) on the occasion of a meeting of the heavenly council (see also Job 2:1; 38:7; Genesis 1:26–27; 1 Kings 22:19–23; Psalm 29:1; 82:1; 89:7 for other biblical references to this vestige of meetings of the ancient pagan pantheon).

36. Here, Abaddon is a poetic synonym for the place of the dead. In Job 26:6, Abaddon appears in parallel conjunction with Sheol, the underworld abode of the dead.

37. Job 1:6, 7 (twice), 8, 9, 12 (twice), 21 (3x); 2:1 (twice), 2 (twice), 3, 4, 6, 7.

38. Job 42:7 (twice), 9 (twice), 10 (twice), 11, 12.

39. Job 38:1; 40:1, 3, 6; 42:1.

40. Job 8:3, 5, 13, 20; 9:2; 12:6; 13:3, 7, 8; 15:4, 11, 13, 25; 16:11; 18:21; 19:22; 20:15, 29; 21:14, 22; 22:2, 13, 17; 23:16; 25:4; 27:2, 9, 11, 13; 31:14, 23, 28; 32:13; 33:4, 14, 29; 34:5, 10, 12, 23, 31, 37; 35:13; 36:5, 22, 26; 37:5, 10, 14; 38:41; 40:9, 19.

41. Job 3:4, 23; 4:9, 17; 5:17; 6:4, 8, 9; 9:13; 10:2; 11:5, 6, 7; 12:4, 6; 15:8; 16:20, 21; 19:6, 21, 26; 21:9, 19; 22:12, 26; 24:12; 27:3, 8, 10; 29:2, 4; 31:2, 6; 33:12, 26; 35:10; 37:15, 22; 39:17; 40:2. The name Eloah, possibly the single form of Elohim, appears frequently (forty times) in the book of Job, and elsewhere in the Old Testament only occasionally (fourteen times) in Deuteronomy 32:15, 17; 2 Chronicles 32:15; Nehemiah 9:17; Psalms 18:31; 50:22; 114:7; 139:19; Proverbs 30:5; Isaiah 44:8; Daniel 11:37, 38, 39; Habakkuk 3:3.

42. Job 5:17; 6:4, 14; 8:3, 5; 11:7; 13:3; 15:25; 21:15, 20; 22:3, 17, 23, 25, 26; 23:16; 24:1; 27:2, 10, 11, 13; 29:5; 31:2, 35; 32:8; 33:4; 34:10, 12; 35:13; 37:23; 40:2.

CHAPTER 11

PSALMS

T he book of Psalms is one of the most beloved books of the Bible. It is also one of the most diverse books and one of the greatest sources of spiritual insight for both Jews and Christians. Psalms is a storehouse of poetic literature that introduces the modern reader to Israel at worship.

THE SETTING OF THE PSALMS

Modern biblical scholarship suggests that in its present form the book of Psalms is the record of the musical life of the Jerusalem temple in the fourth century BCE. That is to say, the individual psalms were sung at that time as a regular part of the temple liturgy, sometimes to the music of the temple band.

1 Chronicles 16:4–7 reports that King David appointed Levites to serve as priests in order to perform specific duties in connection with the ark of the covenant: "to invoke, to thank, and to praise the LORD (Yahweh), the God of Israel." There is also mention in this passage of musical instruments: harps, lyres, cymbals, and trumpets that were blown regularly before the ark of the covenant.[1] Verse 7 is particularly instructive: "Then on that day David first appointed the singing of praises to the LORD (Yahweh) by Asaph and his kindred." Tradition reports that Asaph and his descendants served as influential musicians in the religious life of the Jerusalem

temple. It is likely that Asaph founded a school for singers and musicians, who were thereafter known as "sons of Asaph" (1 Chronicles 25:1, 2; 2 Chronicles 20:14; 29:13). Asaph is also reported to have prophesied with the support of musical instruments (1 Chronicles 25:1).

Whether Asaph, in fact, reaches back to the time of King David or was a figure in the reorganization of the liturgy of the second temple is disputed. Although most scholars are inclined to read these passages as an effort on the part of the Chronicler to afford Davidic authority to practices in the temple at the time of the writing of these verses (fourth century BCE), the passage does at least afford us insight into liturgical practices in Jerusalem at the time of the second temple. These "sons of Asaph" clearly played an essential role in the music and worship of the second temple (Ezra 2:41; 3:10; Nehemiah 7:44; 11:22). In fact, twelve psalms (Psalms 50, 73–83) are identified in the book of Psalms as "psalms of Asaph,"[2] suggesting that they were part of a collection or that they were performed in a manner and style of the musical guild that bore Asaph's name (see also 1 Chronicles 16:7–36, which contains an additional psalm of Asaph; or more accurately a portion of that psalm, 1 Chronicles 16:8–22 = Psalms 105:1–15).

There can be no doubt that many of the practices reported in connection with the revival of temple worship at the time of the second temple reach back into the period of the first temple, but it is not clear that there is an unbroken line of succession and a consistency of temple worship that reaches all the way back to the times of David and Solomon in the tenth century BCE, and especially through the period between 587/586 and 515 BCE, when there was no temple. Yet many of the psalms definitely reach back to an earlier period.

The temple practice of singing psalms as part of the worship of Yahweh obviously survived the destruction of the second temple in 70 CE. The practice was thereafter followed in synagogues, where psalms were used for singing and praying, but never for formal teaching, which was the exclusive function of the books of the Torah and the prophets.

THE ORGANIZATION OF THE BOOK OF PSALMS

The book of Psalms contains one hundred fifty psalms[3] and is divided into five books, which are separated by doxologies (Psalms 41:13; 72:18–19; 89:52; 106:48; 150):

Book 1:   Psalms 1–41
Book 2:   Psalms 42–72
Book 3:   Psalms 73–89
Book 4:   Psalms 90–106
Book 5:   Psalms 107–150 (151)

It is evident that these five "books" were originally five independent collections that circulated or were otherwise known locally. Evidence for this is that there are four psalms that appear twice in almost exactly the same form in our present book of Psalms:

Psalm 14 (book 1)   =   Psalm 53 (book 2)
Psalm 40:13–17 (book 1)   =   Psalm 70 (book 2)
Psalm 57:7–11 (book 2)   =   Psalm 108:1–5 (book 5)
Psalm 60:5–12 (book 2)   =   Psalm 108:6–13 (book 5)

Notice that the first pair of psalms is duplicated in books 1 and 2, the second pair also in books 1 and 2, the third pair in books 2 and 5, and the fourth pair in books 2 and 5. Notice also that Psalm 70 (book 2) is reproduced in only a portion of Psalm 40 (book 1), and that Psalm 57:7–11 (book 2) and Psalm 108:1–5 (book 5), and Psalm 60:5–12 (book 2) and Psalm 108:6–13 (book 5) are in both cases only a portion of the psalms in which each pair is currently contained. This information affords clear evidence of the independent history of the five collections, or five books.

Other notable facts about the five collections or five "books" are:

(1) Book 1 shows a strong preference for using the divine name Yahweh when referring to God, and all but three of the psalms in this collection (1, 2, and 33) are identified as "psalms of David."

(2) Book 2, on the other hand, generally prefers the Hebrew word *Elohim* when referring to God;[4] six of the psalms in book 2 are attributed to the Korahites (44–49), eighteen to David (51–65, 68–70), one to Asaph (50), and one to Solomon (72).

(3) Book 3 also refers to God mainly as *Elohim*; it has eleven (all but Psalm 50 in book 1) of the Asaph psalms (73–83), four of Korah (84–85, 87–88), one of Ethan (89), and one of David (86).

(4) Books 4 and 5 have less noteworthy differences, although there are seventeen psalms of David (101, 103, 108–110, 122, 124, 131, [133], 138–145).[5]

Particularly significant in the remarks above are the fact that only a portion of Psalm 40 (book 1) is parallel to the whole of Psalm 70 (book 2), only a portion of Psalm 50 (book 2) is parallel to only a portion of Psalm 108 (book 5), and only a portion of Psalm 60 (book 2) is parallel to only a portion of Psalm 108 (book 5). This information regarding those psalms that appear twice makes it evident that the transmission of the psalms has been a complicated process and that each of the psalms likely had its own independent history of transmission before being incorporated into one (or two) of the five distinct early collections. This information for those psalms that occur twice gives us some pause about the uncertain history of transmission of the remaining psalms for which we have no parallels.

It is difficult to assign dates to the earlier individual collections or "books" as well as to the whole of the book of Psalms. Nevertheless, by about 100 BCE the book of Psalms seems to have been regarded as sacred scriptures and was no longer open for additional insertions. The fact that the Septuagint has *essentially* the same number of psalms (actually 151 in the Greek Septuagint compared to 150 in the Hebrew Masoretic text) and exactly the same order of the psalms with the same doxologies and almost all of the same superscriptions suggests that this collection of Psalms was fixed not later than 250–150 BCE, the date of the Septuagint translation. The dates of composition of the individual psalms and of the five separate collections are another matter, and in most cases probably beyond the best efforts of modern biblical scholarship.

The psalms are, of course, poetic in their structure and follow the same features of other Hebrew and ancient Near Eastern poetry that we have previously examined, namely, parallelism. We see examples of this parallelism in the book of Psalms:

Synonymous Parallelism (Psalms 19:1–2)

19:1The heavens are telling the glory of God;
and the firmament proclaims his handiwork.
2Day to day pours forth speech,
and night to night declares knowledge.

Antithetic Parallelism (Psalms 20:7–8)

₂₀:₇Some take pride in chariots, and some in horses,
₈but our pride is in the name of the LORD (Yahweh) our God.

Incomplete Parallelism (Psalms 30:1)

₃₀:₁I will extol you, O LORD (Yahweh), for you have drawn me up,
and did not let my foes rejoice over me.

As in the case of other examples of Hebrew poetry that we have already examined, these individual couplets were collected into stanzas of from two to eight lines, and several stanzas were then put together to form a single unit of poetry, in this case a single psalm.

Several of the psalms are acrostics, in which each new line or new unit begins with the next letter of the Hebrew alphabet (א, ב, ג, ד, etc.). Examples of acrostics are Psalms 9–10 (which are obviously one psalm);[6] 25; 34; 37; 111; 112; 119; 145.

There are several types of psalms, which served different purposes or which originated in different types of situations. The following listing is suggestive, not inclusive:

(1) Royal Psalms

These are psalms that were composed for an event in connection with the king, such as a coronation, a wedding, or an occasion for special thanksgiving (Psalms 2; 18; 20; 21; 45; 72; 89; 101; 110; 132; 144:1–11)

(2) Hymns or Songs of Praise

These psalms often begin with a call to praise Yahweh or otherwise summon the assembled community to praise Yahweh[7] (Psalms 8; 19:1–6; 29; 33; 47; 65; 66:1–12; 78; 93; 95–100; 103–106; 111; 113–114; 117; 134–136; 145–150)

(3) Thanksgiving Psalms

These psalms reflect gratitude to Yahweh for a special act of deliverance (Psalms 18; 30; 32; 34; 40:1–10; 66:13–20; 92; 116; 118; 138)

(4) Songs of Zion

These psalms celebrate Yahweh's choice of Mount Zion in Jerusalem as the seat of his earthly presence; see Psalm 137:3 for mention of this category of psalm (Psalms 46; 48; 76; 84; 87; 122; 132)

(5) Laments or Prayers

These psalms usually reflect setbacks suffered in times of national or personal crisis (Psalms 12; 44; 60; 74; 79; 80; 83; 85; 90; 94; 108; 123; 129; 137; 140–143)

(6) Liturgies

These psalms suggest liturgical settings such as antiphonal dialogues (Psalms 15; 24; 50; 68; 81; 82; 95; 115; 132)

(7) Wisdom and Torah Psalms

These psalms offer reflections on issues of life and how to live a good life (Psalms 1; 19:7–10; 37; 49; 73; 112; 119; 127; 128; 133)

The book of Psalms is special among the books of the Jewish Bible as it echoes the voice of the people as they express their faith in the uniqueness and the greatness of their God Yahweh. The collection of psalms reflects the experience of Yahweh in the life of the people, most especially in the theological and liturgical life of the Jerusalem temple, even as it tells of the people's devotion to and adoration for their God. Because it is a collection or an anthology, the book of Psalms does not speak with a single theological voice. Rather the book of Psalms reflects the complexity and the diversity of Israelite religion and Israelite worship.

It is difficult to determine when, where, and for what occasion individual psalms were written. Generally individual psalms contain few specific clues of the sort that would allow scholars to make such determinations beyond the general categories of psalms alluded to above. There are, however, a few psalms that allow us to speculate as to their purpose and even their dates and places of composition. Let us look more closely at three such psalms:

PSALM 2:1–12

The psalm clearly falls into three sections or strophes, each with a different setting. Hence it makes sense to examine each strophe separately.

2:1Why do the nations conspire,
and the peoples plot in vain?
2The kings of the earth set themselves

and the rulers take counsel together,

against the LORD (Yahweh) and his anointed, saying,

₃"Let us burst their bonds asunder,

and cast their cords from us."

The setting for Psalm 2 seems fairly evident. Foreign nations, kings, and rulers are conspiring and plotting against Yahweh and his anointed king. They are determined to break away from Israel, which is currently ruling over them. The historical circumstances are quite clear: we must look for a period during which Israel exercised hegemony over its immediate neighbors. There were, indeed, few such periods.

₄He who sits [enthroned] in the heavens laughs;

the LORD (Yahweh) has them in derision.

₅Then he will speak to them in his wrath,

and terrify them in his fury, saying,

₆"I have set my king on Zion, my holy hill."

In this second strophe the scene shifts to the heavenly court, where Yahweh is looking out over the situation and laughing at those kings and nations who are conspiring against his anointed king. Yahweh addresses these enemies of Israel in wrath and fury, reminding them that it is he, Yahweh, who has installed his anointed king on Mount Zion in Jerusalem.

₇I will tell of the decree of the LORD (Yahweh):

He said to me, "You are my son;

today I have begotten you.

₈Ask of me, and I will make the nations your heritage,

and the ends of the earth your possession.

₉You shall break them with a rod of iron,

and dash them in pieces like a potter's vessel."

₁₀Now, therefore, O kings, be wise;

be warned, O rulers of the earth.

₁₁Serve the LORD (Yahweh) with fear,

with trembling ₁₂kiss his feet,

or he will be angry, and you will perish in the way;

for his wrath is quickly kindled.

Happy are all who take refuge in him.

In this third strophe it is the king, Yahweh's anointed, who is speaking. He proclaims Yahweh's decree that on this day Yahweh has chosen him as his son. In ancient Near Eastern societies, the relationship between a father and a son was used to convey the relationship between a god and a dynastic king. The king was usually understood to be a son of the god(s). Israelites did not, of course, recognize their kings as divine. Divinity was reserved to Yahweh alone. However, the formula in Psalm 2:7 implies that Israel's earthly king was regarded as Yahweh's *adopted* son: "*Today* I have begotten you" (see also 2 Samuel 7:14 and Psalm 89:27–28).[8] The occasion is clear: the setting for this psalm is the day of the king's coronation, on which Yahweh adopted the new king as his own son in fulfillment of the promise made to David in Nathan's oracle (2 Samuel 7:1–17). In this psalm, Yahweh promises success and victory to his newly enthroned king and warns the conspiring foreign kings and rulers to submit themselves to Yahweh and his anointed king.

It is difficult to know exactly for whose enthronement ceremony this psalm was composed, but I do believe that one king best fits the historical circumstances as described in the psalm. It was David and Solomon who established the United Kingdom and established political hegemony over Israel's neighbors. With the death of Solomon came the rebellion of Jeroboam in the north and the gradual disintegration of the small empire that David had conquered and Solomon had consolidated during the brief eighty or so years of the United Kingdom. The enthronement of Solomon's son Rehoboam as king in Jerusalem in about 922 BCE fits the historical circumstances of the psalm.

Mitchell Dahood provides an additional clue to assist us in determining the original setting of Psalm 2 when he says, "The genuinely archaic flavor of the [original Hebrew] language suggests a very early date (probably tenth century [BCE])."[9] This added information supports the argument that this psalm may have been composed for the coronation in Jerusalem of Solomon's son Rehoboam. It is likely that Psalm 2 subsequently served for the coronation of later kings of Judah as well.

Mark 1:11=Matthew 3:17b=Luke 3:22b ("And a voice came from heaven, 'You are my Son, the Beloved, with you I am well pleased,'") all combine elements of Psalm 2:7 and Isaiah 42:1, implying that Psalm 2 was referring to Jesus, but such a reading is retrospective and makes no effort to look at the text of the book of Psalms in its own historical, cultural, and religious context. That said, the survival of Psalm 2 in the period after there were no longer kings or coronations is probably to be credited, at least in part, to the later belief that a future anointed heir of David would at some time in the future once again occupy the Davidic throne in Jerusalem.

PSALM 45:1–17

Psalm 45 is a royal psalm, composed on the occasion of the wedding of an Israelite king to a Tyrian (Phoenician) princess. It is best to look at this psalm a section at a time.

> To the leader: according to Lilies. Of the Korahites. A Maskil. A love song.

> 45:1My heart overflows with a goodly theme;
> I address my verses to the king;
> my tongue is like the pen of a ready scribe.

Psalm 45 begins with a superscription or heading that contains important information, presumably addressed to the director of the royal musicians. The phrase "according to Lilies" probably implies that the psalm is to be sung to the tune of "Lilies," a melody apparently known to the musical director and his singers, but unfortunately not known to us. The psalm is identified as having been composed, collected, or transcribed by a group of temple singers known as Korahites (2 Chronicles 20:19). It is called a *maskil*, a term that appears in the heading of thirteen psalms (32; 42; 44; 45; 52–55; 74; 78; 88, 89; 142). A *maskil* was apparently an artistic song, indicating that it has been composed with particularly artful skill. The psalm is also described as "a love song."

The leader of the singers addresses the king orally:

> 2You are the most handsome of men;
> grace is poured upon your lips;
> therefore God has blessed you forever.
> 3Gird your sword on your thigh, O mighty one,
> in your glory and majesty.

The author's praise of the king is, not unexpectedly, excessive. The king is, after all, presumably the composer's patron.

> 4In your majesty ride on victoriously
> for the cause of truth and to defend the right;
> let your right hand teach you dread deeds.

5Your arrows are sharp
in the heart of the king's enemies;
the peoples fall under you.

The excessive praise continues. The king's majesty is considered sufficient to strike
fear into his enemies and to win victory for the king.

6Your throne, O God, endures forever and ever.
Your royal scepter is a scepter of equity;
7you love righteousness and hate wickedness.
Therefore God, your God, has anointed you
with the oil of gladness beyond your companions;
8your robes are all fragrant with myrrh and aloes and cassia.
From ivory palaces stringed instruments make you glad;
9Daughters of kings are among your ladies of honor;
at your right hand stands the queen in gold of Ophir.

Verse 6 is exceedingly problematic. Although the king was considered to be God's
adopted son, nowhere else in the entire Jewish Bible is the king referred to as "God"
or considered divine. Perhaps our text is defective here, as the royal theology never
ascended to such a level. With slight emendations of the Hebrew text, Mitchell
Dahood translates this verse "The eternal and everlasting God has enthroned you,"[10]
thereby eliminating the problem of the king's divinity. Dahood notes that "the only
evidence for this proposal is its good sense, . . . and . . . the unsatisfactory nature of
the numberless solutions which have been proffered on behalf of this *crux inter-
pretum*."[11] The praise of the king continues in mentioning the eternal endurance of
the king's throne and the king's equanimity and righteousness.

The mention of "ivory palaces" suggests the northern kingdom of Israel.[12] The
bride-to-be is now mentioned in verse 9 for the first time. Princesses are among the
bride's official retinue. The queen stands to the right bedecked in gold from Ophir.
This verse too is somewhat problematic. Dahood's minor emendation of the text
results in a translation that once again makes better sense:

Daughters of kings shall be stationed in your mansions,
the queen at your right hand in gold of Ophir.[13]

It is clear that the phrase "gold of Ophir" is meant to imply that this was the finest gold. The location of Ophir is uncertain, but the southwestern coast of Arabia or the coast of Somalia are likely candidates, in part at least because southern Arabia is the likely location of the person Ophir in the genealogies of Noah (Genesis 10:29; see also 1 Chronicles 1:23). Ophir was apparently considered a source of the best gold as early as the time of King Solomon (1 Kings 9:28; see also Job 22:24 and Isaiah 13:12).

> 10Hear, O daughter, consider and incline your ear;
> forget your people and your father's house,
> 11and the king will desire your beauty.
> Since he is your lord, bow to him;
> 12the people of Tyre will seek your favor with gifts,
> the richest of the people 13with all kinds of wealth.

It is not clear whether these are words of the marriage ceremony itself or simply exhortations to the bride to think not to her past but to her future. Verse 12 likely suggests that the bride is from Tyre in Phoenicia.

> The princess is decked in her chamber with gold-woven robes;
> 14in many colored robes she is led to the king;
> behind her the virgins, her companions, follow.
> 15With joy and gladness they are led along
> as they enter the palace of the king.

The princess of Tyre is now prepared to make her entrance into the palace of the king for the wedding ceremony. She is accompanied by her female attendants.

> 16In the place of ancestors you, O king, shall have sons;
> you will make them princes in all the earth.
> 17I will cause your name to be celebrated in all generations;
> therefore the peoples will praise you forever and ever.

The composer of the psalm or the director of the music now makes a final comment to the king, reminding him also not to look to his past, to his ancestors, but to the sons that his new wife will bear him, stressing thereby the continuity of the royal family. As a final word of flattery, the leader proclaims that the king's name will be celebrated long into the future and that the people will praise his good name forever.

The question now is for whose wedding was Psalm 45 composed. The political connections between Israel and Tyre were strong ever since kings David and Solomon established commercial relations with King Hiram of Tyre (2 Samuel 5:11; 1 Kings 5:1–12). But do we know of a king of northern Israel who married a princess from Tyre in Phoenicia? Indeed, we do. Ahab, the son of Omri and king of Israel from 869 to 850 BCE (1 Kings 16:29–31), married Jezebel, the daughter of Ethbaal, king of the Sidonians (Phoenicia). It is tempting, indeed, to think that we might have in Psalm 45 a song composed for the wedding of Ahab and Jezebel, two people whose names have, indeed, been "celebrated [even if unfavorably] in all generations."

PSALM 137:1–9

137:1By the rivers of Babylon—
there we sat down
and there we wept
when we remembered Zion.
2On the willows there
we hung up our harps.
3For there our captors asked us for songs,
and our tormentors asked for mirth, saying,
"Sing us one of the songs of Zion!"

It is evident that the author of this psalm has recently returned from exile in Babylon and is currently in Jerusalem, where he prays for revenge against both the Edomites and the Babylonians for their respective roles in the destruction of Jerusalem in 587/586 BCE. The reference to "there" four times in Psalm 137:1–3 indicates clearly that the author is no longer in exile in Babylon. Previously the author and his fellow exiles had sat by the rivers of Babylon and wept over the destruction of their beloved Zion, refusing to sing to their Babylonian captors to the accompaniment of their harps.

4How could we sing the LORD's [Yahweh's] song in a foreign land?
5If I forget you, O Jerusalem,
let my right hand wither!

₆Let my tongue cling to the roof of my mouth,

if I do not remember you,

if I do not set Jerusalem above my highest joy.

The exiles had apparently refused to sing their sacred songs while they were in exile in a foreign land for the sole amusement of their Babylonian conquerors. Yet the author of the psalm says to Jerusalem that he will never forget the beloved city. And if I ever do forget, he asks for devastating physical punishment. Memories of Jerusalem were obviously the exile's highest joy.

₇Remember, O LORD, against the Edomites

the day of Jerusalem's fall,

how they said, "Tear it down!

Tear it down!

Down to its foundations!"

₈O daughter Babylon, you devastator!

Happy shall they be who pay you back

what you have done to us!

₉Happy shall they be who take your little ones

and dash them against the rock!

In the final strophe, the returned exile calls for fierce revenge against both Edom and Babylon for their separate roles in the destruction of Jerusalem—against Edom for helping the Babylonians in the sacking of Jerusalem and then rejoicing in that destruction, and against Babylon as the instigator of the devastation. Vengeance obviously spared neither women nor children.

The occasion for the writing of this psalm is the author's reflection on the fall of Jerusalem and the two generations of exile in Babylon, sometime shortly after his return to Jerusalem, sometime around 538 BCE.

CONCLUSIONS

As we have seen, the book of Psalms is the repository of the musical life of Jerusalem's second temple in the fourth century BCE, a record of songs sung to the accompaniment of the temple band composed of harps, lyres, cymbals, lutes, tambourines, strings, pipes, and trumpets. The ark of the covenant before which trumpets had earlier been blown regularly was now gone, likely destroyed or perhaps taken to Babylon at the time of the sacking of the temple in 587/586 BCE.[14] But the musical tradition of Solomon's temple lived on in the second temple.

Like the book of Proverbs, the book of Psalms is divided into several different books, reflecting earlier collections of psalms that were later joined by doxologies in the final version. The existence of two somewhat different versions of four different psalms suggests that the psalms were apparently handed down somewhat freely in the earlier period, probably before the creation of the five distinct written collections. Those who made use of the psalms apparently exercised some freedom in modifying them as seemed appropriate. In addition, the fact that the four psalms that appear twice in the book of Psalms have been modified in their transmission over several centuries should make us wonder about the degree to which still other psalms may have been modified as well over the same period of time. How reliable is our text of the book of Psalms?

The Chronicler credits King David with instituting "the singing of praises to Yahweh." The book of Psalms credits David with having composed seventy-four of the one hundred fifty psalms of the final collection.[15] The attribution is probably more traditional than historical in the same manner in which Solomon is reputed to be the author of Proverbs and Ecclesiastes. Just as Solomon served as the patron of Israelite wisdom, so too did David serve as the patron of Israelite music. It is also noteworthy that the Chronicler afforded Davidic authority to practices in the Jerusalem temple at the time that he was writing his history.

The Chronicler also notes that David's institution of music as a part of temple worship was accomplished in connection with "Asaph and his kindred" (1 Chronicles 16:7). The Chronicler implies that Asaph founded a school for singers and musicians that continued into the period of the second temple. The source of the Chronicler's information is questionable, if not problematic, as there is no report of this in the Deuteronomistic History. The only mention of an Asaph in the entire Deuteronomistic History is to Asaph, a recorder in the court of King Hezekiah of Judah (in 2 Kings 18:18, 37; see also Isaiah 36:3), obviously a different Asaph. The silence of the Deuteronomistic History on the subject of David's establishing the musical tradition of the temple in connection with Asaph is significant and calls our attention to the Chronicler's proclivity for affording Davidic authority to temple practices, which may well be good theology but bad history. The Chronicler's penchant for rewriting history is likely evident once again. Biblical scholarship weighs all of the evidence and comes up empty on a date for Asaph, especially since the twentieth-century doctrine of the inerrancy of scripture is not a canon of sound biblical scholarship.

David's association with music was legendary in Israel, but it was a tradition likely rooted in historic memory and, therefore, reliable. There are in 1 Samuel three stories that tell of David's emergence as an important historical figure: (1) 15:35–16:13, which tells of Yahweh's sending Samuel to Bethlehem to anoint Jesse's seventh and youngest son, David, as king at a time when David was still very young; (2) 16:14–23, which tells the story of how David was summoned to the court of King Saul as a musician skillful at playing the lyre; and (3) 17:1–58, which tells the familiar story of David who, while he was still a boy, slew the Philistine giant Goliath of Gath with his sling, a feat that is elsewhere (probably more accurately), based on the criterion of dissimilarity or embarrassment, attributed to Elhanan (2 Samuel 21:19).[16] The first and third stories have obvious legendary qualities; the second, the tradition that David was a musician in Saul's court, is more likely reliable, as it is in no way designed to enhance David's stature in the way in which the other two were.

Some biblical scholars have been inclined to regard the psalms in book 1 as coming from southern Israel, as the divine name Yahweh appears in Psalms 1–41 a total of two hundred seventy-five times, whereas the generic Hebrew word for God, *Elohim*, appears only fifty times. By contrast the reverse is true in book 2, where *Elohim* is used far more frequently than Yahweh, suggesting to some that these psalms (42–72) may have a northern origin. This theory is complicated by the fact that there was a tendency in the post-exilic period to use the divine name, Yahweh, less and the generic Hebrew word for God, *Elohim*, more. Yet, as we have observed, if that is the case, then why is the purging of the divine name in the psalms not more consistent?

The book of Psalms was written in the same poetic parallelism characteristic of poetry in other books of the Bible and in other ancient Near Eastern poetic literature. We have also witnessed the composition of several alphabetical acrostics in the book of Psalms, with the acrostic in Psalms 9 and 10 extending over both psalms, proving, therefore, that Psalms 9 and 10 are actually a single psalm. In addition, the existence of more than one psalm in some of our canonical Psalms, as is the case in those psalms that appear in two versions, is further evidence that the division of our book of Psalms into 150 psalms is not without its problems.

The identification of psalms by type enables us to see that different psalms had different functions or were composed for different kinds of occasions. The identification of seven types is merely suggestive of the kinds of situations that motivated individuals to compose particular psalms.

Another problem appears at the end of Psalm 72, verse 20, which reads: "The prayers of David son of Jesse are ended," presumably marking the end of a collection of material attributed to King David. Yet Psalm 72 itself is attributed not to David, but to David's son, King Solomon. The final text of the books of Psalms poses many serious challenges for biblical scholars.

I have devoted the final portion of this chapter to trying to date three psalms by gleaning detailed evidence from each to establish its original historical context. The principle is good, but we can never be certain that we have succeeded in our effort. Our identification of Psalm 2 as a coronation hymn for King Rehoboam in 922 BCE, of Psalm 45 as a song for the wedding of King Ahab and Queen Jezebel sometime after 869 BCE, and of Psalm 137 as a psalm composed about 538 BCE by someone who had recently returned to Jerusalem from the Babylonian exile all fit the specific historical circumstances I have identified in each psalm. But were there other historical circumstances about which we have no knowledge that might have served as the occasion for the writing of these three psalms?

The dating of Psalm 2 also took into account Mitchell Dahood's observation that the Hebrew language of Psalm 2 points to a time of composition in the tenth century BCE. Most of us understand that Chaucer's fourteenth-century English, Shakespeare's late sixteenth- and early-seventeenth century English, and Dickens's nineteenth-century English are very different from one another, and different as well from contemporary American English. But few of us have the skills of Mitchell Dahood (1922–1982) to identify a Hebrew text as coming specifically from the tenth century BCE. In like manner, Professor Dahood's helpful emendation of the Hebrew text of Psalm 45:6 affords a sensible reading of that problematic verse and prepares us for some of the issues addressed in greater detail in chapter 13 of this book.

Presumably the degree of authority with which a scholar speaks is subject to peer review, even if the matter eludes the masses. The reason for trusting a trained scholar is that he or she brings the expertise and objectivity to a subject that, at least in theory, each one of us could attain with sufficient time, interest, and serious study. Professor Dahood studied at Johns Hopkins University under the dean of Old Testament studies William Foxwell Albright and served as Professor of Ugaritic Language and Literature at the Pontifical Biblical Institute in Rome until his death in

1982. His credentials establish that he is a reputable scholar worth paying attention to, but they do not mean that Dahood is right with regard to everything that he says.

The lesson here is that reputable scholars attempt to draw their conclusions using all of the information available, relying always on a careful application of the tools of historical criticism. Their conclusions may be sound, but they are not necessarily infallible.

NOTES

1. Psalm 150 contains additional information about instruments that presumably constituted the temple band: trumpets, lutes, harps, tambourines, strings and pipes, clanging cymbals, and loud clashing cymbals.

2. In addition to the psalms that are attributed to the sons of Asaph, individual psalms are attributed to David (Psalms 3–9, 11–32, 34–41, 51–65, 68–70, 86, 101, 103, 108–110, 122, 124, 131, 138, 140–145), to the Korahites (Psalms 42, 44–49, 84, 85, 87, 88), to Heman (Psalm 88), to Ethan (Psalm 89), to Solomon (Psalms 72 and 127), and even to Moses (90).

3. The Greek Septuagint has one hundred fifty-one psalms. Surprisingly Psalm 151 appears in the Hebrew text of the Dead Sea Scrolls, found in 1948 at Qumran on the northwest corner of the Dead Sea.

4. Note, in particular, that where there are parallels, Psalms 53 and 70 generally use "God" (*Elohim*), whereas their counterparts Psalms 14 and 40 use "the LORD" (Yahweh), suggesting the possibility of a southern origin for Book 1, and a northern origin for book 2. Another theory suggests that when individual psalms were copied, the divine name Yahweh was frequently replaced with the more generic *Elohim*; but if that were the case, why was this word modification not done more consistently?

5. Although the attribution of Psalm 133 to David is lacking in the Hebrew Masoretic text and in some manuscripts of the Septuagint, it is supported in 11QPs from the Dead Sea Scrolls. (11QPs is the scholarly designation for the manuscript of the book of Psalms found in cave 11 at Qumran.)

6. Not only does the alphabet extend through both psalms (9 and 10), but they are combined into one psalm in the Septuagint.

7. The word *hallelujah*, familiar to us in English, is a Hebrew word that is quite common in the book of Psalms. *Hallelu-jah* translates into English as "Praise Yah[weh]" (usually rendered in English as "Praise the LORD").

8. 2 Samuel 7:14: "I [Yahweh] will be a father to him [David],

and he [David] shall be a son to me [Yahweh].

Psalm 89:27–28:   "I [Yahweh] will make him [David] the firstborn,
the highest of the kings of the earth.
Forever I [Yahweh] will keep my steadfast love for him [David],
and my covenant with him will stand firm."

9. Mitchell Dahood, *Psalms I (1–50)*, The Anchor Bible (Garden City, NY: Doubleday, 1965), p. 7.

10. Ibid., p. 269.

11. Ibid., p. 273.

12. Amos 3:15 mentions "the houses of ivory" in his condemnation of the northern kingdom in about 750 BCE. Dahood notes that "remains of a palace with ivory inlay have been discovered at Samaria" (p. 274), the capital of the northern kingdom.

13. Dahood, *Psalms I (1–50)*, p. 269.

14. The fate of the ark of the covenant remains a mystery. Speculation about its removal from the temple focuses around King Shishak of Egypt's raid of Jerusalem in the tenth century BCE (1 Kings 14:25–28), the plunder of the temple by King Jehoash of northern Israel in the early ninth century BCE (2 Kings 14:8–14), or Babylonian king Nebuchadnezzar's destruction of the temple in 587/586 BCE (2 Kings 25:13–17). For whatever reason, the Deuteronomistic historian does not list the ark of the covenant among the temple furnishings taken to Babylon by Nebuchadnezzar, perhaps because it had been taken from the temple during one of the earlier raids.

15. The number seventy-four assumes that Psalms 9 and 10 are a single psalm and that Psalm 10 is, therefore, also attributed to David although it understandably has no separate superscription. The Septuagint attributes a total of eighty-five psalms to David, by attributing several more to David but omitting mention of David in two psalms (122 and 124) that the Hebrew text attributes to David.

16. It is not surprising that an accomplishment of this sort would later be attributed to David at a time when he was considered a national hero.

CHAPTER 12

APOCALYPTICISM

Apocalypticism has been defined as "the dualistic, cosmic, and eschatological belief in two opposing cosmic powers, good and evil, God and Satan (or his equivalent); and in two distinct ages—the present, temporal, and irretrievably evil age under Satan, who now oppresses the righteous but whose power God will soon act to overthrow; and the future, perfect and eternal age under God's own rule, when the righteous will be blessed forever."[1]

Let us analyze this long and rather technical definition by dissecting it into its principal components.

COSMIC DUALISM

The dualism of Jewish apocalypticism is not the dualism of Greek philosophy, which juxtaposes spirit and matter. It is rather the metaphysical dualism of good and evil, personified as cosmic forces that are currently involved in a struggle for supremacy within the universe. Cosmic dualism assumes that there are two gods or two great powers, one good and the other evil.

Because of the traditional monotheism of biblical Judaism, the dualism in Jewish apocalyptic literature is less acute than it is in Persian religion, which was probably a major influence on Jewish apocalypticism and in which the good god

Ahura Mazda (also known as Ahriman) was opposed by the apparently equal evil god Angra Mainyu (also known as Ohrmazd).

Satan never appears in the Old Testament as a demonic figure opposed to God. That distinction surfaces only in the deutero-canonical literature of late Judaism, which adopted a modified dualism, in which Satan was always subordinate to God and was sometimes considered to be simply a fallen angel. Yet, in Jewish apocalypticism Satan emerges as both the opponent of God and the tempter and oppressor of humankind. Although God appears in late Judaism to be in full control of the universe, Satan's rule persists. Nonetheless, however powerful Satan may have been in late Judaism, he was never equal with God.

Admittedly, even the modified dualism found in late Judaism is problematic. In some ancient Near Eastern religions that do not have a postmortem judgment, malevolent gods often function in this world to punish bad people and to restore cosmic order. Such a scheme is, of course, central to the ancient Persian religion of Zoroastrianism. This system has been adopted and adapted by late Judaism, wherein God appears to allow Satan considerable leeway to function as a subversive power within the universe. The ultimate result finds heaven, the earth, the underworld, and the entire cosmos engaged in an ongoing struggle between the cosmic forces of good and evil.

APOCALYPTIC ESCHATOLOGY

Combined with this cosmic dualism, we find in Jewish apocalypticism a clear focus on eschatology, a distinct concern about end time. In apocalypticism, there is an interest in both the present age and the future age, sometimes referred to as the Age to Come. Generally speaking, this present age is considered to be irretrievably evil and corrupt because it is under the dominion of Satan, who works his wicked ways with humankind. There appears to be no hope in this present age for the righteous followers of God, because this age is under Satan's rule.

Yet, within the apocalyptic scheme, there is generally hope or even an expectation that God will soon intervene in this present evil age with might and force to engage Satan in a final struggle that will involve the whole of creation. History, as we understand it, will be brought to an end, after which God will inaugurate a new age immediately under his control. The apocalyptic hope of late Judaism is, accordingly, pessimistic with regard to the present age, but optimistic with regard to the future age, the period of God's Rule.

THE ORIGINS OF APOCALYPTICISM

As mentioned previously, apocalyptic thought appears to have originated in Zoroastrianism, the ancient Persian religion, and was subsequently mediated to Judaism initially during the period immediately following the Babylonian exile when Israel was under Persian domination, and thereafter during the Greco-Roman period when religious syncretism was prevalent. From Judaism, apocalypticism was mediated to its daughter religion Christianity, and from Judaism and Christianity to their daughter religion Islam.

The Persian prophet Zoroaster[2] probably lived in the late second millennium BCE[3] and served initially as a priest of the old Persian religion. In founding Zoroastrianism, Zoroaster elevated Ahura Mazda, who was originally an ancient Persian "spirit" or "force" of wisdom, to the position of the one supreme god.[4] The word "Ahura" means "lord," and "Mazda" means "the wise" or "the one who is full of light," so Ahura Mazda literally means "the wise lord" or "the lord who is full of light."

As the one eternal uncreated Being, Ahura Mazda was wholly good and wholly wise, but he was not all-powerful. His power was limited by the power of his opponent Angra Mainyu (or Ahriman), who coexisted with Ahura Mazda as the evil spirit but who was, however, probably destined to perish in the end. Unlike the modified dualism of late Judaism in which Satan was always subordinate to God, the Zoroastrian scheme was more radically dualistic with two apparently equal opposing powers.

Zoroaster believed that the justice of Ahura Mazda would ultimately be administered in the hereafter. Accordingly, on the third day following a person's death, his or her soul would arise at dawn on the peak of Mount Hara, a mythical mountain at the center of the earth, where the person's thoughts, words, and deeds would be weighed in a balance. If the good outweighed the bad, the person's soul would then cross the Chinvat Bridge (the Bridge of the Separator), which spans the abyss of hell and opens at its far end onto paradise, where he or she would ascend to heaven and the presence of Ahura Mazda. If the evil outweighed the good, the soul would fall from the bridge and descend into the fiery underworld, which Zoroaster believed was the place where Angra Mainyu would inflict retribution.

At some undetermined time in the future that will mark the end of the present world order, there will be a general resurrection of all bodies, both good and evil, so that they may undergo a final judgment. Some Zoroastrian texts speak of a twelve-thousand-year history of the universe, from the beginning of the wholly good creation until the time of the Restoration.[5] On the last day, both the good and the evil will undergo an ordeal of fire and molten metal. A molten river will flow from the mountains and consume the wicked in both body and soul and then flow into the underworld, where it will purify hell and destroy Angra Mainyu and the evil spirits. The righteous will survive the fire and find the molten metal harmless.

Subsequent to Zoroaster's death, Zoroastianism appears to have developed a belief that in the final battle between good and evil, a divine savior, born of a virgin mother impregnated by Zoroaster's own sperm, would lead the cosmic forces of good in the final cosmic struggle.

Under the rule of the Achaemenids, who governed the Persian Empire from circa 550 to 331 BCE, Zoroastrianism increased dramatically. Zoroastrian beliefs became widely known in the ancient world and influenced early Ionian philosophers, such as Plato and his school, and likely influenced, as well, some exilic and post-exilic writings of the Old Testament, especially in the period following the death of Alexander the Great in 323 BCE. The greatest influence on late Judaism was, however, on some deutero-canonical literature found in the Apocrypha and Pseudepigrapha of the Old Testament.

There can be little doubt that late Jewish ideas regarding apocalypse, the kingdom of God, a final judgment, the resurrection of the dead, the son of man, the prince of darkness, a savior, and so forth, owe a great deal to Zoroastrianism. The subsequent influence on Christianity and Islam was enormous.

PROTO-APOCALYPTIC TEXTS IN THE OLD TESTAMENT

Under the direction of John Collins, a group of biblical scholars examined texts that were written during the five-hundred-year period between circa 250 BCE and circa 250 CE and that can be classified as apocalypses. On the basis of that study, they offered this definition of the literary genre "apocalypse," a Greek word that means "disclosure" or "revelation":

"Apocalypse" is a genre of revelatory literature with a narrative framework, in which a revelation is mediated by an otherworldly being to a human recipient, disclosing a transcendent reality which is both temporal, insofar as it envisages eschatological salvation, and spatial, insofar as it involves another, supernatural world.[6]

The Greek word *apocalypsis* with reference to a specific literary creation appears for the first time in the opening verses of the New Testament book of Revelation.[7] There are, however, antecedents of the literary genre "apocalypse" as early as the sixth century BCE. Although some of these early proto-apocalyptic writings lack the fully developed cosmic dualism and the apocalyptic eschatology of later apocalyptic literature, they are, nevertheless, important intermediaries between the prophetic and the apocalyptic movements.[8] We find examples of such proto-apocalyptic literature in the opening verses of the book of Ezekiel, in the eight visions found in Zechariah 1–8, in the Little Apocalypse in Isaiah 24–27, in Deutero-Zechariah (Zechariah 9–14), and in Joel 2:28–3:21.

Ezekiel

Ezekiel mentions that in "the fifth year of the exile of king Jehoiachin" (i.e., 593 BCE) "the heavens were opened, and I saw visions of God" (Ezekiel 1:2 and 1:1). In fact, the book of Ezekiel is constructed, in large part, around four detailed reports of visions that describe the prophet's transference to another dimension (Ezekiel 1:1–3:15; 8:1–11:25; 37:1–14; 40:1–48:35). These reports detail Ezekiel's visions of heavenly creatures (1:4–14; 8:3) and spirit possession (37:1; 40:1) that disclosed both Israel's future judgment and Israel's future salvation. Ezekiel's vision of the dry bones that will live again (Ezekiel 37:1–14) and his vision of the New Jerusalem and the new temple (Ezekiel 40:1–48:35) are particularly relevant as examples of proto-apocalyptic literature. The former contains imagery that subsequently developed into belief in the resurrection of the dead; the latter contains imagery that subsequently developed into belief in the future era of God's eternal rule.

Zechariah 1–8

Zechariah 1–8 contains eight visions from the period of circa 520 to 518 BCE (Zechariah 1:1; 7:1),[9] in which an angel transported the prophet to another dimension where he saw various phenomena that the angel then interpreted for him (Zechariah 1:7–17; 1:18–21; 2:1–5; 3:1–10; 4:1–14; 5:1–4; 5:5–11; 6:1–8). These visions point to future events that reflect the priestly perspective of Zechariah, who belonged to temple circles and who, not surprisingly therefore, linked Israel's ultimate deliverance and restoration to the priestly establishment in Jerusalem and to temple worship and sacrifice.

Isaiah 24–27

The four chapters found in Isaiah 24–27 are often referred to as the Little Apocalypse or the Isaian Apocalypse and obviously do not come from Isaiah of Jerusalem, whose prophetic ministry extended over the period from circa 738 BCE until at least 701 BCE. Rather, the material in the Isaian Apocalypse comes from a period at least one hundred or more years subsequent to Isaiah's oracles, specifically from the late seventh or early sixth century BCE, or even later. These four chapters contain a number of themes that were especially popular in later apocalyptic writings: a universal judgment (Isaiah 24:1–23), punishment of the heavenly host and the kings of the earth (Isaiah 24:21–22), the destruction of death (Isaiah 25:8), the resurrection of the dead (Isaiah 26:19), and the future redemption of the exiles of Israel who will eventually be summoned back to Jerusalem (Isaiah 27:2–13).

There are also a number of passages in the Little Apocalypse that have nothing to do with apocalypticism (Isaiah 25:1–5, 10b–12; 26:7–19; 27:2–5). Moreover, some popular apocalyptic themes are conspicuously absent from the Isaian Apocalypse: systematic cosmic dualism, heavenly journeys, and the periodization of history into this age and the Age to Come. It is difficult to decide whether the Little Apocalypse was a coherent composition in its own right or the result of several subsequent editings of the Isaiah manuscript over several centuries. It is not self-evident that Isaiah 24–27 is a coherent sixth-century proto-apocalyptic unit. In fact, much of the apocalyptic material found in Isaiah 24–27 may have been interpolated into the text of the Isaiah manuscript during the period of the second temple, possibly as late as the period of the Ptolemies. Some of the language, vocabulary, and themes found in the Isaian Apocalypse are similar to what we find in the book of Daniel in the second century BCE. In fact, both may reflect knowledge of the same period of trials and tribulations.

Zechariah 9–14

Biblical scholars almost universally agree that Zechariah 9–14 constitutes a writing that is separate and distinct from Zechariah 1–8 and have labeled this subsequent writing Second Zechariah or Deutero-Zechariah. This latter material reflects deep discontent and disappointment with the restoration of the priestly establishment in post-exilic Jerusalem and belief in an impending "day of the LORD (Yahweh)." The phrases "on that day" or "the day of the LORD (Yahweh)" or "a day is coming for the LORD (Yahweh)" appear eighteen times in Deutero-Zechariah (Zechariah 9:16; 12:3, 4, 6, 8, 9, 11; 13:1, 2, 4; 14:1, 4, 6, 8, 9, 13, 20, 21).

In pre-exilic prophecy such language generally refers to imminent events in historical time. In Haggai 2:23, it refers to the future day in which King David's descendant Zerubbabel will rule in Jerusalem as a divine appointee in fulfillment of Yahweh's promise to David (see 2 Samuel 7:16). In Zechariah 2:10–11, it refers to the day in which Yahweh's presence will return to Jerusalem. In Zechariah 3:10, it refers to the time when the people will live with one another once again in peace in Jerusalem. The same sort of language in post-exilic prophecy generally has an eschatological meaning and proclaims the imminent coming of the day of God's judgment upon Israel and the world. In this latter post-exilic context, "the day of the LORD (Yahweh)" will be a day of final destruction with the accompanying deliverance from evil that will come as a result of that destruction. Such references to the imminent "day" appear in greater concentration in Zechariah 12–14 (seventeen times) than anywhere else in the Hebrew Bible.[10]

Scholars have had difficulty in agreeing on a date for the writing of Second Zechariah, ranging from as early as 740–730 BCE to the mid-second century BCE. The references in Zechariah 1:1 to "the eighth month, in the second year of Darius" and in Zechariah 7:1 to "the fourth year of the reign of King Darius, . . . the fourth day of the ninth month, which is Chislev" imply dates of October/November 520 BCE and November/December 518 BCE, respectively, for the period of Zechariah's ministry. Assuming that Deutero-Zechariah was written later, a date as early as the first half of the fifth century BCE seems reasonable for the earliest material. Deutero-Zechariah clearly looks back with disappointment on a situation that Zechariah looked forward to with hope. Zechariah 14 may actually be even later than Zechariah 9–13, perhaps as late as 420 BCE, because it has a more highly developed vision of the eschatological day. In any event, the evidence for a precise dating of Second Zechariah is less certain than scholars would like.

Joel 2:28–3:21

Unlike Hosea 1:1, Amos 1:1, Micah 1:1, Zephaniah 1:1, Haggai 1:1, and Zechariah 1:1, the superscription of the book of Joel (Joel 1:1) affords no mention of Israelite or Judean kings to enable scholars to place the prophet easily into his historical context, possibly because at the time of the writing of the book there were no longer kings of Israel and Judah. We have nothing more by way of identification than the name of the prophet, Joel (which means "Yahweh is God), and of his father, Pethuel (which means "enlarged of God").

In mentioning the restoration of the fortunes of Judah and Jerusalem, Joel 3:1–3 appears to assume that the events surrounding the fall of Judah and Jerusalem in 587/586 BCE were ancient history. So too Joel's possible knowledge of the books of Amos, Isaiah, Micah, and Obadiah suggest a date later than any of those books.[11] Joel also takes for granted the rebuilding of the second temple in 520–516 BCE (Joel 1:9, 14, 16; 2:17; 3:18). Moreover, he refers quite casually to the rebuilt wall of Jerusalem (Joel 2:7, 9). Inasmuch as the rebuilding of the wall of Jerusalem was completed in September/October 445 BCE (Nehemiah 6:15), Joel was clearly written well after that date. References to elders, priests, and the congregation in Joel 1:2, 13–14; 2:15–17 assume the theocratic establishment of post-exilic Judaism in Jerusalem. There is, however, nothing in the book of Joel to suggest that the author had any knowledge of the Seleucid period, so a date of 400 to 350 BCE affords the time frame most probable for the ministry of the prophet and the writing of the book.

Our principle concern here is with the apocalyptic material in Joel 2:28–3:21 and most especially with the meaning of the phrase "the day of the LORD (Yahweh)" in Joel 1:15; 2:1, 11, 31; 3:14. The expression "the day of the LORD (Yahweh)" occurs in the Old Testament in nine verses outside the book of Joel. It is used in oracles against Israel in Ezekiel 13:5 (in reference to a past day); in Amos 5:18, 20 (a day of darkness, not light); in Zephaniah 1:7 (the day is at hand); in Zechariah 14:1 (a day when plunder will be taken); and in Malachi 4:5 (a great and terrible day). It is used against foreign nations in Isaiah 13:6, 9 (against Babylon) and in Obadiah 15 (against all the nations that have harmed Judah). In Joel it occurs three times against Israel: in Joel 1:15 (the day of destruction is near); 2:1 (the day is coming; it is near); and 2:11 (the day is great and terrible); and it is used twice against the nations: in Joel 2:31 (a great and terrible day for those who do not call upon the name of Yahweh); and in 3:14 (the day is near).

There are many additional references to a day for Yahweh, a day of the wrath of Yahweh, a day of Yahweh's fierce anger, a day of Yahweh's vengeance, and the like. As with the examples above, the message is directed against either Israel or one or more of the nations. This distinction is important because in the period of biblical prophecy judgment is directed primarily against Israel, whereas in the more fully developed apocalyptic literature, judgment is directed almost exclusively against Israel's enemies. Accordingly, the earlier messages using these phrases suggest that the day of Yahweh will be directed primarily against Israel's neighbors for threatening the chosen people of God. The day of Yahweh would, accordingly, be a day of victory and celebration for Yahweh's people. Whereas Israel commonly used the term to describe a day of joy in which Yahweh would defeat their enemies, it is possible in the prophetic literature to detect a shift in which the prophets effectively redefined the phrase to refer to Yahweh's judgment against his own people. In the later passages the threat was directed increasingly against Israel for having deserted Yahweh and the covenant. Subsequent to the destruction of Judah and Jerusalem in 587/586 BCE, the day of Yahweh was understood increasingly in apocalyptic terms. The day of Yahweh would be a day of wrath against both Israel and the nations.

Joel seems to have written specifically on the occasion of a devastating plague of locusts, a not uncommon phenomenon in that part of the world (Joel 1:1–12). It is perhaps this natural disaster that led the prophet to understand that the Day of Judgment that Israel's prophets had previously announced was now at hand. Joel was convinced that the day of Yahweh was near and that it would be a day of darkness and gloom, a day of clouds and thick darkness, a day of violent devastation and vehement destruction. There is a cry to blow the trumpet (2:1) to sound the alarm to warn the people of the impending destruction. This time the army that is descending upon the people is not a foreign army; it is rather the army of Yahweh (2:11). There will be "portents in the heavens and on the earth: blood and fire and columns of smoke" (2:30). "The sun shall be turned to darkness, and the moon to blood, before the great and terrible day of the LORD (Yahweh) comes" (2:31).

Following this ominous verse (2:31), there is a sudden shift in Joel's message from threat to promise, because "everyone who calls upon the name of the LORD (Yahweh) shall be saved" (2:32). If the Israelites will only repent and return to Yahweh, Yahweh's army will leave. Judgment will fall upon the nations, and Judah and Jerusalem will be restored (3:20).

As Paul Hanson argues, all of these proto-apocalyptic writings cited above appear to "occupy a transitional position between the more historically oriented per-spective of classical prophecy and the more transcendent view of salvation charac-teristic of the apocalyptic writings."[12]

DANIEL

It is not until we get to the book of Daniel in the second century BCE that we find, especially in Daniel 7–12, the first and only true example of full-fledged apocalyptic literature in the entire Old Testament. It appears that by the time of the second cen-tury BCE, Jewish apocalypticism had, as a result of the religious syncretism char-acteristic of the Hellenistic Age, been infiltrated and influenced by Mesopotamian and Persian influences.

Although this book appears under the name of Daniel, it is actually an anony-mous writing. An ancient wise and righteousness man named Daniel is mentioned in Ezekiel 14:12–20[13] and 28:3; he is also mentioned as King Danel (not Daniel) in the fourteenth-century BCE Ugaritic Tale of Aqhat.[14] The anonymous author of Daniel likely attached Daniel's name to the book to afford it presumed antiquity and, hence, greater authority and, accordingly, provided a setting for Daniel as a Jewish exile in Babylon in the sixth century BCE, probably for the same reasons.

In the authoritative Masoretic text, the book of Daniel is written in two lan-guages: Hebrew in Daniel 1:1–2:4a; Aramaic in Daniel 2:4b–7:28; and Hebrew in Daniel 8:1–12:13. To add to the confusion, the Septuagint Greek translation of the book of Daniel has a good deal of additional material:

> The Prayer of Azariah in Daniel 3:24–45 and the Song of the Three Jews in Daniel 3:46–90 of the Greek version;
>
> Susanna, regarded as apocryphal by Protestants and Jews and as deutero-canonical by Roman Catholics, appears as chapter 13:1–64 of the Greek version;
>
> Bel (Daniel 14:1–22) and the Dragon (Daniel 14:23–42), regarded as apocrypha by Protestants and Jews and as deutero-canonical by Roman Catholics, appears in the Greek version; and
>
> additional compositions linked to Daniel appeared among the Dead Sea Scrolls, such as the Prayer of Nabonidus, and a fragment of the Apocalypse of Pseudo-Daniel.

The apocalyptic material in Daniel 7–12 contains Daniel's four visions:

(1) Daniel 7:1–28 (the vision of the four beasts and the single human being):
     This first vision, written in Aramaic, is dated in the first year of King Belshazzar of Babylon. Modern scholars maintain that the first beast of this vision represents the Babylonian Empire (7:4); the second beast represents the Median Empire (7:5); the third beast represents the Persian Empire (7:6); the fourth beast represents the Greek Empire of Alexander the Great (7:7); and the ten horns of this fourth beast refer to the ten kings of the Macedonian-Seleucid Empire, while the little horn of Daniel 7:8 represents the current king Antiochus IV Epiphanes. Following this sequence, the Son of Man (a single human being), often thought to represent Israel, appears and is given the kingdom (7:13–14). More likely this "one like a human being" is what we would refer to as an angel, a supernatural being, whose eschatological appearance will usher in the future age.

(2) Daniel 8:1–27 (the vision of the ram and the he-goat):
     The second vision is dated to the third year of King Belshazzar and is a restatement of the theme of the first vision, the principal difference being that this time the text is written not in Aramaic, but in Hebrew. In addition, the vision culminates in the desecration of the Jerusalem temple under Antiochus IV Epiphanes and in its subsequent future restoration. The angel Gabriel interpreted this vision for Daniel (8:15–27).

(3) Daniel 9:1–27 (the vision that discloses that justice will be done and that the temple will be reconsecrated):
     The third vision, written in Hebrew, is dated in the first year of King Darius and came to Daniel also from the angel Gabriel. This vision affords a new understanding of Jeremiah's prophecy (Jeremiah 25:11, 12; 29:10) of a seventy-year exile by assuring the Jews that their suffering at the hands of Antiochus IV Epiphanes will soon come to an end. Gabriel tells Daniel that the time of suffering will be seventy weeks of years, or 7×70 years (or 490 years): "Seventy weeks are decreed for your people and your holy city: to finish the transgression, to put an end to sin, and to atone for iniquity, to bring in everlasting righteousness, to seal both vision and prophet, and to anoint a most holy place"—obviously the Jerusalem temple (Daniel 9:24).

(4) Daniel 10:1–12:13 (the final vision describing the course of events from

Cyrus of Persia in 538 BCE to the Syrian king Antiochus IV Epiphanes in 164 BCE):

The fourth vision, also written in Hebrew, is dated in the third year of Cyrus (536 BCE). After rehearsing once again events from the Persian Period, the rise and fall of Alexander the Great, the conflict between the Ptolemies and the Seleucids with their consequences for Judea, and the final evil during the reign of Antiochus IV Epiphanes, Daniel looks at these events against the backdrop of a heavenly struggle that will lead ultimately to the rise of the archangel Michael and the deliverance of the people of Israel (Daniel 12:1), culminating in the resurrection of many of the dead and everlasting contempt and punishment for others (Daniel 12:2).

In these four visions, the angelic mediator Gabriel discloses to Daniel information both about the past and about the future deliverance and salvation that will come at the end time, when God's rule will finally break into history, a salvation that will be the reward of those who remain faithful during the time of persecution and the future judgment.

The cryptic nature of these chapters containing Daniel's apocalyptic visions, set in the context of the sixth century BCE at the time of the Babylonian Empire, may have been a literary device to protect from further persecution those who wrote, those who circulated, and those who heard these subversive words that spoke so powerfully against the Seleucid Empire in general and against Antiochus IV Epiphanes in particular. The author's knowledge of Babylonian and Persian times was at best sketchy, indeed sometimes seriously flawed, indicating his distance from the purported events of the sixth century both in time and in place.

The book of Daniel was written not in Babylonian times as it purports, but rather during the reign of Antiochus IV Epiphanes (175–163 BCE), and more particularly probably after the desecration of the Jerusalem temple in 168 BCE and before its rededication by the Maccabees in 165 BCE. This dating provides a very narrow window of 168–165 BCE for the time in which the book of Daniel was likely written.[15] Additional support for this date in the Greek period is provided by the fact that Daniel 3:5 lists three musical instruments whose names in Aramaic are all loanwords from the Greek: "the Aramaic word for 'lyre,' *qatrōs* (better in the *kĕtîb* as *qîtārôs*) is from the Greek *kitharis* . . . ; the Aramaic word for 'harp,' *pĕsantērîn*, is from the Greek *psaltērion*; and the Aramaic word that is rendered here as 'bagpipe,' *sûmpōnyāh*, is from the Greek *symphōnia*, literally 'accompanying sound.'"[16]

The book of Daniel was, accordingly, written at a time of intense persecution to encourage Jews to resist the oppressive policies under Antiochus IV Epiphanes and to remain faithful to their religion with the expectation that their God would intervene soon to establish the future Age to Come. The doctrine of the resurrection of dead martyrs is clearly asserted. We find also a developed angelology with two named angels, Gabriel (Daniel 8:16; 9:21) and Michael (Daniel 10:13, 21; 12:1). In this regard, Daniel 7–12 is the earliest example of a fully developed Jewish apocalypse.

OTHER JEWISH APOCALYPSES

As we have seen, the literary genre "apocalypse" is generally characterized by a belief in the supernatural world of good and evil otherworldly realms (heaven and hell), the expectation of eschatological (postmortem) salvation, a heightened interest in supernatural beings (including the influence of angels and demons on human life), a final judgment of the dead, and a resurrection of the righteous in glory. Such a worldview obviously existed before the actual writing of Jewish apocalypses. In fact, it was the prior existence of such a worldview that served as the occasion for these apocalyptic writings.

We actually know very little about the mythology of Jewish apocalypticism. The apocalyptic writers undoubtedly had access to a much more fully developed mythology than what we now find in the Jewish Bible. See, for example:

Isaiah 25:8 (he [Yahweh] will swallow up death forever);
Isaiah 26:19 (your dead shall live; their corpses shall rise);
Isaiah 64:1 (O that you would tear open the heavens and come down); and
Isaiah 65:17 (for I [Yahweh] am about to create new heavens and a new earth).

Of these four passages, the first two are from the Isaian Apocalypse (Isaiah 24–27) and the final two are from Third Isaiah (Isaiah 55–66), all relatively late material.

The transition from prophecy to apocalypticism is not entirely clear. As we have seen, there is probably a connection between the "day of Yahweh" in Israel's prophetic literature (see e.g., Isaiah 2:4; see also Psalms 96; 98), and later apocalyptic expectation of a final judgment. Some of the proto-apocalyptic texts we examined above point to a gradual evolution from prophetic to apocalyptic thought.

In addition to the book of Daniel, the only Jewish apocalyptic writing that found its way into the Old Testament canon, we find other Jewish apocalyptic literature from approximately the same period as the book of Daniel and also somewhat later in writings found in the Apocrypha, the Pseudepigrapha, and the Dead Sea Scrolls.

1 Enoch[17]

1 Enoch survives, probably in its entirety, only in an ancient Ethiopic translation (from ca. 500 CE) of a Greek translation of several original Aramaic (and/or Hebrew) writings, some of which are attested in manuscript fragments found at Qumran among the Dead Sea Scrolls.[18] The book purports to be the record of a series of revelations to Enoch, the son of Jared (Genesis 5:21–24), which he passed on to his son Methuselah.[19]

Jewish tradition had apparently invested Enoch with special significance because Genesis 5:24 was understood to imply that Enoch never died, but that he had been transmuted by God into heaven.[20] The wording of this passage in Genesis suggested to later writers something other than death, perhaps even immortality.

It was on that journey to heaven that Enoch presumably "saw" the secrets of the mysteries of the universe and the future of the world and recorded them in writing for posterity. The content of the book is, therefore, twofold: it reports on (1) the nature of the created cosmos and (2) the origin, nature, and final judgment of evil and sin at the culmination of history.

The present book of 1 Enoch likely incorporates several earlier written works of diverse but related material and is, accordingly, a collection of previous traditions and writings. These earlier works are likely reflected in the following outline of the present book:

The Introduction (1 Enoch 1–5) presents the recurring theme of rewards for the elect and the righteous and punishments for the wicked and ungodly sinners when the end of the world and the eschatological judgment come (1:1, 7–9).

1:1The blessing of Enoch: with which he blessed the elect and the righteous who would be present on the day of tribulation at (the time of) the removal of all the ungodly ones. . . . 1:7And the earth shall be rent asunder; and all that is upon the earth shall perish, And there shall be a judgment upon all, (including) the righteous. 8And to all the righteous he will grant peace. He will preserve the elect, and kindness shall be upon them. And they shall all belong to God and they shall prosper and be blessed; and the light of God shall shine unto then. ₉Behold he will; arrive with ten million of the holy ones in order to execute judgment upon all. He will destroy the wicked ones and censure all flesh on account of everything that they have done, that which the sinners and the wicked ones committed against him.

1. The Book of the Watchers (1 Enoch 6–36), probably written before 100 BCE and maybe as early as the second half of the third century BCE, identifies the punishments that will be inflicted on the Day of Judgment upon enemies of the Jews and on all sinners. This section mentions the primordial angelic rebellion (6–11) and Enoch's several journeys through the earth and the underworld (17–36).

₂₇:₁At that moment, I said, "For what purpose does this blessed land, entirely filled with trees, (have) in it midst this accursed valley?" ₂Then, Uriel, one of the holy angels, who was with me, answered me and said to me, "This accursed valley is for those accursed forever; here will gather together all (those) accursed ones, those who speak with their mouth unbecoming words against the Lord and utter hard words concerning his glory. Here shall they be gathered together, and here shall be their judgment, in the last days. ₃There will be upon them the spectacle of the right-eous judgment, in the presence of the righteous forever. The merciful will bless the lord of Glory, the Eternal King, all the day. ₄In the days of the judgment of (the accursed), the (merciful) shall bless him for the mercy which he had bestowed upon them." ₅At that moment, I blessed the Lord of Glory and gave him the praise that befits his glory.

2. The Parables or Similitudes of Enoch (1 Enoch 37–71) were probably written in either the first century BCE or the first half of the first century CE, although scholars have not always agreed on whether the Similtudes are pre- or post-Christian. Central to the Similtudes is the description of events relating to the final judgment of the wicked (38), when the eschatological judge, the Messiah, appears variously as "the Righteous One" (38:1–6).

₃₈:₁The first thing:
When the congregation of the righteous shall appear,
sinners shall be judged for their sins,
they shall be driven from the face of the earth,

₂and when the Righteous One shall appear before the face of the righteous,

those elect ones, their deeds are hung upon the Lord of the Spirits,

he shall reveal light to the righteous and the elect who dwell upon the earth,

where will the dwelling of the sinners be,

and where the resting place of those who denied the name of the Lord of the Spirits?

It would have been better for them not to have been born.

₃When the secrets of the Righteous One are revealed,

he shall judge the sinners;

and the wicked ones will be driven from the presence of the righteous and the elect,

₄and from that time, those who possess the earth will neither be rulers nor princes,

they shall not be able to behold the faces of the holy ones,

for the light of the Lord of the Spirits has shined

upon the face of the holy, the righteous, and the elect.

₅At that moment, kings and rulers shall perish,

they shall be delivered into the hands of the righteous and holy ones,

₆and from thenceforth no one shall be able to induce the Lord of the Spirits to show
    them mercy,

for their life is annihilated.

Elsewhere this eschatological judge or Messiah is called "the Elect One" (40:5; 45:3–4; 49:2, 4; 51:3; 52:6, 9; 55:4; 61:5, 8, 10; 62:1), "the Elect One of Righteousness and of Faith" (39:6), "the Righteous and Elect One" (53:6), "His Anointed" or "His Messiah" (52:4), and "the Son of Man" (46:2, 3, 4; 48:2; 62:5, 7, 9, 14; 63:11; 69:26, 27, 29; 70:1; 71:14, 17), a term common in the New Testament and known also from Daniel 7:13. The Similitudes describe the judgment of everyone, both righteous and wicked, whether dead or alive, as well as the judgment of angels. The son of man in 1 Enoch is regarded as preexistent (46:1, 2; 48:2, 3, 6) and is apparently more than a mere man, likely a supernatural angelic figure.

3. The Astronomical Book or the Book of the Heavenly Luminaries (1 Enoch 72–82) was probably written before 110 BCE and may, given the astronomical views it reflects, come from as early as the Persian period. The book describes astronomical and meteorological beliefs of the Jews shortly before the time of Jesus, including insistence upon a solar year of three hundred sixty-four days rather than Judaism's traditional lunar calendar.

81:1Then he said to me, "Enoch, look at the tablet(s) of heaven; read what is written upon them and understand (each element on them) one by one." 2So I looked at the tablet(s) of heaven, read all the writing (on them), and came to understand everything. I read that book and all the deeds of humanity and all the children of the flesh upon the earth for all the generations of the world. 3At that very moment, I blessed the Great Lord, the King of Glory forever, for he has created all the phenomena in the world. I praised the Lord because of his patience; and I wept on account of the children of the people upon the earth. 4After that, I said:

> "Blessed is the man who dies righteous and upright,
> against whom no records of oppression has been written,
> and who received no judgment on that day."

4. The Book of Enoch's Two Dreams (1 Enoch 83–90) was probably written at the time of Judas Maccabeus (165–160 BCE) or John Hyrcanus (134–104 BCE). The second of Enoch's dreams traces Israel's history from Adam to the time of the Hasmonean revolt (1 Enoch 85–90) and the establishment of the messianic kingdom. This section describes how evil men and fallen angels will be thrown into a fiery abyss, after which the Messiah will appear. In highly symbolic cryptic language, the final verses of the book describe the descent of the Heavenly Jerusalem (90:28–29), the conversion and submission of the Gentiles (90:30), the resurrection of the righteous dead (90:33), and the coming of the Messiah (90:37).

90:28Then I stood still, looking at that ancient house being transformed: All the pillars and all the columns were pulled out; and the ornaments of that house were packed and taken out together with them and abandoned in a certain place in the South of the land. 29I went on seeing until the Lord of the sheep brought about a new house, greater and loftier than the first one, and set it up in the first location which had been covered up—all its pillars were new, the columns new; and the ornaments new as well as greater than those of the first, (that is) the old (house) which was gone. All the sheep were within it.

90:30Then I saw all the sheep that had survived as well as all the animals upon the earth and the birds of heaven, falling down and worshiping those sheep, making petition to them and obeying them in every respect.

90:33All those which have been destroyed and dispersed, and all the beasts of the field and the birds of the sky were gathered together in that house; and the Lord of the sheep rejoiced with great joy because they had all become gentle and returned to his house.

90:37Then I saw that a snow-white cow was born, with huge horns; all the beasts of the field and the birds of the sky feared him and made petition to him all the time.

The highly symbolic nature of 1 Enoch's language is evident in these verses.

5. The Epistle of Enoch or the Book of Blessings for the Righteous and Sorrow for Sinners (1 Enoch 91–105) was probably written sometime in the second century BCE or shortly after 94–79 BCE or 70–64 BCE at a time when the Pharisees were opposed by the Maccabean rulers and the Sadducees (103:14–15). This section reports that the messianic kingdom is temporary in duration, that the final judgment will be consummated at the close of the kingdom, and that there will apparently be a resurrection of only the righteous dead (104:1–13).

104:5You shall not have to hide on the day of the great judgment, and you shall not be found as the sinners; but the eternal judgment shall be (far) away from you for all the generations of the world. 6Now fear not, righteous ones, when you see the sinners waxing strong and flourishing; do not be partners with them, but keep far away from those who lean onto their own injustice; for you are to be partners with the good-hearted people of heaven. 7Now, you sinners, even if you say "All our sins shall not be investigated or written down," nevertheless, all your sins are being written down every day. 8So now I show unto you that light and darkness as well as day and night witness all your sins.

The conclusion (1 Enoch 106–108) repeats the theme of rewards for the righteous and punishments for the wicked. Fragments from the Dead Sea Scrolls suggest that this section was written sometime before the middle of the first century BCE.

108:4I also saw there something like an invisible cloud; (and) though I could see that it was completely dark, yet I could not see the flame of its fire because it was burning brightly; and there were some things like bright mountains which formed a ring (around it) and which were tossing it to and fro. 5Then I asked one of the holy angels who was with me, saying to him, "What is this bright thing? For it is not a heaven but merely the flame of a fire which is burning—and a voice of weeping, crying, and lamenting as well as strong pain." 6And he said unto me, "This place which you see, into it shall be taken the spirits of sinners, blasphemers, those who do evil, and those who alter all the things that the Lord has done through the mouth of the prophets, all of which have to be fulfilled."

Someone obviously brought the several sources of 1 Enoch together in their present form sometime before the creation of our Ethiopic version about 500 CE, and possibly much earlier. It is evident, especially since the discovery among the Dead Sea Scrolls of Aramaic fragments of Enochic passages, that separate Aramaic (and/or Hebrew) sources appeared much earlier. In fact, the material in Aramaic from Qumran attests to a date as early as the first century BCE for at least some portions of the book. Yet the process by which these several writings came together in their present form was obviously complicated and makes it difficult, if not impossible, for scholars to reconstruct with any degree of accuracy the details of that process.

Large portions of the Enochic material belong to the genre of apocalypse: 1 Enoch 17–19; 21–26; 81:1–82:3; and 108 are all journeys to unusual places where visions are interpreted by an angel, somewhat similar to what we find in Ezekiel 40–48 and Zechariah 1–6. It is not entirely clear what holds this material together; there is certainly no single theme or theological outlook to the final composition. The common denominator may be nothing more than that the material has all been attributed to or written in the name of Enoch.

Although 1 Enoch was not included in the Hebrew canon, or even in the Apocrypha (i.e., it was not included in the Greek Septuagint), probably because of its late date, it is very important for an understanding of the eschatological beliefs of late Judaism, of Jesus, and of the writers of the books of the New Testament, especially the Gospels and the Revelation of John. 1 Enoch affords a clear understanding of late Jewish beliefs, at least in some small apocalyptic circles, regarding the nature of the messianic kingdom and the future life, Sheol and the resurrection of the dead, angelology and demonology, the critical issue of the role of the Son of Man in Jesus' teaching, and the early church's interpretation of the role of Jesus in the eschatological age. Without a doubt 1 Enoch clarifies many of the complexities of both intertestamental Judaism and early Christianity. Some of the material found in 1 Enoch is actually alluded to or quoted, probably from a Greek translation, in the New Testament book of Jude 6, 14–15 (see 1 Enoch 6–19). In fact, the author of Jude 14–15 cites 1 Enoch 1:9 as if he regarded it as scripture.

2 Baruch[21]

2 Baruch or the Syriac Apocalypse of Baruch received its name because it is the only complete text of the book that survives in a Syriac manuscript from the sixth century CE. In its opening words, the Syriac Baruch comments that it is a translation from a Greek text, manuscripts of which actually survive in only a few small fragments. Linguistic experts maintain that the Greek text is probably a translation from a Hebrew original. Evidence in support of a Hebrew original is based on several incomprehensible passages in the Syriac version that can best be explained by retranslating the Syriac first into Greek and subsequently into Hebrew. Moreover, presumed wordplays in the Syriac text are evident only when some passages are translated into Hebrew.[22] In addition, several passages from the Hebrew original of 2 Baruch apparently survive in quotations in later Talmudic and rabbinical writings.

Like 1 Enoch, 2 Baruch appears to be a composite work, made up of eight independent Pharisaic writings, probably from the period of circa 50–90 CE:

(1) 1:1–5:6. Jerusalem will be destroyed and the Heavenly Jerusalem will appear.

1:4Behold, therefore, I shall bring evil upon this city and its inhabitants. And it will be taken away from before my presence for a time. And I shall scatter this people among the nations that they may do good to the nations.

4:1And the Lord said to me:
This city will be delivered up for a time,
And the people will be chastened for a time,
And the world will not be forgotten.

4:6Behold, now it is preserved with me—as also Paradise. 7Now go away and do as I command you.

(2) 6:1–9:1. The invasion of Jerusalem by the Chaldeans.

8:1Now the angels did as he had commanded them; and when they had broken up the corners of the wall, a voice was heard from the midst of the temple after the wall had fallen, saying: 2Enter, enemies, and come, adversaries, because he who guarded the house has left it. ₃And I, Baruch, went away. ₄And it happened after these things that the army of the Chaldeans entered and seized the house and all that is around it. ₅And they carried away the people into captivity and killed some of them. And they put King Zedekiah in irons and sent him to the king of Babylon.

(3) 10:1–12:4. Baruch will remain in Jerusalem while Jeremiah goes into exile in Babylonia.

₁₀:₂Tell Jeremiah to go away in order to support the captives unto Babylon. ₃You, however, stay here in the desolation of Zion and I shall show you after these days what will happen at the end of days.

(4) 13:1–20:6. Revelation to Baruch of the impending judgment on the nations.

₂₀:₁Therefore, behold, the days will come and the times will hasten, more than the former, and the periods will hasten more than those which are gone, and the years will pass more quickly than the present ones. ₂Therefore, I now took away Zion to visit the world in its own time more speedily.

(5) 21:2–35:4. The prayer of Baruch and God's answer, signs of the coming judgment, the coming of Messiah and the messianic kingdom, and the resurrection.

₃₀:₁And it will happen after these things when the time of the appearance of the Anointed One has been fulfilled and he returns with glory, that then all who sleep in hope of him will rise. ₂And it will happen at that time that those treasuries will be opened in which the number of the souls of the righteous were kept, and they will go out and the multitudes of the souls will appear together, in one assemblage, of one mind. And the first ones will enjoy themselves and the last ones will not be sad. ₃For they know that the time has come of which it is said that it is the end of time. ₄But the souls of the wicked will the more waste away when they shall see all these things. ₅For they know that their torment has come and that their perditions have arrived.

(6) 36:1–47:1. The apocalyptic vision of the forest, the vine, the fountain, and the cedar and its interpretation; the destiny of apostates and believers; Baruch speaks to the people about his impending death.

41:1And I answered and said:

For whom and for how many will these things be? Or who will be worthy to live in that time? 2I shall now say before you everything that I think, and I shall ask you about the things of which I meditate. 3For behold, I see many of your people who separated themselves from your statutes and who have cast away from them the yoke of your Law. 4Further, I have seen others who left behind their vanity and who have fled under your wings. 5What will, therefore, happen with those? Or how will that last time receive them? 6Their time will surely not be weighed exactly, and they will certainly not be judged as the scale indicates.

44:2Behold, I go to my fathers in accordance with the way of the whole earth. 3You, however, do not withdraw from the way of the Law, but guard and admonish the people who are left lest they withdraw from the commandments of the Mighty One.

(7) 48:1–77:26. The prayers of Baruch, the nature of the resurrection body, and the final destinies of the righteous and the wicked.

48:48But now, let us cease talking about the wicked and inquire about the righteous. 49And I will tell you about their blessedness and I shall not be silent about their glory which is kept from them. 50For surely, as you endured much labor in the short time in which you live in this passing world, so you will receive great light in that world which has no end.

51:1And it will happen after this day which he appointed is over that both the shape of those who are found to be guilty as also the glory of those who have proved to be righteous will be changed. 2For the shape of those who now act wickedly will be made more evil than it is (now) so that they shall suffer torment. 3Also, as for the glory of those who proved to be righteous on account of my Law, those who possessed intelligence in their life, and those who planted the root of wisdom in their heart—their splendor will then be glorified by transformations, and the shape of their face will be changed into the light of their beauty so that they may acquire and receive the undying world which is promised to them. 4Therefore, especially they who will then come will be sad, because they despised my Law and stopped their ears lest they hear wisdom and receive intelligence.

(8) 78:1–87:1. The epistle of Baruch to the nine and a half tribes.

78:1The letter of Baruch, the son of Neriah which he wrote to the nine and a half tribes.

These are words of the letter which Baruch, the son of Neriah, sent to the nine and a half tribes which were across the river in which were written the following things:

₂Thus speaks Baruch, the son of Neriah, to the brothers who were carried away in captivity: . . .

₈₇:₁And it happened when I had finished all the words of this letter and had written it carefully until the end, I folded it, sealed it cautiously, and bound it to the neck of the eagle. And I let it go and I sent it away.

The end of the letter of Baruch, the son of Neriah.

Support for the thesis that 2 Baruch is a composite work is evident in the seemingly contrived way in which these eight individual sections are connected rather artificially, most of them with references to fasts—for example:

5:7 "And we sat there and fasted until the evening"
9:2 "And we rent our garments, we mourned, and fasted seven days"
12:5 "And when I had said these things, I fasted seven days"
21:1 ". . . and I ate no bread, . . . and I drank no water. . . ."
47:2 ". . . and I sat there and fasted."

There are, however, no references to fasts between sections 5 and 6, and between sections 7 and 8.

Scholars have also noted that these separate sections (or books) sometimes deal differently with such issues as the Messiah and the messianic kingdom, the affliction of Israel in the past and the destruction of Jerusalem in the present, as well as several theological issues that were currently being debated in rabbinical schools, such as original sin, free will, good works, the number of those who will be saved, the nature of the resurrection body, and so forth. The views expressed on these issues in different sections of 2 Baruch are at times contradictory.[23]

Like other pseudepigraphical literature attributed to Baruch, 2 Baruch is set in the context of the Babylonian destruction of the Jerusalem temple in 587/586 BCE. As in most pseudepigraphical literature, this setting is fictitious and, in this instance, evidently a veiled reference to the Roman destruction of Jerusalem and the second temple in 70 CE, hence the proposed date for the writing of these individual Pharisaic works during the period of about two decades both before and after 70 CE.

Baruch reports that the fall of Jerusalem to the Babylonians (i.e., the Romans) was a requisite to God's judgment of his people (9–20), but only after everyone who was destined to live has actually lived will the Messiah finally appear. Following his appearance, he will return to heaven, after which the righteous dead will be resurrected and the souls of the wicked will waste away in eternal torment (21–34).

2 Baruch was apparently put together in its present form sometime after the fall of Jerusalem by a Jewish author who had a great deal in common with the Pharisees and who clearly had access to several Pharisaic writings of the period. As a veiled apocalypse, 2 Baruch relates the content of a divine revelation to Jeremiah's secretary Baruch, but there is no cosmic dualism, and neither are there two distinct ages, both hallmarks of Jewish apocalyptic literature.

The author teaches that the present age will improve, especially with the arrival of a messianic kingdom, which will be accompanied by a resurrection of the dead (50–51). There will be a final judgment resulting in the wicked becoming physically worse and the righteous being exalted. In effect, 2 Baruch is evidently an effort, following the destruction of the second temple, to shift the emphasis in Judaism from a temple-centered cultic religion to a Torah-centered nomistic religion in keeping with the teachings of the Pharisees. The book is actually more messianic than apocalyptic.

4 Ezra[24]

The work known as 4 Ezra in Latin manuscripts can be found as chapters 3–14 of the apocryphal book traditionally known as 2 Esdras. 4 Ezra is a Jewish apocalypse containing seven visions and was written for Jews sometime after 100 CE "in the thirtieth year after the downfall of the City" (4 Ezra 3:1), probably a veiled reference to the fall of Jerusalem to the Romans in 70 CE. The book was probably written originally in Hebrew or Aramaic and subsequently translated into what is now a lost Greek version,[25] and was translated subsequently from the lost Greek version into Latin, Syriac, Ethiopic, Arabic (actually two independent Arabic versions), Armenian, and Georgian versions. In a subsequent Latin translation, the originally Jewish 4 Ezra was expanded and Christianized by creating for it a Christian framework, consisting of chapters 1–2 and 15–16, sometimes referred to respectively as 5 Ezra and 6 Ezra.

Although early scholarship on 4 Ezra tended to regard the book as the composite work of several different authors, contemporary scholarship has inclined toward accepting the book as the composition of a single author who likely drew upon earlier literary sources and popular traditions.[26] The original book of 4 Ezra (chapters 3–14) is closely related to the book of Daniel and to 2 Baruch[27] and was, according to most scholars, likely written about 100–120 CE.

The first vision (3:1–5:19) contains in dialogue form Salathiel's (i.e., Ezra's) protest that Israel and the world continue to suffer, perhaps unjustly, to which the archangel Uriel responds that the ways of God are inscrutable (4:1–11) and the end of the present age is coming very soon (4:33–50; 5:1–13). In the mind of the author, Israel's suffering under Roman occupation clearly raised serious questions about the justice of God.

> 5:1Now concerning the signs: Behold the days are coming when those who dwell on earth shall be seized with great terror, and the way of truth shall be hidden, and the land shall be barren of faith. 2And unrighteousness shall be increased beyond what you yourself see, and beyond what you heard of formerly. 3And the land which you now see ruling shall be waste and untrodden, and men shall see it desolate. 4But if the Most High grants that you live, you shall see it thrown into confusion after the third period;
>> and the sun shall suddenly shine forth at night,
>>> and the moon during the day.
>> 5Blood shall drip from wood,
>>> and the stone shall utter its voice;
>> the peoples shall be troubled,
>>> and the stars shall fall.

The second vision (5:21–6:34), also in the form of a dialogue, reports Ezra's second complaint against God for delivering Israel into the hands of oppressors (5:23–30), to which Uriel again responds that man is not able to comprehend the ways of God (5:40), but the rule of the Roman oppressors will soon be followed by a glorious new age (6:7–10).

> 6:25It shall be that whoever remains after all that I have foretold to you shall be saved and shall see my salvation and the end of my world. 26And they shall see the men who were taken up, who from their birth have not tasted death; and the heart of the earth's inhabitants shall be changed and converted to a different spirit. 27For evil

shall be blotted out, and deceit shall be quenched; 28faithfulness shall flourish, and corruption shall be overcome, and the truth, which has been so long without fruit, shall be revealed.

The third vision (6:36–9:25), also in the form of a dialogue, continues to raise the question of why Israel suffers (6:38–59), to which Uriel responds that the messianic kingdom, the end of the world, the general resurrection, and the final judgment are all imminent (7:26–44). This vision ends with a recounting of the signs that will precede the end of this age, including earthquakes, tumult of peoples, scheming of nations, wavering of leaders, and confusion of princes (8:63–9:25). By the end of the third vision Ezra has moved from skepticism about the justice of God to acceptance of the inscrutability of divine providence.

> 7:26For behold, the time will come, when the signs which I have foretold to you will come to pass; the city which now is not seen shall appear, and the land which now is hidden shall be disclosed. 27And everyone who has been delivered from the evils that I have foretold shall see my wonders. 28For my son the Messiah shall be revealed with those who are with him, and those who remain shall rejoice four hundred years. 29And after these years my son the Messiah shall die, and all who draw human breath. 30And the world shall be turned back to primeval silence for seven days, as it was at the first beginnings; so that no one shall be left.

> 7:32And the earth shall give up those who are asleep in it; and the chambers shall give up the souls which have been committed to them.

> 7:36Then the pit of torment shall appear, and opposing it shall be the place of rest; and the furnace of Hell shall be disclosed, and opposite it the Paradise of delight.

The fourth vision (9:27–10:59a) continues the same theme in the form of the story of a woman who is mourning the loss of her only son (9:38–10:24). Following Ezra's submission, Uriel discloses to Ezra the vision of the heavenly Jerusalem (10:25–28).

> 10:25While I was talking to her, behold, her face suddenly shone exceedingly, and her countenance flashed like lightning, so that I was too frightened to approach her, and my heart was terrified. While I was wondering what this meant, 26behold, she suddenly uttered a loud and fearful cry, so that the earth shook at the sound. 27And I

looked, and behold, the woman was no longer visible to me, but there was an established city, and a place of huge foundations showed itself. Then I was afraid, and cried with a loud voice and said, ₂₈"Where is the angel Uriel, who came to me at first? For it was he who brought me to this overpowering bewilderment; my end has become corruption, and my prayer a reproach."

The fifth vision (11:1–12:50) is the last of a series of dream visions and is known as the Eagle Vision, an allegory influenced by or based on Daniel 7, describing the end of the Roman Empire and of this age to be followed by the arrival of the Messiah (12:10–34).

₁₂:₃₁And as for the lion you saw rousing up out of the forest and roaring and speaking to the eagle and reproving him for his unrighteousness, and as for all his words that you have heard, ₃₂this is the Messiah whom the Most High has kept until the end of days, who will arise from the posterity of David, and will come and speak to them; he will denounce them for their ungodliness and for their wickedness, and will cast up before them their contemptuous dealings.

The sixth vision (13:1–58a) reports the arrival of "the man" or "the Son of Man" from the midst of the sea, apparently an angelic figure who was invested with attributes generally associated with Yahweh alone and who will annihilate God's enemies.

₁₃:₂₅This is the interpretation of the vision: As for your seeing a man come up from the heart of the sea, ₂₆this is he whom the Most High has been keeping for many ages, who will himself deliver his creation; and he will direct those who are left.

₁₃:₃₇And he, my Son, will reprove the assembled nations for their ungodliness (this was symbolized by the storm), ₃₈and will reproach them to their face with their evil thoughts and with the torments with which they are to be tortured (which were symbolized by the flames); and he will destroy them without effort by the law (which was symbolized by the fire).

The seventh vision (14:1–48) discloses Ezra's end so that he can be transposed into the heavenly regions to be with the Messiah, as this age is coming to its end very soon, but only after Ezra has dictated for forty days the contents of ninety-four public and secret (exoteric and esoteric, canonical and apocryphal) books, presumably suggesting that the apocalyptic tradition occupies a legitimate place within Judaism.

14:6These words you shall publish openly, and these you shall keep secret. 7And now I say to you: 8Lay up in our heart the signs that I have shown you, the dreams that you have seen, and the interpretations that you have heard; 9for you shall be taken up from among men, and henceforth you shall live with my Son and with those who are like you, until the times are ended.

The author of 4 Ezra believed that the present age was coming to an end and that the new age was imminent. The reign of the Messiah will last for four hundred years (7:28–29). The end of this present age will be preceded by signs and warnings (4:52–5:13; 6:11–28; 7:26–44; 8:63–9:12). There will then follow the resurrection of the dead (5:45; 7:32) and the final judgment (7:33–34; 7:105, 115). The pit of torment and the furnace of hell will appear, and the righteous will be delivered to the paradise of delight (7:36, 78–101).

There is very different eschatology in the Eagle Vision with its announcement of the coming from David's posterity of the Messiah, who will deliver the remnant of the people from Roman oppression and establish God's rule on earth (12:32–34). So too there is a different eschatology in the vision in chapter 13 of "the man" or "the Son of Man" rising from the sea in which a preexistent supernatural angelic figure will destroy God's enemies and then gather the ten lost tribes of Israel.

In various places, the book mentions God's son the Messiah who will rise from the offspring of David, the messianic kingdom, signs that will precede the end of the world, the resurrection of the dead, the final judgment, and the rewards and punishments of souls after death. Unlike 2 Baruch, 4 Ezra is an apocalypse par excellence.

Sibylline Oracles[28]

The Sibylline Oracles are a collection of Jewish and Christian apocalyptic writings composed over a nine-hundred-year period between the second century BCE and the seventh century CE. These books were apparently written in imitation of the now lost pagan sibylline books and possibly in imitation of the oracles at Delphi. The oracles contain collections of ecstatic prophecies presumably delivered by sibyls or divinely inspired seeresses or prophetesses, apparently designed to win pagans initially to Judaism and subsequently to Christianity.

Because of the authority attached to the pagan sibylline oracles and prophecies in Greece and Rome, Hellenistic Jews living in Egypt and elsewhere seem to have composed their own oracles in the same literary form of hexameter verses in the Homeric Greek dialect, beginning in the second century BCE, as a way of disseminating Jewish teachings and the Jewish religion. In their present form, we actually have three types of oracles:

(1) Jewish oracles
(2) Jewish oracles edited and reworked by Christians
(3) oracles written originally by Christians

The oracles are seldom devoid of Christian editing and/or redaction, making difficult the task of determining what is uniquely Jewish in the Sibylline Oracles—our primary objective in this section. In spite of that challenge, it is still possible to recover at least some of the earliest (Jewish) material with some measure of confidence, even though the oracles were obviously not preserved in the order in which they were written.

Some of the Sibylline Oracles were apparently composed in Egypt, perhaps in Alexandria (books 3, 5, and 11–14); some can probably be traced to Syria (books 4, 6, and 7); some may have originated in Asia Minor, possibly Phrygia (books 1 and 2); and at least one (book 8)[29] is traceable to just about anywhere in the Near East subject to Roman rule. Whatever their individual places of origin, all of the oracles were revised by later Christian editors in other uncertain geographical settings.

In their present form, the Sibylline Oracles contain Greek and Roman mythology (including influence from Homer and Hesiod); Jewish legends (including material about the Garden of Eden, Noah, and the Tower of Babel); thinly veiled references to contemporary historical figures such as Alexander the Great and Cleopatra; a long list of Roman emperors; and Gnostic and early Christian homilies and eschatological writings.

Scholars are in general agreement that of the oracles preserved in our collection, only books 3, 4, and 5 seem to have significant Jewish elements; and so we turn our attention to them.

Book 3 contains Jewish oracles from the period of Roman supremacy in Egypt and Palestine in the second century BCE. The fact that the book approves of a Ptolemaic king as a divinely ordained savior (3:652–656) suggests Egypt as its place of origin. This oracle contains allusions to the building of the Tower of Babel (3:97–109), the establishment of the Solomonic kingdom (3:167), the conquests of

Alexander the Great (3:171–173), a history of the Jews up to the time of Cyrus the Great (3:218–294), prophecies against Antiochus IV Epiphanes (3:399), and predictions about the imminent judgment of the sinful world culminating in the coming of a savior king (3:652–656).

> 3:652 And then God will send a King from the sun [i.e., an Egyptian king]
> 653 who will stop the entire earth from evil war,
> 654 killing some, imposing oaths of loyalty on others;
> 655 and he will not do all these things by his private plans
> 656 but in obedience to the noble teachings of the great God.

The eschatology of the third oracle is very similar to what we find in the books of Isaiah and Psalms. Its reference to last times includes the coming of Beliar,[30] probably in the form of Nero (3:63–74), the smell of brimstone from heaven (3:60–61), and the collapse of the heavens accompanied by a stream of fire that will burn earth and sea and melt the heavenly vault (3:80–90), culminating in God's judgment of the world (3:91–92). The principal theme of Sibylline Oracles 3 lies, however, in its condemnation of idolatry and sexual abuses (3:762–766), especially homosexuality, and in the support of the temple (3:657–668). The eschatology of book 3 focuses on the anticipation of an idyllic king or kingdom (3:49–50, 767–795).

> 3:53 All men will perish in their own dwellings
> 54 when the fiery cataract flows from heaven.
> 55 Alas, wretched one, when will that day come,
> 56 and the judgment of the great king immortal God?
> 57 Yet, just for the present, be founded, cities, and all
> 58 be embellished with temples and stadia, markets and golden
> 59 silver and stone statues, so that you may come to the bitter day.
> 60 For it will come, when the smell of brimstone spreads
> 61 among all men. But I will tell all in turn,
> 62 in how many cities mortals will endure evil.

> 3:84b . . . An undying cataract
> 85 of raging fire will flow, and burn earth, burn sea,
> 86 and melt the heavenly vault and days and creation itself
> 87 into one and separate them into clean air.
> 88 There will no longer be twinkling spheres of luminaries,

89 no night, no dawn, no numerous days of care,

90 no spring, no summer, no winter, no autumn.

91 And then indeed the judgment of the great God

92 will come into the midst of the great world, when all these things happen.

3:49 For a holy prince will come to gain sway over the scepters of the earth

50 forever, as time presses on.

3:767 And then, indeed, he will raise up a kingdom for all

768 ages among men, he who once gave the holy Law

769 to the pious, to all of whom he promised to open the earth

770 and the world and the gates of the blessed and all joys

771 and immortal intellect and eternal cheer.

Book 4 contains an attack by a first-century CE Jew on the pagan sibyl who served earlier as the mouthpiece of Apollo (4:4–5). There is also a reference in book 4 to the destruction of the temple and the city of Jerusalem in 70 CE (4:115–16, 125–27). Book 4 is Jewish throughout, treating the history of great empires from the time of the Assyrians to Alexander the Great (4:49–101). It paints a picture of the joy of the righteous and the dire fate of the wicked (4:24–46). The book ends with an eschato-logical passage (4:152–92) containing an exhortation to conversion and baptism (4:162–78) and a description of the eruption of Mount Vesuvius in 79 CE as God's punishment of the Romans for their destruction of Jerusalem in 70 CE (4:130–35). These details suggest a date of the final version of book 4 about 80 CE. The book ends with a description of the final fiery conflagration (4:171–78) and the resurrec-tion of the dead and the final judgment (4:179–92). This book is probably the most Jewish of the Sibylline Oracles.

4:40 For the entire race of men is slow of faith. But when

41 the judgment of the world and of mortals has already come,

42 which God himself will perform, judging impious and pious at once,

43 then he will also send the impious down into the gloom in fire,

44 and then they will realize what impiety they committed.

45 But the pious will remain on the fertile soil

46 and God will give them spirit and life and favor at once.

4:171 But if you do not obey me, evil-minded ones, but love

172 impiety, and receive all these things with evil ears,

173 there will be fire throughout the whole world, and a very great sign

174 with sword and trumpet at the rising of the sun.

175 The whole world will hear a bellowing noise and mighty sound.

176 He will burn the whole earth, and will destroy the whole race of men

177 and all cities and rivers at once, and the sea.

178 He will destroy everything by fire, and it will be smoking dust.

179 But when everything is already dusty ashes,

180 and God puts to sleep the unspeakable fire, even as he kindled it,

181 God himself will again fashion the bones and ashes of men

182 and he will raise up mortals again as they were before.

183 And then there will be a judgment over which God himself will preside,

184 judging the world again. As many as sinned by impiety,

185 these will a mound of earth cover,

186 and broad Tartarus and the repulsive recesses of Gehenna.

187 But as many as are pious, they will live on earth again

188 when God gives spirit and life and favor

189 to these pious ones. Then they will all see themselves

190 beholding the delightful and pleasant light of the sun.

Book 5 also contains a reference to the destruction of the Jerusalem temple in 70 CE (5:411–13). Although the Jewish element predominates in this book, it is, nevertheless, impossible to determine the relative dates of composition of the various elements. There are several references to a savior figure who is represented as coming from heaven (5:108–109; 5:155–61; 5:256–59; 5:414–28). A restored and glorious Jerusalem is found in 5:249–55 and 5:420–27. Book 5 contains no mention of the resurrection of the dead. Because of the prominence of the Nero legend (5:33–34; 5:93–110; 5:138–40; 5:147; 5:150–51; 5:363–64; 5:367), book 5 was probably written about 80 CE.

5:256 There will again be one exceptional man from the sky

257 (who stretched out his hands on the fruitful wood),[31]

258 the best of the Hebrews, who will one day cause the sun to stand,

259 speaking with fair speech and holy lips.

5:414 For a blessed man came from the expanses of heaven

415 with a scepter in his hands which God gave him,

416 and he gained sway over all things well, and gave back the wealth

417 to all the good, which previous men had taken.

THE DEAD SEA SCROLLS

In 1947, two teenage Bedouin goat herders accidentally stumbled upon a major archaeological discovery when they found seven leather scrolls stored in clay jars in a cave on the northwest corner of the Dead Sea. Subsequent exploration in the area led to discoveries in ten additional caves, with caves 1 and 11 yielding several relatively intact manuscripts and cave 4 yielding thousands of fragments from more than five hundred manuscripts. Among these manuscripts and fragments are examples of every book of the Old Testament except the book of Esther (some of them in multiple copies), books from the apocrypha and the Pseudepigrapha (including Tobit, Ecclesiasticus [or Sirach], 1 Enoch, Jubilees, some fragments of the Testament of the Twelve Patriarchs),[32] and several hitherto unknown writings apparently peculiar to the sect that produced the scrolls.

The so-called Dead Sea Scrolls apparently came from a community that had settled near the caves at a site known as Khirbet Qumran on the northwest corner of the Dead Sea from the second half of the second century BCE until the Romans destroyed the community during the first Jewish revolt (66–70 CE). The people who lived at Qumran were Essenes, a communal religious group previously known to us only from the writings of Philo of Alexandria (ca. 20 BCE–ca. 50 CE), Flavius Josephus (37 CE–ca. 100 CE), and Pliny the Elder (23–79 CE). The Essenes were likely an offshoot of the Hasidim, who during the Maccabean period broke away from the temple cult in Jerusalem when the Hasmonean rulers assumed not only secular rule in Jerusalem but also the Jerusalem temple's high priesthood. The founder of the group, known in the scrolls as the Teacher of Righteousness, apparently broke with someone called the Wicked Priest, possibly Jonathan Maccabeus or Simon Maccabeus, presumably because the Hasmoneans had no legitimate right to assume Jerusalem's high priesthood.

The Essenes apparently believed that their community had retreated to the desert to prepare the way for the Lord, in fulfillment of the prophecy of Isaiah 40:3.

> When these become a community by these norms in Israel, they shall separate
> themselves from the session of the men of deceit by going out into the wilderness
> in order to make His way there; as it is written "In the wilderness make clear the
> way of . . . level in the desert a highway for our God." (1QS 8:13–14)[33]

The Qumran community, which consisted of about two hundred members, considered itself a priestly community and referred to itself as "sons of Zadok" (1QS 5:2),
doubtless a claim that at least some of its members were the legitimate priestly community. The group, whose way of life at Qumran is described in the *Rule of the Community* (1QS) found in cave 1, pursued a rigorous ascetic life in the desert likely
because of their observance of the laws of priestly purity and because of their belief
that they were, in the dualistic scheme of things, "the sons of light" and their enemies were "the sons of darkness" (1QS 3:20–22), or alternatively that they were the
"lot of God" and their enemies were the "lot of Belial" (1QM 1:1–7).[34] The Qumran
community had a distinctly eschatological orientation, believed that it was living in
the last days, and expected that God's judgment was imminent. We read, for
example, in 1QS 3:19–21:

> From a spring of light (emanate) the generations of truth and from a well of dark-
> ness (emerge) the generations of deceit. And in the hand of the prince of lights is
> the rule over the sons of righteousness, and in the ways of light they walk. In the
> hand of the angel of darkness is all the rule over the sons of deceit, and in the ways
> of darkness they walk.[35]

The dualism of Qumran, most especially the dualism of light and darkness, is found
nowhere in ancient Judaism apart from the scrolls.[36]

Although the Qumran community was evidently eschatological in its outlook
and showed a strong interest in apocalypses, we find among the scrolls no clear
example of an apocalypse that we did not know previously. There is no clear evidence that a member of the sect composed a new apocalypse. They did, however,
produce and preserve copies of several apocalyptic books, among them Aramaic
fragments of all sections of 1 Enoch except the Similitudes.

The persistent importance of the dualism of the sect is reflected in some of their
original writings but most especially in *The Scroll of the War of the Sons of Light
against the Sons of Darkness* (1QM). Moreover, many of the original Essene writings reflect elements of cosmic dualism and eschatology. For example, the opening

column of the *War Scroll* lists the adversaries in the ensuing war as the Sons of Light; the sons of Levi, Judah, and Benjamin; and the exiles in the desert against the Sons of Darkness and the army of Belial; the troops of Edom, Moab, Ammon, and Philistia; and the "Kittim of Asshur" (probably the Romans) (1QM 1:1–7). The *War Scroll* is not a realistic guide to warfare. In fact, it relied primarily on divine and angelic help rather than on military power for the victory of the Sons of Light and for God's ultimate defeat of Belial.

Rule books for the sect governed the life of the members of the community as they awaited the imminent end of days and the struggle with the cosmic forces of evil. According to the *War Scroll*, that final battle would be conducted by the priests, headed by the chief priest. Most scholars understand that this final war, in the mind of the author of the *War Scroll*, would be against the Romans (the Kittim of the scroll) and that this war against Rome would be eschatological.

Unlike most Jewish apocalypses, the claims of the Qumran community were not made in the context of revelatory visions. Yet the Essenes believed in the punishment of the wicked after death by the Angels of Destruction in the everlasting Pit, the resurrection of the righteous dead, a final judgment (CD 20:17–22),[37] and a universal conflagration (1QH 3:24–26).[38] The community seems to have entertained various, sometimes even conflicting views regarding the coming of a messiah: alternatively a future Davidic king, the anointed one of Aaron and Israel, the messiahs of Aaron and Israel (two figures?), along with "the prophet" (1QS 9:11). The Essenes apparently expected figures who would represent prophet, king, and priest, although the functions of these messiahs are nowhere clearly explained.

> They shall be judged by the first regulations in which in the beginning the men of the community were instructed, until the coming of a prophet and the Messiahs from Aaron and Israel (1QS 9:10–11).

The Qumran community lived in accordance with the teachings of their founder, the Teacher of Righteousness, who afforded them the correct and revealed interpretation of the Torah, by which they were expected to live during this current period of Belial's dominion (1QS 1:1–3:12; 5:1–20). They understood that their entrance into the community served as a resurrection from death to life (1QS 1–2), a transition that was usually reserved for the final judgment.

CONCLUSIONS

In the course of this chapter, I have relied on scholarly definitions of "apocalypse" (p. 317) and "apocalypticism" (p. 313), the one definition reflecting the phenomenon, the other the literary genre in which we find specific written examples of the phenomenon. In spite of these relatively specific definitions, we have sometimes found it difficult to classify some books. Are they protoapocalyptic? Are they full-blown apocalypses? Is there, in fact, no visionary revelation at all in some? What exactly is it that constitutes the apocalyptic? The answers to these questions are by no means self-evident.

One of the major challenges in identifying or classifying apocalyptic literature is that we do not find all of the same elements of apocalypticism in the books we examined. Moreover, it is often difficult in apocalyptic literature to understand what is going on in the minds of some of the writers, as the language of apocalyptic literature is particularly difficult to "decode" or understand. Apocalypses frequently report personal visions of the supernatural world in language that is intentionally veiled, highly symbolic, and sometimes even cryptic.

Although there are mythological elements in every religion, and although we are certainly accustomed to seeing mythology in classical Judaism, there is generally a much more highly developed mythology in Jewish apocalyptic literature than in any other material in the Jewish Bible, whether in the law, the prophets, or the writings. The presence of so much highly developed mythology in the apocalyptic literature is probably the result of Judaism's borrowing ideas from other religious traditions, in particular from Zoroastrianism in the case of Jewish apocalypticism. The elaborate angelology, complete with named archangels, references to a final judgment, a general resurrection of the dead, and the fiery pit of torment all point to probable contact with Zoroastrian mythology. That this borrowing of ideas was more common in the period after Alexander's conquest is not surprising, inasmuch as religious syncretism was a hallmark of the Hellenistic age.

The visions of the Jewish apocalypticists are qualitatively different from the visions of most of the classical prophets of the eighth, seventh, and sixth centuries BCE. The calls of Amos, Hosea, Isaiah, and Jeremiah are relatively easy to understand as they often reflect circumstances in the natural order of their personal lives and their historical times. The visions of 1 Enoch and 4 Ezra and the Sibylline Oracles, and even of Ezekiel, make us wonder whether we are sometimes dealing with individuals with a psychotic disorder such as schizophrenia or, perhaps, with a series of bizarre dream sequences.[39]

An important methodological issue in this chapter has been the dating of various apocalyptic writings, because it appears likely that the conditions for the emergence of apocalypticism in Judaism did not exist until the post-exilic period or even later during the Hellenistic age. We have seen, in fact, that a number of books in the Jewish apocalyptic literature, such as Daniel, 2 Baruch, 4 Ezra, and the Sibylline Oracles, sometimes purport to be set within the context of the Babylonian exile, following the fall of Jerusalem in 587/586 BCE. Specific references in some of these books to subsequent events, such as the fall of the Babylonian Empire, the rise of the Persian Empire, and the subsequent rise of Alexander the Great and the Seleucid Empire through the rule of Antiochus IV Epiphanes are transparent indicators that these books could not have been written in the earlier time in which they purport to have been written.

Contemporary biblical scholarship does not acknowledge such a detailed predictive component in biblical prophecy. Rather, as we have seen earlier, biblical prophecy was not predictive and spoke about the future only as a necessary consequence of the present. Detailed references to specific events in the distant future are clear indicators that a particular book was written sometime after these specific events had already occurred and that the author was probably trying to win greater acceptance for the authority of his more recent writing by projecting it into the distant past and then demonstrating the "ancient" author's clear ability to predict in detail the distant future. The method of such writings is eminently transparent.

Modern biblical scholarship, based on its rationalistic historical methodology, disallows a supernaturalist reading of these books that contain detailed predictions of historical events hundreds of years into the future. With respect to those books that purport to speak within the context of the fall of Jerusalem in 587/586 BCE, the references are generally understood to relate rather to the desecration of the Jerusalem temple in 168 BCE or to the fall of Jerusalem to the Romans in 70 CE. When so understood, these books make a great deal of sense in their own historical setting.

Moreover, the dating of many of the Jewish apocalypses to the period between the second century BCE and the first century CE has affected the dating of other material as well. The Little Apocalypse in Isaiah 24–27 and the material referred to as Deutero-Zechariah are more like the book of Daniel and the late Jewish apocalypses than they are like the biblical books within which they have sometimes been inserted. This observation has led scholars to determine that these are distinct and later writings, not integral to the books within which they were subsequently inserted and currently appear.

It is purported that apocalypses are revelations that have been mediated by an otherworldly being to a human recipient, disclosing transcendent reality regarding eschatological salvation and the supernatural world. These are not the qualities of biblical prophecy, so when such apocalyptic material appears in earlier prophetic books, its presence there is suspect and demands an alternative explanation.

Another important principle that we have observed in this chapter is the fact that biblical scholars do not limit their study to the books of the Jewish and Christian canon, the Old Testament, especially in their study of the late period of ancient Judaism. From the early periods of Israel's history, we have no Jewish literature except the biblical books themselves. Therefore, when possible, scholars draw upon literature from Israel's neighbors in Egypt, Mesopotamia, Canaan, and Arabia in order to understand Israelite religion within the larger social, political, and economic context of the ancient New Eastern world. In the case of the apocalyptic literature, scholars look outside the Bible to contemporary extant Jewish literature in the Apocrypha, the Pseudepigrapha, and the Dead Sea Scrolls. The books of the canon cannot be understood properly without studying them within their larger contexts.

As we have seen, apocalypticism is relatively uncommon in the canonical books of the Old Testament, but it was not at all uncommon in late Judaism of the second century BCE and later, as is evident from its frequent appearance in books of the intertestament period, including the literature of the Essene community at Qumran.

NOTES

1. Martin Rist, "Apocalypticism," in *The Interpreter's Dictionary of the Bible*, vol. 1 (New York: Abingdon Press, 1962), p. 157.

2. The Persian form of his name was Zarathustra. Zoroaster is a later Greek rendering of the name. Zoroaster's teachings are preserved in the Gathas or the Hymns of Zoroaster. For an English translation of the hymns of the prophet, see Jacques Duchesne-Guillemin, *The Hymns of Zarathustra* (Boston: Beacon Press, 1963).

3. Persian tradition places Zoroaster's birth at circa 660 BCE, but the date is uncertain. A date closer to 1000 BCE seems more likely, although by no means certain. Mary Boyce, *A History of Zoroastrianism*, Handbook of Oriental Studies/Handbuch der Orientalistik, vols. 1 and 2 (Leiden: E. J. Brill, 1975 and 1982).

4. In much the same way in which Muhammad elevated Allah as the one supreme god in Mecca.

5. Mary Boyce's *Textual Sources for the Study of Zoroastrianism, Textual Sources for the Study of Religion* (Chicago: University of Chicago Press, 1984) cites the relevant sources.

6. John J. Collins, *Apocalypse: The Morphology of a Genre*, Semeia, vol. 14 (Missoula, MT: Scholars Press, 1979), p. 9.

7. "The revelation (*apocalypsis*) of Jesus Christ, which God gave him [John] to show his servants what must soon take place; he made it known by sending his angel to his servant John, who testified to the word of God and to the testimony of Jesus Christ, even to all that he saw" (Revelation 1:1–2).

8. See Paul D. Hanson, *The Dawn of Apocalyptic: The Historical and Sociological Roots of Jewish Apocalyptic Eschatology* (Philadelphia: Augsburg Fortress Press, 1984). This volume is helpful in tracing the emergence of the Jewish apocalyptic movement.

9. Zechariah 1:1: "In the eighth month, in the second year of Darius, . . ."; Zechariah 7:1: "In the fourth year of King Darius, . . ."

10. Amos 5:18–24 also emphasizes this notion of impending judgment.

11. Joel 3:16a may allude to Amos 1:2; Joel 3:10 to Isaiah 2:4b and/or Micah 4:3b; Joel 3:17b to Isaiah 52:1b; and Joel 3:3 to Obadiah 11. See Hans Walter Wolff, *Joel and Amos*, trans. Waldemar Janzen, S. Dean McBride Jr., and Charles A. Muenchow (Philadelphia: Fortress Press, 1977), pp. 10–11 for a full discussion of Joel's use of language from earlier prophetic figures.

12. Paul D. Hanson, "Apocalypses and Apocalypticism," in *The Anchor Bible Dictionary*, vol. 1 (New York: Doubleday, 1992), p. 281.

13. Ezekiel 14:14 mentions Daniel's name between the names of two other ancients, Noah and Job.

14. For an English translation of "The Tale of Aqhat," see James B. Pritchard, *Ancient Near Eastern Texts Relating to the Old Testament with Supplement* (Princeton, NJ: Princeton University Press, 1969), pp. 149–55. In this tale, the ancient sage and saint Danel is Aqhat's father and is probably the man to whom Ezekiel is referring and hence the man alluded to in the biblical book of Daniel.

15. The passage Daniel 11:40–45 is not historical. It affords an incorrect prophecy (based perhaps on Ezekiel 38:17–23; 39:4–5), regarding the death of Antiochus IV Epiphanes somewhere between the Mediterranean Sea and Mount Zion, affording us, thereby, the latest possible date (*terminus ad quem*) for the writing of the book. Antiochus IV Epiphanes actually died in 164 BCE in Persia during his eastern campaign.

16. Louis F. Hartman and Alexander A. Di Lella, *The Book of Daniel*, The Anchor Bible (Garden City, NY: Doubleday, 1978), p. 157.

17. R. H. Charles, "1 Enoch," in *The Apocrypha and Pseudepigrapha of the Old Testa-*

ment in English, vol. 2, ed. R. H. Charles (Oxford: Clarendon Press, 1963), pp. 163–281; E. Isaac, "1 (Ethiopic Apocalypse of) Enoch," in *The Old Testament Pseudepigrapha*, vol. 1, ed. James H. Charlesworth (Garden City, NY: Doubleday, 1983), pp. 5–89. All quotations from 1 Enoch are from the Charlesworth volume.

18. Of the five major portions or sources of 1 Enoch as identified in this section, fragments of four of them have been found in the caves near Qumran. No portion of the Parables or Similitudes of Enoch has been found, leading some scholars to speculate that the Similitudes of Enoch may be a later Christian addition to the book, a view not supported by most scholars, who consider the Similitudes as being Jewish and probably datable no later than the first century CE.

19. In Genesis 4:17–18, Enoch is by contrast the son of Cain and the great-grandfather of Methushael (= Methuselah), not his father as in Genesis 5:21.

20. "Enoch walked with God; then he was no more, because God took him" (Genesis 5:24).

21. R. H. Charles, "2 Baruch, or the Syriac Apocalypse of Baruch," in *The Apocrypha and Pseudepigrapha of the Old Testament in English*, vol. 2, pp. 470–526; A. F. J. Klijn, "2 (Syriac Apocalypse of) Baruch," in *The Old Testament Pseudepigrapha*, vol. 1, pp. 615–52. All quotations from 2 Baruch are from the Charlesworth volume.

22. A. F. J. Klijn, "2 (Syriac Apocalypse of) Brauch," p. 616. See also F. Zimmermann, "Textual Observations on the Apocalypse of Baruch," *Journal of Theological Studies* 40 (1939): 151–56; and F. Zimmermann, "Translation and Mistranslation in the Apocalypse of Baruch," *Studies and Essays in Honour of Abraham A. Neuman*, ed. M. Ben-Horin et al. (Leiden: E. J. Brill, 1962), pp. 580–87.

23. R. H. Charles, "2 Baruch," p. 474. See also Richard Kabisch, *Jahrbücher für protestantische Theologie* (1891), pp. 66–107.

24. G. H. Box, "IV Ezra," in *The Apocrypha and Pseudepigrapha of the Old Testament in English*, vol. 2, pp. 542–624; Bruce Metzger, "The Fourth Book of Ezra," in *The Old Testament Pseudepigrapha*, vol. 1, pp. 517–59. All quotations from 4 Ezra are from the Metzger volume.

25. Given the popularity of this work, it is unclear why the Greek text disappeared, perhaps as early as the second century.

26. G. H. Box identified chapters 3–10 as the Salathiel Apocalypse, the earliest material, which he dated to about 100 CE. To this, Box claims, three appendixes were subsequently added: chapters 11–12 (the Eagle Vision), chapter 13 (the Son of Man vision), and chapter 14 mainly (the Ezra legend). By contrast Bruce Metzger leans toward recognizing the whole of 2 Ezra 3–14 as a single composition. Various scholars have suggested the following as possible preexisting sources: 4 Ezra 4:35–37; 5:1–13; 6:18–27; 6:49–52; 7:78–99; 9:43–10:3; 13:1–13; 13:40–47.

27. Like 2 Baruch (see above, pp. 332–36), 4 Ezra also has a similar structure with fasts serving as the division between the seven visions or divisions of the book:

5:20 "So I fasted seven days, mourning and weeping, as Uriel the angel had commanded me;"

6:35 "Now after this I wept again and fasted seven days as before, in order to complete the three weeks as I had been told;"

9:26 "So I went, as he directed me, into the field that is called Ardat; and there I sat among the flowers and ate of the plants of the field, and the nourishment they afforded satisfied me;"

[10:59b "So I slept that night and the following one, as he had commanded me"];

12:51 "But I sat in the field seven days, as the angel had commanded me; and I ate only of the flowers of the field, and my food was of plants during in those days;"

[13:58b "And I stayed there three days"].

The two passages in brackets, 4 Ezra 10:59b and 13:58b, serve as divisions between visions, but they are technically not fasts. In addition to this feature of fasts separating sections of their respective books, 2 Baruch and 4 Ezra have a good deal of common terminology.

28. See especially H. C. O. Lanchester, "The Sibylline Oracles," in *The Apocrypha and Pseudepigrapha of the Old Testament in English*, vol. 2, pp. 368–406; and J. J. Collins, "Sibylline Oracles," in *The Old Testament Pseudepigrapha*, vol. 1, pp. 317–472. References in this section come from J. J. Collins's edition.

29. Sibylline Oracles 8:131–138 was obviously written in Egypt.

30. Beliar or Belial is the head of the demonic powers and is widely attested in the pseudepigraphic literature. He is the equivalent of Satan, the angel of wickedness.

31. Sibylline Oracles 5:257: "who stretched out his hands on the fruitful wood" is clearly a Christian allusion to Jesus' crucifixion. So too 5:256 may also reflect Christian influence.

32. Among them an Aramaic Testament of Levi that is not a part of the Testament of the Twelve Patriarchs, and a fragment of a Hebrew Testament of Naphtali that is longer than the corresponding Greek text found in the Testament of the Twelve Patriarchs.

33. The Dead Sea Scroll notation system 1QS refers to a manuscript found in cave 1 at Qumran, in this case the so-called Manual of Disciple or the Rule of the Community.

34. 1QM refers to a manuscript found in cave 1 at Qumran and generally known as the *War Scroll*.

35. P. Wernberg-Møller, *The Manual of Discipline* (Grand Rapids, MI: Eerdmans, 1957).

36. See also 1QS 2:19: "Thus they shall do year after year, all the days of the reign of Belial."

37. CD, the *Damascus Document* was already known before the discovery of the Dead Sea Scrolls from a copy that was found at the Cairo Genizah in Egypt at the beginning of the twentieth century. A *genizah* is a repository for old scrolls that cannot be discarded because they contain the divine name.

38. 1QH is a collection of Thanksgiving Hymns found in cave 1 at Qumran.

39. Dreams are often bizarre and contain elements of both the real and the surreal. A major difference is that most of us do not believe that our dreams reflect contact with the supernatural world or serve to predict events in the future, whereas our biblical forebears assumed both. I suspect that much of the apocalyptic literature was informed by dreams in which authors often wove together what was real with what was certainly surreal.

CHAPTER 13

THE TEXT OF THE OLD TESTAMENT

Most people who pick up their Bibles and read the book of Genesis assume that they are reading something that Moses wrote about 3,260 years ago, or at least a reliable English rendering thereof. Most people believe that if they were to turn to the book of Isaiah, they would find from start to finish authentic teachings of Isaiah of Jerusalem from about 2,750 years ago.

Nothing could be further from the truth. The text of the Old Testament currently available, even in Hebrew, has a far more complicated history than most people assume. At best, we may be reading a text of the Old Testament that was current at about the time that Jesus lived, some two thousand years ago, many hundreds of years removed from the earliest manuscript of almost every biblical book. Even that representation is a simplistic understanding of the situation. We are, in fact, usually reading an English translation of a manuscript that is only about a thousand years old—very far removed in both time and place from the writings of our earliest biblical authors.

In this chapter, I hope to look briefly at the ways in which the text of the Old Testament evolved until it was relatively fixed, at least in its consonantal form by the end of the first century CE. I say "in its consonantal form," because at the end of the first century CE Hebrew was written only with consonants and with no spaces between words. The intervening vowel sounds that were spoken between the consonants achieved written status much later in the form of dots and dashes above and below the consonants. The fixing, or relative fixing, of the consonants was helpful, but even this process was more complicated than most students of the Bible realize.

Imagine, for a moment, what it would mean if English were written with only consonants and with no spaces between words, as is the case in biblical Hebrew. To understand the challenge, just try to read this sentence:

mgnfrmmntwhttwldmnfnglshwrwrttnwthnlycnsnntsndwthnspcsbtwnwrds

If you are having difficulty, just look at the beginning of this paragraph. The context in which you find the consonants may or may not help you to decide which vowels to add.[1]

We must, however, begin our discussion of the development of the text of the Old Testament long before the period when the standardization of the consonants and the adding of vowels became issues. We should remind ourselves from previous discussions in earlier chapters of the complicated process by which some biblical books seem to have evolved into their present forms.

Earlier in this volume we reviewed the cases for and against Moses' authorship of Genesis, Exodus, Leviticus, Numbers, and Deuteronomy and came to the conclusion that not only did Moses not compose these five books, but that the process by which these books were created is enormously complicated and difficult to unravel.[2] Scholars have generally identified four sources or strata in the Pentateuch, named respectively as J, E, D, and P, and have advanced theories regarding the composition of the Pentateuch and its ultimate division into five scrolls because of how much writing could be contained on a single scroll. We cannot assume that we understand exactly the process by which the Pentateuch came into its present form, but we do know that the process was far more complicated than the traditional view that Moses sat down toward the end of his life and simply wrote for posterity the five books, the view that we find expressed for the first time in late Judaism, probably in Ecclesiasticus, written shortly after 200 BCE.

In the same manner, we know that the book of Isaiah is certainly not the work of a single author but that there are at least three or possibly even four separate components that were joined together in antiquity: (1) material from the second half of the eighth century BCE dealing with the teachings and ministry of Isaiah of Jerusalem in chapters 1–39;[3] (2) material from the end of the Babylonian exile about 540 BCE from an anonymous prophet known as Deutero-Isaiah in chapters 40–55;[4]

(3) material from an anonymous prophet (or prophets) from the period after the Babylonian exile in about 520–515 BCE known as Trito-Isaiah in chapters 56–66; and (4) possibly a distinct unit from as late as the second century BCE known as the Isaian Apocalypse in chapters 24–27, or minimally, material edited into the book of Isaiah by a late redactor.[5]

Likewise, the Zechariah scroll clearly contains the teachings of two distinct individuals: (1) the visions and oracles of Zechariah from 520–518 BCE in chapters 1–8;[6] and (2) writings from an individual or school from the late fifth century BCE in chapters 9–14.[7]

We have also shown that the teachings of Qoheleth are probably found in Ecclesiastes 1:1–12:8 and that 12:9–14 reflects the hand of a later, more orthodox editor, who was probably trying to soften the radical skepticism of the original book.[8] So too the prophecy of Amos of Tekoa from about 750 BCE can be found in chapters 1:1–9:10, whereas the material in Amos 9:11–15 comes from about two hundred years later during the time of the Babylonian exile.[9]

Our book of Psalms was composed from several older collections of psalms, each of which had its own history of transmission and each of which obviously suffered modifications in its transmission.[10]

These few examples are but the tip of the iceberg. It is, in fact, safe to assume that no book of the Old Testament comes down to us in its original form. The books were copied by hand in antiquity, and copyists often took liberties in editing the material they were copying or in adding new material to older writings, especially in the period before about 200 BCE. These early scribes were not concerned with transmitting material in exactly the same form in which they received it. They were concerned with the current relevance of the books they were passing on to a new generation, not with preserving accurately material for subsequent submission to a committee that would consider each book for possible inclusion in a canon of sacred scriptures. Rather, the early copyists were preserving and updating earlier traditions. They did not understand that they were writing the books of the Bible.

Historical accuracy, as we have come to understand that concept, was not a consideration of the writers or the copyists. Ancient writers worked with what was available to them. In the earliest period that often meant tradition passed down orally in the tents of nomads, when storytelling was an art and the only source of information from bygone years. Storytelling combined elements of history with legend, and the appropriation of ancient Near Eastern mythology from foreign lands was common.

Oral traditions and even the writings of antiquity reflect the thinking of their own time. They were not intended or designed to suit the standards that we would ideally apply to modern historical writings.

In other words, the process by which the thirty-nine books of the Old Testament were initially written and subsequently transmitted is enormously complicated and often beyond the reach of modern scholars to comprehend in detail. At best we have good working hypotheses that attempt to explain the available data within the limits of historical reason. Scholarly opinion may, after a period of time, cluster around a single theory, but invariably new generations of scholars call into question old theories. We have, at best, a sound method and a tested process. It is the conclusions that are so often elusive.

In saying this, I do not intend to present a pessimistic viewpoint but rather a realistic picture of what we do and do not, can and cannot, know. I mean only to urge the reader to exercise caution about the conclusions we reach—more specifically in the context of this chapter, the relationship of our present text of the Old Testament to what preceded.

TEXTUAL CRITICISM

Textual criticism is the scholarly discipline concerned with the critical study of ancient biblical manuscripts for the purpose of trying to reconstruct the earliest possible version of the Hebrew text of the several books of the Old Testament.[11] Specifically, scholars analyze, compare, and evaluate ancient manuscripts of the Jewish Bible in an effort to trace the history of the transmission of the text. This scientific discipline involves a systematic, precise, and technical study not only of ancient Hebrew manuscripts, but also of ancient translations (or versions), including an effort to reconstruct the Hebrew text that underlies each of these translations or versions.

More specifically, textual critics ask whether there was ever a single original Hebrew textual tradition, and if so, can we reconstruct it? The simple answer to that question is that there may have been an original Hebrew text of each of the books of the Bible, but it is quite another matter to claim that we are able to reconstruct that original Hebrew text. A more realistic goal might be to try to establish the textual form of the books of the Old Testament in the period of the fourth or third centuries BCE. It is unrealistic to imagine that we could possibly penetrate beyond that time and reconstruct the "autograph" of any given book. In fact, it is apparent that the texts of the various books of the Old Testament existed in several different forms at a relatively early period. The methodological problems involved in re-creating something called the autograph or the archetype or the original book are formidable, rendering the task not only elusive, but essentially impossible.

A comparison of passages such as 2 Samuel 22 and Psalm 18; Psalm 14 and Psalm 53; Psalm 40:13–17 and Psalm 70; Psalm 57:7–11 and Psalm 108:1–5; Psalm 60:5–12 and Psalm 108:6–13[12] indicates that textual variants occurred very early in the history of the transmission of the texts, long before the complete versions of these books first appeared. So too a comparison of large portions of 1 and 2 Samuel and 1 and 2 Kings with 1 and 2 Chronicles illustrates the nature of the challenge. The differences between such parallel passages within the Old Testament and among even the various presumably authoritative and standardized Masoretic manuscripts afford some idea of the challenges involved in trying to reconstruct a very early stage in the history of the transmission of the text. Textual critics discovered relatively early that the task is virtually impossible.

Until the middle of the twentieth century, most study of the Hebrew text began with an examination of the Masoretic text or the "received text," although it is essential to understand from the outset that, in spite of its status as the "received text," *the Masoretic text is not intrinsically superior to other textual traditions*. Coupled with a study of the Masoretic text, there has always been the question of the relative authority of the Greek Septuagint and the Samaritan Pentateuch. It was, however, the discovery of the Dead Sea Scrolls more than a half century ago that completely changed the playing field in textual criticism of the Old Testament.

THE DEAD SEA SCROLLS

It is impossible to overstate the importance of the discovery of the Dead Sea Scrolls in 1947 for their role in advancing an understanding of the history of the transmission of the text of the Old Testament. Several relatively well-preserved scrolls were found in caves 1 and 11 at Qumran; in addition, cave 4 yielded thousands of fragments from as many as five hundred different scrolls. With the single exception of the book of Esther, all of the books of the Hebrew Bible are represented among the Dead Sea Scrolls, some in multiple copies.[13] Although work on the scrolls is an ongoing process, some observations are in order.

Even though most of the scrolls from Qumran bear considerable resemblance to the consonantal form of the later Masoretic text, they are not all homogeneous. Manuscripts of the Dead Sea Scrolls that are not of a Masoretic type usually bear similarities to either the Septuagint or to the Samaritan Pentateuch. There are, in addition, a few manuscripts of an independent type, reflecting an apparent blending of Masoretic, Septuagint, and Samaritan readings, or readings not otherwise found in ancient manuscripts. Variations among multiple manuscripts of the same biblical book indicate that the scribes who generated the Qumran manuscripts were obviously not involved in a program of rigorous transmission of a single standardized text. Indeed, textual variants, whether unintentional or deliberate, suggest that the scribes who produced the Dead Sea Scrolls were not scrupulous in their transmission of these texts.

The scribes who wrote the manuscripts that were produced at Qumran were presumably Essenes, but not all of the manuscripts that were found at Qumran were actually written there. A study of the ancient style of writing within the scrolls indicates that some of them are actually older than the founding of the Qumran community in circa 150 BCE, suggesting that the Essenes took some of the scrolls with them to Qumran when they moved from Jerusalem to the desert. Where did these earlier scrolls come from? Some scholars have suggested that they were taken to Qumran from the temple library in Jerusalem, but it is impossible to know for sure. Archaeologists have identified a room at Qumran that served as a scriptorium or official writing room. Yet it is evident that even the scrolls that were written at Qumran were copied from already existing texts, presumably from manuscripts taken from Jerusalem to Qumran by the Essene founders of the community.

What is not clear is what the Dead Sea Scrolls tell us about the prior history of the books of the Hebrew Bible or about the status of the text of various books within rival sects. We can only speculate, for what it is worth, that the situation among the Essenes was not exceptional and that other scribes of the same period and even earlier probably also lacked a sense that they should be transmitting a single standardized text. There is no evidence to support the view of some scholars that the texts of the scrolls in the temple library in Jerusalem had already been standardized. Moreover, it is possible that some differences among the manuscripts can be ascribed to theological differences or outlooks among rival Jewish sects, something that is particularly evident in the case of the Samaritan Pentateuch.[14]

It is also clear that the Qumran scrolls are about a thousand years older than our previously oldest extant manuscripts of the Hebrew Bible and that they are, therefore, invaluable for assisting scholars in understanding better the status of the text of the biblical books in the period from about 250 BCE to about 68 CE, at least among the Essenes of Qumran, and perhaps beyond the sect itself, although that is less evident.

A complete Isaiah scroll from cave 1, known as 1QIs(a) and containing all sixty-six chapters of our book of Isaiah, has many textual corruptions.[15] In addition, the paragraph divisions of the text of this manuscript are different from the paragraph divisions of later Masoretic texts. The orthography (i.e., the spelling of words) of this Isaiah scroll is also different from the spelling or system of writing of the Masoretic text. In addition, this scroll shows signs of having been corrected at some point in time by a later scribe. Those corrections range from adding individual vowel consonants to inserting between the lines or in the margins of the manuscript some relatively lengthy passages. These editorial changes appear to be more than simple corrections; they sometimes seem to be deliberate changes, and some of them reflect departures from, not accommodations to, the standardized Masoretic text. Many of the changes reflect insertions dealing with the form of the divine name, likely reflecting later or peculiarly sectarian developments in the manner in which members of the Qumran sect addressed God. The meaning of some of the signs and crosses in the margins of the Isaiah scroll remain an enigma.

A second Isaiah scroll was also found in cave 1 and is known as 1QIs(b). This manuscript shows variations from the first Isaiah scroll, supporting the view that the Essenes obviously did not have a single fixed or standardized text of Isaiah. From the variants, it seems improbable that the scribes intended to create a standardized text and simply failed at the effort. 1QIs(b) is actually closer to the standardized Masoretic text than is 1QIs(a). The existence of 1QIs(b) demonstrates that there already existed at Qumran in pre-Masoretic circles a text of Isaiah similar to the one that the Masorites subsequently adopted as their own. In other words, the later Masorites clearly knew and preserved an earlier textual tradition and did not simply create a new standardized text. That is not to say that there was a continuous tradition of an authoritative text from a much earlier period. The choice of the Masorites provides us with no information whatsoever about the antiquity or the reliability of this particular manuscript tradition. It simply tells us that there was a proto-Masoretic text at the time of the establishment of the Qumran community in about 150 BCE. The similarity of 1QIs(b) to medieval manuscripts of the Masoretic text shows that there was obviously a good deal of care involved in transmitting one particular consonantal text, perhaps as early as about 250 BCE. Other manuscripts indicate, however, that there was more than one textual tradition in use at Qumran.

What we learn from the Dead Sea Scrolls is that the Essenes actively engaged in transcribing biblical texts, that their texts had no fixed form, and that discrepancies, divergences, and inconsistencies in their manuscripts apparently posed no serious theological problem for the sect. It is also interesting that the Qumran scrolls preserve a collection of different texts, including not only proto-Masoretic but also proto-Samaritan, proto-Septuagint, and independent types.

JAMNIA

Following the fall of Jerusalem in 70 CE, many of the rabbinical scholars under the leadership of Rabban Johanan ben Zakkai retreated to Jamnia, a former Philistine city on the Mediterranean coast, and proceeded to address the challenge of conserving, adapting, and reinterpreting Judaism apart from Jerusalem and the temple cult. The theory that there was an actual Council at Jamnia in 90 CE had its origin in the late nineteenth century and was the prevailing view among scholars for much of the twentieth century.[16] There is, however, no Jewish, Christian, or classical textual support for this theory; and it has more recently been largely abandoned.

The upside of the theory of such a council is that it led to the abandonment of the earlier misconception that the canon of the Old Testament had been fixed either by Ezra or by the Great Assembly (or the Great Synagogue) several centuries earlier, probably before 250 BCE. Some scholars attributed to the Council of Jamnia the closing of the Old Testament canon, and a few even projected the view that the text of the Old Testament from a single recension had been standardized by action of the council. The residue of the theory of a Council of Jamnia is that it continues to invite the misapprehension that official action on matters of canon, text, and other issues was taken at specific meetings on particular dates in or about 90 CE. There is no evidence for this view.

We know that, from the period of the second century CE, Christianity solved many of its divisive issues with formal votes of bishops at synods or councils of the church; Judaism, however, did not. The term "Council of Jamnia," therefore, invites a serious misapprehension about Judaism and the role of the rabbis who gathered at Jamnia over a period of many generations, who debated important issues and expressed agreement on some and disagreement on others. Unlike Christianity, Judaism did not divide over these discussions and disagreements.[17] The meetings of the rabbis at Jamnia were more like conversations and discussions at a school or academy than they were like the debates and binding votes of bishops at a council convened officially to resolve a theological dispute or division within the church. In fact, the rabbis often reached consensus over a period of time without formal votes.

What we do know about these conversations at Jamnia from a review of the Mishnah[18] and the Tosefta[19] is that they covered such issues as the calendar, especially as it pertained to the Sabbath and other festivals, ritual cleanness, prayer, regulations regarding the family, and so forth. Apart from discussions about Ecclesiastes, the Song of Songs, and the book of Jesus Son of Sirach (or Ecclesiasticus), there was apparently little discussion about the canon and none regarding the standardization of the text of the Old Testament.

THE SCROLLS FROM WADI MURABBA'AT

Not far from the caves of Qumran, biblical scrolls were found in 1951 in a cave in the area of Wadi Murabba'at. Letters, contracts, and coins found in the same cave suggest that the scrolls belong to the period of the Bar Kochba Revolt of 132–135 CE.

The biblical manuscripts, including fragments of the Pentateuch and the book of Isaiah, are very similar in form to the Masoretic text. In a cave in the same general area, scholars subsequently found a leather scroll in Greek with fragments of the books of Jonah, Micah, Nahum, Habakkuk, Zephaniah, and Zechariah, presumably a portion of a scroll containing the twelve minor prophets. Study of Habakkuk 1–2, the best-preserved portion of this scroll, suggests that it was a pre-Christian revision of the Septuagint, very similar in form to the Greek texts of Aquila of Sinope, Symmachus the Ebionite, and Theodotion of Ephesus from the second century CE,[20] and similar to the text of the Greek Old Testament used by Justin Martyr in Rome in his *Dialogue with Trypho* in the mid-second century. It is interesting to note that during the second century both Jews and Christians were apparently familiar with a common Greek translation of the Hebrew Bible and that this translation was itself a revision of the Septuagint from Alexandria, Egypt.

THE MASORETIC TEXT

The Masoretic text is regarded as the standard authoritative text of the Hebrew Bible, but it achieved that status only after a very long period of time. By the second century BCE and perhaps even earlier, in addition to proto-Masoretic texts, there were families of biblical manuscripts that reflected significant deviation from the Masoretic family, such as proto-Septuagint sources, the Greek Septuagint, proto-Samaritan sources, the Samaritan Pentateuch, and some of the Qumran scrolls.

The Masoretic text reflects a distinct but not necessarily more original family of manuscripts, but even then no two Masoretic manuscripts are exactly alike, especially in the case of manuscripts from the first centuries of the Christian era and earlier. The Masoretic text receives its name from the fact that it was the Masoretes[21] who added vowels to the consonantal framework of the text of the Hebrew Bible. It was, however, not until the rabbinic period (ca. 200–ca. 500 CE) that scribes made a serious effort to standardize the text of the Hebrew Bible by developing systems for counting the words and letters in a particular manuscript in order to provide ways of assuring the accurate transcription of biblical texts.

Tradition maintains that it was Ezra who started the scribal tradition by copying the text of the Pentateuch (Ezra 7:6), but that tradition is probably legendary. Although the Masoretes developed mechanisms to guarantee the accurate preservation of the text, it is not clear exactly when that process began and over how long a period of time it evolved, but it likely extended over a period of about a thousand years.

Inasmuch as the Masoretic text appears in many different forms, it is more accurate to refer to Masoretic texts as a family group rather than to give the impression that there was a single Masoretic text at an early date. In the first century CE, the sect known as the Pharisees played a major role in the preservation of this text, and some think that it may have been the Pharisees who were initially responsible for establishing the Masoretic text as authoritative. But it was actually between circa 500 and circa 1000 CE that the Masoretic text was carefully prepared and preserved by succeeding generations of biblical scribes in individual academies, sometimes involving many generations of the same family.

In spite of the best efforts of the Masoretes, the mechanisms for the faithful transmission of the text were never totally foolproof. It appears that different forms of the text of the Hebrew Bible existed in Babylonian and Palestinian rabbinic academies until the Palestinian system of vocalization ultimately prevailed, although only after considerable modification of the text had taken place. Competition among rabbinic schools over the manner of the vowel pointing of the manuscripts forced the Masoretes in Tiberias to produce between circa 780 and circa 930 CE a completely new and more detailed method of pointing the consonants with dots and dashes above and beneath consonants to represent the various vowel sounds. This Tiberian vocalic system is still familiar to anyone who studies biblical Hebrew. The existence of competing rabbinic schools in Spain, France, Italy, and Germany during the medieval period further compounded the problem of the transmission of the biblical text.

Although uniformity of manuscripts was an abstract ideal for the Masoretes, the presence of textual variants persisted because there were so many texts within the proto-Masoretic group. It was only with the development of printing toward the end of the fifteenth century that the Masoretic text was fully stabilized. The first printed edition of the complete text of the Old Testament was done in 1488 in Soncino, Italy, a small city not far from Milan. The authoritative edition of the Masoretic Text is generally considered the *Biblica Hebraica Stuttgartensia*, based on the 1008 CE Leningrad manuscript, a text that is now available in machine-readable (i.e., computer) form.

THE SAMARITAN PENTATEUCH

In theory the Samaritan Pentateuch goes back to the time of the division of the northern kingdom of Israel from the southern kingdom of Judah in 922 BCE. Scholars have argued, however, that the Pentateuch came into its present form sometime after the Babylonian exile, perhaps about 400 BCE, so the Samaritan Pentateuch should be understood as a northern version of that Judean collation of J, E, D, and P. Accordingly, at some uncertain point in the post-exilic period, perhaps when Alexander the Great permitted the Samaritans to build their temple on Mount Gerizim, the Samaritans accepted as canonical only the Pentateuch, the first five books of the Hebrew Bible—Genesis, Exodus, Leviticus, Numbers, and Deuteronomy—in a version that introduced Samaritan readings into the text, such as the final commandment in the Decalogue commanding the building of the altar on Mount Gerizim.

In 1616 the first copy of the Samaritan Pentateuch became available to European scholars, but its status has been a matter of disagreement ever since the time of its rediscovery. The Samaritan community still survives in very small numbers, perhaps a mere two hundred people, in Nablus in the area of Mount Gerizim, near Shechem, and in Holon, near Tel Aviv.

The discovery at Qumran of 4QEx(a)[22] affords an example of an ancient Hebrew text related to the Samaritan text, establishing the antiquity of a proto-Samaritan Pentateuch as an early alternative to the Masoretic text.

THE TARGUMS

The targums were translations of biblical books, especially the Pentateuch, from Hebrew into Aramaic. These translations were created to provide in the synagogues an understanding of the biblical texts to laymen who were no longer able to under-stand the books in the original Hebrew. These targums also provided an opportunity to hear for the first time the words of the sacred scriptures in the vernacular, even before the translations into Greek beginning in about 250 BCE. The earliest transla-tions into Aramaic were done orally, initially during the period of the second temple.

Although a few fragments of Aramaic targums survive among the Dead Sea Scrolls in the form of 4QTgLe, 4QTgJob, and 11QTgJob,[23] it is primarily during the rabbinic period beginning in the second century CE that older traditional Aramaic translations were written down in Babylonia and Palestine and serve as our written targums: the Targum of Onqelos from Babylonia,[24] which since the Middle Ages has been regarded as the most authoritative translation into Aramaic of the Pentateuch, and the Targum of Jonathan, a translation of the prophets, from Palestine.

THE VERSIONS

To make sense of ancient texts of the Old Testament as they survive in languages other than Hebrew, those texts must first be retranslated back into Hebrew to deter-mine whether they reflect deviations from known Hebrew readings. Until recently, scholars paid a great deal of attention to these versions, because before the discovery of the Dead Sea Scrolls, our oldest Hebrew manuscripts were from the Middle Ages, whereas some manuscripts of the Greek Septuagint, the Aramaic Targums, the Syriac Peshitta, and the Latin Vulgate could be dated to the fourth or the fifth cen-turies CE.

We now have Hebrew manuscripts that are much older than these ancient versions, so the value of these translations is now much less than it was before the discovery of the Dead Sea Scrolls. Nevertheless, among the ancient translations, the Septuagint remains particularly important because that translation dates to the period circa 250–circa 150 BCE, even if the actual manuscript evidence for the Greek Septuagint is several centuries later. Among these ancient versions, the Latin Vulgate appears to be very close to the Masoretic text; the quality of the Syriac Peshitta varies from book to book—some are very literal, others mere paraphases of the Hebrew, although they are generally closer to the Masoretic text than is the case with the Greek Septuagint.

THE SEPTUAGINT

The Septuagint is the translation from Hebrew into Greek of authoritative Jewish literature for the benefit of the Hellenized Jewish community in Alexandria, Egypt, at a time when members of that diaspora community were presumably no longer able to understand their holy books in the original Hebrew. The books included in this Greek translation include not only all of the books that eventually became the Hebrew Bible, but additional books that are now characterized by Roman Catholics as deutero-canonical and by Protestants and Jews as apocryphal.[25]

The quality of the text of the Greek Septuagint varies significantly from book to book. Some translations are very literal (e.g., Psalms and Ecclesiastes), others are mere paraphrases (e.g., Isaiah, Esther, Job, Proverbs, Isaiah, and Daniel). This range of texts raises the question of whether a particular book in the Greek Septuagint is merely a free rendering of the Hebrew text or rather a good translation of a variant Hebrew text. There is no way to know.

Given the early date of the translation into Greek (ca. 250–ca. 150 BCE), the Septuagint is one of the most important sources for establishing the text of the Old Testament. Along with the Dead Sea Scrolls, the Samaritan Pentateuch, and the Masoretic text, the Septuagint is one of our important independent witnesses to a relatively early stage in the development of the text of the Old Testament.

It is often argued that in those instances in which the Septuagint is shorter than the Masoretic text, it is the Septuagint that reflects the earlier stage in the development of that particular book. This appears to be the situation in the case of Jeremiah,

1 Samuel 17–18, and in the chronological elements of 1–2 Kings. As a rule, longer versions of a text tend to reflect a later stage in that text's development.

THE TEXT OF THE OLD TESTAMENT

It is relatively clear that by the end of the first century CE there were three principal textual traditions, one that served as the basis of the Masoretic text, one that served as the basis of the Samaritan Pentateuch, and one that had served as the Hebrew basis of the Greek Septuagint. Relatively minor variations existed within each of these three textual traditions after 100 CE, although each tradition continued to survive independently. It has been suggested that the three families of text may reflect the status of the manuscript traditions in the three principal centers of Judaism at the turn of the millennium: Palestine, Babylonia, and Egypt. This view is, however, now complicated by the fact that elements of all three textual traditions have been found at Qurman.

What is more difficult to determine is the history of the text before circa 150 BCE, because there is so little evidence from that earlier period. What data there are can be interpreted in many different ways. Because of the evidence discussed at the outset of this chapter, we are able to understand the somewhat complicated process by which some individual books were put together (e.g., the three Isaiahs into a single Isaiah manuscript, the two Zechariahs into the Zechariah manuscript) and the complicated process by which five distinct collections of Psalms were collected into our single book of Psalms, reflecting in the process some duplication of individual psalms in which cases there are variations between the two members of the doublets.

It is, however, hard to imagine that there was ever a single authoritative copy of every book of the Old Testament, especially considering the complicated history of such books as Isaiah, Zephaniah, Ecclesiastes, Amos, and so on, and the absence at an early time of any notion of a "canon" of sacred scripture. It seems much more probable that there were multiple versions of each book at a relatively early date. Moreover, it is likely that much of the "organization" and/or "codification" of our current thirty-nine books of the Hebrew Bible took place in the period of the second temple, possibly beginning as early as the time of Ezra's return from exile in Babylonia, at least in the case of the Pentateuch; but much of this is conjecture.

It is evident that the earliest copyists of what became the books of the Bible were much more than copyists. They took liberties, sometimes considerable liberties, to insert changes or additional material into the text, thereby serving not only as copyists, but as editors, and to some extent as authors of late or even the completed or final versions of our biblical books. Later copyists apparently exercised much less freedom in editing the text that they were copying, particularly as the text itself was achieving a somewhat more authoritative status.

By the end of the first century CE, the texts were relatively fixed, but they were in three relatively distinct forms. The Masoretic text was increasingly regarded as the received text of rabbinic Judaism; the Greek Septuagint had been adopted by the Hellenistic Christian community and had basically been abandoned by the Jews; and the Samaritan Pentateuch was the authoritative text of the Samaritan sect, which was by now essentially a schismatic movement or a distinct religion fully alienated and estranged from what had become the religious center of Judaism in Jerusalem. The Essene community, which preserved exemplars of all three forms, did not survive the Roman war and abandoned their buildings at Qumran and their scrolls to the caves to the west of their community, where they remained undisturbed from about 68 CE until their discovery in 1947.

A reconstruction of the history of the text of the Hebrew Bible is dependent on the evidence that has survived from antiquity, so a reconstruction can never be comprehensive and definitive, especially inasmuch as the information is more and more scarce the further we reach back into history.

CONCLUSIONS

Introductory textbooks rarely deal with the issue of textual criticism, except perhaps in a cursory way. Yet it is the work of textual critics that is elemental to all methodological considerations involved in a study of the Old Testament. It matters considerably whether or not we are in touch with the words of Isaiah of Jerusalem when we read the whole of the book of Isaiah. It matters not only who wrote the Pentateuch, but what exactly we are reading when we open our Bibles, not only in English, but even in Hebrew (and Aramaic) for those few who actually have access to the canonical books in their original languages.

It was difficult to decide whether an examination of textual criticism and the text of the Old Testament should be the first or the final chapter of this volume. Both could easily be justified. I decided to keep this chapter until the end of this book when its importance and impact could be more fully appreciated. Textual criticism is obviously foundational to all biblical scholarship. Everything else that we do depends on having a relatively clear understanding of what we are reading when we open the pages of the Old Testament, whether in Hebrew or in English.

Few scholars are trained in the intricacies of textual criticism, because few people have the skills or the patience required to study the text of the Bible book by book, word by word, consonant by consonant, vowel by vowel, in an effort to determine the family to which a particular manuscript may belong, or where in the history of the transmission of the text a particular manuscript belongs, or how and why the textual tradition developed as it did.

Beginning with the rabbinic period, there are discussions that enable us to understand somewhat better some aspects of the process, but we have nothing of value in the period before about 1000 CE except for some manuscripts and fragments of manuscripts from Qumran. Piecing together a comprehensive theory from an examination of the evidence from the Dead Sea Scrolls is an enormous challenge. A study of this material affords us only a glimpse, although an important glimpse, that enables us to recognize that there is, at least, evidence from the period between circa 250 BCE and 68 CE of Masoretic type manuscripts, of Samaritan type manuscripts, and of Septuagint type Hebrew manuscripts that underlie our Greek translation. To complicate matters further, there are among the Dead Sea Scrolls some independent type manuscripts as well.

We now have a better understanding of the process by which the Masoretic text became, over a period of many centuries, the standard Hebrew text. We also have a clear understanding that there is no evidence to suggest that the Masoretic text reflects the best or the earliest textual tradition of the Old Testament. It was simply the text preferred in rabbinic circles during the period when scribes were developing procedures that eventually led to the subsequent standardization of the text. The fact that no two Masoretic manuscripts are exactly alike reflects some of the difficulties involved. It was only with the advent of mechanical printing of the Hebrew Bible just a few centuries ago that such standardization could and did occur, yet even then not everyone agreed on what manuscript should serve as the source of the printed word.

Textual criticism takes us back only so far and cannot help us to understand the processes by which the Pentateuch was created and the books of Isaiah, Zechariah,

Ecclesiastes, Psalms, and Amos were put together in their present form. The fact that biblical scholars are convinced that manuscripts were modified by copyists quite freely in the early history of their transmission is disconcerting, if not alarming, for it means that we are likely far removed from the earliest written versions of many, if not most, of the books of the Bible when we pick up our modern translations.

The implications of textual criticism cannot be overestimated and should give us considerable pause as we open any and every book of the Bible and wonder about the integrity, authenticity, and authority of what we are actually reading. It is, after all, only the final product that has achieved canonical status, with not even a glance at the long process by which our canonical books assumed their present form. At best, the efforts of textual critics are able to put us in touch with the families of manuscripts of the Bible as they were known in the period shortly before the birth of Jesus of Nazareth. The earlier stages in the development of the manuscript tradition of our canonical books are difficult, if not impossible, to reconstruct.

What would be very helpful for both scholars and laypersons would be a Bible that clearly reflects developments in the biblical texts; that shows us what an original version of Ecclesiastes and Amos may have looked like by identifying clearly later editorial additions; that shows the distinctions between Isaiah of Jerusalem, Deutero-Isaiah, and Trito-Isaiah and between Zechariah and Deutero-Zechariah; that identifies what are likely the various components of the Pentateuch; and that reflects what are probably appropriate emendations in the Masoretic readings based on variants in the Samaritan and Septuagint texts and on informed scholarly conjectures when the Masoretic text is otherwise problematic. From what we have learned in the course of this study, it is time to abandon our rather slavish adherence to the Masoretic text for scholarly study and even for a devotional reading of the Old Testament. Our contemporary translations should reflect not tradition and established practices, but the best results of biblical scholarship.

NOTES

1. Recall, for example, that in the case of Proverbs 30:1, some scholars have suggested a minor emendation to the Masoretic text that would change the meaning of the word usually translated as "the solemn word" or "the oracle" to read instead "of Massa" (see p. 292, n. 2, pp. 271–72).

2. See chapter 1, pp. 43–56.

3. Ibid., pp. 189–98.

4. Ibid., pp. 207–21.

5. Ibid., p. 318.

6. Ibid., p. 188.

7. Ibid., p. 319.

8. Ibid., pp. 273–78.

9. Ibid., pp. 165–72.

10. Ibid., pp. 295–312.

11. Although textual criticism began with the study of biblical manuscripts, primarily with manuscripts of the New Testament, it is not limited to the study of the Bible. Its principles can be, and generally are, applied to the study of any text for which there are multiple written traditions with textual variants. From these variants, the textual critic tries to establish the lost original text of a document, generally referred to as the archetype or the autograph. The methods of textual criticism have been applied, for example, to Homer's *Iliad* and *Odyssey*, to Plato's *Republic*, and even to the plays of William Shakespeare.

12. See above, p. 297.

13. There is also no material from Nehemiah among the Dead Sea Scrolls, but Ezra-Nehemiah was at the time a single scroll.

14. For a discussion of the way in which the move toward Christian orthodoxy influenced the editing of manuscripts of the New Testament, see Bart D. Ehrman, *The Orthodox Corruption of Scripture: The Effect of Early Christological Controversies on the Text of the New Testament* (New York: Oxford University Press, 1991). A similar process likely accompanied the transmission of the books of the Old Testament.

15. The identification of this scroll as 1QIs(a) reflects the convention by which scholars identify the Dead Sea Scrolls. The "1" indicates that this particular scroll came from the first cave in which scrolls were found. The "Q" is an abbreviation for Qumran. "Is" is an abbreviation for Isaiah, and "(a)" indicates that this was the first of more than one Isaiah scroll found in cave 1.

16. Heinrich Graetz, *Kohelet oder der Solomonische Prediger, übersetzt und kritisch erläutet* (Leipzig: 1871). See also George Foot Moore, *Judaism in the First Centuries of the Christian Era: The Age of the Tannaim*, vol. 1 (Cambridge, MA: Harvard University Press, 1927), pp. 83–92.

17. I do not mean to imply that sectarian Judaism did not continue to exist. Indeed, it did. In fact, it is more accurate during this period to refer to Judaisms rather than Judaism.

18. The Mishnah is a collection of the oral interpretations and teachings of about one hundred fifty rabbis from circa 50 BCE to circa 200 CE compiled in writing circa 200 CE.

19. The Tosefta is a work similar to the Mishnah containing a codification of teachings of the rabbis.

20. In the first half of the third century, Origen of Alexandria (185–254 CE) prepared the *Hexapla*, an extraordinary feat of biblical scholarship, designed to gather in one place alternative and apparently competing editions of the Old Testament. The text of Origen's *Hexapla* was in six columns (hence its name) and contained different versions of the Jewish scriptures: (1) a Hebrew text (probably the Masoretic text); (2) the Hebrew text transliterated into Greek characters; (3) the translation of Aquila of Sinope from circa 130 CE; (4) the translation of Symmachus the Ebionite from the late second century; (5) the Septuagint; and (6) the translation of Theodotion of Ephesus from circa 180–190 CE.

21. The Hebrew word Masorah literally means "tradition" or "transmission" and refers, therefore, to the rules that govern the writing of biblical manuscripts.

22. 4QEx(a) refers to the first manuscript of the book of Exodus discovered in cave 4 at Qumran.

23. An Aramaic translation of Leviticus found in cave 4 at Qumran, an Aramaic translation of Job found in cave 4 at Qumran, and an Aramaic translation of Job found in cave 11 at Qumran, respectively.

24. Although associated with Babylonia, many scholars believe both on linguistic grounds and on similarities to Palestinian teachings that the Targum of Onqelos originated in Palestine in the first or early second century CE.

25. The books of the Apocrypha are not the same for everyone. Books included in all Orthodox and Catholic Bibles but not in Protestant and Jewish Bibles are: Tobit, Judith, Additions to Esther, Widsom of Solomon, Ecclesiasticus (sometimes referred to as the Wisdom of Jesus, the Son of Sirach), Baruch, Letter of Jeremiah, Additions to Daniel (including the Prayer of Azariah and the Song of the Three Jews, Susanna, and Bel and the Dragon), and 1 and 2 Maccabees. In addition, the Greek Orthodox Bible includes the Prayer of Manasseh, Psalm 151, 1 Esdras, 3 Maccabees, and 4 Maccabees (in an appendix). Slavonic Orthodox Bibles include the Prayer of Manasseh, Psalm 151, 2 and 3 Esdras, and 3 Maccabees.

BIBLIOGRAPHY

Astruc, Jean. *Conjectures sur les mémoires originaux dont il paraît que Moïse s'est servi pour composer le livre de Genèse. Avec des remarques qui appuient ou qui éclaircissent ces conjectures* [Conjectures on the Original Documents that Moses Appears to Have Used in Composing the Book of Genesis. With Remarks that Support or Throw Light upon the Conjectures]. Brussels: [published anonymously], 1753.

Bellinzoni, Arthur J. *The Future of Christianity: Can It Survive?* Amherst, NY: Prometheus Books, 2006.

Blount, Charles. *Miracles, No Violation of the Laws of Nature.* London: 1683.

Box, G. H. "IV Ezra." In *The Apocrypha and Pseudepigrapha of the Old Testament in English*, vol. 2. Edited by R. H. Charles. Oxford: Clarendon Press, 1963, 542–624.

Boyce, Mary. *A History of Zoroastrianism.* Handbook of Oriental Studies, vols. 1 and 2. Leiden: E. J. Brill, 1975 and 1982.

———, ed. *Textual Sources for the Study of Zoroastrianism.* Textual Sources for the Study of Religion. Translation by Mary Boyce. London: Rowman & Littlefield, 1984.

Cappel, Louis. *Arcanum Punctationis Revelatum* [The Secret of the Pointing Revealed]. Leiden: Erpenius, 1624.

———. *Critica Sacra* [Sacred Literary Criticism]. Paris: 1650.

Charles, R. H. "1 Enoch." In *The Apocrypha and Pseudepigrapha of the Old Testament in English*, vol. 2. Edited by R. H. Charles. Oxford: Clarendon Press, 1963, 163–281.

———. "2 Baruch, or the Syriac Apocalypse of Baruch." In *The Apocrypha and Pseude-*

pigrapha of the Old Testament in English, vol. 2. Edited by R. H. Charles. Oxford: Clarendon Press, 1963, 470–526.

Collins, Anthony. *A Discourse of Free-Thinking Occasioned by the Rise and Growth of a Sect Called Freethinkers.* London: 1713; Whitefish, MT: Kessinger Publishing, reprinted 2007.

Collins, John J. *Apocalypse: The Morphology of a Genre.* Semeia, vol. 14. Missoula, MT: Scholars Press, 1979.

———. "Sibylline Oracles." In *The Old Testament Pseudepigrapha*, vol. 1. Edited by James H. Charlesworth. Garden City, NY: Doubleday, 1983, 317–472.

Copernicus, Nicolaus. *De revolutionibus orbium coelestium* [On the Revolutions of the Heavenly Spheres]. Nuremberg: Johannes Petreius, 1543.

Crenshaw, James L. "Proverbs, Book of." In *The Anchor Bible Dictionary*, vol. 5 (O–Sh). New York: Doubleday, 1992, 513–20.

Dahood, Mitchell. *Psalms I (1–50).* The Anchor Bible. Garden City, NY: Doubleday, 1965.

Descartes, René. *Discours de la Méthode pour bien conduire sa raison, et chercher la verité dans les sciences* [Discourse on the Method of Rightly Conducting the Reason, and Searching for Truth in the Sciences]. Leyden: Ian Maire, 1637.

Driver, S. R. *The Book of Genesis.* Twelfth edition. Edinburgh: T & T Clark, 1954. First published in 1926.

Duchesne-Guillemin, Jacques. *The Hymns of Zarathustra.* Boston: Beacon Press, 1963.

Duhm, Bernard. *Das Buch Jesaja, übersetzt und erklärt.* Fourth edition. Göttingen: Vanderhoeck & Ruprecht, 1922. First published in 1892.

Ehrman, Bart D. *The Orthodox Corruption of Scripture: The Effect of Early Christological Controversies on the Text of the New Testament.* New York: Oxford University Press, 1991.

Eichhorn, Johann Gottfried. *Einleitung in das Alte Testament* [Introduction to the Old Testament], 3 vols. Leipzig: Weidmann, 1780–1783.

Galilei, Galileo. *Dialogo sopra i due massimi sistemi del mondo* [Dialogue concerning the Two Chief Systems of the World]. Florence: Gian Battista Landini, 1632.

Gaster, Theodor H. *The Oldest Stories in the World.* Boston: Beacon Press, 1959.

Glanville, Stephen Ranulf Kingdon. "Instructions of 'Onchsheshonqy.'" In *Catalogue of Demotic Papyri in the British Museum*, vol 2. London: 1955, 2–66.

Graetz, Heinrich, *Kohelet oder der Solomonische Prediger, übersetzt und kritisch erläutet.* Leipzig: C. F. Winter, 1871.

Hamilton, Victor C. "Satan." In *The Anchor Bible Dictionary*, vol. 5 (O–Sh). New York: Doubleday, 1992, 985–89.

Hanson, Paul D. "Apocalypses and Apocalypticism." In *The Anchor Bible Dictionary*, vol. 1 (A–C). New York: Doubleday, 1992, 279–80.

————. *The Dawn of Apocalyptic: The Historical and Sociological Roots of Jewish Apocalyptic Eschatology*. Philadelphia: Augsburg Fortress Press, 1984.

HarperCollins Study Bible, New Revised Standard Version. New York: HarperCollins, 1993.

Hartman, Louis F., and Alexander A. Di Lella. *The Book of Daniel*. The Anchor Bible. Garden City, NY: Doubleday, 1978.

Hobbes, Thomas. *The Leviathan*. London: Andrew Crooke, 1660.

Isaac, E. "Ethiopic Apocalypse of Enoch." In *The Old Testament Pseudepigrapha*, vol. 1. Edited by James H. Charlesworth. Garden City, NY: Doubleday, 1983, 5–12.

Kabisch, Richard. "Das Vierte Buch Esra." In *Jahrbücher für protestantische Theologie* (1891), 66–107.

Kaufmann, Yehezkel. *The Religion of Israel*. Translated by Moshe Greenberg. Chicago: University of Chicago Press, 1960.

King, Martin Luther, Jr. "Our God Is Able." In *Strength to Love*. Philadelphia: Fortress Press, 1963.

Klijn, A. F. J. "2 (Syriac Apocalypse of) Baruch." In *The Old Testament Pseudepigrapha*, vol. 1. Edited by James H. Charlesworth. Garden City, NY: Doubleday, 1983, 615–52.

Krentz, Edgar. *The Historical-Critical Method*. Philadelphia: Fortress Press, 1975.

Lanchester, H. C. O. "The Sibylline Oracles." In *The Apocrypha and Pseudepigrapha of the Old Testament in English*, vol. 2. Edited by R. H. Charles. Oxford: Clarendon Press, 1963, 368–404.

La Peyrère, Isaac de. *Prae-Adamitae* [Men before Adam]. Amsterdam: Louis and Daniel Elzevier, 1655.

Lindblom, Johannes. *Prophecy in Ancient Israel*. Philadelphia: Fortress Press, 1962.

Metzger, Bruce. "The Fourth Book of Ezra." In *The Old Testament Pseudepigrapha*, vol. 1. Edited by James H. Charlesworth. Garden City, NY: Doubleday, 1983, 517–59.

Moore, George Foot. *Judaism in the First Centuries of the Christian Era: The Age of the Tannaim*. Cambridge, MA: Harvard University Press, 1927.

Morin, Jean. *Biblia graecae sive Vetus testamentum secundum Septuaginta* [The Greek Bible of the Old Testament according to the Septuagint]. Paris: 1628.

————. *Exercitationes biblicae de Hebraei Graecique textus sinceritate* [Exercises regarding the Reliability of the Text of the Hebrew and Greek Bibles]. Paris: 1663, 1669, and 1686.

————. *Exercitationes ecclesiastiae in utrumque Samaritorium Pentateuchum* [Ecclesiastic Exercises in the Samaritan Pentateuch]. Paris: 1631.

————. *Pentateuchus hebraeo-samaritanus* [The Hebrew-Samaritan Pentateuch]. Paris: 1645.

————. *Pentateuchus samaritanus* [The Samaritan Pentateuch]. Paris: 1645.

Myers, Jacob M. *Ezra Nehemiah*. The Anchor Bible. Garden City, NY: Doubleday, 1965.

New Revised Standard Version Bible, the Division of Christian Education of the National Council of Churches of Christ in the U.S.A. New York, 1989.

Pfeiffer, Robert H. *Introduction to the Old Testament.* New York: Harper & Brothers, 1948.

Philo. *Volume VI: On Abraham.* Loeb Classical Library. Cambridge, MA: Harvard University Press, 1959, 2–135.

———. *Volume IX: The Contemplative Life.* Loeb Classical Library. Cambridge, MA: Harvard University Press, 1954, 104–69.

Pope, Marvin H. *Job.* The Anchor Bible. Garden City, NY: Doubleday, 1965.

Pratt, James Bissett. *The Religious Consciousness: A Psychological Study.* New York: Macmillan, 1946.

Pritchard, James B. *Ancient Near Eastern Texts Relating to the Old Testament with Supplement.* Princeton, NJ: Princeton University Press, 1969.

Reimarus, Hermann Samuel. *Von dem Zwecke Jesus und seiner Jünger* [The Aims of Jesus and His Disciples] *Noch ein Fragment des Wolfenbüttelschen Ungennannten* [Anonymous Fragments]. Braunschweig: Gotthold Ephraim Lessing, 1778.

Rist, Martin. "Apocalypticism." In *The Interpreter's Dictionary of the Bible,* vol. 1 (A–D). New York: Abingdon Press, 1962, 157–61.

Schweitzer, Albert. *The Quest of the Historical Jesus.* Translated by W. Montgomery, with an introduction by James M. Robinson. New York: Macmillan, 1968.

Scott, R. B. Y. *Proverbs Ecclesiastes.* The Anchor Bible. Garden City, NY: Doubleday, 1965.

Simon, Richard. *Histoire critique des principaux commentateurs du Nouveau Testament depuis le commencement du Christianisme jusques à notre temps* [Critical History of the Principal Commentators of the New Testament from the Beginning of Christianity until the Present Time]. Paris: 1693.

———. *Histoire critique des versions du Nouveau Testament* [*Critical History of the Versions of the New Testament*]. Paris: 1690.

———. *Histoire critique du texte du Nouveau Testament* [Critical History of the Text of the New Testament]. Paris: 1689.

———. *Histoire critique du Vieux Testament* [Critical History of the Old Testament]. Paris: 1678; Rotterdam: Reinier Leers, 1685.

———. *Nouvelles Observations sur le texte et les versions du Nouveau Testament* [New Observations on the Text and the Versions of the New Testament]. Paris: 1695.

———. *Réponse aux Sentiments de quelques théologiens de Hollande* [Response to the Opinions of Some Theologians from Holland]. Paris: 1692.

Spinoza, Baruch. *Tractatus theologico-politicus* [*Theological-Political Treatise*]. Hamburg: Henry Kunraht, 1690.

Strauss, David Freidrich. *Das Leben-Jesu* [The Life of Jesus], 2 vols. Tübingen: C. F. Osiander, 1835 and 1836.

———. *Hermann Samuel Reimarus und seine Schutzschrift für die ernünftigen Verehrer*

Gottes [Reimarus and His Apology or Defense for the Rational Worshippers of God]. Bonn: Strauss, 1862.

Tarnas, Richard. *The Passion of the Western Mind: Understanding the Ideas That Have Shaped Our World View*. New York: Ballantine Books, 1991.

Torrey, Charles C. *Ezra Studies*. Chicago: University of Chicago Press, 1910.

———. *The Chronicler's History of Israel: Chronicles-Ezra-Nehemiah Restored to Its Original Form*. New Haven, CT: Yale University Press, 1954.

Ussher, Archbishop James Ussher of Armagh. "Chronology or Annales Veteris et Novi Testamenti." In *Annals of the Old and the New Testament*. London: 1650.

Wernberg-Møller, P. *The Manual of Discipline*. Grand Rapids, MI: Eerdmans, 1957.

Wilckens, Ulrich. "Über die Bedeutung historischer Kritik in der modernen Bibelexegese." In *Was heisst Auslegung der Heiligen Schrift?* Regensburg: Friedrich Pustet, 1966.

Wolff, Hans Walter. *Joel and Amos*. Hermeneia Series. Translated by Waldemar Janzen, S. Dean McBride Jr., and Charles A. Muenchow. Philadelphia: Fortress Press, 1977.

Zimmermann, F. "Textual Observations on the Apocalypse of Baruch." *Journal of Theological Studies* 40 (1939): 151–56.

———. "Translation and Mistranslation in the Apocalypse of Baruch." In *Studies and Essays in Honour of Abraham A. Neuman*. Edited by M. Ben-Horin et al. Leiden: E. J. Brill, 1962, 580–87.

CITATIONS

Old Testament citations are listed according to the order of the Jewish Canon

Hosea

1:1, 173, 320
1:2–6, 174
1:8–9, 174
2:2–15, 174
2:16–23, 175
2:19–23, 175–76
3:1–3, 174
3:2, 175
5:8–14, 172
9:7, 175
11:8–9, 175
13:10–11, 172
13:16, 172–73

Joel

1:1, 173, 320
1:1–12, 321
1:2, 320
1:9, 320
1:13–14, 320
1:14, 320
1:15, 320
1:16, 320
2:1, 320, 321
2:7, 320
2:9, 320
2:11, 320, 321
2:15–17, 320
2:17, 320
2:28–3:21, 320–22
2:30, 321
2:31, 320, 321
2:32, 321
3:1–3, 320

3:3, 351n11
3:10, 351n11
3:14, 320
3:16a, 351n11
3:17b, 351n11
3:18, 320
3:20, 321

Amos

1:1, 165, 173, 320
1:1–9, 357
1:2, 351n11
1:3–2:16, 168
1:3–5, 168
1:6–8, 168
1:9–10, 168
1:10, 357
1:11–12, 168
1:12, 280
1:13–15, 168
1:19:8a, 171
2:1–3, 168
2:4–5, 168
3:2, 168
3:15, 312n12
5:18, 320
5:18–24, 351n10
5:20, 320
5:21–24, 168–69
6:8, 170
7:1–3, 169
7:4–6, 169
7:7–9, 169, 200
7:10–15, 165–66
7:14–15, 83

7:16–17, 166–67
8:1–3, 169, 200
8:8b–15, 179
9:1–4, 169
9:8a, 165, 170
9:8b, 165
9:8b–15, 171–72
9:9–10, 172
9:11–15, 172, 357

Obadiah

1, 351n11
8, 258
9, 280
15, 320

Micah

1:1, 173, 320
3:9–12, 202
4:3b, 351n11

Habakkuk

1–2, 363
3:3, 294n41

Zephaniah

1:1, 173, 320
1:4–6, 235
1:7, 320

Haggai

1:1, 320
2:23, 214, 319

3:16, 266

3:19–20, 266

3:21, 263

4:1, 263

4:5–9, 266

4:10, 263

4:20, 263

5:1, 263

5:7, 263

5:20, 263

6:16–19, 265

7:1, 263

7:4–5, 266

7:24, 263

8:1–36, 266

8:22–13, 266

8:22–29, 266

8:32, 263

9:1–6, 266

10:1–5, 266–67

10:1–15:33, 266

10:1–22:16, 263, 266

16:1–22:16, 267

16:8, 267

16:10, 267

16:12, 267

16:15, 267

22:17–18a, 269

22:17–24:22, 263, 267

22:19, 269

22:20, 269

22:20–21, 268

22:21, 269

22:22, 269

22:24, 269

22:28, 269

22:29, 269

22.25, 269

23:1–2, 269

23:1–6, 268

23:4–5, 269

23:6–7, 269

23:6–8, 268

23:8, 269

23:9, 269

23:10–11, 269

23:15, 263

23:19, 263

23:19–21, 268

23:26, 263

24:11, 269

24:13, 263

24:21, 263

24:23–24, 270

24:23–34, 263

24:23b–26, 270

25:1–29:27, 263, 270

25:11–14, 270–71

25–27, 270

27:11, 263

28:1–2, 270–71

28:6, 270–71

28:12, 270–71

28–29, 270

30, 289

30:1, 271–72, 290, 371n1

30:1–4, 260, 292n2

30:1–33, 263, 271

30:5, 294n41

31, 289

31:1, 271, 290, 292n2

31:1–8, 261

31:1–9, 263, 272

31:3–5, 272

31:10–14, 272–73

31:10–31, 263, 272

Job

1:1–2:13, 281

1:2, 282

1:2–3, 282

1:6, 293–94nn35, 37

1:6–11, 282

1:7, 294n37

1:8, 294n37

1:9, 294n37

1:12, 282, 294n37

1:13–17, 282

1:18–19, 282

1:20–21, 282

1:21, 294n37

2:1, 293–94nn35, 37

2:1–8, 282

2:2, 294n37

2:3, 294n37

2:4, 294n37

2:6, 294n37

2:7, 294n37

2:9, 282

2:11, 280

INDEX

Aaron, 99, 115n15, 158

Abaddon, 284, 294n36

Abdon, 237

Abel, 76n4, 79n29

Abijah (Abijam) (king), 152

Abimelech (of Israel) (king), 119, 120–21, 141, 143, 145

Abimelech of Gerar (king), 52, 57n11, 186nn1, 3

Abinadab, 125

Abner, 125

Abraham, 57nn10–11, 68, 70, 75, 77n18, 79n33, 100, 102, 186n3, 279, 280

    Abram becoming Abraham, 80n40

    as an archetype, 65, 74

    associated with holy trees, 71, 79n34, 100

    comparison of similar stories about, 182–83

    God's covenant with, 66, 68, 71, 116n18, 141, 184, 248–49

    King David gaining area promised to, 127, 139

    as a prophet, 158, 184

    and Sarah, 52, 66, 69, 78n26

Abram, 52, 71, 74, 78n25, 138

    Abram becoming Abraham, 80n40

Absalom, 128–29, 145, 237

absolute monotheism, 210–11

Accuser (the Satan). *See* Satan

Achaemenids (governor), 316

acrostic poems, 272, 279

    in Psalms, 299, 309

Acts of Solomon, 118, 131, 132, 142, 176, 223, 237

Adam, 24, 60, 61, 62, 74, 75, 76nn1, 3, 4, 143

    representing all humankind, 76nn2, 5, 143, 150nn33–34

Admah, city of, 175, 180n8

Adonijah, 129

adulteress, marriage to, 174, 175

Age to Come, 314–15, 318, 325

agnostic skepticism, 277

Agur (son of Jakeh), 263, 271, 290